Fenton Bresler .... orked exten-
sively in all sec .... and criminal
matters. He w. .... and maga-
zines, with a weekly column in the London *Evening Standard* and
a monthly column in the *Daily Telegraph*. His many books include
biographies of Lord Chief Justice Lord Goddard and Georges
Simenon.

FENTON BRESLER

NAPOLEON III

A Life

HarperCollins*Publishers*

For Frédéric Constant

HarperCollins*Publishers*
77–85 Fulham Palace Road,
Hammersmith, London W6 8JB

www.**fire**and**water**.com

This paperback edition 2000
1 3 5 7 9 8 6 4 2

First published in Great Britain by
HarperCollins*Publishers* 1999

ISBN 0 00 638814 0

Set in Sabon

Printed and bound in Great Britain by
Omnia Books Limited, Glasgow

TABLE OF CONTENTS

PART THREE

POWER AT LAST

PART FOUR

THE SECOND EMPIRE

PART FIVE

THE END

ILLUSTRATION CREDITS

Colour

Napoleon I and his family at St Cloud in 1810 by Louis Ducis (Châteaux de Versailles et de Trianon/© photo RMN-Gerard Blot); Maria Laeticia Bonaparte ('Madame Mère') by François Gérard, 1804 (Musée de Malmaison/AKG London); Hortense, Queen of Holland by Jean-Baptiste Regnault, 1810 (Musée de Malmaison/AKG London); Louis Bonaparte, King of Holland, and his son Napoleon Louis, after Jean-Baptiste Wicar (Musée de Versailles/Roger-Viollet, Paris); Napoleon III by Franz-Xavier Winterhalter, 1853 (Musée Napoléonien, Rome/Roger-Viollet, Paris); Miss Howard by Henriette Cappelaere, c.1846–59 (Château de Compiègne/© photo RMN); Empress Eugenie and her ladies-in-waiting by Franz-Xavier Winterhalter, 1855 (Château de Compiègne/Roger-Viollet, Paris); Visconti presenting Napoleon III with the plans for the 'New Louvre' by Ange Tissier, 1853 (Musée du Louvre/Roger-Viollet, Paris); Reception of the Siamese ambassadors by Napoleon III and Empress Eugenie on 27 June 1861 by Jean Léon Gerôme (Châteaux de Versailles et de Trianon/© photo RMN); Sovereigns visiting Paris for the Universal Exhibition of 1867 by Charles Porion (Château de Compiègne/© photo RMN); Napoleon III at the Battle of Solferino by Ernest Meissonier, 1860 (Château de Compiègne/AKG London); Napoleon III and Bismarck after the Battle of Sedan, illustration by Camphausen, 1878 (Mary Evans Picture Library); Napoleon III and the Prince Imperial (Château de Compiègne/Roger-Viollet, Paris); Empress Eugenie and the Prince Imperial at Chislehurst by James Tissot (Château de Compiègne/Roger-Viollet, Paris)

Black and white illustrations

Josephine de Beauharnais, drawing by Eugéne Isabey, 1798 (Musée des Arts Décoratifs/Roger-Viollet, Paris); Joseph Bonaparte by Robert Lefevre (Musée Napoléonien, Rome/Roger-Viollet, Paris); The Duc de Reichstadt, lithograph (Roger-Viollet, Paris); Arenenberg Castle (Roger-Viollet, Paris); King Louis-Philippe, attributed to Pierre-Roch Vigneron (Musée Carnavalet/Roger-Viollet, Paris); The future Napoleon III, drawing by Alfred d'Orsay, 1839 (AKG, London); The future Napoleon III in exile at Ham, engraving by Leguay after a drawing by Philippoteaux (Mary Evans Picture Library); The Château de Ham (Roger-Viollet, Paris); Louis Napoleon Bonaparte proclaimed President of the French Republic, lithograph of 1849 (Roger-Viollet, Paris); Barricades on the rue Royale in Paris in 1848 (Roger-Viollet, Paris); Doctor Henri Conneau (Roger-Viollet, Paris); The Duc de Persigny (Roger-Viollet, Paris); The Duc de Morny (Roger-Viollet, Paris); Napoleon III and Eugenie in 1861 (AKG, London); The Comtesse de Castiglione (Roger-Viollet, Paris); Marguerite Bellanger (Mary Evans Picture Library); Jerome Bonaparte, ex-King of Westphalia, in later life (Roger-Viollet, Paris); Joseph Charles Paul Bonaparte ('Plon-Plon') (Mary Evans Picture Library); Princess Mathilde (Roger-Viollet, Paris); The Royal and Imperial visit to the Crystal Palace, 20 April 1855 (photo by Negretti & Zambra/The Royal Archives, © Her Majesty The Queen); Napoleon III watching the two-year-old Prince Imperial being photographed on a pony (Popperfoto); The Prince Imperial as a young man (Mary Evans Picture Library); Napoleon III in 1865 (AKG, London); Archduke Maximilian of Austria and his wife Charlotte in 1865 (Hulton Getty Picture Collection); French prisoners of war in German camps after the Franco-Prussian War (AKG, London); Part of the original draft of the 'Ems Telegram' (AKG, London); Empress Eugenie in 1880 (Roger-Viollet, Paris); The last photograph of Napoleon III (AKG, London); Exterior of Camden Place (*Illustrated London News*/Mary Evans Picture Library); Napoleon III's study at Camden Place (Hulton Getty Picture Collection)

EUROPE IN 1848

NORWAY

North Sea

Edinburgh

DENMA

GREAT BRITAIN

HANOVE

Amsterdam

HOLLAND

Rhine

London

BELGIUM

B

Paris • Sedan

BAVARIA

BADEN

Strasbourg • WÜRTTEM

Seine

Loire

B

Tours •

FRANCE

SWITZERLAND

Rhône

Geneva

Lyons •

SARDINIA

Turin

Solf

PARMA

TUSCANY

Biarritz •

Toulouse •

MASSA & CARRARA

LUCCA

Nice •

Flore

Marseilles •

TU

MONACO

Corsica

Madrid •

S P A I N

PORTUGAL

SARDINIA

Mediterranea

NORTH AFRICA

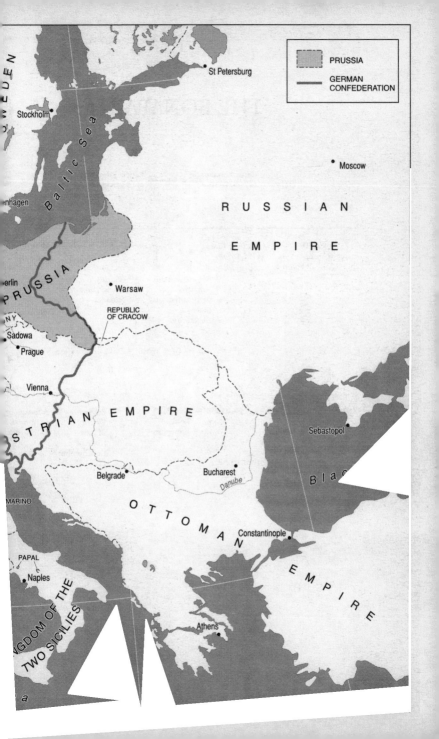

▨	PRUSSIA
▬	GERMAN CONFEDERATION

St Petersburg

Stockholm

Moscow

Baltic Sea

nhagen

RUSSIAN

EMPIRE

erlin

PRUSSIA

Warsaw

REPUBLIC
OF CRACOW

NY

Sadowa

Prague

Vienna

Sebastopol

STRIAN EMPIRE

Belgrade

Bucharest

Danube

Bla

MARINO

OTTOMAN

Constantinople

PAPAL

Naples

EMPIRE

GDOM OF THE

TWO SICILIES

Athens

a

THE BONAPARTES

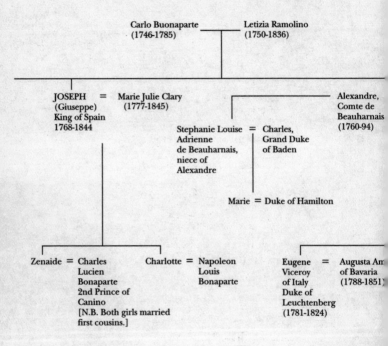

Carlo Buonaparte
(1746-1785)

Letizia Ramolino
(1750-1836)

JOSEPH = Marie Julie Clary
(Giuseppe)   (1777-1845)
King of Spain
1768-1844

Stephanie Louise = Charles,
Adrienne   Grand Duke
de Beauharnais,   of Baden
niece of
Alexandre

Alexandre,
Comte de
Beauharnais
(1760-94)

Marie = Duke of Hamilton

Zenaide = Charles   Charlotte = Napoleon
          Lucien   Louis
          Bonaparte   Bonaparte
          2nd Prince of
          Canino
          [N.B. Both girls married
          first cousins.]

Eugene = Augusta Am
Viceroy   of Bavaria
of Italy   (1788-1851)
Duke of
Leuchtenberg
(1781-1824)

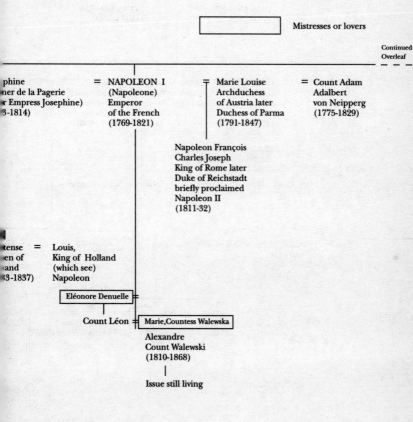

Continued
Overleaf

Mistresses or lovers

phine
ner de la Pagerie
r Empress Josephine)
3-1814)

= NAPOLEON I
(Napoleone)
Emperor
of the French
(1769-1821)

= Marie Louise
Archduchess
of Austria later
Duchess of Parma
(1791-1847)

= Count Adam
Adalbert
von Neipperg
(1775-1829)

Napoleon François
Charles Joseph
King of Rome later
Duke of Reichstadt
briefly proclaimed
Napoleon II
(1811-32)

tense
en of
and
3-1837)

= Louis,
King of Holland
(which see)
Napoleon

Eléonore Denuelle =

Count Léon = Marie, Countess Walewska

Alexandre
Count Walewski
(1810-1868)

Issue still living

THE BONAPARTES

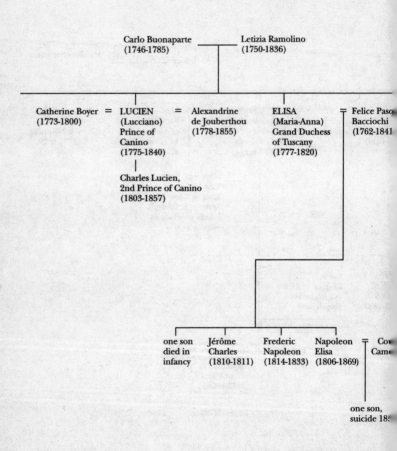

Carlo Buonaparte
(1746-1785)

Letizia Ramolino
(1750-1836)

Catherine Boyer = LUCIEN
(1773-1800)   (Lucciano)
                    Prince of
                    Canino
                    (1775-1840)

= Alexandrine
   de Jouberthou
   (1778-1855)

ELISA
(Maria-Anna)
Grand Duchess
of Tuscany
(1777-1820)

= Felice Pasc
   Bacciochi
   (1762-1841

Charles Lucien,
2nd Prince of Canino
(1803-1857)

one son
died in
infancy

Jérôme
Charles
(1810-1811)

Frederic
Napoleon
(1814-1833)

Napoleon
Elisa
(1806-1869)

= Co
   Came

one son,
suicide 18!

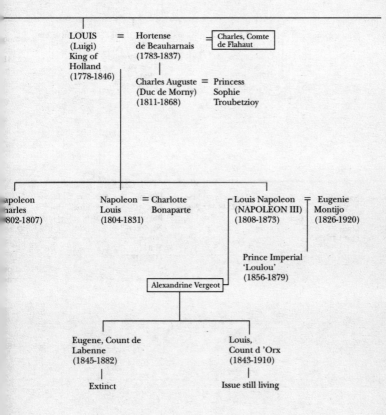

THE BONAPARTES

Mistresses or lovers

Continued
Overleaf

LOUIS
(Luigi)
King of
Holland
(1778-1846)

= Hortense
de Beauharnais
(1783-1837)

= Charles, Comte
de Flahaut

Charles Auguste = Princess
(Duc de Morny)   Sophie
(1811-1868)   Troubetzioy

Napoleon
Charles
(1802-1807)

Napoleon = Charlotte
Louis   Bonaparte
(1804-1831)

Louis Napoleon = Eugenie
(NAPOLEON III)   Montijo
(1808-1873)   (1826-1920)

Prince Imperial
'Loulou'
(1856-1879)

Alexandrine Vergeot

Eugene, Count de
Labenne
(1845-1882)

Louis,
Count d'Orx
(1843-1910)

Extinct

Issue still living

THE BONAPARTES

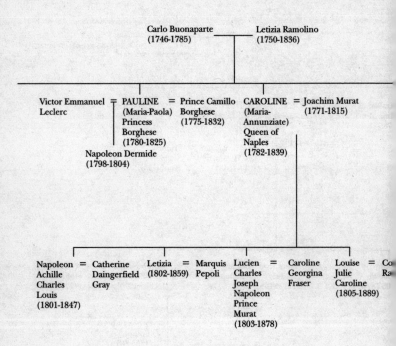

Carlo Buonaparte
(1746-1785)

Letizia Ramolino
(1750-1836)

Victor Emmanuel = PAULINE = Prince Camillo   CAROLINE = Joachim Murat
Leclerc   (Maria-Paola)   Borghese   (Maria-   (1771-1815)
                   Princess   (1775-1832)   Annunziate)
                   Borghese   Queen of
                   (1780-1825)   Naples
                                                 (1782-1839)

Napoleon Dermide
(1798-1804)

Napoleon = Catherine   Letizia = Marquis   Lucien =   Caroline   Louise = Co
Achille   Daingerfield   (1802-1859) Pepoli Charles   Georgina   Julie   Ra
Charles   Gray   Joseph   Fraser   Caroline
Louis   Napoleon   (1805-1889)
(1801-1847)   Prince
                                              Murat
                                              (1803-1878)

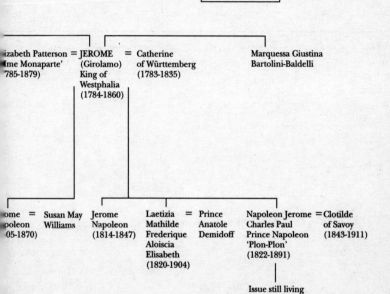

Mistresses or lovers

Elizabeth Patterson 'Mme Monaparte' (1785-1879) = JEROME (Girolamo) King of Westphalia (1784-1860) = Catherine of Württemberg (1783-1835)

Marquessa Giustina Bartolini-Baldelli

Jerome Napoleon (1805-1870) = Susan May Williams

Jerome Napoleon (1814-1847)

Laetizia Mathilde Frederique Aloiscia Elisabeth (1820-1904) = Prince Anatole Demidoff

Napoleon Jerome Charles Paul Prince Napoleon 'Plon-Plon' (1822-1891) = Clotilde of Savoy (1843-1911)

Issue still living

INTRODUCTION

This book tells the story of Napoleon III, nephew of Napoleon I, the great soldier and emperor, one of the most famous men in history, whose name, image and basic life story are known to almost everyone. By contrast, Napoleon III is practically unknown to the present generation. Even in his lifetime, he was a mystery to many and remains so today more than a century after his death.

No one could ever have called him classically handsome. The nose was too big and he was only of medium height, with the top of his body too large for his legs. Everyone agreed that he looked better on horseback than on foot, but his well-trimmed moustache and small, pointed beard gave him a romantic, brooding allure and his eyes were of a clear, piercing blue. He grew up in exile in southern Germany and German-speaking Switzerland after fleeing Paris, as a child of seven, after his uncle's defeat at Waterloo in 1815, and his voice was tinged throughout his life with a slight German accent. It was deep, dark and enticing. He was not so much charming as a charmer. Even Queen Victoria, at first wary of this man so closely related to her country's greatest recent enemy, fell beneath his spell. 'He is endowed with a wonderful self-control,' she confided to her journal, 'great calmness, even gentleness, and with a power of fascination, the effect of which upon all those who become more intimately acquainted with him is most sensibly felt.'

Hortense Cornu, a woman who knew him well and was one of the few close women friends whom he did not take to bed, admitted freely: 'His intellectual character has great excellences – and great deficiencies. He has no originality or invention: he has no power of reasoning or discussing: he has few fixed or general principles of any kind.

'But,' she claimed, 'he is exceedingly mild and kind: his friendships are steady, though his passions are not. He has in a high degree decision, obstinacy, dissimulation, patience and self-reliance. What we call a sense of right and wrong he calls prejudice. His courage and determination are perfect but he is exceedingly indolent and procrastinating. Everything wearies him. He gets up bored, he passes the day bored, he goes to bed bored.'

Yet another woman with whom perhaps remarkably he did not go to bed, Valerie Masuyer, a lady-in-waiting to his mother, did not agree. 'His silence and calm hide a passionate temperament,' she said. 'His heart is ingenuous and yet, like his mind, it is tortuous. Though he never fell in love for the sake of loving, yet his heart is inclined to be captured by an adventure for the joy of being in a conspiracy.'

Except for one thing, no one ever knew his inner thoughts. 'If I had married him, I swear I'd have broken open his head to see what was in it,' said his cousin, Princess Mathilde Bonaparte, to whom he was once engaged and always remained close.

What was that one thing that everyone knew about him? His all-compelling sense of destiny. This man came from exile and ignominy to rule France, first as Prince-President then as Emperor for twenty-two years, from 1848 to 1870. Under his benevolent dictatorship, the nation grew in artistic fulfilment, industrial wealth and international influence, until catastrophic defeat at the Battle of Sedan in a totally unnecessary war with the newly emergent power of Germany cast her back into the shadows.

'Germany' as a nation did not exist until after Napoleon III surrendered at Sedan in September 1870; it was then merely a loose confederation of self-governing states sharing the same language and ethnic origin. There was no separate German nation. It was primarily Prussia, the most powerful of those self-governing states that fought the decisive war with France, rather than 'Germany'.

Germany did not become a legal and political entity until the German Empire was triumphantly proclaimed five months later beneath the glittering chandeliers of the one-time royal palace at Versailles on the outskirts of Paris, with France humbled and humiliated as never before in her history. In a splendid ceremony, the seventy-four-year-old King Wilhelm of Prussia was declared the first German Emperor, while the ex-French Emperor languished as a prisoner of war in Wilhelm's summer palace.

Napoleon's defeat triggered the birth of modern Germany, which leads directly into the entire course of subsequent European history. The seeds of two World Wars were planted on the battlefield of Sedan.

This book's primary aim is to present a fascinating man, in all his fullness, to a modern audience. His life reads like a cross between an old-fashioned novel and a modern film script. Early despair and high adventure culminating in glittering success enjoyed to the full (including compulsive sex with many women and genuine love for only a few); followed by ever-increasing failure and loss of touch, partly caused by intermittent and painful illness; catastrophic defeat in battle and death three years later in an English country house near London. Furthermore, important new evidence indicates that his death was caused not so much by the kidney stones that had plagued him for several years as by incompetence at the highest level of the British medical profession.

Over the years there have been many biographies, translated into several languages, but not one has yet concentrated on the human side of this many-faceted human being. It is easy to dismiss Napoleon as a failure, albeit a magnificent one. That has been the theme of nearly all the biographies to date. But that is grievously to underrate him and ignore both the real value of his achievements and the complexity of his character. It is not only that, as the late Professor D. W. Brogan of Cambridge University has written, 'France was forced into the modern world by Napoleon III'; he also gave us the glittering splendour of the Second Empire which he created and whose legacy in art, literature and sheer style still prevails. The man deserves to be better known to a new generation of readers.

In France, in recent years, a major reassessment has begun, albeit without much enthusiasm.* Ever since Victor Hugo, author of *The Hunchback of Notre Dame* and *Les Misérables*, branded him 'Napoléon le Petit' in a scathing attack published in exile in 1852, most French biographers and historians have written ill of him. 'No more than a military parade crossing a masked ball' is the memorable phrase of Ferdinand Bac in 1932.

The paradox is that France as a nation forgave Napoleon I,

---

* For instance, in 1979, Professor Alain Plessis wrote in his *De la fête impériale au mur des fédérés*, published in English six years later by Cambridge University Press as *The Rise and Fall of the Second Empire*: 'It is certain that the caricatured portrait drawn by his first biographers can no longer be accepted. Today, historians are generally agreed that Napoleon III deserves greater credit.' This is hardly ecstatic praise.

despite his crashing defeat at Waterloo, but it has never brought itself to forgive his nephew for the disaster at Sedan in 1870. Almost no French city or small town is without its Place Napoléon, Boulevard de l'Empereur or other memorial to Napoleon I but there is hardly a single square, boulevard, street or avenue in the whole country that is named after Napoleon III, and all public places that did bear his name during his reign were swiftly changed after his fall.

Now that is gradually changing. In his 1990 biography, *Louis Napoléon le Grand*, Philippe Séguin, a leading French politician, argued that Napoleon III was a patriotic visionary with surprisingly modern ideas well ahead of his time. He claims that he was a sort of nineteenth-century General de Gaulle dedicated only to fulfilling his country's greatness. Such an enigma is he that, in early 1997, the distinguished French journalist Alain Minc published a book, *Louis Napoléon revisité*, in which, although agreeing that Napoleon was ahead of his time, he comes to exactly the opposite conclusion. He seeks to argue persuasively, over 238 pages, that, far from being a precursor of the right-wing Charles de Gaulle, Napoleon III was a nineteenth-century version of the left-wing François Mitterrand.

Napoleon III played his cards so close to his chest in the poker game of his life that even today his own countrymen are in dispute as to what sort of a person he really was.

At least nowadays they are engaged in the debate. Thierry Lentz, one of his most recent French biographers, wrote in 1995: 'Napoleon III was for a long time unappreciated and disliked. Later historians took hold of his personage and his reign to reduce them deliberately to a parenthesis, an unfortunate and ill-fated accident along the inescapable path of the country towards a republic.

'Only today does Napoleon III have his rightful place in history, without excesses of criticism or of praise.'

But, apart from Philippe Séguin and Alain Minc, this 'rebirth' has largely been the work of an academic mafia whose books have not been widely read and who have made little impact upon the French general public. In 1993, the Paris-based Academy of the Second Empire, an elitist French 'fan club' for a famous historical figure, prevailed upon the Parisian civic authorities to rename a small open space outside the Gare du Nord railway station Place Napoléon III; you would still be hard-pressed today to find a single taxi-driver who knows about the new name. (Ironically, I *have* found an avenue Miss Howard, named after his most famous mistress, on a new housing estate built in the grounds of her demolished mansion just outside Paris. The French have their own logic.)

Hitherto, many French biographers have tended largely to ignore foreign biographers, as if their own kind alone had virtue and understanding. It has been much the same in Britain. Some of our biographers have paid lip-service to the need to seek out the views of their French colleagues but, when one actually reads their books, one cannot find much evidence of it.

I have tried to make the best of both worlds. I have looked beyond the available biographies, into original sources, some of which are noted in the Acknowledgements, all of which have proved to be invaluable. For much of my life, while continuing to practise at the English Bar, I have worked as an investigative writer. I have, therefore, treated this biography in exactly the same way: as a work of investigation. I have been a detective of sorts, following a trail of clues, some not easy to uncover. I have visited the principal places where Napoleon III lived, worked and loved. I have talked, in France and England, to the people of today about this man from the past. The story is told as much as possible in the words of Napoleon III himself and his contemporaries – as well as our contemporaries.

One final word: to read – and, one hopes, enjoy – this book, you do not have to be a student of nineteenth-century European history. Dealt with at length, as in most other biographies, the details of that half-forgotten interplay between long-dead rulers and politicians many of whose countries no longer even exist, can be remarkably boring for a non-academic reader. As with a Tolstoy novel, you almost need a glossary to remind you who everyone is. For me, the Europe of over a hundred years ago is the backdrop against which Napoleon III functioned: he alone takes centre stage.

As a book of serious historical research, this is a reinterpretation of Napoleon III's character based on modern insights and a greater use of the foreign material available. I have approached it in the manner of a barrister preparing a 'heavy' case for court: by the time he rises to his feet in front of the judge, he has made himself an expert on the subject, sometimes more so than the so-called 'expert witnesses' who are to give evidence and who are to be cross-examined.

But I emphasise at the very start that this book is aimed not only at those who like historical biography but at the wider public who want to read an interesting story and meet an intriguing character.

ACKNOWLEDGEMENTS

THIS BOOK HAS TAKEN me four and a half years to research and write, although in a sense the research has taken me much longer than that, going back to my school days when I first became fascinated with Napoleon III. When, in the summer of 1994, I was discussing the subject of my next book with Sally Riley, a close friend and astute literary agent (though not mine), she said that I should write the book I had always wanted to write; and that is what I have at last done. My first grateful acknowledgement must therefore go to her.

Thereafter, in addition to the many biographers, memoir-writers, historians and journalists, most of them long dead, whose works I am happy to mention in the Bibliography, I must thank a wide range of different people who have helped me greatly. When writing about a man who died well over a century ago, inevitably the first group to whom I must express my indebtedness are librarians, archivists and specialist booksellers: Simon Blundell, Librarian at the Reform Club in London, which has one of the finest private collections of books in the country; Mme Nicole Effroy at the Library of the Cercle de l'Union Interalliée in Paris; Christa Gross of the Napoleon Museum in Arenenberg, Switzerland, where Napoleon III spent much of his developing years; the helpful staff at the Archives Nationales in Paris; the Musée du Second Empire in Compiègne; the Library of the Royal Society of Medicine, with its bound volumes of Victorian copies of the *Lancet* and the *British Medical Journal*; the Local Studies Section of Bromley General Library, Kent; and Kensington Public Library, West London, with its issues of the last century's *Times* readily available on micro-film, and its unique collection of out-of-print biographies gathered from public libraries all over the capital and stored in its basement; Roy Hopper, Librarian at Chislehurst Public Library, who went far beyond the call of duty in searching out long-forgotten literature on Camden Place, where Napoleon III died, and on Nathaniel William John Strode, who was then, at least in theory, its owner; Miss Ann Yarnold, Librarian at Farnborough Hill School, Hampshire, which was for many years the final home of his widow, the Empress

Eugenie; Mme Nadine Massias of the Bibliothèque de Bordeaux and Jacques Pons and Mme Ursch of the Archives Départementales des Landes in south-west France, who kindly helped with local information about Napoleon III's illegitimate sons, the Comte de Labenne and the Comte d'Orx; Christophe Bourachot, the enterprising owner of the Librarie des Deux Empires in Paris, a bookshop where anyone researching anything to do with either of France's two Empires is certain to find something of value; Gibert Joseph, the venerable bookshop on the Boulevard St Michel, which for generations has supplied students, both young and old, with books they often cannot find elsewhere, and – of course – the stall-holders on the banks of the Seine where, if you are lucky, you may find a somewhat tattered literary relic that you had given up hope of ever finding.

I am proud to acknowledge my gratitude to Her Majesty The Queen for graciously allowing access to documents in the Royal Archives at Windsor Castle, and for permitting extracts from those documents to be published here. I must also express my indebtedness to Lady de Bellaigue, Registrar of the Royal Archives, for her assistance and helpful suggestions.

The following people spent time with me and gave me the benefit of their comments and knowledge: Mme Marie-Hélène Gémain d'Orx, Napoleon III's great-great-granddaughter, who talked stylishly and openly about him and his descendants; Sir David Innes Williams, MD, MChir. (Cambridge), FRCS, Mr Grant Williams, MS, MSc., FRCS and Mr James F. Bellringer FRCS (Urol.), three consultant urologists who have assisted me greatly with their specialist medical knowledge; Alain Boumier and Charles Griffiths of the Académie du Second Empire in Paris, N. E. Pearson, the Chislehurst Golf Club's Secretary, and William M. Mitchell, its historian; Dr. Paul Kuapman, the Westminster Coroner; Father Cuthbart, Prior of St Michael's Abbey, Farnborough; the distinguished French biographer and magazine editor, Pierre Assouline, an old friend, who pointed me in many useful directions; Ms Julia Cowper-Smith, who talked to me about her great-grandfather, Nathaniel Strode; Laurent Lemarchand, Assistant Press Secretary at the French Embassy in London, who helped with both the meaning of a specialist French expression and the current value of mid-nineteenth-century French currency; Eric Salandre, a fervent admirer of Napoleon III at Ham where he was imprisoned 'in perpetuity' on his way to final power; Pierre Laperrade, owner of the Hôtel des Voyageurs in Gavarnie, where Napoleon III was alleged to have been conceived, who supplied much useful local information.

I must also mention the Tourist Offices at Boulogne-sur-Mer, Cauterets, Compiègne, Ham, Martinique, Plombières and Sedan, which provided a lot of information it would have been difficult to find elsewhere.

Finally, I must say how grateful I am to my editor, Richard Johnson of HarperCollins, and to my agent, Jonathan Lloyd of Curtis Brown, who have both been patient and loyal throughout the long saga that this book has entailed.

PART ONE

NAPOLEON I AND THE FIRST EMPIRE

Chapter One

Roots: Martinique and Corsica

N APOLEON III'S ROOTS WERE not in mainland Europe but in two starkly contrasting islands thousands of miles apart. One was the small, lush Caribbean island of Martinique, first colonised by the French as far back as 1635. The other was the rugged, mountainous Mediterranean island of Corsica, bought by the French in a starkly commercial transaction from the Italian city-state of Genoa in 1768 after which it took them a whole year to conquer – but not entirely subdue – the armed opposition of islanders fighting for their independence from both France and Italy.

The future emperor's maternal grandparents came from Martinique and were of pure French stock. His grandmother was born on 23 June 1763 and was baptised Marie Josephe Rose Tascher de la Pagerie. Although called Rose during the first thirty-two years of her life, she is known to history as Josephine, first wife of Napoleon I. As ever completely taking over anything and everything that came his way, Napoleon told her within weeks of their first meeting in the autumn of 1795 that thenceforth her second name, Josephe, should be made more feminine and beguiling as 'Josephine' and that she should answer in future to nothing else.

Her own grandfather, Gaspard Joseph Tascher de la Pagerie, had emigrated from France in 1726 as a young man, hoping to make his fortune in the French Caribbean islands, then considered part of the Americas. The colonies were rich in sugar cane, then the only source of sugar in the world, and the expression 'rich as a Creole' was a familiar one in eighteenth-century France. But the amiable, lightweight Gaspard made no fortune for himself or for his wife and five children. His most noteworthy achievement was to marry his good-looking but equally indolent son, Joseph Gaspard, to Rose Claire des Vergers de Sannois, of nobler blood, stronger character – and supposedly considerable wealth. With her, at the almost unmarriageable age of twenty-five, came the sugar plantation at Les Trois Îlets, lying about twenty miles across the bay from the island's capital, Fort Royal (now Fort de France and the closest resemblance to Paris in the tropics).

Life was good for the young Josephine and her two younger sisters. As with most colonial expatriates, her family lived in far grander style than would have been possible in the country of their origin. There were plenty of slaves, the house was large and comfortable, they were high in the pecking order of island society. And there was always the balmy warmth of an island paradise: 'a patch of emerald on a sapphire sea', as a modern travel brochure might say. She and her sisters could play in the shade of mango and custard-apple trees. As her most recent biographer, Evangeline Bruce, has written, 'The memory of the island's brilliant birds and tropical bougainvillea, the jasmine and the orchids would remain with her all her life and, when she was Empress of France, be recreated in her greenhouses and aviaries.' A modern visitor to her future home at Malmaison just outside Paris can still see the remains of her once-splendid conservatories.

At twelve, she went for four years to a convent boarding-school where she learned the social graces of deportment, embroidery, dancing and music – but not much else. 'Her voice is sweet, she plucks prettily at the guitar and, showing a general aptitude for music, she could with proper instruction perfect her singing, playing and dancing,' wrote her father without too much enthusiasm. A mulatto fortune-teller told her one day that she would be unhappy, she would be widowed, she would marry again and she would become 'more than a queen' in France.

Once back home from school on the plantation at Les Trois Îlets, this broad prophecy seemed destined to be unfulfilled. Her mother's father had died, leaving not a fortune, as everyone expected, but horrendous debts – of which her philandering, feckless father already had enough of his own. What to do? There was only one solution: the sixteen-year-old Josephine, sweet-natured and generous but, at that stage, chubbily pretty rather than beautiful, must make a 'good marriage'.

And so, at least in financial terms, she did. Vicomte Alexandre de Beauharnais had been born on the island in 1760, three years before Josephine, while his father, the Marquis François de Beauharnais, was Governor and Lieutenant General of all the French colonies in the Caribbean. Returning to France at the end of his father's tour of duty, he had been brought up in Paris and by 1779, at the age of nineteen, he was a dashingly handsome young man in his white and silver infantry uniform. Unfortunately, he was also self-centred, snobbish and already a womaniser.

He needed a wife badly. His mother had left him considerable wealth but, unless he married, he would have to wait until he came of age before he could inherit. Josephine's aunt, who just happened to be his father's mistress (they eventually married after nearly forty years together when the marquis was eighty-two and she was fifty-seven), suggested her dowryless niece as a suitable bride. Indeed, any of the three young sisters would have done. 'Bring us whichever daughter you consider most likely to suit my son,' the Marquis de Beauharnais wrote to Josephine's father, enclosing a marriage document in which the space for the name of the bride was left blank.

In October 1779, after Josephine and her father had undertaken the two-month voyage between Martinique and France, the two young 'lovers' met for the first time. She was quite happy with what she saw but, although he conceded that she had a very pleasing temperament, he complained to his father that she was rather less pretty than he had been led to believe.

Nevertheless, on 13 December 1779, they were married. Almost from the very beginning they were both unhappy for they had hardly any points of mutual contact: she was gauche and unsophisticated while he was worldly and well-educated – and there was no love between them to fill the gap. They had two children, Eugene, on 3 September 1781, and Hortense, mother of Napoleon III, on 10 April 1783, but by the time Hortense was born, the marriage had ended. In the previous September, soon after Josephine had become pregnant, Alexandre left without warning and returned to Martinique as aide-de-camp to the then governor, accompanied by his current mistress. Husband and wife never lived together again.

Three years later, in February 1785, Josephine obtained a legal separation with custody of Eugene until he was five after which

Alexandre would oversee his education, permanent custody of Hortense and a substantial annual allowance. By then she was living at the Abbaye de Penthemont, officially a convent in the rue de Grenelle in a fashionable part of Paris but, in reality, simply a good address in which aristocratic young women, experiencing problems with their husbands, could rent suitably secluded accommodation.

In the two years that she lived there, Josephine virtually reinvented herself: she restyled herself upon the other women in the place, many coming from the most illustrious families in France. She looked after her figure, she learned anew how to dress and to walk, adding style and a Parisian elegance to her natural Caribbean grace. She is 'a fascinating young person,' wrote one of her visitors, 'a lady of distinction and elegance, perfect of manner, endowed with a multitude of graces and with the loveliest of speaking voices'. Napoleon I (hereafter referred to as Napoleon) was later to say that her lilting voice, with its slight Creole accent, was 'like a caress'.

Leaving her 'convent' home in September 1785, Josephine quickly developed two new characteristics. Firstly, she was almost never out of debt until her death twenty-nine years later: she had acquired a taste for the grand style of living which thenceforth she pursued resolutely, whether or not in sufficient funds. Secondly, until she finally found, in the early 1800s, true marital happiness with Napoleon, she became almost as sexually promiscuous as her first handsome, philandering husband. She would never acquire chocolate-box beauty and most of the many paintings of her that survive, especially from her days as Empress, are simply too bland to make any impact; but a watercolour sketch by Jean-Baptiste Isabey in the late 1790s (no one seems sure of the date) shows her as she must really have been: retroussé nose, warm, sensuous eyes, marvellous lips, her chestnut-coloured hair brushed loosely forward across the temples and forehead in a style that seems remarkably casual and modern. One can easily believe she was the one woman for whom Napoleon, despite all his mistresses and many ephemeral affairs, felt the greatest love of his life.

Josephine also knew her family duty. In the summer of 1788, when she learned that her father, Joseph, was ill and her only sister lay dying, she sold some of her most precious belongings, including her harp, to pay for her and five-year-old Hortense's passage home to Martinique. They were still on the island when the French Revolution began on 14 July 1789 with the storming of the Bastille in Paris. It was not a good time for a *vicomtesse* and her daughter to be in France, especially as Josephine found life extremely agreeable on the family plantation at Les Trois Îlets, coupled with frequent visits to balls and Government House suppers at Fort Royal.

But it was only a question of time before the shock waves of the Revolution reached Martinique. Armed insurrection broke out on the island and hearing, on yet another pleasant visit to Fort Royal in early September 1790, that the capital was due to be attacked by insurgents on the very next day, Josephine hastened down to the harbour clutching Hortense's hand.

It was definitely the time to go. As they dashed across the open country that is now the beautifully set out Parc de la Savane, a cannonball landed only a few feet from them: today tourists can see on that spot a white marble statue of Josephine in her robes as Empress of France. Riding at anchor in the harbour was a French naval frigate under the command of a young officer whom Hortense, in her memoirs written some thirty years later, describes discreetly as 'a captain whom my mother knew': in fact, the Comte Scipion du Roure was one of Josephine's many lovers. He took them on board, without luggage or money; on the long voyage home across the Atlantic, seven-year-old Hortense showed early the physical bravery that was later to be her hallmark – and that of her son, Napoleon III.

To help pass time as the ship struggled through the waves, Hortense used to entertain the crew with Caribbean songs and dances but, after a while, the rough wooden deck wore ever-widening holes in her only pair of shoes. Yet, rather than disappoint the sailors, she continued to dance, even though the soles of her feet were cut and bleeding.

The France to which mother and daughter returned in late October 1790 was still comparatively safe for aristocrats and, for some time, Josephine, who remained dependent financially upon her estranged husband, took up again her pleasure-loving life. King Louis XVI still sat, however uneasily, upon the throne, the aristocrats still kept their titles and people with money who had not been lucky (or clever) enough to leave the country, tried to carry on their lives as if the Bastille had never been attacked.

The worst excesses of the Revolution were yet to come – but they were not all that far distant.

The darkest days of the French Revolution are familiar to anyone interested in history, but it is worth revisiting briefly the tumultuous event that has essential relevance for the whole subsequent history of France, including the life of Napoleon III.

On 10 August 1792, the Parisian mob stormed the Tuileries Palace dragging off Louis XVI, his queen, Marie-Antoinette, and their young children to prison and butchering the king's Swiss Guard with such brutality that it turned the stomach of the young Napoleon who, then a young artillery officer, watched the scene with horror.[1]

In early September 1792 came the infamous September Massacres when hundreds of so-called 'traitors' held in the prisons of Paris simply because they were aristocrats, priests or were wealthy were slaughtered without trial or scruple: 'I am the man you are looking for,' said the Archbishop of Paris stepping forward trying to halt the bloodshed, only to be struck across the face with a sword and have a pike plunged into his chest as he fell to the ground.

On 21 September 1792, the National Convention, the country's new governing body, formally abolished the monarchy and proclaimed a republic in which the only title permitted was 'Citizen'.

On 21 January 1793, Louis XVI was guillotined in the Place de la Concorde (then called the Place de la Révolution), to the drums beating loudly to drown his plea that his blood should be the last to flow in France. On 30 June 1793, a law was passed declaring that 'Liberty, Equality, Fraternity' were to be carved on public buildings: surprisingly, this famous motto of the Revolution did not appear any earlier and, to this day, no one knows who first coined it. On 16 October 1793, Marie-Antoinette was beheaded after apologising to her executioner for treading on his foot as she stumbled on to the scaffold: 'I beg your pardon, monsieur,' she said. 'I did not do it on purpose.' Those were the last words she spoke.

---

[1] Years later, in exile on St Helena, he was to recall: 'Never since has any battlefield given me the same impression of so many corpses as did the sight of the masses of dead Swiss ... I saw some very well-dressed ladies committing the worst indecencies on their bodies.'

During these terrible years, the death toll mounted and heads tumbled into the baskets beneath the guillotines set up in Paris and other major cities, as if the whole country had gone berserk with blood lust.

Finally, on 10 June 1794, the infamous Law of 22 Prairial allowed 'the enemies of the people' to be summarily executed without even the mock trials which had previously been the norm and, over the following seven weeks, 1,366 people died.

This latest orgy of death proved too much for a nation now at last losing its appetite for mindless killing and, on 28 July 1794, a rat-faced lawyer named Maximilien Marie Robespierre, the last and most powerful of the revolutionary leaders and the most feared man in France, was taken, with his closest supporters, to the Place de la Révolution and, amid scenes of shameless rejoicing, beheaded. 'You monster spewed out of hell,' one woman screamed at him. 'Go down into your grave burdened with the curses of the wives and mothers of France ... The thought of your execution makes me drunk with joy.'

At last, the blood-letting was over.

Josephine rode out the worst horrors of the Revolution by bending with the wind and adapting to the new lifestyle forced upon her. She let herself be called *Citoyenne* Beauharnais, dropping the title of vicomtesse and the too-aristocratic 'de', and encouraged her children, like all good young republicans, to learn a trade: twelve-year-old Eugene was apprenticed to a carpenter and ten-year-old Hortense to a seamstress.

Paradoxically, Alexandre, her estranged husband and, by birth, far more aristocratic than she, embraced passionately the cause of the Revolution. In modern terms, one would call him a dedicated 'champagne socialist'. In the Revolution's early days, he gladly accepted the reduced role of the king and of his own class and, after the fall of the monarchy, he was even happy to fight for his country's new rulers against the invading armies of Austria and Prussia, sent by their sovereigns to save the French sovereign and his family. He was promoted general and made Commander-in-Chief of the Army of the Rhine. 'He possesses energy, a stubbornness of disposition, a depth of intelligence, a longing to win fame and an overpowering ambition,' said a friend.

9

But, perhaps like his grandson over half a century later, he did not have the ability with which to fuel and maintain his ambition. When called from the garrison city of Strasbourg to relieve beleaguered Mainz, not too far distant, he delayed until it was too late. A Revolutionary commissioner sent out to investigate reported that the general had preferred to 'make a fool of himself at Strasbourg by chasing after whores all day and giving balls for them at night'. In March 1794, he was arrested in Paris as 'a friend of tyranny and an enemy of liberty' and thrown into a former Carmelite convent converted into a prison.

Desperately, Josephine petitioned for his release. She did all that she could. Then she received an anonymous letter, warning that she was herself in danger. A less courageous woman might have fled but, 'Where should I go without compromising my husband?' she wrote to an aunt. The following month, she too was arrested and taken to the same Carmelite prison.[1]

At first, their young children came every day to see them in their cells in different parts of the prison. Later they were not even allowed to write. 'We tried to make up for this,' recalled Hortense in her memoirs, 'by writing at the bottom of the laundry list, "Your children are well" but the porter was barbarous enough to erase it. As a last resort, we would copy out the laundry list ourselves so that our parents would see our writing and know that at least we were still alive.'

On 23 July 1794, Alexandre was executed. His last letter to Josephine is a remarkable document. He declares his loyalty to the Revolution that is about to take his life and denies that he has ever betrayed it. He urges her to fight for his rehabilitation – but begs her to postpone her labours because, if he were rehabilitated too soon, that would discredit the Revolution by revealing that it had killed innocent people. 'In the midst of revolutionary tempests,' he explains, 'a great nation seeking to pulverise its chains must ever be watchful and more afraid of sparing a guilty man than of striking the innocent.'

After this special pleading for his killers, he ends: 'Farewell, dear

---

[1] In a last desperate celebration of life, they each took, as many other prisoners did, a lover from among their fellow captives. Josephine's was the future General Hoche whose name is now given to one the most famous avenues in Paris.

friend. Console yourself in our children. Console them by enlightening their minds and, above all by teaching them that by their courage and patriotism they may efface the memory of my execution and recall my services and my claims to our nation's gratitude. Farewell, you know those I love. Be their comforter and by your care prolong my life in their hearts. Farewell, I press you and my dear children for the last time to my breast.'

The letter so moved Hortense that she kept it for the rest of her life and reprinted it, in full, in her memoirs.

Josephine also prepared to die, but five days after Alexandre's execution Robespierre was beheaded on the same scaffold. On 6 August 1794 the *Veuve Beauharnais* was freed to return home to her children.

France after Robespierre in the mid-1790s was in many ways similar to Europe and the United States after World War One in the 1920s: everyone who could afford it – and many who could not – gave themselves over to having a good time. That certainly applied to Josephine. Still alluring at thirty-one, although it was said that she never opened her mouth too wide for fear of showing her unfashionably darkened and unsightly teeth, she used her charm – and perhaps much more besides – to wheedle generous compensation out of State officials for her late husband's confiscated property while influential friends put profitable business deals her way.

'Her even temper,' wrote a contemporary, 'her easy-going disposition, the kindness that filled her eyes and was expressed not only in her words but in the very tone of her voice . . . all this gave her a charm that counter-balanced the dazzling beauty of her rivals.'

But it was not charm alone that sustained this warm, sensuous woman from the Caribbean. Within less than a year of her husband's death, probably in May or June 1795, she had become the mistress of one of the most powerful men in France at that time. This was the handsome virile figure of forty-year-old Paul Barras, once a vicomte but now a leading member of the government and a general commanding the Army of the Interior. In August 1795, with his help, she made the down payment on a pretty little house of her own at 6, rue Chantereine, now renamed rue de la Victoire in honour of Napoleon's later victories.[1]

---

[1] The house itself was demolished in 1859 as part of her grandson's rebuilding of Paris.

Her relationship with Barras lasted only a few months but it served to bring her into contact with Napoleon Bonaparte, then a twenty-six-year-old brigadier general in the artillery. That summer this Corsican-born outsider, then still spelling his name Napoleone Buonaparte in the way of his island ancestors, had decided that his flagging military career needed a boost. According to military historian Correlli Barnett, he 'crawled to the influential in Paris' – among whom was General Barras. Barras had first noticed his brilliance at Toulon two years earlier when his inspired use of cannon-power, at a time when many French artillery officers had left the country, forced an invading British force to leave that vital naval sea-port. At Barras's sumptuous weekly receptions in the summer of 1795 Buonaparte several times met the general's charming hostess but, at that stage, he was merely one admirer among many.

But, on 5 October 1795 – still known to historians as '13 Vendé-miaire' as it was called in the Revolutionary calendar that still prevailed – the young brigadier general 'saved the Republic' (to use Barras's own expression) by his ruthless suppression of an armed royalist revolt in the streets of Paris. Robespierre's death had not brought political stability to France. Many royalists believed that their time had come at last. Their forces outnumbered government troops by six to one and they proclaimed defiantly that on this day they were going to march on the National Convention at the Tuiler-ies Palace and seize power. The previous evening Barras had summoned Buonaparte to his office and asked brusquely: 'Will you serve me? You have three minutes to decide.' The young artillery officer had not hesitated. He ordered the big guns to be brought in.

One cannon was posted so as to rake the rue St-Honoré, the approach road to the Tuileries, 8-pounders were placed at all exits from the street and more guns kept in reserve to take the rebel column in the flank, in case it still managed to force a way through. At 5.00 pm the rebels arrived. Seven hours later the victorious Buonaparte reported to his elder brother, Joseph: 'We killed plenty of them. They killed thirty men of ours and wounded sixty. We have disarmed the (rebel) districts and all is calm. As usual with me, I was not wounded. Happiness is mine!'

In Correlli Barnett's telling words, 'The Paris mob, since 1789 the ultimate arbiter of Governments, had yielded to military force, henceforward the ultimate arbiter instead.' It was a lesson that Napoleon Bonaparte – and later his nephew Napoleon III – were never to forget.

Napoleon's 'whiff of grape-shot', to use Thomas Carlyle's famous expression, not only saved the Republic but ensured overnight his own personal fame. Promoted to the gold-laced uniform of a full general, he took over from Barras as Commander-in-Chief of the Army of the Interior and Military Governor of Paris when, some three weeks later, the National Convention, having voted itself out of existence, handed over the government of France to five Directors – with Barras as their leader.

And what of Josephine? Round about this time, although no one knows the exact date, she ceased to be Barras's mistress. She was not the sort of woman to remain for long without a powerful protector in those difficult times. She knew the new general slightly from Barras's glittering weekly receptions and he had occasionally been a guest at her charming little house on the rue Chantereine. Now she chose to send him this somewhat strange note: 'You no longer come to see a friend who is fond of you. You have quite forsaken her. This is a mistake, as she is tenderly attached to you. Come to lunch with me tomorrow. I need to see you and to talk to you about matters of interest to you. Goodnight, *mon ami, je vous embrasse. Veuve Beauharnais.*'

That same evening, he sat down and wrote a hurried reply. 'I cannot imagine the reason for the tone of your letter. I beg you to believe that no one desires your friendship as much as I do, no one could be more eager to prove it. Had my duties permitted, I would have come in person to deliver this message. Buonaparte.'

Both these letters were written using the formal 'vous'. They did not 'tutoyer' each other, as with family, close friends – or lovers. But soon that was to change. 'I was not insensible to women's charms,' Napoleon said later on St Helena, 'but I had hardly been spoiled by them; I was shy with them. Mme de Beauharnais was the first to give me confidence.' He admitted that he was 'struck by her extraordinary grace and her irresistibly sweet manner. The acquaintance was shortly to ripen into intimacy.'

The date of this 'ripening' is unknown but it was obviously the night before he wrote (jumbling together, in his rush for words,

13

both personal forms of address) one of the most passionate love letters in history:

'Seven in the morning. I awaken full of you. Your portrait and the memory of yesterday's intoxicating evening have given no rest to my senses. Sweet and incomparable Josephine [note: no longer "Rose"], what a strange effect you have upon my heart! Are you displeased? Do I see you sad? Are you worried? Then my soul is grief-stricken and your friend cannot rest. But ... I cannot rest either when I yield to the deep feeling that overpowers me and I draw from your lips and heart a flame that burns me.

'Ah! last night I clearly realised that the portrait I had of you is quite different from the real you! You are leaving at noon and in three hours I shall see you. Until then, *mio dolce amor*, receive a million kisses but do not send me any for they will sear my blood.'

Within less than three months, they were married. Napoleon was hopelessly in love. Josephine was not; but she found him *drôle* (entertaining), one of her favourite words, and she was flattered by his attentions. Besides she was getting no younger and his star was rising: on 2 March 1796, he was named Commander-in-Chief of the Army of Italy soon to be dispatched to fight the Austrian armies in Austrian-controlled northern Italy.

One week later, on the evening of 9 March, two days before the Army of Italy was due to depart, Josephine and Napoleon were married by the light of a single candle at a simple civil ceremony in the mayor's office of the Second Arrondissement of Paris.[1] She wore his wedding present: a simple necklace of hair-fine gold from which hung a gold enamelled medallion bearing the prophetic words: '*Au Destin*' (To Destiny).

Five years later, her daughter, Hortense, was to marry one of Napoleon's younger brothers and the link between relaxed Martinique and turbulent Corsica in the ethnic make-up of their son, the future Napoleon III, would be complete.

*   *   *

[1] Anyone wanting to see the unchanged exterior of this building at 3, rue Antin, now a bank, can find it easily: three turnings on the right down from the Opéra Garnier past the Café de la Paix. Two plaques are on the wall, one commemorating the wedding itself and the other its 200th anniversary on 9 March 1996.

Napoleon's own attitude to his Corsican origins varied. He did not have an ounce of French blood in his veins from either of his parents: Carlo, a nimble-minded lawyer with a sharp, sensuous, Italian-looking face, or Letizia, petite and dynamic with dark brown eyes, chestnut hair and a strong, firm nose. Both their ancestors had come two centuries earlier from Italy and they were accepted as part of the island's native nobility. As a youngster, Napoleon had hated the French nation. 'I was born as my fatherland lay dying,' he once said bitterly. He believed that France had destroyed Corsica's one real chance of independence in crushing the guerrilla war that had broken out after it bought the island from Genoa a year before his birth, a war in which Carlo Buonaparte himself had fought on the side of the guerrillas.

The future emperor was born on 15 August 1769 in a house which still exists in the appropriately renamed Place de Letizia in modern Ajaccio. His original first name of Napoleone virtually proclaimed his family's hatred of the French, for he was named in honour of an uncle killed fighting against the French. Although pregnant, Letizia had insisted on going with Carlo to war and sharing his perils amid the rocks of his mountain redoubt: 'Bullets whistled past my ears,' she later recalled, 'but I trusted in the protection of the Virgin Mary, to whom I had consecrated my unborn child.'

On the day that the Corsicans were decisively defeated at the Battle of Ponte Nuovo, his mother felt the unborn Napoleon moving inside her 'as if he wanted to fight before he was even born'.

The future French emperor carried this enmity with him to the military academy at Brienne in north-eastern France, to which his father (who had by then made his peace with the conquerors) brought him at the age of nine. Only then did Napoleone reluctantly learn to speak French instead of his native Corsican. But for several years, his proud nature, poverty[1] and alien birth earned him few friends among his fellow officers.

---

[1] Carlo Buonaparte died in 1785, aged thirty-five of stomach cancer and, with his strong Corsican sense of family duty, Napoleon, then only sixteen, made himself responsible for his widowed mother, four brothers and four sisters. He thought his elder brother, Joseph, too lightweight for the task, a view reflecting his brother's lack of ability which he never changed.

At first, the French Revolution made little impact upon him. He used the time when France's rulers were fighting for their own lives to return home on long periods of leave to try and unite his countrymen in a new war for Corsican independence but they remained, as ever, hot-blooded, stubborn and hopelessly divided among themselves. In June 1793, with no money and nothing left except the clothes they wore, he and his family were forced to flee the island. They were branded outlaws in their own homeland.

At last, Napoleon's love for Corsica was dead. 'Among all the insults hurled against me, that of "Corsican" is the most mortifying,' he said. On St Helena, he recalled that, when Paul Barras advised him to marry Josephine, one reason that he gave was that 'the marriage would make people forget my Corsican name and make me wholly French'.

And, indeed, within a short time of his marriage, he 'Frenchified' both his Christian name and surname, dropping the final 'e' from his Christian name and 'u' from Buonaparte. Letizia, his strong-willed mother (and a totally different person from Napoleon III's other grandmother, the sweet-tempered but pleasure-loving Josephine), was bitterly opposed to the change. Later, on St Helena, Napoleon was to pay moving tribute to Letizia: 'Losses, privations, fatigues, she sustained and faced them all. She had the head of a man on the body of a woman.' But now he told his brother Joseph: 'Please tell Mama not to keep calling me Napoleone. Napoleone, always Napoleone! That makes me lose patience!' Corsica had become for him just another Mediterranean island, like Malta or Corfu.

But towards the end of his life, in exile on his rock in the South Atlantic, he relented. As so often happens, when the final clouds begin to gather in the sky, he went back, in his mind, to his roots. The modern Corsican historian, Jutta Schutz, reports him as saying on St Helena: 'Providence created in me a Corsican rock from which all strokes of Fate simply run off like water.' In those last years, he often felt homesick for Corsica. He was certain that the earth smelt different there and that, even with his eyes closed, just by the smell alone, he would recognise his native island.

And it has returned the compliment. In Ajaccio today, two splendid statues in marble commemorate him; the house in which he was born has been lovingly preserved; there is a Musée Napoléonien in the Town Hall and his parents' bodies lie buried in the Cathedral.

The veneration continues even unto the next generation. There is no avenue Napoleon III left in modern mainland France but there is one in modern Ajaccio.

Chapter Two

Parents

WITHIN WEEKS OF GIVING Josephine the wedding present bearing the words 'To Destiny', Napoleon seems to have realised for the first time what that destiny was to be. In May 1796, in the face of withering artillery fire from Austrian soldiers entrenched on the other side of a small river, his troops stormed their way across a vital bridge at the Italian town of Lodi and opened up the way to the major city of Milan, which they entered triumphantly five days later.

By his personal bravery at Lodi, Napoleon not only earned from his men the affectionate nickname of 'the Little Corporal' but he became aware, to the full extent, of his remarkable powers of leadership. 'From that moment,' he said on St Helena, 'I first foresaw what I might be. Already I felt the earth flee from beneath me, as if I were being carried into the sky.' Thinking back to that time half a century later, the venerable Marshal Auguste Marmont, then a young officer fighting alongside him, recalled: 'We marched surrounded by a kind of radiance whose warmth I can still feel as I did fifty years ago.'

Napoleon later boasted to his brother, Joseph: 'I am destined to change the face of the world,' and, on St Helena, reflecting on his life, he admitted: 'I wanted to rule the world – who wouldn't have in my place? The world begged me to govern it.'

And so he followed his destiny, one which buried at least one million Frenchmen and countless others besides. Within four years of his victory at Lodi, on 9 November 1799 (famous in all French – and some English – history books and biographies as 18 Brumaire, its date in the Revolutionary calendar[1]), he made himself dictator

---

[1] This dated from 22 September 1792 which became the year 1 and introduced new months (such as Brumaire) and new, ten-day weeks.

of France, albeit not yet emperor but with the title of First Consul. Having returned secretly from Egypt, where he had been leading the French armies in a grandiose campaign to establish French dominance in the Middle East,[1] he overthrew the Directory in a surprise coup d'état, casting Paul Barras and his four fellow Directors out into the political wilderness. A Second and a Third Consul were also appointed but they were mere subordinates. At the age of thirty, supreme political and military power were solely in his own hands.

As a symbol of his new status, he moved into the Tuileries Palace, the old home of the kings of France. He took over Louis XVI's rooms on the first floor and gave Marie Antoinette's former apartments on the ground floor to Josephine. 'I was never made for so much grandeur,' she confessed to her daughter Hortense. 'I will never be happy here. I can feel the Queen's ghost asking what am I doing in her bed.'

But Napoleon had no such scruples. On their first night at the Tuileries, he picked up his wife and carried her into Marie Antoinette's old bedroom, where he too was to sleep and the executed queen had entertained her husband. 'Come on, little Creole,' he said. 'Get into the bed of your masters.'

With the supreme power that Napoleon had acquired came the passionate desire for an heir. Napoleon had adopted Josephine's two children as his own and he was very fond of them. Even when Hortense later became a queen, he always began his letters to her: '*Ma fille.*'

Yet, however close he felt to them, they were not of his blood. Above all else, he needed and craved for his wife to give him a son. But Josephine was in her late thirties and, despite all her 'fertility cures' and frequent visits to the stimulating waters of the bustling spa town of Plombières that still exists today, she remained obstinately barren. The marital tension was mounting. On one occasion when Napoleon suggested going hunting and she tearfully protested that all the female deer were pregnant, he said in front of everyone:

[1] 'This little Europe does not supply enough of glory for me,' he had said. 'I must seek it in the East; all great fame comes from that quarter.' In fact, the Egyptian campaign proved only a partial success blighted almost at the start by Admiral Nelson's brilliant victory at the Battle of the Nile in August 1798 when all but four of the French ships were taken or destroyed.

'Come, we shall have to give up the idea. Every creature here is pregnant except Madame.'

Josephine knew with every barren day that passed that her marriage was in ever-increasing peril: all she could do was continue to have faith in the waters at Plombières, and hope.

It was at Plombières in 1801 that Josephine finally thought of the idea that would at once secure her husband an heir of his own blood, albeit at one stage removed, and, at the same time, take the pressure off her, as she approached her fortieth birthday, to provide an heir. She suggested to Napoleon that Hortense, then eighteen and a pretty, talented, blue-eyed girl, should marry his favourite younger brother, Louis Bonaparte, then aged twenty-three. An heir by that couple, united to him by love and blood, would surely prove the next best thing to a son of his own; and indeed, seven years later, their third son, the future Napoleon III, was born. It was all part of his maternal grandmother Josephine's grand design.

Napoleon readily accepted the idea. At the time, it seemed to him the perfect solution, and the two young people involved – despite their considerable reservations – reluctantly agreed to do as they were told.

Louis Bonaparte, born Luigi Buonaparte in Ajaccio on 2 September 1778, was handsome in a swarthy, Corsican way and the best looking of the five Bonaparte brothers. He had always been close to Napoleon. At the age of eleven, after their father's death, he had gone to live with him in his army lieutenant's billet and had virtually been brought up by him: Napoleon gave him catechism lessons for his first Communion and cooked their meals. 'Louis has just the qualities I like,' wrote Napoleon at about that time. 'Warmth, good health, talent, precision in his dealings and kindness.'

As a teenager, Louis had been dashing and brave and utterly devoted to his brother: at the age of seventeen, he saved his life at the Battle of Arcona during the Italian campaign by galloping to rescue him, under fire, from a treacherous marsh into which his horse had bolted.

Said Napoleon on St Helena: 'In Italy, my brother's courage was brilliant and he remained indifferent to the praises which his valour provoked. He was a strict disciplinarian without thinking of his own personal safety. At the passage of the River Po, he placed himself at the head of the attacking columns. At Pizzighittone he was the first in the breach. At the assault of Pavia he was on horse-back at the head of the sappers and grenadiers who were ordered to destroy the gates with their hatchets. In a shower of bullets, he remained on horseback because he thought it was his duty to be mounted in order to make a better reconnaissance of the city.' Napo-leon III obviously derived his personal bravery from *both* his parents.

But it was also during the Italian campaign that an incident seems to have occurred that warped Louis' character and affected his temperament for the rest of his life. Whether it was, as British biographers have variously maintained, an injury in battle, the onset of a particularly painful form of rheumatism, or a crisis caused by a sudden awareness of his supposed (but unsubstantiated) homo-sexuality, something undoubtedly happened that, within a few years, was to make him sullen, moody and, as Napoleon himself later admitted, 'always complaining'. Two distinguished French his-torians, André Lebey writing in 1909 and Adrien Dansette in 1961, both cite Napoleon on St Helena as giving a remarkably basic reason for his brother's marked change of character: namely, the disastrous effects of a bad attack of *mal de Naples*, a venereal disease contracted by Louis as 'the unfortunate reward of the favours of a certain Countess C. at Brescia'.

Whatever the truth, even so 'understanding' a biographer as the Victorian Blanchard Jerrold, Napoleon III's first official biographer and one always anxious to portray any Bonaparte in the most favourable light, can only describe Louis as 'even in those early days a morose, self-contained man'. It took several weeks before he agreed to become his brother's stepson-in-law, after which he sent his bride-to-be a twenty-page letter setting out the details of his sexual adventures to date (omitting the countess in Brescia) and requesting a similar confession from her. Perhaps a little tartly, she replied that she had nothing to confess.

That was undoubtedly true.

Described by a contemporary witness as 'an exquisite blonde with amethyst eyes, supple waist and harmonious gestures', Hortense de Beauharnais had inherited all her mother's charm and sweetness of nature. She was also a considerable painter and musician; her stir-ring march *Partant pour la Syrie* became a favourite battle song of her stepfather's soldiers and later the national anthem of her son's Second Empire.

In 1801, she was at the perfect marriageable age for someone in her position. She had recently refused several suitors whom she did not like and Napoleon himself had inadvertently been responsible for her losing the one husband whom she wanted.

She was known to have fallen in love with twenty-nine-year-old Colonel Christophe Duroc, Napoleon's most trusted aide-de-camp, and it was also known that he returned her affections. One evening before Josephine's marriage suggestion Napoleon asked Louis Antoine Bourrienne, his private secretary: 'Where is Duroc?' 'He has gone to the Opéra,' was the reply. 'As soon as he returns,' said Napoleon, 'tell him he can have Hortense. The wedding must take place within the next forty-eight hours. I will give him 500,000 francs and the command of a division at Toulon. They are to go there the day after the wedding. I want no sons-in-law around me here in Paris and I wish to know this very night whether that suits him.'

Not surprisingly, Duroc, a handsome, proud man who was later killed in battle and whose statue can be seen today, with other French military heroes, lining the outer wall of the Louvre along the rue de Rivoli in Paris opposite the rue de l'Echelle, reacted angrily to Napoleon's peremptory words. 'In that case, he can keep his daughter and I am off to the whorehouse!' he told the obsequious Bourrienne.

Then, only weeks after that unhappy incident, the same Bourrienne came to Hortense with the suggestion that she marry Louis, a man for whom, in her own words, she did not care particularly.

In her memoirs, written some sixteen years later, she could still recall what he said. Bourrienne's message deserves to be recounted in full, for it is a masterpiece of moral blackmail and Machiavellian astuteness:[1]

---

[1] These memoirs, begun in exile in 1817 and substantially completed by 1820, were never meant for outside eyes but only for those of 'a few intimate friends whom I wish to know me better'. In fact, they remained in the private possession of her family for over a century, during which time Napoleon III himself read and re-read them. Apart from unauthorised and unreliable extracts published in France in the mid-nineteenth century, they were finally only published, with the permission of Prince Napoleon, then head of the Bonaparte family, in Paris in as late as 1927. They were published in London during the following year but only in abridged form and in a poor translation. Largely overlooked by both French and British biographers and historians, the original French version forms a unique and valuable record of Hortense's life.

'I have been commissioned to suggest something to you which your mother and the Consul desire ardently. They wish to unite you to Colonel Louis Bonaparte. He is kind and affectionate. His tastes are simple. He will appreciate you to the fullest degree, and is the only suitable husband for you. Look about you. Who is there you would care to marry? The time has come when you must consider the matter seriously. No one until now has appealed to you, and even if your heart made a choice that did not meet with your parents' approval, would you be prepared to disobey them? You love France. Do you want to leave it? Your mother could not bear the thought of your union with some foreign prince who would separate you from her for ever. Her misfortune, as you know, is that she can no longer hope for children. You can remedy this and perhaps ward off a still greater misfortune. I assure you intrigues are constantly being formed to persuade the Consul to obtain a divorce. Only your marriage can tighten and strengthen those bonds on which depend your mother's happiness. Will you hesitate?'

Hortense asked for a week to consider the matter. Some British historians dismiss her as the equivalent of a poor little rich girl: pampered and selfish. For instance, Robert Sencourt, writing in 1933, described her as: 'Talented, capricious and indulgent, she was one of those women who pine for lack of sympathy and whose nerves never allow them to charm except when they have their own way.' That waspish judgement is unfair. In later life, she was to prove a steely survivor and, even at that stage, as she explains in her memoirs, she saw it 'as a question of sacrificing my romantic fancies to my mother's happiness. I could not hesitate between the two.'

At the end of the week, she told Bourrienne that she would marry Louis. 'Strange to say, from that day,' she recorded, 'I became calm. All my agitation seemed to have passed from me to my mother. Too well aware of my ideas on marriage not to suspect the reasons underlying my acceptance, she wept continuously. Her glances seemed to say: "You are sacrificing yourself for me." I realised that in order to console her, I must seem satisfied.'

For his part, Napoleon chose to play the gruff soldier. 'Well! So Louis is courting you, is he? That ought to suit you and your mother too. There, I give my consent!' And that was all he said.

On 3 January 1802, Hortense and Louis were married in a civil ceremony at the Tuileries Palace followed by a religious service the following day in a small house on the rue de la Victoire, now long since demolished, that Napoleon gave them as a wedding present. For reasons that are perhaps easy to understand, Josephine, who genuinely loved her daughter, wept uncontrollably throughout both proceedings. Louis' comment in his own memoirs is brutal: 'Never was there a ceremony so sad, never did a husband and wife feel more sharply a presentiment of all the horrors of a forced and ill-assorted marriage.'

Although it is fashionable nowadays not to quote Blanchard Jerrold, who is generally dismissed as a glorified Victorian hack, it is a fact that, as Jerrold's own biographer in the *Dictionary of National Biography* concedes, he did have the great advantage of knowing Napoleon III personally and of talking to him about, among many other things, his parents. Jerrold's assessment of their marriage seems as fair now as when he penned it in 1874. After quoting Louis' brutal comment in his memoirs, he continues: 'But we may believe that at the time they acquiesced with good grace. Both had been disappointed in love; Hortense had been wounded in her pride by the conduct of Duroc; Louis had suffered the morbid elements of his character to obtain a mastery over him. But they stood in relation to one another at the altar much as most couples stand where the marriage is made by the families of the young people as a prudent, worldly settlement in life.

'The aversion, with all its bitterness, came afterwards.'

From the beginning, the marriage was a total disaster. The two were a complete mismatch. The person whom Hortense held most dear in the world was Josephine; yet within days of their wedding Louis, who shared the clannish dislike of all Napoleon's siblings for their sister-in-law, told her: 'You are the daughter of a mother without morals. I do not wish that you have any contact with her. You shall not see her except in my presence and only when family convenience requires it.' Hortense ignored the decree but it made it even less possible for her to love this soured, bad-tempered man.

Yet she did her duty. Within a month, she was pronounced pregnant. Six months later, Napoleon was proclaimed Consul for

Life with the right to nominate his successor: the need for an heir became even more pressing.[1]

Hortense had calculated with her obstetrician (Jean-Louis Baudelocque, after whom a hospital in Paris is now named) the date of her baby's expected arrival. 'He told me that women often made mistakes of two and even three weeks, especially if it were a boy,' she wrote in her memoirs, 'and that he would not be surprised if the event took place on 1 October. As I had been married on 3 January, that would have made just three days less than nine months after my marriage. Surprised and laughing, I hastened to tell this to my husband but he replied glowering: "If such a thing happened, I would never see you again as long as I lived." – "What," I exclaimed in despair, "can it be that you suspect me?" – "No, I know the truth. But it is on account of what people would say."' (This is because Lucien, another Bonaparte brother jealous of Napoleon's success and resentful of Josephine and her daughter, had repeated to Louis on his wedding day the popular – and untrue – rumour, partly fed by the British wartime propaganda machine, that Hortense was already pregnant with Napoleon's own child.)

In fact, it was not until the evening of 9 October 1801, in a new and much more splendid house on the rue de la Victoire given them by Napoleon,[2] that Hortense gave birth to a baby boy. Her nurse and her waiting women cried out: '*Voilà notre Dauphin!*' and, when Napoleon came two days later to see his nephew and step-grandson for the first time, he was delighted. With typical arrogance, he ordered that the child be called Napoleon Charles.

The birth of a son did nothing to make Louis' and Hortense's marriage any happier. We know from a letter written by Louis to his wife fifteen years later that sexual intercourse, suspended at the start of Hortense's pregnancy, was not resumed between them until a full two years later. Officially, they still lived together as man and wife but they did not actually sleep together again until a period

---

[1] Napoleon, forever presenting himself as a champion of the people, a role that Napoleon III was later assiduously to follow, only accepted the title after a national referendum (then called 'plebiscite') had shown its overwhelming approval by a massive majority of 3.5 million to 8,000.

[2] Nowadays a synagogue stands upon the site.

of some two months in the spring of 1804, as a result of which their second son was born, on 11 October 1804. Again at Napoleon's command, the child was given the first name of Napoleon but his parents were graciously allowed to choose his second name of Louis.

But by then there had been a fundamental change in the status of all of them. Five months earlier, on 18 May 1804, the logical result of the build-up of the last few years had come to a triumphal conclusion and Napoleon's compliant Senate had proclaimed him Emperor of the French. Again, he had insisted on a national referendum to back this up by popular acclaim and this time even fewer Frenchmen had voted against than two years earlier had opposed his becoming Consul for Life: 3,000 Noes instead of the original 8,000.

An emperor must have a nominated heir and, indeed, the referendum had specifically given its overwhelming consent to an 'hereditary' Empire. No one contemplated for a moment that France could possibly ever be ruled by a woman; so the Senate decreed that if, at his death, Napoleon had no legitimate male heir, the succession should go first to his elder brother, Joseph, and his male descendants and then to Louis and his male descendants, provided that Napoleon had not previously adopted any son or grandson of his brothers aged at least eighteen – which could only be a long time off. Joseph Bonaparte only had two daughters and it was generally accepted that his wife was past child-bearing age, so the moral was clear: Louis and his two-year-old son, Napoleon Charles, were, for the foreseeable future, next in line to rule the Empire; after the death of Joseph.

There is no doubt that Napoleon dearly loved his step-grandson/ nephew, and that is the correct manner in which to express the way in which he regarded the relationship between himself and all Hortense's eventual three sons. A few months later, he confided to Pierre Louis Roederer, at the time a trusted adviser: 'Joseph's daughters don't even know yet that I am called Emperor – they still call me Consul. Whereas little Napoleon, when he goes past the grenadiers in the garden shouts to them "Long live *Nonon* the soldier!"' (*Nonon* is a French word for grandpa.) And he added significantly: 'I love Hortense . . . If she asked to see me when I was in Council, I would go out to her. If Madame Murat [his own sister, Caroline Murat] asked for me, I would not. With her, I always have to take up positions for a pitched battle. They [his brothers and sisters] say my wife is untrustworthy and her children's attentions insincere. Well, I like them. They treat me like an old uncle. That sweetens my life. I'm growing old, I'm thirty-six.'

At Napoleon's splendid over-the-top Coronation at Notre Dame in Paris on 2 December 1804, with everyone dressed up at huge expense (an estimated eight million francs) in pure comic-opera finery with sumptuous robes and headdresses created especially for the occasion, little Napoleon Charles stood nervously in pride of place in the front row with his mother's right hand protectively on his shoulder. In David's famous painting of the scene in the Louvre, he is depicted looking on as Napoleon, having crowned himself with the Pope sitting uselessly beside him, places the Imperial crown on the kneeling Josephine's head.[1]

'I swear to rule for the interests, happiness and glory of the people of France,' said Napoleon as part of his Coronation Oath; and he had used that same vital word 'glory' when accepting his earlier nomination as Consul for Life.

Those two references to 'glory' are an indication of the psychological appeal of Napoleon I, and later of Napoleon III, to the French nation: it appealed to the average French person's desire, above all else, for national glory; for France to be perceived as the finest, the best, in whatever context she is engaged. General de Gaulle trumpeted the same message in the 1960s. Even today's French politicians use it as an essential part of their platform. By contrast, no British politician has ever promised glory to the electorate. It has never been part of a British sovereign's Coronation Oath to swear allegiance to the achievement of glory as a sacred mission.

No British sovereign or politician would dream of making a

---

[1] One can also see Joseph and Louis Bonaparte, now princes in satin and velvet, standing on the left of the picture. Louis is second from the left. 'If Father could only see us now!' Napoleon had whispered to Joseph as the brothers processed into the cathedral. Incidentally, one should not be misled by Napoleon's mother sitting in the middle of the picture smiling benignly down on the proceedings. That was poetic licence by David: in fact, the redoubtable Letizia refused to attend because she was angry with Napoleon for his disapproval of her favourite son Lucien's love-inspired but 'unsuitable' marriage to the widow of a bankrupt businessman.

similar claim but to Napoleon I and Napoleon III such boasting came easily.

How was the marriage of Louis and Hortense faring amid all this pomp and glitter?

The answer is not very well. After their second child's birth, there was no resumption of sexual intercourse between them. When Hortense returned to St-Leu, the country home which Louis had purchased some time after their marriage, she found that he had raised the walls around the house by several feet and put a sentry box under her bedroom window. He had also walled up all doors but one leading into her quarters, had the side gate into the grounds bricked in, forbade her ladies-in-waiting to walk in those grounds and hired spies to read their correspondence.

But this was not all. To her understandable dislike of his malevolent character, there now was added physical revulsion. Louis had contracted an appalling new illness for which he was always seeking (unsuccessfully) a cure at various fashionable spas. It caused his right hand to wither so that soon he was only able to write with a pen strapped to the lower part of his arm. The once handsome young soldier had, at twenty-six, become a querulous, ageing invalid.

Hortense began to spend more and more time with her mother and less and less time with her husband.

The year 1805 saw Napoleon's power nearing its peak. Abroad, he had brought Italy, the Netherlands and the states of western Germany under his rule. At home, he was an absolute monarch with even his brothers and sisters calling him 'Sire' and 'Votre Majesté'. On 2 December 1805, the first anniversary of his Coronation, he achieved his greatest military feat: victory against the combined armies of Austria and Russia at Austerlitz. The British historian Alastair Horne, in his 1996 account of Napoleon's last ten years in power, claims that it was Austerlitz that started the clock ticking towards his destruction: 'If Austerlitz raised Napoleon to the pinnacle of his success, it also turned his head and filled it with the delusion that no force or combination of forces could now stop him conquering the world.'

But such thoughts played no part in the lives of Louis and Hortense. Quite the opposite. In June 1806, Louis became King of

Holland, put on the throne by his Imperial brother as part of his policy of having those he thought – or, at least, hoped – that he could most trust as nominal local rulers of his fast-expanding empire. Hortense was now Her Majesty the Queen of Holland but it made her no happier. She hated the cold, foggy weather of the flat, low-lying country where she was now forced to live and the status of king made Louis even more unpleasant to live with.

Napoleon, despite all the demands on his time and energies, yet perceived his 'daughter's' misery and did his best to try and help. In a quite extraordinary letter to Louis on 4 April 1807 from Schloss Finkenstein in east Prussia, where he was both preparing for another major attack on the Russian army and living an idyllic life with his latest mistress, the beautiful Polish countess Marie Walewska, he wrote: 'Your quarrels with the Queen are known to the public. Show in your private life the paternal and soft side of your character, and in your administration the sternness you display at home. You treat your young wife as though she were a regiment. You have the best and worthiest wife in the world, and yet you are making her unhappy.

'Let her dance as much as she likes, she is just the age for it. I have a wife who is forty and from the field of battle I write to her to go to balls. You wish a wife who is only twenty, who sees her life passing away with all its illusions, to live in a cloister or, like a nurse, to be always washing her child.

'I should not say all this to you if I were not interested in you. Make the mother of your children happy. There is only one way: show her thorough respect and confidence.

'Unfortunately you have a wife who is too virtuous: if she were a coquette, she would lead you by the nose. But she is a proud wife who grieves and revolts at the bare idea that you have a bad opinion of her. You should have had a wife like some I know in Paris. She would have deceived you and at the same time kept you at her knees.'

We will never know if this letter might have had some lasting effect for within days Louis and Hortense were temporarily united by tragedy: their four-and-a-half-year-old son Napoleon Charles, their first-born, became ill. A soreness of the throat developed into a brittle cough; the doctors diagnosed croup, a severe infection of the larynx, and, despite all their efforts, in the early hours of 5 May 1807 the little boy died. Both parents, weeping and on their knees at his bedside, were for a while united in their grief but not for long: they journeyed together to the royal palace of Laeken in French-occupied Austrian Netherlands (now modern Belgium) where Josephine joined them. Louis soon left to return to Holland.

Hortense was inconsolable in her grief. By nature, she instinctively cast herself in the role of victim of life's many miseries – but yet with a steely will to survive. While never forgetting her high social status, she tended to smile bravely through her tears. In the very first paragraphs of her memoirs, begun at the age of thirty-four, she wrote, in somewhat cloying prose: 'My life has been so brilliant and so full of misfortunes that people have interested themselves in me. The world has praised me and blamed me according to circumstances, but always with exaggeration because my high rank has allowed too few people to approach me so as to be able to judge me properly. I believe that I have merited neither a eulogy too flattering nor a criticism too severe. My heart has always guided me in all that I have done, and can one's heart go wrong when it is pure? . . .

'As for my children, it is not from me that they ought to learn the unhappiness their father has caused me. I have suffered so much for them, I have so cherished them that, if ever they were to know the truth, they would love me the more. As for myself, it will be sad, no doubt, to retrace the most beautiful years of my youth lived in tears; but there will be perhaps a sort of comfort in rediscovering, amid the dangers that I have been able to avoid, the little good that I have been able to accomplish.'

With the death of her young child, it will perhaps come as no surprise that her writing became even more tortured.

'It was towards me that he turned his pale and ravaged face,' she writes in her memoirs. 'It was I whom his lips, ready to close for ever, seemed to call. It was the name of his mother that I saw framed on those discoloured lips, as he breathed his last. And I survived! How can God allow a mother to outlive her child?'

And so it continued. Finally, on 20 May, Napoleon wrote to her as her 'affectionate father' pleading with her to put rational bounds to her sorrow. 'Don't destroy your health; distract your attention and learn that life is so thickly strewn with so many rocks and may be the source of so many misfortunes that death is not the worst of evils.'

On 2 June, he wrote again: 'You have not written a line to me in your just and heavy grief. You have forgotten everything as though you had not to suffer other losses. I am told [almost certainly by Josephine] that you care no longer for anything and that you are indifferent to everything: I perceive the truth of this through your silence. This is not well, Hortense. This is not what you used to promise. Your son was everything to you. Your mother and I, then, are nothing? Had I been at Malmaison [Hortense and Josephine had by then returned to Josephine's favourite residence just outside Paris] I should have shared your distress, but I should also have insisted that you give yourself back to your best friends.

'Adieu, my child. Be cheerful. We must be resigned. Keep your health so that you may fulfil all your duties. My wife is quite grieved at your condition: give her no more sorrow.'

At the suggestion of Dr Nicolas Corvisart, Napoleon's personal physician, who was a good doctor but tended to say what he knew his illustrious patients wanted to hear, Hortense had agreed to leave Napoleon Louis, her surviving two-year-old son, with Josephine at Malmaison while she tried to find new hope and a new will to live, alone with only a small entourage, in the remote, mountainous region of the Pyrenees in south-west France. Napoleon immediately perceived that this might be a marvellous opportunity for his brother, who was after all also mourning the loss of a son, to attempt a meaningful reconciliation with his wife. 'They are babies. They really must be brought together again. There is not the thickness of a sheet of paper between them,' he told Josephine.

So he persuaded Louis, who was always seeking a new cure for his various ailments, to follow Hortense down to the south-west and, while visiting other spas in the area, to try and spend some time with her – quietly, far from the normal pressures of their everyday life.

Josephine also was delighted. Like an old mother hen, she clucked her satisfaction to her daughter. 'I want the King [i.e. Louis] to travel by the same road which you have taken,' she wrote in a letter of 4 June. 'It will be a consolation for both of you, my dear Hortense, to meet. All the letters I have received from him since your departure are full of his affection for you. You have too sensitive a heart not to be touched by this.'

Her mother wanted her to be happy. Her adoptive father, of

course, wanted her happiness as well, but he also needed a second young male heir to his throne. And he was not to be disappointed. It was this visit of Hortense and Louis to south-west France in the summer of 1807 that led to the birth of Napoleon III in April of the following year.

Chapter Three

Birth (1808)

THE FUTURE NAPOLEON III was born at one o'clock in the morning of 20 April 1808 at his mother's home in Paris at 8, rue Cerutti[1] after Hortense had endured a twenty-two-hour labour. 'He was so weak that I feared I should lose him at birth,' she later wrote. 'They were obliged to bathe him in wine and wrap him up in cotton wool to keep him alive.'

But it was soon clear that the child would survive and horsemen rode night and day to give the news to the Emperor down at Bayonne, near the Spanish frontier. He had massed his armies all along the border to intimidate the Spanish king into abdicating, a manoeuvre which, after a few tense weeks, was to succeed. The slovenly Carlos IV was prevailed upon to go into luxurious exile upon which Napoleon, playing chess with the crowned heads of Europe, gave his throne to his own elder brother, Joseph, Louis having (typically) vexed him by refusing to leave Holland for this new and larger kingdom. Yet, despite the pressing demands on his time and patience, Napoleon, on learning of the new baby's arrival, at once wrote to Hortense, again as her 'affectionate father', to tell her of his delight: 'I hear you are happily delivered of a boy. It has caused me the greatest joy. I only now want to be assured that you are going on well.'

He ordered a salvo of guns to be fired in salute by every regiment along the entire frontier.

At his command, the baby was named Charles Louis Napoleon but 'Charles' was quickly dropped and the future ruler of France was thereafter always called Louis by his intimates and friends,

---

[1] The building no longer exists. It is simply an open stretch of roadway where the rue Pillet-Will cuts into the rue Cerutti, now named rue Laffitte.

which is how he will henceforth be referred to.[1] He was the first baby to be born a prince of the First Empire and stood next in line of succession to the throne after his only surviving elder brother, Napoleon Louis, who was three-and-a-half years older. When writing about the new-born child's later life, commentators often overlook that he was born within the very inner circle of Imperial power; but, as Hortense herself shrewdly observed, 'The birth of a second possible heir to the throne fitted in admirably with the Emperor's plans.'

Horsemen also rode through the night to the royal palace at Amsterdam to tell King Louis of Holland that his third son had been born. His reaction was more muted than that of his brother: 'I have begged Mamma [Letizia], and I have requested Madame de Boubers, to give exact accounts of your health. I hope they will soon acquaint me with your complete convalescence . . . I will beg you to let me know what the Emperor has written to you. I should like the little one only to be christened so that he may be solemnly baptised here but I subordinate my wishes to yours and to that of the Emperor. Adieu, Madame.'

The reason for this coldness was two-fold. Firstly, Louis had reverted to being his former, moody self and he and Hortense were once again estranged. They had not lived together as man and wife since their return to Paris from the Pyrenees in late August the previous year, after which she had refused to accompany him back to Holland.

Secondly, Hortense's pregnancy had been officially announced in early September 1807 and Louis – like everyone else – had expected the baby to be born some nine months later, in May 1808. In fact, he had written to his wife: 'I hope you will reach your time without accident. I have communicated to the Legislative Body the news that you are pregnant. I shall not be able to go to Paris in May. Although I have got through the winter, I could not bear Paris. I must resign myself to live like an invalid.'

So why was the baby born in April? Louis knew that, after several

---

[1] The boys' names are somewhat confusing because of Napoleon's insistence that all three of his nephews should have his own name as one of their Christian names. In fact, within the family, Napoleon Charles, the first-born, was called 'Charles', Napoleon Louis, the second-born, was called 'Napoleon' and Charles Louis Napoleon was called 'Louis'.

years of absence from Hortense's bed, they had finally had sex together on 12 August 1807. As he later wrote to her, 'On 12 August, I met you again at Toulouse and threw myself into your arms.'

Louis sat there, lonely in his cold, dank palace, mulling over the dates. Going forward in time from 12 August 1807, when he could have been the father, a normal pregnancy would have produced a baby on around 12 May 1808. But working backwards from 20 April 1808, when the baby was actually born, it seemed that the pregnancy began on around 25 July 1807 – when he was at the spa town of Ussat-les-Bains in the Pyrenees and Hortense was at Gavarnie, a small village high up in the mountains some fifty miles away.

So why did her baby arrive nearly three weeks early, in the eighteen days between 20 April and the expected approximate date of 12 May 1808?

Most people would simply say that little Louis was born prematurely, with no suggestions of impropriety. Babies are born premature for all kinds of reasons. Indeed, Vincent Cronin, Napoleon's best-known British biographer, has written that the Emperor himself may have been born before his expected time; and no one would ever have accused the virtuous and deeply religious Letizia of adultery.

(Eighteen days either way, even three or four weeks, prove nothing. That is certainly the position in English law. For instance, in 1939, in the leading case of *Clark v. Clark*, the Divorce Court President Sir Boyd Merriman, whom older barristers still remember as a stern, highly suspicious judge of the old school, ruled that a baby, extremely premature in appearance and weighing only 2.5 lb, born only 174 days after the last date on which sexual intercourse could have taken place between a husband and his wife, *was* the husband's son and refused him a divorce on the grounds of her adultery. If Louis, born on 20 April 1808, had been conceived on 12 August 1807, Hortense's pregnancy would have lasted for 240 days: seventy-six days longer than in *Clark v. Clark*.)

Furthermore, the Code Napoléon, enacted in 1804, accepted the legitimacy of a child born in France after a pregnancy lasting between 180 and 300 days. So what was the problem?

To King Louis' suspicious mind there was only one answer:

Charles Louis Napoleon Bonaparte was not his son.[1] The child must be illegitimate and the son of some unknown lover of Hortense. He continued for some years to deny that the baby was his child, although eventually he mellowed and grudgingly accepted him as his son.

King Louis was, however, not the only one to doubt the baby's legitimacy. Because of the discrepancy in the dates, the scurrilous French political pamphlets of the day readily accused Josephine's daughter of having betrayed her husband. So also did some of the Emperor's own brothers and sisters, eager to use any weapon with which to attack Josephine, whom they had always considered as 'soiled goods' and an unfit wife for their illustrious brother. In vain, Hortense insisted that the child *was* premature, citing his frail and weakened condition at birth and insisting that his early delivery was brought on by a bumpy carriage ride over cobblestones the afternoon before, when she was taking her older son Napoleon Louis to a children's ball.

But many at court, happy to believe the worst of this pampered daughter of Josephine, branded her an adulteress, as she well knew. Over a decade later, as if to give her reply, she wrote in her memoirs: 'I learned later that the surgeon said afterwards, "Queens have the right to give birth before their proper time. They never count like anybody else."' We have it on the authority of Blanchard Jerrold, writing soon after Louis' death, that Hortense never intended her memoirs to be published. So why put that in that vital little quotation? Obviously, the allegation still rankled.

Until the young Louis began his long struggle for power after the death in 1832 of François Charles, King of Rome and Napoleon's only legitimate son (by his second wife, Marie-Louise of

---

[1] Louis, who had never forgotten the rumours that Napoleon had had sexual relations with his own stepdaughter, was so pathologically distrustful of his wife – and so reckless – as to reply to Napoleon when he wrote to congratulate him on the baby's birth: 'I thank Your Majesty for the letter that you have been kind enough to send me on the safe delivery of a child to the Queen. I shall willingly conform to Your Majesty's desires as to the names to be given to his son.' Was that use of the word 'his' instead of 'my' a Freudian error or a deliberate insult? Napoleon, who was already having enough troubles with his maverick brother, who was increasingly behaving as if he were the king of an independent country and not merely the puppet ruler of a satellite state, chose to ignore it.

Austria), it really did not matter whether or not King Louis was his father. But once Napoleon's own son was dead, the exact circumstances of *his* paternity became of profound importance. His hopes of one day becoming ruler of France rested almost entirely on his being the nephew of the great Napoleon and a true Bonaparte. As he wrote to a friend in 1834: 'I know that I am everything because of my name, nothing because of myself. I owe everything to my heredity.' That is why accusations of illegitimacy became of such wounding intensity. When Victor Hugo, the radical novelist and poet, was banished in the early 1850s, his first work in exile was *Les Châtiments* in which he poured scorn on the new Emperor: 'whose name is a theft and whose birth a falsity'.

So all Louis' major biographers – except for Blanchard Jerrold who simply ignored the whole matter – had, at an early stage, to tackle the question: 'Was he, or was he not, the son of Louis Bonaparte?'

The answer from most French and British writers has been a somewhat unenthusiastic 'Yes.' In France, André Lebey wrote in 1909: 'One arrives then at the conclusion that it would seem he was the son of Louis Bonaparte; but one cannot be sure. Queen Hortense's tomb at the mournful little church of Rueil outside Paris keeps its secret.' In 1961, Adrien Dansette, perhaps Louis' greatest French biographer, wrote: 'It is very difficult in such a matter to arrive at any certainty. In the present state of our knowledge of the facts, it would seem impossible to refuse King Louis the benefit of the old adage: "The father is he who went through the marriage ceremony."' In 1990, Philippe Séguin came to much the same halfhearted verdict: 'One finds oneself in the impossibility of attributing the paternity to any third party, and King Louis is the only man certain to have shared the bed of Queen Hortense at around the time of her conception.'[1]

In Britain, Dr F. A. Simpson, writing in 1909, was rather more bullish: 'The whole weight of the evidence is in favour of the belief

[1] In 1992, Françoise Wagener, Hortense's most recent French biographer, simply dodged the issue. She called the accusation that the queen had been unfaithful while in the Pyrenees 'vulgar' and 'absurd' and did not examine, even for one second, the relevant evidence – on either side.

that Louis Napoleon was actually the son of Louis of Holland.' But later writers have not been so sure. In 1972, Professor W. H. C. Smith of London University concluded: 'There seems to be no basis in fact for this charge of bastardy, although it is a close-run thing arithmetically.' In 1979, Jasper Ridley, the most recent British biographer, merely observed: 'All that can be said with certainty is that it is very unlikely that it will ever be possible to prove whether Louis Bonaparte was, or was not, the father of Napoleon III.'

In 1995, Thierry Lentz simply shrugged his shoulders: 'In essence, it matters little whether the King of Holland was or was not the true father of Napoleon III. The doubt has no political import-ance.'

It is hard to agree with him. It may not be 'politically' important but, if one is primarily interested in Louis as a human being, it is vital to know who his father was and if his own deep belief in his Bonaparte ancestry was founded on reality or delusion.

It is worth examining the basic facts gathered from various sources using in particular one major piece of evidence that almost every previous writer seems to have substantially ignored: namely, Hortense's own account of the summer of 1807 recorded for pos-terity in her memoirs.

There are three essential matters to consider:

(1) The chronology of events.

On 18 June, Hortense, accompanied by her lady-in-waiting Mme Adele de Broc, her schoolfriend Mlle Louise Cochelet, her two court chamberlains and her equerry Count Charles Bylandt-Palstercamps, plus their respective servants, arrived at Cauterets in the Pyrenees. Their original destination had been the spa town of Bagnères but they had soon moved on. In her memoirs, she explains why: 'When we arrived at Bagnères, the beautiful valley of Campan appeared to me too cheerful. The enchanting landscape was not in keeping with my state of mind. What I needed was stern and wild scenery in harmony with profound grief. So I stayed only a few days at Bagnères and went on to Cauterets where the mountains, huddling closer together as they increase in height, make Nature wilder and more imposing.'

On 26 June, she allowed Louis to join her in the house she had rented on the Place St-Martin. Again, she explains why: 'The letters that I had received from my husband touched me. His grief seemed

alike to mine, and for the first time we understood each other . . .
I wrote to him in friendship; I felt that I had need to reassure him
for in all sincerity I had completely forgiven him. He repeated so
often that in the last two months he had come to see life differently,
that he now wished only to make me happy and that it was I, and
I alone, who could give him the necessary courage to perform his
various duties that, in the end, I relented.'

So, from 26 June to 6 July, they lived together again under the
same roof. But there was no sexual intercourse. 'I was still wholly
absorbed by my grief. I believe that he genuinely wanted to be kind
and attentive but, despite all that he tried to do, all the defects of his
unhappy disposition persisted in coming to the surface. I trembled at
the thought of having again to suffer at his hands. I begged for
time.' So Louis went off to take the waters at Ussat-les-Bains but
kept up the pressure for a reconciliation (which, of course, would
have entailed a resumption of marital intercourse) with a barrage
of letters. 'His only wish was to effect a reconciliation between us
and he was resolved, so he wrote, to see me consent to this with
joy.'

Until then Cauterets had been ideal for Hortense. She had the best
of both worlds: the refreshing spa waters, imposing mountainous
countryside all around and the bustling ambiance of a fashionable
tourist centre on her doorstep. The town remains today a busy
small resort, although more popular now for its winter sports facilities than for its few remaining spas, but in the early 1800s it was
described as 'the meeting-place for the pleasures of the world and
of fashion. At night, the café terraces are lit, one chats, one applauds
the jugglers, the acrobats and the tightrope walkers who perform
in the streets. Players at whist and backgammon enjoy themselves
in the Casino and dancers fill the ball-rooms.'

Yet after a while, this poor little rich girl – which, at that stage
of her life, she undoubtedly was – decided that she needed a change
of scene.

On 10 July, on horseback and accompanied only by Mme de
Broc and one of her chamberlains, she left Cauterets for a long
excursion in the Pyrenees and down into Spain where they moved
around in 'an old-fashioned carriage drawn by six mules that might
have dated from the days of the Goths'. For the first time, she
travelled incognito and not as a queen. She found it all immensely

refreshing and invigorating. It was with considerable reluctance that, on 19 July, she returned to Cauterets.

'My husband was waiting at Toulouse to take me back with him to Paris,' she writes in her memoirs, 'but I was enjoying my solitary wanderings so much that I asked him to go on ahead and allow me to remain by myself a little while longer in my mountains. I would rejoin him in Paris.'

Within less than a week, on the morning of that vital date of 25 July, she was off again; this time on a trip which is usually depicted as a personal caprice – a visit to the Grande Cascade, one of the highest waterfalls in Europe, high above the village of Gavarnie in the Upper Pyrenees where water pours down over a sheer drop of 440 metres. But, as her memoirs make clear, this was not an expedition for pleasure alone: she also had royal duties to perform. After visiting the Grande Cascade, she was going on to the nearby town of St-Sauveur where she was to lay the foundation stone for a bridge bearing her name over the River Gave. No one ever mentions this 'work' element of her journey. It is totally ignored both by French and British writers.

In fact, the two regional Prefects and other local dignitaries wanted to accompany her on this semi-official expedition but, as she explains, 'I did not like the idea of admiring the beauties of nature surrounded by all these people. Not wishing to offend anyone, I sent all my household to accompany them along the usual road and promised to meet them at the waterfall.' She herself left at three o'clock in the morning, accompanied (so she claims) only by Mme de Broc, an artist named Pierre Thiénon attached to her husband's household who was to take sketches along the way, a professional guide and some local stalwarts as helpers, for they were undertaking a hazardous journey.

They did not take the Prefects' easy route along a proper road but crossed the mountains themselves, scaling a dangerous glacier in the process. No woman had made the arduous journey before and it was a formidable achievement. In fact, it proved almost too much for Pierre Thiénon: 'Madame,' he told Hortense at one point, 'rather than undertake this trip again, I would prefer to be shot on the spot!'

Hortense thought it was all marvellous fun. 'I was astonished at having undertaken so daring a task simply to escape the companionship and idle chatter of the two Prefects; but my nervous energy was simply incredible. The moment when we saw green vegetation on our long and perilous way down was an instant of real rejoicing.'

Hortense and her small party arrived early in the evening down at Gavarnie, almost a full half day ahead of the Prefects and the other local worthies travelling along the safer but longer route. They spent the night at the village inn and this is where, according to Hortense's enemies, the future Napoleon III was conceived: far from prying eyes down in fashionable Cauterets but high up in the mountains, alone with an unknown lover in the romantic setting of a remote mountain inn.[1]

In her memoirs, Hortense herself writes about her brief stay in Gavarnie: 'We arrived at six o'clock in the evening at the inn. The artist went to bed. I made two or three sketches, and later in the evening while walking about the little village with Adele [de Broc] I stopped to watch a man preparing a display of fireworks to be held in my honour on the following day. I was delighted to have escaped these so-called "festivities" and I no longer regretted my tiredness.'

In fact, this haughty young woman – she was still only twenty-four – had already decided not to wait for the Prefects and the other dignitaries.

'The next morning I admired from near at hand Gavarnie's own waterfall placed in a wondrously beautiful *cirque* [a bowl-shaped hollow surrounded by mountains], and I left the village at the moment that the "important people" arrived.'

But she did not totally ignore them or her royal duties. 'Nevertheless, I decided to wait for them at St-Sauveur where we sat down together at a big formal banquet, although that is the sort of thing I hate, and I then laid the foundation stone for a new bridge across the River Gave. The next morning, I returned to Cauterets. I left with Mme de Broc at the break of day leaving the authorities all

---

[1] The inn, now known as the Hôtel des Voyageurs, still exists and nearly two centuries later understandably seeks to keep alive its reputation as the possible setting for a famous night of illicit love. Pierre Laperrade, the present owner, has been kind enough to send me extensive local documentation on the subject, including extracts from two local history books which deal specifically – but sadly inconclusively – with the 'historical enigma' of his establishment.

still sleeping in their beds, for which no doubt they have never forgiven me. I admit that I was wrong. One should be able to know how to support the inconveniences of one's position but perhaps I have an excuse in the need for calm and solitude that I have already explained.'

A queen still only in her early twenties and the adopted daughter of the most powerful man in Europe, she was, at this period, undoubtedly arrogant, wilful and rude. But are those the words of a young woman masking an adulterous encounter? Almost enjoying her grief and her unhappiness, was she even all that interested in the physical enjoyment of sex?

Whatever may have happened during her brief time away, she found on her return to Cauterets a letter from her husband saying that he did not want to return to Paris without her and virtually demanding that she join him at Toulouse 'as soon as possible'.

She did not exactly hurry to his side. She lingered two more weeks in Cauterets before finally, on 10 August, leaving on the two-day journey to Toulouse where, as we know, Louis 'threw himself' into her arms. At first, all went well with the reconciliation. In a letter to her brother, Eugene, ten days later, she wrote: 'I am with the King, and we are getting on well together. I don't know whether it will last but I hope so, for he wants to treat me better, and you know I have never deserved ill-treatment.'

On 27 August, they returned to Paris and it was soon confirmed that Hortense was pregnant. Dreading a return to Holland, she easily persuaded the malleable Dr Corvisart to advise the Emperor that it would be better for her unborn baby if she stayed in Paris. Napoleon readily agreed, not only because of his genuine love for his 'daughter' but also because he wanted a child potentially so close to the French throne to be born in France. For his part, King Louis, furious with both this insult to his own regal dignity and the intrusion into his intimate family life, stormed back to Holland without his wife. Apart from a brief two months in 1810, they were never to live together again, and even on that final occasion there was no resumption of marital intercourse.

(2) If Louis Bonaparte was not the baby's father, who was?

Several possible candidates have been named over the years but on any reasonable basis, in the light of what we know today, none of them really fits the bill.

The candidates are as follows:

Count Charles Bylandt-Palstercamps, Hortense's thirty-four-year-old Dutch equerry – but it is proved that he returned to Holland on 14 June, several weeks before her visit to Gavarnie;

The Marquis de Castellane, one of the two local Prefects – but Hortense's own memoirs reveal that she found this forty-eight-year-old, physically unattractive man unbearably pompous, and that she deliberately left before dawn on her journey to the Grande Cascade to avoid his company;

Charles Henri Ver Huell, a brave forty-three-year-old Dutch admiral who knew both Hortense and her husband – but Adrien Dansette has found a letter signed by him placing him, beyond doubt, still in Holland on 24 July, the day before she left for the Grande Cascade;

Another Dutchman named Ver Huell, whose age and first name no one now seems to recall, was undoubtedly in the Pyrenees around that time on his way to Madrid to assume his duties as Dutch Ambassador to Spain. But there is no evidence that he even met Hortense on the journey;

Count Elie Decazes, a handsome twenty-seven-year-old widower who, rather like Hortense mourning the death of her son, was travelling in the region following the recent death of his young wife. He undoubtedly visited Hortense at Cauterets, as she openly admits in her memoirs, and some writers have made him the most likely candidate. But this is to overlook the fact that he was an ambitious schemer who used his good looks to further his career[1] by paying court to the bored wives of influential men, and was far too astute to take any of them to bed. He did not visit Hortense for sexual reasons but to ask for her help in persuading her husband to give him the vacant post of his private secretary. Louis did as Hortense suggested, which is inconceivable if this most jealous of all men thought that there was the slightest chance of Decazes having cuckolded him.

Hortense did eventually take a lover by whom, in September 1811, after she had ceased all pretence at living with her husband, she had an illegitimate son, who later became famous as the Duc

---

[1] He ended up as Chief of Police of Paris then Prime Minister of France under Louis XVIII, the restored Bourbon king after Napoleon's defeat at Waterloo.

de Morny and a right-hand man to his half-brother, Napoleon III. This was the dashing Count Charles de Flahaut, 'as brave on the battlefield as in bed,' as French historian Alfred Fierro has written, a tall, handsome officer, two years younger than Hortense, with impudent blue eyes, a bold nose and a fine pair of legs that looked good in tight military breeches.

Flahaut was an experienced and skilled philanderer. The illegitimate son of Napoleon's wily Foreign Secretary, Talleyrand, he had first met Hortense in 1804 at a society ball and this unhappily married young woman had, despite herself, quite promptly fallen in love with him. 'I saw him almost every day. The moment I caught sight of his grey horse in the distance my heart began to beat,' she admits in her memoirs.

But the two French biographers who have perhaps done most research on the subject, André Lebey and Adrien Dansette, both agree that their love affair did not take physical form until 1810, by which time Hortense's marriage was dead beyond any real hope of redemption, and the young Louis was two years old.

But even if Hortense and Flahaut had wanted to make love in the Pyrenees in the summer of 1807, it would have been a physical impossibility. Flahaut, later to be a full general at twenty-seven and Napoleon's devoted aide-de-camp, was serving with his regiment in Germany and Poland for the whole of 1807 and well into 1808.

(3) Was there any similarity between King Louis and 'his' son?

In 1830, when the king was fifty-two and young Louis twenty-two, Valerie Masuyer, Hortense's lady-in-waiting, wrote in the private notebooks which, like other fashionable women of the day, she kept: 'The King has a very beautiful head ... His son Louis resembles him greatly, especially the top part of the face; the profile of the two of them is exactly the same. It is the eyes and the mouth that he owes to his mother.'

This physical resemblance to the king was confirmed thirty years later by Alfred Maury, librarian at the Tuileries Palace. In his memoirs, he tells how he was passing by Napoleon III's study one day in 1860 and saw an usher opening the door for a man 'who looked just like the Emperor. The resemblance was striking.' The usher said that the visitor was Comte de Castelvecchio, recently appointed the chief collector of taxes in the Alpes-Maritimes Department. 'And he added, with a laugh: "That's the Emperor's brother! He is the natural son of King Louis."' [In fact, François Louis Gaspard, Comte de Castelvecchio, was born in Rome in April 1826, son of ex-King Louis and 'a lady of the highest Roman society whose identity', according to Professor Jean Tulard's monumental *Dictionnaire du Second Empire* published in 1995, 'it has not been possible to this day to discover.' He was a beneficiary in his father's will and Napoleon III, ever conscious of family loyalty, appointed him to several high administrative posts. He died in 1869 but the *Dictionnaire* speaks of 'photographs still in existence which show an undeniable resemblance to Napoleon III'.]

But there was not only a physical resemblance between the two men who shared the Christian name Louis. Although, as with any father and son, there were important differences of character, there were also fundamental similarities. The older Louis had none of the charm of the younger Louis but both were introspective and subject to moods of deep melancholy. Both were also physically brave and with a strong sense of duty. 'From the moment I set foot on the soil of the kingdom, I became a Dutchman,' the new King of Holland said in his first speech to the Dutch Parliament. Napoleon may have written to him, with his customary disdain: 'All the world knows that without me you would be nothing.' Yet in the four years that Louis was King of Holland he consistently defied his Imperial brother and tried to stand up to him as the head of an independent nation.

But he shared with his son a deep flaw in resolve. They both tended, ultimately, to shrug their shoulders and – almost with an audible sigh – let fate take command.

When finally King Louis realised, in July 1810, that he could never win the battle for 'his' nation's sovereignty as a truly independent power, he suddenly lost interest, threw in the towel and abdicated, fleeing into exile. Just as, when facing overwhelming defeat on the battlefield of Sedan in September 1870, Napoleon III surrendered without even attempting to escape and provide a rallying-point for those of his countrymen desperate to fight on, which some Frenchmen today still consider a viable possibility.

Within a week of King Louis' abdication, Holland ceased to be a kingdom and was incorporated into France. Within two days of Napoleon III's personal surrender, his Empire collapsed and his wife and son had to flee into exile.

What about Napoleon III himself? Did *he* think he was Louis Bonaparte's son? After all, he knew all about the scurrilous allegations that were made: during the Second Empire any publication questioning his legitimacy was banned in France.

No British writer has ever before given Louis' own views on the subject of his birth. I found the answer in a tattered old book picked up in a second-hand book-stall on the banks of the Seine near Notre Dame. Ferdinand Bac was a French writer whose father, Charles Henri Bac, was both Louis' personal friend and first cousin, being the illegitimate son of Jerome Bonaparte. In his *Napoléon III inconnu*, published in 1932, Bac quotes directly what the Emperor said to his father.

He believed that he was Louis' son. 'I have made my calculations,' he said.

At the end of the day (as English lawyers are wont to say), it is proved to my mind beyond all reasonable doubt that Napoleon III was, indeed, the son of Louis Bonaparte, brother of the great Napoleon. As a barrister, I am confident that I could take on the case in a modern court of justice – and win.

Chapter Four

Early Childhood
(1808–15)

IN HIS BIOGRAPHY, *NAPOLEON III*, published in 1972, Professor William Smith writes: 'When the Empire fell, Louis was seven and it seems unlikely that he can have remembered much either of the institution or of his uncle.' That flies in the face of what Louis himself wrote, in later life, on the value of childhood in forming the character of an adult, and on his own childhood.

Decades before the birth of modern psychiatry and Freudian views on the importance of childhood, he wrote in 1839 at the age of thirty-one: 'Every man is the slave of the memories of his childhood. He obeys all his life, without question, the impressions he received when he was a boy, the trials and influences which he had to face.'

A few years later he wrote to his childhood friend, Hortense Cornu, with whom he remained close the rest of his life, 'You are right in saying that childhood and youth are two great saints canonised by death: but allow me to add that the people one knew during the first years of life are like the precious relics of those great saints, and share their atmosphere of affection and adoration.'

Outstanding among those 'precious relics of great saints' were his mother (but sadly not his father, whom he hardly knew as a child), his doting maternal grandmother the Empress Josephine (his paternal grandmother, Letizia Bonaparte, by then 'Madame Mère' was far too austere and aloof) and, perhaps above all, the Emperor himself. For Napoleon was more like a combined surrogate father and grandfather than an uncle to the young Louis: he was truly his ultimate role-model. 'How can pygmies like ourselves,' he wrote to his cousin, Prince Napoleon, in 1865, 'really appreciate at its full worth the great historical figure of Napoleon? It is as though we stood before a colossal statue, the form of which we are unable to grasp as a whole.'

This was not posturing. Until the ultimate catastrophe of Waterloo, he was a close and privileged member of Napoleon's inner family circle. A charming painting by Louis Ducis in 1810, to be seen today at the Palace of Versailles, shows a seated Napoleon, looking like an indulgent uncle, surrounded by his young nieces and nephews (his sister Caroline's three children and his brother Louis' two sons), with the future Napoleon III, then aged two, enjoying pride of place on the Emperor's knee. Furthermore, we know from a few fragments of autobiography entitled *Souvenirs de ma vie*, which his official biographer Blanchard Jerrold found among his papers after his death, that he had clear memories of the 'precious relics' of his childhood saints. 'When having reached a certain age,' he wrote, 'one looks back to the earliest days of childhood, one sees only isolated scenes that have struck the imagination. They are real pictures that have fixed themselves in your memory but which it is impossible to connect.'

The earliest 'picture' was of his baptism in November 1810, when he was not yet three years old. 'The Emperor was my godfather and the Empress Marie-Louise [Napoleon's second wife, whom he married in April 1810] was my godmother.

'Then my memory carries me to Malmaison. I can still see the Empress Josephine in her salon on the ground floor, covering me with her caresses, and even then flattering my vanity by the care with which she repeated my childish *bons mots*. For my grandmother spoiled me in every sense of the word whereas my mother, from my tenderest years, tried to correct my faults and develop my good qualities. I remember that once arrived at Malmaison, my brother and I were masters, to do as we pleased. The Empress, who loved flowers and conservatories passionately, allowed us to cut the sugar canes to suck them, and she always told us to ask for everything we wanted.'

Then there was the Emperor. 'I often went with my brother, who was three years older than me, to have breakfast with the Emperor. They used to lead us to a room whose windows opened on to the Tuileries Gardens. As soon as the Emperor entered, he came over to us, lifted us up with his two hands by the head and put us like that standing on the table. This altogether exceptional manner of picking us up terrified my mother, since [Dr] Corvisart had assured her that it was a very dangerous way of handling two small children.'

It was a childhood virtually without a father. He almost never saw Louis Bonaparte and, although Napoleon himself was happy – even after the birth of his own son, François Charles, the King of Rome, in March 1811 – to play the role of surrogate male parent, he also had battles to fight and countries to conquer. When he was at home, Louis and his brother – with or without their mother – were never long absent from the Emperor's palace: whether at the Tuileries in central Paris, St Cloud on the outskirts of the capital, or Fontainebleau, forty miles deep into the country. But for long periods of time, Napoleon was almost as absent a surrogate father as his brother was an absent biological father.

Blanchard Jerrold had, alone of all Louis' biographers, the great benefit of many hours spent with him in his last exile in Chislehurst talking about his life and early days. His assessment is authoritative and convincing: 'Louis, the future Emperor, was from his birth to manhood, his mother's child.'

And, despite the continuing unhappiness and complexities of her own private life, she did not make too bad a job of it. His early childhood was undoubtedly happy and highly privileged, but Hortense ensured that he was surprisingly unspoilt.

He had, it is true, a nanny, a vivacious brunette named Marie Bure (always called in the family 'Madame Bure') who was a strong influence throughout his early childhood, beginning with feeding him at her own breast, along with her own baby son.[1] He later shared with his older brother Napoleon Charles no less than three governesses, but his was still a remarkably egalitarian upbringing.

'I want,' Hortense told Louise Cochelet, her lady-in-waiting and a former schoolfriend, 'to make my sons understand that, in spite of the glitter which surrounds them, they are subject to all the vicissitudes of life. They must repose on the solidity of their greatness and I teach them to rely only on themselves', just as she and

---

[1] Pierre Bure grew up to be a great friend and loyal supporter of his foster brother and, when Louis had two illegitimate sons by a country girl, it was Pierre who set up home with her and brought the boys up as his own. Louis never forgot his debt to Pierre and later made him Treasurer of his Imperial Household.

her brother, Eugene, had done in their own non-Imperial childhood.

Despite her obvious enjoyment of her regal lifestyle, Hortense retained many of the democratic sentiments of her father and of his fellow early Revolutionaries. Like all Napoleon's supporters, and she was genuinely one of his most passionate admirers, she believed that the Empire was, unlike the Bourbon monarchy, directly linked to the ordinary people of France. Although, paradoxically, the rest of the Bonapartes were far more 'dignified' in their private dealings with each other than their born-to-the-purple Bourbon predecessors had ever been, using full titles and 'vous' instead of 'tu' except in the most intimate circumstances, she wanted her children to be brought up differently. She told the boys' governesses and servants not to address them as 'Your Royal Highness' but to call the elder boy simply 'Napoleon' and the younger child 'Louis', as she did herself.

Brought up in this warm atmosphere, both brothers were bright, high-spirited, affectionate boys but Louis appears to have been the more remarkable and engaging child of the two. Josephine called him 'Oui-oui' because of his childish attempts to pronounce his first name, and the nickname – which, of course, also means 'Yes, yes', a reference to his pleasing personality – stuck. Hortense kept among her most valued possessions – which her tearful son found after her death – a note that he had written to her after he fell off his rocking-horse: '*Petite maman, Oui-oui a fait pouf dans le dada. Oui-oui n'a pas bobo – il aime maman beaucoup à coeur. Oui-oui.*' (Little Mummy. Oui-oui fell off his gee-gee. Oui-oui did not hurt himself. He loves Mama very much.)

There are several stories from various sources of his generosity to the poor, not a frequent characteristic of young royalty at that time. Louise Cochelet, for instance, tells how one day, when Louis was about four, he suddenly came upon a child chimney sweep, his face all covered with black soot, in the house on rue Cerutti where he spent his early years. Frightened, he cried out in terror at 'the little black man', whereupon Madame de Boubers, his chief governess, took him on her knee and told him that he should have pity, not fear, for the poor child forced by poverty to earn his living in that hard and difficult way. Louis was deeply moved. A few months later, the same little chimney sweep, while cleaning chimneys in the middle of the night, by mistake came down into the bedroom where the two princes were sleeping. This time, Louis was not frightened: he got out of his bed, went over to the desk where his money was kept and handed it all over to the little black-faced boy.

He was a born charmer. His adoring grandmother, Josephine, who often happily looked after the boys while their mother, whether for reasons of health or pleasure, was off visiting one or more of her favourite spas, never tired of writing to tell her of his latest little exploit. Two examples from her letters will suffice to give the flavour of what this bubbling, intelligent little boy was really like.

The first is when Louis was five years old: 'The Abbé Bertrand [his first tutor] was making him read a fable where there were allusions to metamorphoses. Having had the word explained to him, he said to the Abbé: "I should like to be able to change myself into a little bird. I would fly away when it was time for my lesson with you but I would come back when M. Hase [his German teacher] came."

'"But that is not very kind towards me," said the Abbé.

'"Oh," Oui-oui replied, "I was talking about the lesson, not the man."

'Don't you agree,' wrote Josephine, 'that this retort was very *spirituel*? It would be impossible to get out of the difficulty with more finesse and grace.'

The second is when Louis was about six: 'Two days ago, seeing Madame Tascher [a distant relative] leaving to join her husband at the waters, he said to one of my ladies: "She must be very fond indeed of her husband to leave grandmamma."'

His natural gift of effortless charm remained with him throughout his life. 'He was a charming child,' agrees Hortense Cornu, 'as gentle as a lamb, affectionate, caressing, generous (he would even give away his clothes to anyone in need), witty, quick in repartee and with the sensibility of a girl; but easily puzzled and intellectually lazy ... He had not a trace of arrogance and would throw himself unreservedly into the arms of the first person he met, overwhelming them with caresses beyond rhyme or reason, so that people said he must have a warm and loving heart.

'*But*,' she adds with surprising candour, '*there was nothing in it. He forgot you as soon as you were out of his sight.*' (My emphasis.)

Even as a child, Louis knew how to use his charm to help him get what he wanted. The Abbé Bertrand let him shirk his lessons and his mother's friends could refuse him nothing when, as Blanchard Jerrold uncritically puts it, 'his light blue lacklustre eyes turned on them with a look of kindness and goodwill'.

It was not a joyous time for Hortense. Blanchard Jerrold was probably not exaggerating when he wrote: 'The period ranging between the birth of Louis and the fall of Napoleon in 1814 was the most tumultuous, the most trying, probably the most unhappy of Hortense's stormy life.'

The baby's birth had done nothing to improve the state of her marriage. Napoleon, angry at his brother's continued refusal to come to Paris to see his latest son, wrote him an irate letter reproaching him for his behaviour. This served only to fan Louis' crude suspicions that Hortense was using her double connection with the Emperor to plot against him. 'Madame,' he wrote her on 29 August 1808, 'our unhappy quarrels have been the cause of all my family troubles ... My only consolation is to live away from you, to have nothing to do with you and nothing to expect of you. Adieu, Madame ... Adieu forever.'

So Hortense was left in limbo, married but with no husband while the man she loved but did not dare to go to bed with (Charles de Flahaut) was hundreds of miles away serving with his regiment and, as she suspected, having many affairs.

Louis also found the situation insupportable. Finally, on 24 December 1809, he came to Paris to ask a family council at the Tuileries to sanction a formal separation from Hortense with his having custody of their older child, Napoleon Louis. But only ten days earlier that same council had approved (i.e. rubber stamped) the Emperor's own reluctant request for a divorce – and one official break-up of a marriage was sufficient damage to the Imperial family's prestige. Louis' request was refused.

Hortense's attitude to the divorce of her mother is interesting. One cannot help feeling sadness for Josephine. Aged forty-six, and after thirteen years of barren marriage, she was obviously not going to have any more children and Napoleon was by now convinced he must have a male heir of his own blood, preferably, for dynastic (and snobbish) reasons, by a princess of a ruling royal house of Europe. They genuinely loved each other and, if Josephine had by then given him a son, there certainly would have been no divorce. But love, like patriotism, is not always enough.

Once Napoleon had told Josephine of his decision ['I still love you,' he said, 'but in politics there is no heart, only head.' She burst into tears and fainted.], he summoned Hortense. She relates the scene in her memoirs. 'You have seen your mother,' he said. 'She has spoken to you. My decision is made. It is irrevocable. All France desires a divorce and claims it loudly. I cannot oppose my country's will. So nothing will move me, neither prayers nor tears.'

'Sire,' replied Hortense in a tone that she describes as cold and calm, 'you are the master to do as you will. No one will oppose you. Since your happiness demands it, that is enough. We shall know how to sacrifice ourselves . . . My mother will submit, I am sure of that; and we shall all go, taking with us the memory of the kindnesses you have shown us.'

At this, Napoleon burst into tears. 'What! Will you all leave me, will you all abandon me! Don't you love me any longer? If it were only my own happiness, I would sacrifice it for you; but it is the happiness of France! Pity me rather for being obliged to sacrifice my most cherished affections.'

By now, Hortense was also in tears. 'Take courage, sire,' she said. 'We shall need our own in order to bear no longer being your children. But I assure you that we shall know how to be brave. We shall think that by going away we remove an obstacle to your plans and your hopes.'

And there was much in similar vein from both of them, and at further tearful meetings when Eugene, her brother, arrived from northern Italy where he was viceroy. Napoleon implored them both to stay but they were adamant that they must depart.

It did not work out like that. By then the exact terms of the divorce had been announced: Napoleon was being remarkably, and properly, generous. Josephine was to keep the title of Empress, her palace at Malmaison near Paris and her country home near Evreux were to be hers absolutely and she was assured of a large annual income. Ever the realist, Hortense decided to stay after all, and persuaded her brother to do the same.

This is how, with somewhat cloying language, she explains their decision: 'We were won over by the Emperor's solicitude for his wife's reputation at the very moment he was leaving her. The conduct of the husband dictated that of the children. They would have done wrong not to imitate it. Whatever it might cost us [sic], we resolved to let our thoughts dwell only on the honourable future assured to our mother . . . Our wishes would be subordinate to her interests.'

She proved as good as her words. When five months later, on 2 April 1810, Napoleon married, with sumptuous ceremonial at Notre Dame, the Archduchess Marie-Louise of Austria, a chubby blonde nineteen-year-old with childbearing hips, Hortense was one of those who carried the new bride's train. It was the same train that Josephine had worn six years earlier at her coronation.

Nine days later, Hortense showed again her taste for realistic compromise, a quality that her younger son was to show he had inherited in ample measure. For, despite all the bitter things that she had said about her husband, she left two-year-old Louis behind in Paris 'on account of his delicate health' and went with her older son to live with King Louis in that hated palace in Amsterdam. She had been ordered by Napoleon to make a last attempt at reconciliation, anxious by whatever private means to try and placate his increasingly troublesome brother. As ever, she obeyed the Emperor, even though the recently wounded Charles de Flahaut, returned to Paris, implored her not to go.

But the would-be reconciliation, in which sex played no part, lasted less than two months. It was the end. Pleading ill-health and leaving little Napoleon Louis behind with his father, Hortense fled Holland for the last time. She went to her favourite spa at Plombières and then, after a few days, went down to another spa at Aix-les-Bains to join her mother. As her carriage trundled along towards the outskirts of Aix, she saw on the road ahead two men on horseback galloping to greet her. One was Josephine's equerry – and the other was Charles de Flahaut. 'My heart beat violently,' she writes in her memoirs, 'but I hid my emotion and displayed only surprise.'

The following month was idyllic. 'The sight of M. de Flahaut, who spent his days at my mother's, aroused an emotion which became more and more difficult to hide and which was too intense for my enfeebled health. For the first time since I knew that I loved him I now saw him constantly . . . I have always looked back on that quiet and gentle month as the happiest time of my life.'

It was then, in those balmy days of the mid-summer of 1810, that they became lovers at last.

By then, Louis had abdicated and there was no longer a political reason for Napoleon to keep Hortense tied to the ex-King of Holland. He officially approved their separation, gave Hortense – for whom he still had great affection – the use of all Louis' property in France and settled a large annuity upon her and her children. Furthermore, although she was no longer Queen of Holland, he decreed that she was still to be known as 'Queen Hortense' and her two sons were to be once again princes of France.

In November 1810, little Louis, then aged two-and-a-half, was baptised in a splendid ceremony at Fontainebleau. But by now there was a subtle change in his importance: Marie-Louise, the new Empress, was already pregnant with Napoleon's own child. Five months later, on 28 March 1811, she gave birth to François Joseph Charles, his only legitimate child,[1] and a hundred and one guns roared out in salute. 'I am at the summit of my happiness,' said the Emperor and created the baby King of Rome.

By then, Hortense was herself pregnant, but in the greatest secrecy. She never lived openly with Flahaut but she was bearing his child. On 21 October 1811, the birth of Charles August-Louis Joseph Demorny was registered at the Town Hall of the Third Arrondissement in Paris. His parents were stated to be Auguste Jean Hyacinth-Demorny and his wife, Emilie Coralie. In fact, he was Hortense and Flahaut's love-child and was brought up by Flahaut's mother, Adele de Souza. After all, she had experience in such matters: Charles had been the product of her own affair, as a married woman, with Napoleon's ex-Foreign Secretary, Charles Maurice de Talleyrand.

No one knew about the baby except for Napoleon, alerted by his secret police. He was furious with Flahaut and immediately ordered him back to active service, with the whole event hushed up. Flahaut thereafter maintained a kind of contact with his son

---

[1] He had at least three illegitimate children, one daughter and two sons, the youngest of whom, Comte Alexandre Walewski, born in 1810 and the son of a married Polish countess, was later to be for several years Napoleon III's Foreign Secretary.

but Hortense seems never again to have seen him. She did not tell Josephine about the birth and does not mention the baby in her memoirs. Her son Louis did not know that he had a half-brother (who later, as the Duc de Morny, became his most trusted minister) until going through her papers after her death twenty-six years later.

The new child did not bring Hortense and Flahaut any closer. Napoleon saw to it that the handsome young officer was for long periods of time stationed away from Paris. Besides he was a gallant soldier whom he needed at the front.

Soon, however, there were greater problems for Hortense, and all of France, to bear. In June 1812, Napoleon led his army into Russia and by September he had entered Moscow but he found the city in flames and three-quarters destroyed. He stayed until October, hoping to induce the Russians to sue for peace, but when they refused he decided to withdraw to winter quarters. Sadly for his army, the cold weather descended earlier and more bitterly than usual and caught his 100,000 men in its grip, killing first the horses and then his poorly equipped and undernourished soldiers. The Russians harried the retreating French troops relentlessly and, by the time that the rearguard finally staggered from Russian soil in mid-December, only one thousand of the Grande Armée were fit for battle. It was the beginning of the end. Napoleon had at last overreached himself and even his soldiers, for the first time, felt the full bitterness of defeat.[1]

After the disastrous retreat from Moscow, Napoleon raised a new army and attempted to inspire them again with his passion. At first, the next year's campaign went reasonably well, although without the triumphant dynamism of previous years. For instance, in early May, Napoleon succeeded in defeating a combined Russian and Prussian army at Lützen in Saxony but he was unable to follow up his victory and destroy the fleeing enemy because of the weakness of his cavalry.

In the days following the Battle of Lützen, Hortense, whatever her other failings, once again showed her devotion to her children.

[1] My late grandmother's own grandmother told her that she remembered the bedraggled remnants of Napoleon's army straggling through her village in Poland. She said that they looked worn out, as if all they wanted to do was get home.

Six-year-old Louis had a bad toothache and a tooth had to be taken out. The extraction – undertaken, of course, without anaesthetic – was not an entire success, and the little boy was still bleeding after two days. Only then did Madame Bure, his nanny, tell Hortense. Without a word, she took the boy in her arms and held him tightly against her bosom until he fell asleep and the bleeding stopped. Then she put him to bed herself and sat up beside him until late in the evening.

Finally, she went to her own room but she could not sleep. She kept seeing her son with blood-stained mouth standing before her. She got up and hastened to his bedroom where she found both Louis and Madame Bure sound asleep. But there was a persistent trickle of blood from the sleeping child's lips. Without waking the nanny, Hortense placed her finger firmly on the bleeding gum to stop the flow of blood and remained like that until day-break. As Blanchard Jerrold wrote sixty years later, 'The wound was closed – and her son was saved!' (Louise Cochelet independently relates this incident in her memoirs.)

Back on the battlefield, two more indecisive victories followed in Germany – at Bautzen and Dresden – but far worse was to come. In August 1813, Austria joined what history books call 'the Fourth Coalition' of Russia, Britain, Prussia and Sweden arrayed against Napoleon. With the Duke of Wellington's British troops advancing against the other side of France from Spain, it was an awesome display of combined military might. When Hortense returned with her children to Paris that autumn from her usual round of spas and comfortable country houses, she found a city transformed and demoralised. Everyone knew that the war was going badly.

At the 'Battle of Nations' at Leipzig in mid-October 1813, the French army of 160,000 men had to face Allied forces of 320,000 men, better equipped, fresher and in better spirit. It was a disaster for the French. When, after four days of slaughter, Napoleon had to order the retreat, 50,000 of his soldiers lay dead on the battlefield. The edifice of his military infallibility had collapsed.

By now, Wellington's troops had crossed the Spanish frontier and were threatening western France while the Russian, Prussian and Austrian armies pressing on across the German states were preparing to invade eastern France. For the first time since the early days of the Revolution, French soldiers were not waging wars of conquest in foreign lands but gearing up to defend their own homeland.

Even so, 1814 began surprisingly well. For two months Napoleon, though still badly outnumbered, waged a brilliant campaign, winning several important victories. But the country knew that the régime continued in peril. Hortense stopped her sons' normal dessert after dinner so that they should have a sense of contributing towards the national struggle.

Nonetheless, it came as a total surprise when her maid awoke her on the night of 28 March 1814 with the frightening news that the Allied armies were at the very gates of Paris. They had outflanked Napoleon's armies and were demanding the surrender of the city. Napoleon sent messages that he was hastening back to defend his capital but panic quickly spread. His own wife, the Empress Marie-Louise, fled, taking his young son with her.[1] Only Hortense, of his immediate family, remained but when, on the next evening, a high-ranking officer told her that he could no longer guarantee her safety or that of her children, she agreed that they too must go.

On 1 April, they arrived, as refugees, to join Josephine at her country home near Evreux some sixty miles north-west of Paris. Three days later, Napoleon abdicated at Fontainebleau and surrendered to the Allies. On 24 April, Louis XVIII, the obese, arrogant younger brother of the guillotined Louis XVI,[2] arrived in Calais, and, on 3 May, supported by Allied soldiers, he entered Paris. The following day, Napoleon landed on Elba, the small island of his first exile, which was to be his personal kingdom and which he was never – at least, in theory – to leave.

There are those who claim that Hortense's role in the next ten months before Napoleon's return from Elba does her no great credit. To be blunt, she collaborated shamelessly with the restored

[1] Napoleon never saw her – or his son – again. Within months, she had taken a lover, the swashbuckling Austrian general Count Adam von Neipperg, who had a black patch covering the socket of an eye lost in battle against Revolutionary France twenty years earlier. She gave him three children and, as soon as Napoleon died in May 1821, she married him.

[2] Louis XVII, the young son of Louis XVI, never in fact reigned. He died aged ten of tuberculosis in prison in Paris in June 1795, two years after his parents had been executed.

Bourbons and their influential foreign friends. Soon returned with Josephine and her children to Malmaison, she quickly made herself amenable to the country's new rulers. The King of Prussia and his two sons came to visit her at Malmaison,[1] as did the most powerful of all the foreign leaders in Paris, the Russian Tsar Alexander I. It was not long before gossipmongers were prattling about the surprising new friendship that had sprung up between the thirty-seven-year-old married Alexander and the forty-one-year-old Hortense, whose lover, Flahaut, was now far away.

When Josephine, having caught a chill, died suddenly on May 29 (her last words were: 'Bonaparte . . . Elba . . . the King of Rome') Alexander was the only foreign dignitary waiting at Malmaison to comfort the distraught Hortense.

Even little Louis, now aged six and still partly traumatised by the dramatic events of the past few months, realised how close Alexander had become to his mother. During one of the Tsar's visits, he sidled up to him and quietly placed on his finger a ring which Hortense's brother, Eugene, had given him. When Hortense asked what he meant by that, he replied: 'I only have this ring which Uncle Eugene gave me. I have given it to the Emperor because he has been so kind to you, dear Mamma.' Alexander is said to have smiled, placed the ring on his watch-chain and said that he would always keep it in remembrance of this noble act of generosity shown by someone so young.

Before finally leaving to return home, Alexander personally intervened with Louis XVIII to ensure that he fully implemented the terms of the Treaty of Fontainebleau which had followed Napoleon's abdication and assured Hortense of generous financial provision. Louis agreed that she should receive her allotted 400,000 francs a year for herself and her children and, although removing her status as a queen, he conferred on her the title of Duchesse de St-Leu, the name of Louis Bonaparte's former country estate that Napoleon had handed over to her at the time of her official separation. Added to the net four million francs which she had inherited under Josephine's will, she at least had no financial worries.

---

[1] The Prussian king's younger son, seventeen-year-old Prince William, who now met for the first time six-year-old Louis, was fifty-six years later, as King William I, to accept his surrender at Sedan.

But she had another worry: Louis Bonaparte had returned to France and was claiming custody of Napoleon Louis, his older son, then aged ten. She fought viciously to keep him, even obtaining a private interview with Napoleon's arch enemy, the restored Bourbon king, to beseech his help, but Louis replied that he could not intervene in the judicial process.

On 8 March 1815, the court gave judgement in Louis Bonaparte's favour and ordered that Napoleon Louis must be sent to him within three months. But the court's authority did not long endure. Eleven days later, Louis XVIII was fleeing once more into exile. The following evening, on 20 March 1815, Napoleon returned in triumph to his capital.

Hortense had first heard of Napoleon's escape from Elba on 5 March when Lord Kinnaird, a British friend and famous art collector, galloped up to her carriage and said that he had just heard that Napoleon had landed at Golfe Juan near Cannes five days earlier. He warned her that she and her sons were in danger from supporters of the restored king who thought that she had something to do with Napoleon's escape.

She took the warning seriously and bundled her children into hiding.

At just under seven years old, Louis began the cloak-and-dagger life he was to know for much of the next thirty years. For that same evening, Louise Cochelet took the two boys out of the house in rue Cerutti by the back-garden gate and, telling them to keep absolutely quiet, guided them through the dark streets to a carriage. There a manservant was waiting to take them to the simple home on the boulevards skirting Paris where a former house-maid of Hortense's brother, Eugene, lived.

To the youngsters it was a great adventure. In *Souvenirs de ma vie*, Louis writes: 'When the first news of the landing of the Emperor came, there was great irritation among the Royalists and the King's bodyguard against my mother and her children. The rumour ran that we were to be assassinated. One night our governess came, and with the help of a valet de chambre, took us across the garden of my mother's house to a little room on the boulevards where we had to remain hidden. It was the first sign of a reversal of fortune. We were fleeing for the first time from the family roof; but our young years prevented us from understanding the meaning of events and we thoroughly enjoyed the experience.'

Hortense stayed in the house on the rue Cerutti for another five days but then she too sought shelter, in the home of a friend whom she had known since their days together as children on Martinique.

Yet when Napoleon, dusty and emotional from his triumphant nineteen-day journey from the south, stepped down from his carriage into the great courtyard of the Tuileries Palace, one of the first to step forward to greet him with a low curtsy was Hortense in full court gown. Not surprisingly, he returned her greeting coldly. His warmth was reserved for her sons: 'Where are they?' he asked. 'Why are they not here?'

The next morning she brought them, rescued from their hiding place, to see their uncle. He embraced them with tears in his eyes and took them to the open window where the crowd outside roared its greeting. For a few moments there was silence in the room. Then he burst out: 'I would never have thought you would forsake my cause!' and unleashed a tirade of recriminations to which Hortense could only stammer inadequate replies.

One final cutting remark made her burst into tears: 'You should not have stayed in France. A crust of black bread should have been preferable. When one has shared in the elevation of a family, one must share in its misfortunes.'

But her tears had their effect. His attitude softened. 'Come, come,' he said, 'you have not a single good excuse to make but you know that I am an indulgent father. There! I forgive you. We won't speak of it any more.'

And that was that. The Empress Marie-Louise, then safely back in her native Austria and ensconced with her glamorous one-eyed lover, refused to come to Paris or send Napoleon's four-year-old son, the King of Rome. So Hortense became effectively the First Lady of France, acting as hostess for the Emperor and her children treated virtually as his own. They were present with Hortense on all state occasions and, in particular, at a great ceremony that took place on 1 June when Napoleon, dressed in all his Imperial glory in white satin and wearing the sumptuous cape he had last worn at his coronation, swore a solemn oath to uphold the new liberal constitution he had granted and, to the cheers of thousands of spectators, 50,000 armed soldiers marched past in salute.

Napoleon claimed that he had returned in peace and that he wanted no more wars, but the Allied powers had issued a formal declaration: 'Napoleon Bonaparte has placed himself beyond civil and social relations and, as the enemy and disturber of the peace of the World, he has delivered himself to public punishment.' They massed their armies in what is today Belgium, preparing to invade France from the north-east; despite his continued talk of peace, Napoleon had no choice but to strike before they had completed their plans.

On Sunday 11 June, he invited Hortense and her sons to the sort of private family luncheon at the Tuileries that he had always held on the day before leaving to join his armies at the start of a campaign. He was relaxed and at his ease. In the evening, he received his ministers and then he asked Hortense to bring the boys to say goodbye. Both children were muted: they sensed that something momentous was afoot and Louis is said to have begged his uncle not to go on this latest campaign because 'those wicked Allies will kill you!' This brought tears to Napoleon's eyes. He turned to Marshal Soult, his old companion in arms who was to join him on the campaign, and said: 'Embrace the child, Marshal. He has a good heart. Perhaps one day he will be the hope of my race.'[1]

Seven days later, on the battlefield of Waterloo, a few kilometres outside Brussels, Napoleon met his last and most crushing defeat.

---

[1] Blanchard Jerrold relates this incident in his *Life of Napoleon III*, published in 1874 but it is fashionable for some modern writers to doubt its authenticity as being almost too good to be true. Yet it first appeared in print as far back as 1840 in *Lettres de Londres*, a pamphlet written by Comte Persigny, a close friend and supporter of Louis, then a prince in exile plotting to return to France and seize power. The pamphlet is undoubtedly a piece of pro-Louis propaganda but that does not mean that everything it says is untrue. If Persigny had wanted to invent the incident, he could easily have made the marshal anonymous or named one who was by then safely dead, but Soult was very much alive and well at that time. His career had not ended with Napoleon's defeat. In 1840, aged seventy-one, he was a senior minister in the strongly anti-Bonapartist government of King Louis-Philippe and it is highly improbable that Persigny would have risked publishing the story, if he knew that Soult could deny it, which he did not. As Dr F. A. Simpson wrote in 1909, 'That such a wholly unnecessary risk of denial should have been incurred does seem to show that the story had some basis of fact.'

The shattered remnants of his army staggered back across the frontier into France and, on the morning of June 21, Napoleon himself, dishevelled and exhausted, returned to Paris.

The next day he abdicated for a second time. 'My political life is over and I proclaim my son, under the title of Napoleon II, Emperor of the French.' But he 'reigned' for only a few days. The four-year-old child in Vienna was not even told what had happened.

It was now that Hortense came into her own, and showed a courage and selflessness that one cannot but admire. The fallen Emperor asked if he could join her at Malmaison, which she now owned and where he had known so much happiness in the early days with her mother, Josephine. Her friends advised her to be 'sensible' and not risk making herself unacceptable to Louis XVIII and the Allied leaders who would soon be returning to Paris.[1] But, 'I answered that I could never abandon the man whom I had called my father and, now that he was unhappy, was the time to prove my gratitude. Strengthened by the approval of my own conscience, I should put myself above the opinion of the world and it did not worry me that others might think badly of me if I was at peace within myself.'

She sent her sons to hide in a small apartment over a hosiery shop on the Boulevard Montmartre, where she knew the owner could be trusted, and left the next day (25 June) for Malmaison.

Napoleon arrived during the morning. 'I went to greet him with a heavy heart, thinking how this same spot, which he had visited at the height of his glory and happiness, saw him again today at the lowest level of misfortune, for he did not even find the loving friend of other days, so tender and devoted. I, the daughter of that dear friend, was only able to offer him my affection and respect. I was deeply conscious of how insufficient that was.'

The next morning, he asked her to come and see him. She found him walking alone in the garden. He wanted to talk about Josephine. 'I cannot get used to this place without her!' he said. 'Every minute I expect to see her come down a path to gather the flowers she loved so much. Poor Josephine! There was only one

---

[1] They proved correct. On his return to Paris, Tsar Alexander, for one, refused to see Hortense.

subject we ever argued about: her debts, and for sure I scolded her enough about them!

'But she was the most enchanting being I have ever known. She was a woman in every sense of that word: vivid, lively, with a tender heart.' Hortense had to turn away so that he could not see her tears.

He remained at Malmaison for four days, although it was dangerous to stay so long. The Allied troops were advancing on Paris and Blücher, the Prussian general, had ordered him to be captured dead or alive. Napoleon was in a state of turmoil, not knowing what to do. Finally, he decided to go to America and told Hortense to follow him with the boys as soon as she could, so that they could all live there together.

On 29 June came the time to depart. He asked her to bring her sons to say goodbye, as he had done before Waterloo. She was not happy about this, fearing that they might be attacked on the way from their hiding place on the Boulevard Montmartre, but she could not refuse the Emperor's last request. That afternoon they were brought to him, and Louis later told Blanchard Jerrold that he remembered the Emperor's tears as they embraced.

Then Napoleon bade farewell to Hortense, and to his mother who, with the same courage that she had shown fifty years earlier when following her husband into battle in the mountains of Corsica while pregnant with her unborn son, had now come to bid him a tearful goodbye. It was quickly over. Followed by his officers, Napoleon walked swiftly to the gate. With one last look back, he clambered aboard the waiting coach, and set off for Rochefort, on the western coast of France, where he planned to board a French ship for the United States.

On reaching Rochefort four days later, he found the port blockaded by a British warship, the *Bellerophon*, and two smaller vessels. He rejected the idea of trying to slip past them, hidden in the cargo of a neutral ship, as degrading. After ten days of uncertainty and torment, he decided to surrender to the British and throw himself upon their mercy.

On 13 July 1815, he sent a message to Captain Maitland of the *Bellerophon* that he intended coming aboard his ship two days later and wrote this letter to the dissolute and overweight British Prince Regent, later to become George IV: 'I come, like

Themistocles,[1] to throw myself on the hospitality of the British people. I place myself under the protection of their laws.' The Prince Regent did not reply to his letter.

Still hoping for a reply from the Prince Regent, Napoleon formally surrendered to Captain Maitland on 15 July and next day the ship set sail for England. There, as the ship rode at anchor off Torbay, he was told that the British Government had decided that he was not to be allowed to set foot on British soil but was to be transferred to another British ship, the *Northumberland*, and taken into permanent exile on the remote British island colony of St Helena in the South Atlantic.

On 9 August the *Northumberland* left on its long journey of 5,000 miles and two months later, on 16 October 1815, Napoleon and the four brave stalwarts who had chosen to go into exile with him arrived on the small rocky island that was to be his prison for the rest of his life.

Looking through his campaign field glasses at the tiny island's steep cliffs as they came slowly into view, Napoleon muttered, almost as if to himself: 'It's not an attractive place. I should have done better to remain in Egypt.'[2]

Just over two weeks after Napoleon had left Malmaison at the end of June, Hortense and her sons, recalled from yet another secret hiding place, followed him into exile. The White Terror, a brief, bloody episode in French history, whose ferocity British writers tend to ignore, was about to begin. It was a pro-Bourbon monarchist version of the Revolutionary Terror of ten years earlier. Royalist extremists were determined to wreak their vengeance on those who had rallied to Napoleon's cause on his return from Elba. In mid-July 1815, the murders and assassinations began.

Count Elie Decazes – the same man alleged to have been with Hortense on the night Louis was conceived in the village inn at

---

[1] Themistocles, the famous Athenian statesman who, when condemned to death by his former supporters, placed his life in the hands of the Persian king – once his fiercest enemy – who received him with honour.

[2] It was from Egypt that he had returned secretly in the autumn of 1799 to launch the coup d'état that made him First Consul and transformed him overnight from a high-ranking general into the master of France.

Gavarnie – was now, in his determinedly upward career, the new Police Prefect of Paris. Genuinely fearing for her life and at the same time serving his new Bourbon masters who wanted the ex-Emperor's immediate family safely out of Paris, he ordered Hortense and her sons on the evening of 17 July to leave the city that very night. 'Just as I was entering my carriage', says Hortense in her memoirs, 'I was informed that members of the Royal Bodyguard, acting of their own volition, had left ahead of me with instructions to ambush me. I trembled for the lives of those dearest to me.'

However, neither the king himself nor the Allied Armies of Occupation wanted any martyrs. As Hortense coolly observes, 'They wished me ill but they did not want to kill me. The balance was difficult to maintain.' General Baron von Muffling, the Prussian Military Governor of Paris, provided a military escort to the gates of Paris and Field Marshal Prince von Schwarzenberg, the Austrian Military Commander whose headquarters had taken over the ground floor of her mansion on the rue Cerutti, offered her an escort of Austrian cavalry to take her on to the Swiss frontier.

It was not only the White Terror that Hortense had to fear or the renegade members of the Royal Bodyguard riding to ambush her. Groups of disaffected French soldiers, hostile to the fallen Emperor, were also known to be marauding the countryside. But Hortense would only accept the protection of a single Austrian cavalry officer, Captain Count Eduard von Woyna, the Prince von Schwarzenberg's twenty-year-old aide-de-camp. 'As long as all these people are French, I have no reason to fear them,' she said.

She was quickly to be proved wrong.

PART TWO

THE PATH
TO POWER

Chapter Five

Growing Up in Exile
(1815–29)

W ITHIN THREE MONTHS OF the midnight flight from
Paris, Hortense's elder son, eleven-year-old Napoleon
Louis, was reclaimed by his father in delayed execution
of the earlier court order giving him custody. A robust, level-headed
child, he quickly settled into a strict but agreeable lifestyle with
ex-King Louis in his two magnificent *palazzi* in Rome and Florence. For Hortense and the seven-year-old Louis, it was a different
story. They were on the move for six years before finally she was
able to establish a settled, permanent home for them in Switzerland.

It was a traumatic experience for both but, at least, Hortense
had known adversity before, in her own childhood. For Louis, it
was a new experience and one that he never forgot.

In that turbulent month of July 1815, the child who, as a two-
year-old, had sat on the lap of the emperor and lived in Imperial
splendour was now, with his mother and brother, fleeing as fugitives
for their lives. The White Terror was to claim many victims that
year, among them several of Napoleon's marshals and generals. But
apart from Napoleon's brother-in-law, Joachim Murat, the King of
Naples, who was captured and shot, Hortense and her sons were
the only members of Napoleon's inner family circle to be in real
physical danger.

Joseph Bonaparte, the Emperor's oldest brother, had managed
to escape, with most of his wealth intact, to the United States.
Ex-King Louis had – typically – not budged from his comfortable
exile in Rome during the whole 'Hundred Days', that period
between Napoleon's re-entry into Paris as emperor on 1 March and
22 June when he abdicated for the second time. Lucien Bonaparte

had come from Rome to aid his brother but had afterwards returned safely there, under Austrian protection, with Madame Mère. Jerome, the youngest brother, had fought courageously at Waterloo but had reached Austria unscathed to resume his life of a wastrel, the family's playboy. The brothers' three sisters were also safely many hundreds of miles away, in Italy or Austria.

None of this was of any solace to Hortense. With her two boys and accompanied only by a lady-in-waiting, an equerry, the boys' nanny (Madame Bure) and Captain Count von Woyna, her small party trundled in three carriages along the dusty roads of central and eastern France towards Geneva and the safety of Swiss soil. 'The idea that fighting might take place under my very eyes made me tremble,' she later wrote.

In fact, it very nearly happened at Dijon, which they reached three days later. As they entered, Hortense heard a woman shout from a doorway: 'There she is!' and soon she saw notices in the streets proclaiming that she was someone who had brought misfortune upon France.

After arrival at her hotel, three Royal Bodyguard officers forced their way into her room and declared that she was under arrest. 'Madame,' they said in front of her two terrified sons, 'our orders are that you are not to leave this spot.' Anti-Bonapartist crowds yelled abuse in the streets outside and for a while the situation was ugly. But the local Austrian commander, called hurriedly to the scene by Woyna, placed Hortense and her party under his personal protection and the following morning, flanked by an escort of Austrian cavalry, they left the town through sullen crowds.

Frustrated and angry, the Royal Bodyguard's leader shouted at Woyna: 'I shall send a courier to Paris! They shall know about your behaviour. You have prevented me from carrying out my orders. A woman who has done us so much harm! To let her go free! It is disgraceful!'

That evening, bedraggled and dispirited, they reached Geneva. Louise Cochelet, the Abbé Bertrand and other members of Hortense's staff were waiting for them, but their problems were far from over. The Geneva authorities would not let them stay: Hortense was a political embarrassment. Where could she go? Her passports only extended as far as Geneva. As a temporary respite, she moved back into France and travelled down to her beloved Aix-les-Bains: surely there, with the Austrians occupying most of the region, they would be safe for a while?

Almost immediately there was one piece of good news: Charles de Flahaut rode into town. Hortense's joy was short-lived. Her lover had stood by Napoleon during the Hundred Days and fought bravely at Waterloo but now he, too, was on the run. The local Prefect warned Hortense that, for his own safety, Flahaut should not stay. After three days he departed, leaving Hortense in tears.

She and her sons remained in Aix for four deeply unhappy months. The White Terror was at its peak. Scores were being killed or arrested. Marshal Brune was assassinated in Avignon, Marshal Ney, famously the 'Bravest of the Brave', was arrested (later to be executed) and Flahaut's cousin, the young Count Charles de la Bédoyère, was surprised on a secret visit to Paris to see his pregnant wife and shot.

Even in Aix-les-Bains, Hortense and her children were constantly under surveillance from royalist spies. By the autumn it was clear that they could not long remain. In late October 1815, the Austrian commander told her that, regrettably, he could no longer guarantee her safety.

The Allied Governments had by then issued a declaration that 'the places of residence of the members of Bonaparte's family must be subject to restrictions because where they live cannot fail to concern the maintenance of public order'. Their aim was to disperse the leading Bonapartists over the face of Europe so that they could not easily collaborate in plotting a second return by Napoleon,[1] so they grandly said that Hortense could live in Switzerland – where no other member of the fallen Emperor's family was allowed to live.

But where in Switzerland? The Swiss authorities, with political power divided between local cantons and the Federal Government at the capital, Berne, could not agree among themselves as to where she should go.

Hortense's cousin, Stephanie de Beauharnais, had married the

[1] In fact, the only substantial attempt at rescuing Napoleon from St Helena was engineered in 1818 by his eldest brother, Joseph, then living comfortably in exile in the United States as a wealthy gentleman-farmer in New Jersey. It was a total failure. The Allies had chosen well their remote island prison for the man who had once ruled most of Europe.

Grand Duke Charles of Baden, now a part of the modern Federal German Republic but then an independent state in southern Germany. So, tiring of Swiss indecision, Hortense prevailed upon her cousin to obtain her husband's permission for her to live in the Baden town of Constance on the shores of Lake Constance. After a difficult journey in which the inhospitable Swiss twice arrested her – in front of young Louis – they finally arrived at Constance on the evening of 7 December 1815.

There, at least for a while, they had something like a home. By then, though, two disastrous events had occurred in Hortense's private life. Firstly, she had foolishly opened some letters that had arrived for Flahaut after he had left Aix-les-Bains and, to her horror, discovered that they were passionate love letters from another woman: they were from a famous and beautiful actress who had obviously been his mistress for some time. After a typical orgy of sanctimonious self-pity, she wrote him an anguished letter of reproach and went up into the mountains where she remained for five hours, silent and alone. Hortense and Flahaut were never again to be lovers. Two years later, having fled to Britain, he married the wealthy but neither very pretty nor very young Scottish noblewoman, the Hon. Margaret Mercer Elphinstone, and they had two children. The present 8th Marquess of Lansdowne is their direct descendant.

Secondly, no sooner had Hortense lost her lover than she lost her older son. In early October 1815, exercising his rights to custody under the court order of the previous March, Louis Bonaparte sent two of his men to bring Napoleon Louis to him in Rome.

It was not only Hortense who grieved. 'I cannot describe,' Louise Cochelet writes in her memoirs, 'the grief I felt at seeing Prince Napoleon tear himself from the arms of his mother and his young brother, who burst into tears. I did not know how to calm the grief of my dear Prince Louis or to amuse him when he was left so terribly alone. He grieved so much that he fell ill.'

At seven and a half, Louis was from now on to be a mummy's boy, with no elder brother or father to share in helping him to grow up: the burden was placed on Hortense. But it was a two-way dependency. Hortense Cornu, who was to survive Louis and was particularly close to him throughout his childhood and early manhood, told Blanchard Jerrold: 'This docile, sympathetic and observant boy was his mother's great comfort. Louis repaid this devotion with a passionate affection.' This mutual love was to endure for the rest of their lives. One has only to read their letters to realise the warmth and intensity of their tenderness for each other. Even towards the end of Hortense's life, when Louis was in his late twenties, he would often start: 'My dearest *Maman*' and would always end: 'I embrace you with all my heart', or: 'I love you with all my heart.'

For her part, she once wrote to him: 'The only thing I need is you and the sun.'

Even his wife, Eugenie, whom he did not even meet until over ten years after Hortense died, was jealous of this long-lasting love. In February 1912, nearly thirty years after Louis' own death, she said coldly to Ferdinand Bac: 'The Emperor always manifested with regard to his mother an extraordinary veneration. I do not know if she deserved it.'

Hortense and the young Louis remained in Constance for seventeen boring months, living in a rented house in the suburbs. Even the normally bland Blanchard Jerrold admits: 'It is hardly possible to imagine a duller winter place than Constance. In the dead of winter, we can conceive no more terrible prison than the ruins of its walls encompass' – especially to such a sun-loving nature as the Creole Hortense.

Hortense still encouraged Louis to have no pretensions of rank and he remained as friendly and generous as ever. One day, when out walking with a neighbour's son, he met two boys begging in the street. He had no money, so he gave them his boots and jacket and returned home barefoot and in shirtsleeves.

They still had no permanent home. On 12 February 1816, France had passed a law banishing from its territory all members of the defeated Emperor's family on pain of death, and Hortense records how Louis received the news: 'With tears running down his cheeks, he exclaimed: "What? Can it be, *Maman*, that we shall never see France again?"' Hortense wanted to settle in Baden and buy her own home on the lakeside near Constance but, under pressure from the French Government, her cousin-in-law, Grand Duke Charles, forbade her: she could only live in a rented house. Feeling the need for 'a small corner of land that is really my own', she began to explore the possibilities of buying a place of her own in Switzerland where she knew that, at least in principle, the Allied powers would permit her to live, if only she could find a canton whose government would allow it.

In the summer of 1816, while on a reconnaissance with Louise Cochelet, she came across a small, dilapidated castle called Arenenberg (Fools' Castle), near the little town of Ermatingen in German-speaking Switzerland. It was on the southern shore of Lake Constance almost opposite Constance itself. Brooding and romantic on a hill above the lake, with magnificent views over the water and the surrounding countryside, it needed substantial enlargement and modernisation. Money, however, was not a problem.[1] Hortense fell in love with it at once – or, at least, with its potential.

On 10 February 1817, she signed the contract of purchase. It would be several months before it was ready for occupation, and then only as a part-time summer residence. Situated in the canton of Thurgau, the cantonal government said that she and her son could not live there all the year round unless the Allied powers gave their specific consent. Shrewdly, Hortense insisted upon a clause in the contract that the purchase would be rescinded if such consent was not forthcoming.

It took four years for consent to come through; it only did so after Napoleon's death on St Helena in May 1821. Only then did the Allied powers take a more relaxed view as to where the Emperor's close family could be permitted to live. Their reasons for not accepting Arenenberg until then are revealed in an extraordinary letter written by the young Stratford Canning (later 1st Viscount Stratford de Redcliffe) – a ruthless career diplomat who was then British Minister to Switzerland – to Lord Castlereagh, the British Foreign Secretary, soon after Hortense had signed the purchase contract:

---

[1] The bulk of Hortense's very substantial fortune came from her inheritance from Josephine which consisted mainly of property outside France and produced an annual income of about £400,000 tax free at today's values. She also had a lot of valuable jewellery. Her wealth, however, never prevented her or, later in life, Louis, from periodically complaining about cash-flow and instituting a determined but temporary economy drive.

We would have no adequate means of controlling either the correspondence or the movements of Madame de St-Leu.[1] The position selected on the banks of Lake Constance, at the very extremity of Switzerland, renders observation difficult. The police of the canton is too weak to be depended on. The employment of secret agents would be attended with expense, and from the remoteness of the situation would be exposed to continual failure.

Arenenberg, although to prove a delightful summer home over the next few years, was not an immediate answer to Hortense's need for a full-time home. In February 1817, the very month that she signed the Arenenberg contract, it became clear that was what she urgently needed, for Grand Duke Charles of Baden finally gave in to French pressure and wrote to Hortense, as her 'very devoted cousin', that she and her son would have to leave his domain.

Where were they to go? 'I was once more a homeless wanderer,' she later wrote despairingly.

Her brother, Eugene, came to the rescue. He was living as a royal duke in Bavaria where he was happily married to the king's daughter. This was one of the few dynastic marriages engineered by Napoleon that actually worked. He had always been close to his sister, so now he bought her a house in Augsburg, Bavaria's third largest city, and said that she could live there for as long as she liked, certainly until at least the Arenenberg problem was resolved. He knew that his father-in-law, the liberal King Maximilian, would, as ruler of the most powerful country in southern Germany, stoutly withstand whatever opposition might emerge from France or the Allied Powers.

So, on 6 May 1817, Hortense and Louis left Constance and moved, with their household of sixteen 'courtiers in exile' plus servants, to Augsburg. It was then, as it still is today, a cultivated and animated city, but Hortense took the opportunity to write self-pityingly in her memoirs: 'It was the town of my choice because

---

[1] Although many still accorded her the courtesy title of 'Queen' and 'Majesty', her legal title had now reverted to 'Her Highness the Duchess of St-Leu' conferred upon her by King Louis XVIII soon after his first Restoration and never formally rescinded. This was much to the annoyance of her permanently estranged husband, ex-King Louis, whose legal title was the lower-ranking 'Count of St-Leu', without either 'Majesty' or 'Highness'.

I had been told that there was no social life there. I had retired from the world and all I wanted was tranquillity and kindness. I found both there.'

At least, she was able to sit down and begin her memoirs.

At first, living in Augsburg made little difference to the young Louis. He was still only nine years old, a sensitive, dreamy little boy with an angelic face and a determination to please. His tutor, the amiable Abbé Bertrand, did not worry too much about formal lessons. He still called Louis by his nickname 'Oui-oui' and left him most of the time to his own devices, preferring to chat with Hortense, flirt discreetly with her ladies or write long and learned letters on French mediaeval heraldry to other elderly clerics.

If anything, Hortense played a larger part in her son's education than did his professional mentor. No one seems to have thought of starting to teach him Latin or arithmetic or French grammar – nor even German which was, after all, the language of the people among whom they had been living for the past two years. But Hortense – unlike most other wealthy mothers of the time – still spent many hours a week in his company. She taught him drawing, for which he had a natural aptitude, and she painted him herself: a delightful sketch still exists of the pretty little boy, his tousled hair sticking out from beneath a large, wide-brimmed hat, his eyes dark and soft. She also encouraged him, although he was not physically robust, to take up riding and swimming. He may have been a mother's boy but she did not want him to be a namby-pamby.

Above all, in her house crowded with furniture, paintings and other relics of the First Empire brought from her former palace on the rue Cerutti in Paris, Hortense set out, even at this very early age, to instil in Louis – and his elder brother, although in his case mainly by correspondence – a passionate pride in the name Bonaparte and in the achievements of the Emperor now living in remote exile. 'You and your brother', she wrote to the teenage Napoleon Louis then living in Florence with his father (who did not share his wife's devotion to his brother's glory), 'are assuredly heirs of Napoleon, after the King of Rome ... In our present condition, uncertain of what you may become, never weary of hoping. Keep your eyes peeled, look out for propitious moments ... Everywhere "flights of fancy" arise which can raise the heirs of a great and illustrious man to the skies.'

It was heady stuff but little boys still had to be educated and by the autumn of 1819 Hortense became reluctantly aware that Louis, by then eleven, was learning virtually nothing with the charming but hopelessly disorganised Abbé Bertrand. She was too kind-hearted to turn the old gentleman out of her household but she found a new tutor for Louis. He was a different kind of person altogether, a tight-lipped, humourless twenty-six-year-old scholar named Philippe Le Bas. He was warmly recommended by her old schoolfriend Louise Cochelet's brother but he still seems an odd choice. He was the son of a Revolutionary leader and close friend of Robespierre who had committed suicide in prison rather than meet the same fate on the guillotine. With a permanently pained expression on his face and a nasty little moustache, he had grown up hating royalty, aristocrats, the rich and even the middle class. Yet here he was, tutor to the grandson of an aristocrat (the Vicomte Alexandre de Beauharnais) whose execution his own father must have greeted with delight.

It shows both Hortense's generosity of spirit and Le Bas' dexterous mental processes that he was able, with a young wife and child to support, to overcome his moral scruples. He presumably told himself that it was his duty to teach a pampered little prince the stern realities of life.

Le Bas took up his duties at Arenenberg in June 1820, and was almost at once appalled. Within two weeks, he wrote to his stepfather: 'I cannot hide from myself the fact that my task will be anything but an easy one. My pupil is twelve years old and has aptitude but he is not well advanced. I might even say that his knowledge on a great many points is practically nil. He has a complete distaste for study. It would have been much more satisfactory to me, had I taken him in hand at the age of seven or eight. As it is, I find myself in the position of an architect who is asked to make habitable an ill-built house: he has to pull it down, even to lay the foundations afresh, if he would attain his object. Still I must not lose courage; though I see little love of work in my pupil, I have at least found more docility than I expected, a desire to please me, a fear of dissatisfying me and an excellent heart. With qualities such as these, one has something to build on.'

Four weeks later, he was writing: 'At twelve years of age, my pupil is like a seven-year-old and the simplest notions are to him strangers. It takes him half an hour to explain to me what a "verb" is.' But he was beginning to have more confidence in Louis' basic intelligence: 'With patience, things will improve.'

It was not only patience that Le Bas prescribed. Poor little Louis, used to a remarkably easy life with Abbé Bertrand, when he would often get up as late as 9 o'clock in the morning, now had a far more rigorous timetable. He had to get up at 6.00 am, walk in the mountains until 7.00 am and then do three hours of grammar and Latin, all on an empty stomach. He was allowed an hour off for breakfast at 10.30 am. At 11.30 he resumed work with lessons in arithmetic, German and Greek. From 3.00 to 4.00 pm his man-servant took him swimming in the lake, which was followed by a history or geography lesson from 4.00 to 6.00 pm. After dinner at six and a walk, one more hour was spent, from 8.00 to 9.00 pm, going over the lessons of the day again, and at 9.00 pm the exhausted child was allowed to go to bed.

Not surprisingly, Louis found this new regimen of nine-and-a-half hours' work a day a great strain, and he became highly nervous and agitated. Instead of showing understanding, Le Bas merely reckoned that his pupil was out of sorts because of the physical toll of riding and swimming – and promptly stopped them. In future, Louis' only recreation was to be walks with his tutor, during which he would be taught botany and astronomy. Not a minute of this twelve-year-old's day was to be wasted!

In the autumn of 1820, the household moved from their summer home at Arenenberg back to Augsburg and Le Bas actually increased Louis' working hours. His daily work schedule increased from nine-and-a-half hours to eleven-and-a-half. It gave the poor child bad dreams: he awoke in the night screaming with terror. Abbé Bertrand had let him keep a candle burning all night because he was afraid of the dark, but Le Bas now ordered the candle removed. It may have been harsh but the nightmares – and the screaming – ceased.

His studies also began to improve so Hortense now insisted that the child's workload be eased a little and that, before going to bed, he should spend an hour with her and her ladies in the drawing-room. Le Bas thought it 'a waste of time' but could say nothing.

In April 1821, soon after his thirteenth birthday, and at Le Bas' own suggestion, Louis began attending the High School (Gymnasium) in Augsburg as a day boy. Dating from 1581, the school had a high reputation but it was hard for Louis to do all his lessons in German instead of in his native French.[1] Yet he did remarkably well: in February 1822, at the end-of-term examinations, he came fourth out of the sixty-six boys in his class.

By then, Hortense, in the greater freedom allowed her after Napoleon's death in May 1821, had left her brother's house in Augsburg and gone to live full-time at Arenenberg. She transferred all her paintings and other relics of the Napoleonic era to the house, completing the process of turning it into a Swiss version of Malmaison.[2] Much to his dismay, Louis had to stay behind in term-time in Augsburg with Le Bas and his wife, Clemence. Yet he continued to make good academic progress: 'You were a very good pupil,' one of his old teachers told him when he visited the Gymnasium as emperor of the French some forty years later.

But Hortense missed her son badly and in 1823, when he was still only fifteen, she took him away from school and brought him home to Arenenberg. Le Bas and his wife came with him and officially Philippe remained his tutor, but his heyday had passed.

Ex-King Louis, although now even more irascible and almost a permanent invalid, had mellowed towards Hortense and had several times allowed their older son, Napoleon Louis, to visit his mother and younger brother. Not unreasonably, he now insisted that Louis should visit him at Marienbad, a spa town in Bohemia (today the Czech Republic) where he was taking the waters. Accordingly, in August 1823, Louis, accompanied by his tutor, spent an enjoyable month with his father and older brother, but Le Bas did not like it at all. He was continually complaining in his letters to his wife and stepfather that Louis was doing almost no work. It did not

---

[1] The slight German accent with which, in adult life, he spoke his native tongue dates from this schoolboy period. A natural linguist, he also later spoke fluent English and Italian – with a slight French accent.

[2] The house, later given to the canton of Thurgau by Napoleon III's widow, is now converted into a Napoleon Museum and visitors can see for themselves various rooms on the ground floor in which the walls are still hidden by curtains hanging from a central point in the ceiling in imitation of an army tent. This was a direct copy from Malmaison where it was a feature much liked by Napoleon.

occur to him that having a good time was also part of growing up.

On their return, things did not improve because both parents had arranged to spend an extended winter with their sons in Rome. This was Hortense's and Louis' first winter together in the Eternal City and both were to love it so much that they would spend all their winters there, with one exception, for the next seven years. Rome had become the exiled Bonapartes' safe haven: except for ex-King Joseph, still living in the United States, all Napoleon's surviving brothers and sisters – and his mother – now rented or owned elegant *palazzi* in Rome.

Life in Rome was fun for the wealthy exiles and Hortense did not see why her younger son should be exempt from this pleasure. Having ensured for him a solid grounding in formal education, she now thought it was time for Louis to ride, hunt and go to balls with other young men and women in Roman high society. The ever-weary Le Bas complained to his family, 'My pupil goes to bed late and gets up late. He works little and lazily until luncheon, rides at midday, comes in tired at three o'clock, yawns over his studies until five and then goes to pass the rest of the day at his father's.'

They were still in Rome the following spring when Hortense's much-loved brother, Eugene, died unexpectedly in Bavaria at the age of forty-three. She was devastated and hurried back, with Louis, to attend his funeral. On their way, they crossed the River Rugone, the same (Latin) Rubicon that Julius Caesar had crossed when marching on Rome to make himself dictator. Louis was greatly impressed and ordered the carriage to stop. He alighted and filled a small bottle with water from the river. Twenty-seven years later, when planning the coup d'état of December 1851 that made him President for Ten Years shortly before becoming emperor, he gave it a code name: 'Rubicon'.

Because of her continuing grief for her brother, Hortense, for the first time since she had bought the place, spent the whole winter at Arenenberg. The following autumn, however, they were off again to Rome and in March 1826 they were still enjoying what they considered the good life. But Le Bas disagreed. 'Our life is a sadly squandered one,' he wrote to his stepfather, 'and our studies suffer from it. I can hardly find one or two hours a day in which my pupil is free for work. I have protested to *Madame la Duchesse* and she has admitted that I am right but she does nothing to remedy the situation.

'It would have made me so happy to have seen the dear boy as distinguished by his knowledge as he will still be by his good qualities and fine character. But, alas, the highroads are not the places for a solid education! One must resign oneself to a superficial manhood when we turn wanderers at this time of life.'

But when they returned to Arenenberg, Le Bas still found no improvement. Hortense always seemed to be entertaining. Her home seemed to be permanently full of royal cousins, writers, musicians, poets, eminent figures from society and survivors of the First Empire. In July 1827, he complained bitterly to his stepfather of 'the comedies, the shows, the parties on the water and in carriages; everything that it is possible to invent in order to waste time. I never feel so lonely as when I am in high society.'

It could now be only a matter of time before the inevitable parting of the ways. In early September 1827, Hortense brusquely gave notice to Le Bas, dismissing him on 1 October. She thanked him somewhat unenthusiastically for his services but said that she could no longer afford to keep him. Moaning to his stepfather that he had not been given three months' notice, he returned to Paris and eventually became a celebrated academic.

'How boring that man was!' Louis, now nineteen, commented to a friend.

For the next two years, Louis marked time. Freed from all tutorial restraint, he concentrated on having a good time. He was young, quite handsome – especially as he well knew, on horseback – with a slight military moustache (the famous short, pointed beard did not come until much later) and an enticing voice. Sex was early one of his pleasures and the French historian, André Castelot, tells us that Louis first fell in love at the age of twelve, with a little girl in Augsburg. He wrote out her name in cress seeds in a flower-bed but Le Bas angrily raked it out with a pickaxe.

The following year, he did more than write a girl's name in seeds. Aged only thirteen, he lost his virginity to a chambermaid named Eliza at Arenenberg.

It was not only precocious physical lust. Louis could also be romantic and gay – in the old-fashioned sense of the word. For instance, at fifteen, he was walking along the banks of a river at Mannheim with his three pretty young cousins, the daughters of Grand Duke Charles of Baden. They were talking about the Golden Age of chivalry which the girls claimed to be dead. Louis protested that was not true and, at that very moment, a flower decorating the hat of one of the girls was caught by the wind and carried into the water. 'My dear Louis,' said Marie, the youngest girl. 'Here is a good opportunity for a chivalrous knight to show his courage!'

Without hesitation, he dived fully dressed into the river and rescued the flower.

A year later, when still a schoolboy in Augsburg, he fell in love with a girl sitting at a window and, although they did not exchange a word and never saw each other again, he later told Valerie Masuyer, his mother's lady-in-waiting, that he would remember that girl all his life.

According to André Castelot, in his mid-teens Louis became such a menace to the 'little peasant girls' around Arenenberg that an official complaint was made to his mother, but she merely smiled indulgently.

Sexual activity was not his only exercise. A very good horseman, he was also a first-class swimmer, a good gymnast, a fair fencer and an excellent shot. In other words, although perhaps more highly sexed than most, he was a perfectly normal, aggressively athletic young man of his wealth and class. The two years following his tutor's dismissal passed very amiably for him, whether at Arenenberg in the summer or at Rome in the winter, although arguably not for the girls whom he deflowered or whose hearts he broke.

In April 1829, he became twenty-one. One of the new circle of young friends that he met in Rome later that year was Lord Fitzharris, later 3rd Earl of Malmesbury and one of Queen Victoria's more mediocre Foreign Secretaries. In his memoirs, he gives this graphic description of Louis as he first knew him: 'A wild, harumscarum youth riding at full gallop down the streets to the peril of the public, fencing and pistol-shooting, and apparently without serious thoughts of any kind, *although even then he was possessed with the conviction that he would some day rule over France* [my italics] . . . He was a very good horseman and proficient at athletic games, being short but very active and muscular. His face was grave and dark but redeemed by a singularly bright smile.'

I have italicised the sentence about Louis being convinced even then that some day he would rule over France because frankly I do not believe it. Lord Malmesbury wrote his book fifty-five years after the incident, in 1884, with the dubious value of hindsight. It was then the accepted view, and still is today, that Louis had his impassioned belief in his destiny as future ruler of France almost from the moment that he emerged squalling from his mother's womb. But that simply was not so. Lord Malmesbury got it right in his preceding words: 'apparently without serious thoughts of any kind'.

That was the *real* Louis at the age of twenty-one.

It is, of course, true that Hortense brought him up with a deep pride in his ancestry and with vague notions of his possible role as *one* of the heirs to the great Napoleon but, as we have already seen, she herself called them 'flights of fancy'. It is also true that Louis, if only because of his early childhood so close to the Emperor, had a built-in awe of him: 'In Paris I was so young that it is only in my heart that I have any memory of him,' he wrote to his aged grandmother, Letizia, when Napoleon died. 'When I do wrong, if I think of this great man, I seem to feel his shade within me telling me to be worthy of his name.'[1]

But there was a limit to this veneration of the past. The young Louis lived very much in the present and, even if he looked to the future, he saw immediately ahead of him two almost equally youthful figures, one four years older and the other two years younger. His brother, Napoleon Louis, had recently cemented his position in the family's hierarchy by marrying Charlotte, daughter of the Emperor's oldest brother, ex-King Joseph; and François Joseph Charles, Napoleon's only legitimate son, had technically ruled for a few days as Napoleon II after Waterloo and was the emperor's designated heir.

The Austrians had tried to remake François Joseph Charles as one of their own, with an Austrian name (Franz Josef Karl), an

---

[1] He never changed. Forty-four years later, when dictating his will to a lawyer's clerk, he proclaimed: 'It is the soul of my illustrious uncle that has always inspired and maintained me.'

Austrian title (Duke of Reichstadt) and a totally Austrian lifestyle. He lived like a prisoner in a golden cage in the ornate palace in Vienna of his grandfather, the Austrian Emperor. In 1829, when the French poet, Barthélemy, arrived seeking an audience to hand over an epic poem dedicated to Napoleon, the Duke's tutor, Count Maurice Dietrichstein, refused him access. 'You must understand that the Prince hears, sees and reads only what we want him to hear, see and read,' he explained. 'He is not a prisoner but ... he is in a very special position.'

François Joseph Charles was generally known to be not very well but no one knew the exact state of his health, not even his doctors. In 1830, they diagnosed him as having a diseased liver whereas in truth he was slowly dying from tuberculosis.

To the outside world, he was a mystery. As Blanchard Jerrold has written, 'Both Louis and his elder brother looked towards the sick young man at Vienna with reverential respect. They never ceased to hope that the day would come when he would be delivered out of his bondage, and they would be able to do homage to him as their sovereign.'

And he cites this letter from Louis to François Joseph Charles: 'My dear Cousin, – I enquire in every quarter for news of your health, and the doubt in which I am left by indirect reports causes me the greatest anxiety. If you knew all the attachment we have for you, and the extent of our devotion, you would understand our grief in not having direct intercourse with one whom we have been taught to cherish as a kinsman and to honour as the son of the Emperor Napoleon.'

Dietrichstein confiscated this letter and the sad young Duke never saw it. Yet the fact remains that these two young people, François Joseph Charles of uncertain health and Napoleon Louis of robust good health, stood solidly before Louis in the official order of succession to the empty Imperial throne of France – and that was without counting his uncle, ex-King Joseph, a vigorous sixty-one-year-old with another fifteen years to live, and his own father ex-King Louis who was only fifty-one.

Few people knew Louis better throughout his life than Hortense Cornu, the daughter of one of his mother's maidservants. Never a snob, he once wrote to her: 'I wish you were a man! You understand things so well and, apart from a few details, I think like you do.'

Two months after his death in final exile in January 1873, Hortense Cornu told an English journalist: 'The Emperor frequently said to me, not when he was a child but at the age of nineteen and twenty, "What a blessing that I have two before me in the succession, the Duke of Reichstadt and my brother, so that I can be happy in my own way instead of being, as the head of my house must be, the slave of a mission."' That comment perhaps helps to refute the traditional view that Louis *always* believed that one day he would rule France.

In fact, that only came about after Napoleon Louis and François no longer stood in his path and were both – prematurely – dead. That was soon to happen.

Chapter Six

The Call to Destiny
(1830–32)

T HE YEAR 1830 SAW Louis longing for some dashing military role. It was an era when romantically charged young men of good family and ample means yearned to go to war to support oppressed peoples trying to achieve their nationhood. In the two previous years, the misanthropic ex-King Louis had refused to let either of his sons join the Russian army to help the Greeks in their War of Independence against Turkey in which the poet Lord Byron had died: 'Fight only for France,' he had told them. As a poor substitute, in June 1830, Louis joined the Swiss military academy at Thun to study artillery (Napoleon's field of expertise) and engineering.

In a sense, he was playing at soldiers. The Swiss army had not fought a battle for over 300 years but, as he wrote to Hortense, 'The exercise does me much good. I have double my ordinary appetite.' Like the other volunteers, he marched up to thirty miles a day with a pack on his back and slept in a tent at the foot of a glacier.

But in France, there was no play-acting. Louis XVIII, the ageing Bourbon king restored by the Allies after Waterloo, had died in his sleep in 1824 and been succeeded by his younger brother, the Comte d'Artois, then aged sixty-seven, who reigned as Charles X. It was a disaster. A repressive, religious bigot, he had learned nothing from the French Revolution or the fact that his eldest brother, Louis XVI, had been beheaded. The Duke of Wellington, looking on from England, commented shrewdly: 'There is no such thing as political experience. With the warning of James II before him [the British king exiled in 1688 for claiming that he ruled by 'Divine Right'], Charles X is setting up a Government by priests, through priests, for priests.'

On 27 July 1830, the people of Paris finally rose in revolt. For three days they fought in the streets until finally Charles' own troops deserted and the King, 'continuously weeping', fled to England. Charles had alienated all sections of the community: the working classes, the middle classes, the professional classes, the armed forces and the intelligentsia. The widely popular and revered Marquis de Lafayette, then aged seventy-three, who had fought on the side of the people in both the American War of Independence and the French Revolution, could easily have been appointed President of a new French Republic, but he refused the honour. He said that France needed a popular monarchy headed by a prince who would be true to the spirit of the Revolution.

There was one obvious candidate: Louis-Philippe, the Duc d'Orléans and head of a younger Bourbon line. As a young man, he had fought in the Revolutionary armies before fleeing into exile during the Reign of Terror. On 31 July 1830, his name having been put forward by Lafayette, he accepted the French Parliament's invitation to serve as 'Lieutenant-General of the Kingdom'. Ten days later, on 9 August, after Charles X had formally abdicated, he took the oath as 'Louis-Philippe I, King of the French by the Grace of God and the Will of the Nation.'

Unfortunately, he did not strike a dashing figure. He had won his Revolutionary colours a long time ago; now he was a fat, fifty-seven-year-old bourgeois, the idol of the bourgeoisie itself, happier with an umbrella than a sword. With a pear-shaped body and a pudding face, he knew his limitations. He set out to be a 'Citizen-King'. But that was not really the French style and, for a brief while, it looked as if a Bonaparte might once again rule over the nation. In the working-class districts of Paris, there were cries of '*Vive Napoleon III!*' (the nineteen-year-old Duke of Reichstadt, Napoleon's only legitimate son, then living in Vienna) and a new young generation, who had not known personally the blood-letting of war, thought only of the glory of France under the great Emperor. At the military academy in Thun, Louis could only look on with envy. 'We are very quiet in our little corner where further afield people are fighting for our dearest interests,' he wrote to Hortense.

At least, the Bonapartes hoped that now they might be allowed to return as private citizens to France but that possibility was soon denied them. In September 1830, the Law of 1816 was renewed banishing all family members on pain of death. A Bonapartist revival seemed as remote as ever.

In October, Hortense and Louis (on leave from the academy) left Arenenberg, as usual, to spend their customary winter of balls and frivolity in Rome. Nothing seemed untoward but it was to prove a journey that changed their lives. En route, they stopped in Florence to visit Napoleon Louis; the impact on Louis was at once profound. He virtually became a man overnight instead of the perpetual adolescent, and the next few months were to cement the process. For he found his brother transformed: the twenty-six-year-old Napoleon Louis had turned into a young revolutionary. All he could talk about was his excitement at the July Revolution in France and his hopes of how it would inspire a massive nationalist uprising that would blaze across Italy. He appealed to his younger brother to become involved: how could he resist the splendour of a call to arms that the great Napoleon himself would not have refused?

At this stage, one needs to pause for two different passages of explanation: one dealing with Italy and the other with the nature of the relationship between Louis and his brother.

The Italy of 1830 was not the Italy of today. There was no Italian nation. The country was divided. Much of the Italian peninsula was under Austrian domination. It was stratified, like layers in a cake, into the kingdom of Piedmont and the Austrian provinces of Venetia and Lombardy in the north, the self-governing duchies of Tuscany, Parma, Lucca and Modena in a thick wedge below, the Papal States ruled directly by the Pope in a diagonal spread across the centre, and the kingdom of Naples and Sicily in the far south. The Italian peninsula was virtually a large Austrian colony for the Austrians pulled the strings that animated the King of Naples and Sicily, their influence prevailed in the so-called 'independent' duchies (most of whose rulers were members of the Austrian Emperor's family), and even the Pope looked to the Austrian army for help when his subjects became restless. Only in Piedmont was there a native king who was truly independent.

The Austria of those years was not the small, comparatively minor mid-European state of today. Then it was an ageing giant that had existed under the name of the Holy Roman Empire ever since 962 when its first Emperor, Otto I, was crowned. For over

700 years it had expanded across central and eastern Europe, down into Italy and the Balkans, but it had become corrupt and a shadow of its former military might. Defeated by Napoleon I at Austerlitz in December 1805, it had, at his insistence, changed its title to the Austrian Empire. Thereafter it hung desperately on to its shrinking remaining power.

The Austrians – and the Pope – ruled by military dictatorship buttressed by a ruthless secret police. There was no liberalism, no freedom. Napoleon had lost the Battle of Waterloo but, in the peninsula, he had won the battle for men's minds: the Kingdom of Italy which he had created (and over which Eugene de Beauharnais, Hortense's brother, had ruled as an able viceroy) lingered in people's minds as a memory of past achievement and as a spur to new endeavour.

Since Napoleon's defeat, secret societies had spread all over Italy and none was more powerful than the *Carbonari*. This was the first resistance movement of modern times, sworn to secrecy in mystic initiation ceremonies and operating in small cells of individuals so that any police agent infiltrating the organisation could, at best, discover only a few names. Its aim was to expel the foreigner and create a united Italy. All classes thronged to join it: nobles, officers, peasants, priests – anyone in whom liberal and patriotic ideas had taken firm root.

And, as he revealed to his younger brother in November 1830, Napoleon Louis was a member. He had taken the secret oath as a *Carbonaro*.

Justice has not perhaps been done to an explanation of the nature of the relationship between Louis and his brother. Torn apart fifteen years earlier, when their father had sent his minions to bring the older boy to live with him in compliance with the French High Court's custody order, it has been largely assumed that they lived separate lives during boyhood and adolescence, and had little influence upon each other.

This is not necessarily the case. Like many a younger brother, Louis idolised his older brother who had always been the more dominant and outward-going of the two. A strikingly handsome young man with a well-balanced mind, logical and eloquent, he 'was every inch the Emperor,' according to Valerie Masuyer, who met him for the first time during that visit to Florence.

He was entirely different from Louis, a man of action rather than a dreamer. Expansive and extrovert, he yet had a practical side. He owned, of all things, a successful paper plant at Serravezza, near La Spezia, south-east of Genoa, for which he had designed all the machinery, and he had not only written a history of Florence but invented a new method of producing steel. Furthermore, he took very seriously his role as the oldest of the new generation of male Bonapartes in direct line of succession to Napoleon's throne. He really seems to have believed that one day he might be emperor: the thought never seems to have occurred to him that it might be his younger brother. Nor was he alone in this view: his uncle, ex-King Joseph, according to the 1804 Law of Succession, next in line after Napoleon's own male heirs (of whom there was only one, the young Duke of Reichstadt), obviously thought that his older nephew was the man of the future. Four years earlier, in 1826, he had shown his approval of Napoleon Louis as potential successor to the unmarried and childless Reichstadt by sending his young daughter, Charlotte, from their comfortable home in exile in the United States to marry her own first cousin.[1]

None of this was lost on Louis. Throughout his life, he was to show a need for someone to point him the way ahead, someone with a character stronger than his who would open his eyes to his own potential, someone who would both lead him and upon whom he could rely.

The truth is that he was destined never to be the support for someone else's failings: it was always the other way around.

And so it proved now with Napoleon Louis. Louis left Florence a passionate convert to the cause of Italian freedom. Historians have argued about whether he actually went so far as to follow his brother's example and join the *Carbonari*. It does not matter. He had become, at the very least, a highly committed supporter.

The Rome in which Louis and his mother arrived in the last week of November 1830 was in a state of political ferment. Pope Pius VIII was dying and his death on 1 December that year left a dangerous power vacuum that was to endure for two months before his

---

[1] Joseph himself had no sons and none of his three daughters had any hopes of succession. The 1804 Law of Succession only envisaged *male* heirs.

successor, Gregory XVI, was elected. To the patriots it seemed a perfect moment to strike, and the city was a hotbed of plots and counter plots, most of them highly amateurish. The whole thing had, to modern minds, an air of comic opera.

All his life, Louis was to love the devious delights of conspiracy and intrigue but, at twenty-two, he had not yet learned discretion. Either unaware that he was under constant surveillance by the Pope's secret police or simply not concerned, he openly rode about the streets with the saddle of his horse trimmed with the red, white and yellow colours of the banned flag of United Italy.

Finally, on 11 December 1830, he was seen to be involved in a minor skirmish with armed police in the Piazza Colonna outside what is now the Parliament of modern Italy. He escaped unharmed, but wounded in the exchange of bullets was a twenty-seven-year-old doctor from Milan named Henri Conneau, the son of a Frenchman and an Italian woman who was later to be his personal physician and, according to French historian Jean-Claude Lachnitt, 'undoubtedly his closest friend'. Conneau would reappear at significant moments in Louis' life, and in the events surrounding his death.

Later that same evening, fifty uniformed members of the Papal Guard surrounded the Palazzo Ruspoli which Hortense had rented for the winter. Their colonel, accompanied by four guardsmen, mounted the stairs to the first floor *salon* and, bowing to the ex-queen, announced that her son must leave Rome with him immediately: he had orders to escort him out of the Papal States.

As he embraced his mother and told her not to fear for his safety, Louis whispered in her ear that one of the revolutionaries, a new friend of his, was sheltering in his quarters. Would she take care of him? She muttered her agreement; he kissed her and left.

Having rejoined his brother in Florence, the two young hotheads – despite all their father's entreaties to stop this dangerous nonsense – declared openly their support for the revolutionary forces. Louis wrote to a friend: 'You will have heard that I have been forced to leave Rome: apparently the Cardinals were afraid of me. Some people say that I am much hurt by this insult but they are mistaken. There are governments by which it is an honour to be persecuted.' His youthful enthusiasm screams out from the printed page.

The brothers' parents were in despair. Ex-King Louis, who had by now become deeply religious, accused them of embracing the cause of the Anti-Christ while Hortense raised more worldly arguments against their headstrong action.

'The Italians may no doubt in a moment of excitement shake off a burden that oppresses them,' she wrote to her sons on 8 January 1831, 'but I do not believe that they have the means of contending alone and for long against the efforts directed against them . . . Is it common sense to think that so small a part of an empire can withstand superior forces? Short-sighted people can neither foresee nor judge. You must beware of their alluring suggestions.'

She conceded that her sons bore 'a magical name' but the holders of such a name 'should properly appear in revolutions only to re-establish order by giving security to nations and counterbalancing the exclusive power of kings. Their role is to wait with patience but if they ferment troubles, they will only experience the fate of adventurers who have been used and who are deserted.'

Those words were to prove prophetic.

In mid-January, open revolt broke out in the Duchy of Modena and later in the northern part of the Papal States where, in the regional capital of Bologna, the Pope was formally deposed and a provisional government proclaimed. On 25 January, ignoring their father's orders to stay in Florence,[1] the two brothers departed to join the revolutionaries. Hortense, hastening up from Rome in her anxiety for their welfare, was perplexed to find they had not ridden ahead, as usual, to meet her on the road. Her heart beat fast with apprehension: where on earth were they?

A letter was waiting at her hotel. 'Your affection will understand us,' Louis – as always closer to his mother than his sibling – had written. 'We have accepted engagements and we cannot depart from

---

[1] The two young men were fighting the Austrians as well as other forces, which made ex-King Louis concerned about his own position. In general, Bonapartes were not welcome in Florence. Napoleon I had deposed Grand Duke Ferdinand, the Austrian Emperor's brother, and put his own sister Elisa on the throne. She had ruled solely in French interests and one reason why the returned Ferdinand had allowed Louis to live in Florence was that his abdication as King of Holland had earned him the reputation of being the only one of Napoleon's crowned siblings to stand up to him. He therefore enjoyed a highly privileged position, which he did not want to endanger.

them. The name we bear and the engagements we have accepted oblige us to help a suffering people that calls upon us.' Later he wrote again, this time exultantly: 'For the first time I know what it is to live! Before I have done nothing but vegetate. A fairer or more honourable position than ours cannot be imagined.'

He acquitted himself well in battle. At San Lorenzino, his men had forced some Papal troops to retreat, leaving a few men lying wounded on the ground. As he rode up, one of these wounded soldiers fired at him but missed. Louis drew his pistol and advanced upon him but, on reaching him, said that he would spare his life. As he turned his back to ride away, the soldier grabbed a gun from a wounded companion and aimed at him but Louis' sergeant-major rushed forward and ran the man through with his sabre before he could pull the trigger.

Hortense's tears had been justified. The revolutionaries were only using the naïve young brothers. They hoped that the name of Bona-parte would bring hundreds, if not thousands, of recruits to their cause and, to some extent, this proved true. But, on a broader scale, they knew that they were hopelessly outnumbered and that their only hope of armed support could come from Louis-Philippe of France. He was, after all, the 'Citizen King' raised to power by the July Revol-ution that had directly spawned their movement. They based their strategy on the hope that he would commit his soldiers to their aid.

That was the last thing the cautious new king was going to do. The veteran Austrian Chancellor Metternich not only made it clear that any French intervention in Italy would produce a sharp response from his country, still one of the most powerful in Europe. He also instructed the Austrian Ambassador in Paris to point out that the active presence of the two young Bonaparte princes gave the whole affair the appearance of a serious Bonapartist movement, which, as he well knew, was the last thing that Louis-Philippe, still shaky on his throne, would wish to countenance.

In truth, the revolutionaries completely misread the scene. Increasingly desperate for French help, and with the two princes having served their initial purpose in adding the glamour of their name to their enterprise, they now cynically dropped them and requested them to withdraw from their struggle. In fact, it did not help them because Louis-Philippe still did not send a single soldier to fight alongside them. Hortense was proved correct in her warning that the heroic brothers would 'experience the fate of adventurers who have been used and who are deserted'.

On 5 March, Louis wrote sadly to his mother: 'The intrigues of Uncle Jerome and Papa have been so successful that we have been obliged to leave the Army.' The Revolution was doomed. Austrian and Papal troops were sweeping all opposition before them. The two princes, in fear of their lives – the Austrians had put them under sentence of death – became fugitives. Nor could they return to Florence, as the Grand Duke, under pressure from his Austrian masters, had banned them from re-entering any part of his domain of Tuscany.

Hortense was distraught. She did not know where her sons were or even if they were still alive. Ex-King Louis, her estranged husband, was useless: he simply burst into tears and exclaimed how terrible it all was. But Hortense proved that she was made of sterner stuff. She realised that, even if she found her sons alive, she would have immense difficulty in finding a country that would give them asylum. Many of Europe's royal heads of state regarded them as hot-headed apostles of revolution and even the Swiss Republic had announced that, for the moment, they would not be welcome. She calculated that only Britain, with its long liberal traditions, held out any hope of giving them at least temporary shelter.

Lord Seymour, the British Minister to the Grand Duke of Tuscany stationed in Florence, was an old friend. Hortense threw herself upon his mercy and begged his help. A kindly man, he gave her three British passports – for 'Mrs Hamilton and her two sons' – and assured her that he would inform his Government that they would be arriving on British shores.

Armed with these vital documents, without which travel across Europe would have been impossible, Hortense set out from Florence on 10 March to rescue her two sons.

It was undoubtedly her finest hour as a mother.

Hortense, however, was never to see her older son again. On 17 March, while in hiding, twenty-seven-year-old Napoleon Louis died of measles in his brother's arms[1] at Forli, a small town in the

---

[1] One does not often think of measles as a fatal illness, but the fourth edition (1996) of the *Penguin Medical Encyclopaedia* states: 'By itself, the measles virus is not often dangerous; but during the attack the patient is abnormally vulnerable to all sorts of bacteria. Most deaths from measles are in fact due to secondary bacterial infection.'

northern Papal States. 'Why did I not die in his place?' an anguished Louis wrote later to their father.

It is not being disloyal to Louis' memory to observe that, if it *had* been the other way around and Napoleon Louis had survived, the older brother might have become emperor and the history of the Second Empire and, indeed, of the world would have been very different.

But for now Louis' own life continued to be at risk. When at last Hortense found him, two days later, at Pesaro on the Adriatic coast, he was seriously ill himself, having caught measles from his brother. Wiping away her tears, she proceeded to save his life.

The story of their epic escape across half of Europe is dramatic, powerful, and nowadays almost totally forgotten. Austrian troops were marching on Pesaro and it was impossible for Hortense and Louis to remain there. Wrapped warmly in blankets, Louis managed to stagger to his mother's coach and the two fled south to the seaport of Ancona where they had to stop. Louis could go no further.

The triumphant Austrians, pressing down on Ancona from Pesaro, were expected to arrive at any day. What to do? Austrian ships were blockading the harbour but neutral vessels were allowed through, so Hortense obtained a passport for her son from officials of the revolutionary government still precariously in control of the city and booked Louis a place on a Greek vessel due to sail that night for Corfu. Making a great fuss she had his luggage put aboard; when the Austrian army entered Ancona the next day, they were told that Louis had got safely away to Corfu.

In reality he was lying delirious and in high fever in his mother's apartment in the Palazzo Leuchtenberg, a sumptuous building put at her disposal by her nephew, the son of her late brother, Eugene. She let it be known that she herself had now been taken ill and withdrew to her private quarters. Unknown to the outside world, Louis lay restless in his narrow bed in a small inner room that opened out of her own bedroom.

But then came potential disaster: the newly arrived Austrian commander-in-chief demanded that Hortense vacate the *palazzo* so that he could take it over for himself and his staff. Defiantly, she rejected the demand and said that, although prepared to hand over the public rooms, she would not surrender her private quarters. The

Austrian general accepted the compromise and, for the next eight days, his office was right next door to Hortense's bedroom, separated from Louis' bed in its little inner room only by the thickness of a wooden double door.

For all that time, Louis dare not speak, not even in a whisper. They could not risk the sound of a man's voice betraying his presence. When, as frequently happened, he could not stop himself coughing, Hortense herself put her hand on his mouth to stifle the noise. As soon as the crisis in his condition passed and a loyal doctor pronounced him fit to travel, Hortense told the Austrian general that her own health had improved and that she was ready to leave. Courteously he gave her a pass through the Austrian lines.

At four in the morning on Easter Sunday 1831, Louis dressed himself in the livery of one of his mother's lackeys, as did the young Marquis Zappi, an Italian revolutionary aristocrat whom Hortense was also courageously helping to escape. At dawn, her carriage, followed by another containing her small retinue, trundled out of the courtyard of the Palazzo Leuchtenberg through ranks of sleeping Austrian soldiers, with Louis and the young Italian marquis travelling as her footmen.

Once safely through the Austrian lines, two of Hortense's real servants changed into 'gentlemen's clothes' and sat proudly in her coach as if they were the two sons named in the British passports of 'Mrs Hamilton'. That deception had to be maintained throughout their travels in the Papal States and onwards through Tuscany because Louis was well known in the region because of his revolutionary activities.

At midnight on Easter Sunday, they crossed the frontier from the Papal States into Tuscany. As they pressed on through the darkened countryside, all seemed to go well, but when they arrived at the village of Camoscia at about two in the morning they found it was impossible obtain fresh horses. They would have to stop: their hard-ridden horses were too weary to continue.

It would have been too risky to try and find lodgings in the village inn, so Hortense rested in her coach, and the future emperor of France, only recently recovered from a near-fatal illness, had to try and get some sleep lying on a stone bench outside in the street, together with the *real* servants.

Starting before dawn the next day, they travelled along narrow byroads, changing horses and drivers as often as they could, until they reached a remote village deep in the Tuscan hills. At last, they were able to spend the night in comparative security and the following day would see them safely out of Tuscany.

There was one more hurdle to overcome. The city of Siena lay implacably in their path: there was no way round it and there was only one road through it. The problem was that Hortense and Louis had always stopped there on their annual journeys down to Rome in happier days and the possibilities of recognition – and arrest – were great.

Hortense, showing the bravery she had exhibited throughout, decided to brazen it out and ride through the city with no attempt at disguise. If she were stopped, so be it: she would simply lie and say she had no idea where her son was. As for Louis, he jumped down from his mother's carriage before it reached the city's gate and, still dressed as a lackey with his face half-covered by the wide brim of a large hat, he made his way through the many small streets to the gate on the other side. Some way down the main road he waited anxiously for his mother's coach to appear. Two hours passed and there was no sign of it. What had happened? Had she been arrested? Instead of saving himself and pressing on on foot, Louis ran back towards the city only to see Hortense's coach coming into view. Unable to obtain fresh horses in the city, she had been forced to wait while the existing horses had a well-earned rest.

That was the end of the danger. Soon they were out of Tuscany and Louis and the Marquis Zappi changed places and clothes with the two footmen and resumed their role as 'Mrs Hamilton's' sons. Finally, on 17 April 1831, the small party reached France, a country which Hortense and Louis had not seen for sixteen years. It was hardly a triumphal homecoming. They were now once again, at least technically, at risk of arrest and execution, this time, under the 1816 French Law of Banishment for the Bonapartes. Still on an emotional high from her adventures in Italy, Hortense determined to confront the king and endeavour to obtain better terms for Napoleon's family in exile.

She calculated correctly that Louis-Philippe owed her a service, since during the First Empire she had obtained from Napoleon a pension of 400,000 francs a year for Louis-Philippe's mother, the Dowager Duchess of Orleans. To his credit, he agreed to see her but in the strictest secrecy and, with never too firm a grasp on his own personal dignity, in the most ridiculous of circumstances.

Louis was confined to his hotel bedroom with a recurrence of his measles but, on 26 April, the king received Hortense alone in a room at the Palais Royal that was so small there was hardly enough space for them to squeeze in. Hortense and Queen Amelie sat on the bed, the king and his sister, Madame Adelaide, took the only two chairs while the aide-de-camp, whose bedroom it was, leaned against the door to stop anyone coming in.

Little was accomplished: Louis-Philippe expressed his regret at the necessity for the Bonapartes' continuing exile and agreed to help Hortense with her claims for compensation for the property she had left in France. For the most part, he simply spoke in platitudes – as was often his wont.

It was clear that the two visitors could not long be permitted to remain on French soil. Despite strict attempts at secrecy, it was soon known that they were in Paris and their presence in the capital within less than a year of Louis-Philippe's accession to the throne was a destabilising factor to the new régime. On 5 May, the tenth anniversary of Napoleon's death, a demonstration in his honour took place in the Place Vendôme around the Column that Napoleon had raised to his own greater glory and, through the open windows of their hotel in the nearby rue de la Paix, Hortense and Louis could hear the loud cries of 'Vive l'Empereur!'

The next day, they were politely asked to leave France.

On 10 May 1831, after a terrible four-hour crossing in which they were both seasick, they arrived at Dover. Immediately they came up to London where they took rooms in a hotel and then rented a house at 30, George Street in the heart of the fashionable West End. They were in England for three months during which time Louis, with the help of the eminent physician, Dr Henry Holland, fully regained his health.

Their time in London was pleasant, it uneventful. Louis' cousin, Christine, daughter of Napoleon's younger brother, Lucien, had married Lord Dudley Stuart and she readily introduced them into the 'best' London society. Hortense, who had recently shown the steely side to her nature, now happily reverted to her former lifestyle as a social gadabout while Louis, also reverting to type, amused himself with several affairs.

One of these brief liaisons was with a beautiful young girl known only to history as Sarah Godfrey. As usual Louis appears briefly to have been genuinely emotionally involved. He grew his moustache long because he thought Sarah would like it but, on discovering that she did not, he at once trimmed it. She sang English songs for him and he sang Neapolitan folk-songs for her. It was all very agreeable, perhaps too much so. In the end, he had to invent a reason for not marrying her, explaining with a sob in his voice that, as a nephew of Napoleon whose greatest enemy had been England, he could not possibly marry an Englishwoman.

It was all very different from holding his dying brother in his arms and sleeping rough on a bench in an Italian street.

The idyll could not last. By the end of August they had returned to Arenenberg which, only ten months earlier, they had left to visit a healthy and robust Napoleon Louis in Florence and then travel on to their usual frivolous winter season in Rome.

But now many things had changed. His brother's death had had a profound effect upon Louis. With anxieties increasing about the exact state of the Duke of Reichstadt's health, Louis had become to many people, in his new role as his father's sole heir, the likely new Bonapartist pretender of the next generation. To mark his appreciation of this changed situation, he reversed the order of his Christian names and, for the next seventeen years, signed himself Napoleon Louis, as had his brother, instead of Louis Napoleon. It was as if he was announcing to the world that he was one stage nearer to signing himself merely 'Napoleon', with full Imperial dignity.

The Duke of Reichstadt was still alive and only twenty. No one knew his precise state of health but he was still the acknowledged head of the Bonaparte family and official pretender to the Imperial throne of France. For all his playing around with his Christian names, Louis was still formally only fourth in line of succession – after Reichstadt and Napoleon's two elderly brothers.

Yet there had undoubtedly been a sea-change in Louis' status, and in his own awareness of that new status.

To some extent, he reverted to his dilettante ways as a sophisticated version of a country playboy, but his life was no longer a single-minded pursuit of pleasure. In June 1832, he published his first book, *Rêveries politiques*, in which he set out his newly acquired political doctrines. During the lifetime of his older brother, he would hardly have given a single thought to the matter.

Now, building upon the Napoleonic legend that Napoleon himself had created posthumously in his memoirs, *Le Mémorial*, dictated in exile on St Helena and published two years after his death, Louis claimed that Europe was in the throes of a bitter struggle between tyranny and liberty, with Napoleon and his successors on the side of liberty.

The Emperor had been his own supreme propagandist, standing the true facts of history upon their head. 'Greatness has its beauties but only in retrospect and in the imagination,' he had once written to a fellow soldier, and *Le Mémorial* proves that to be correct. 'I have cleansed the Revolution, ennobled the common people and restored the authority of kings,' he fancifully claimed.

In *Rêveries politiques*, his nephew expanded on this improbable theme. Louis argued that the worst enemy of liberty was not the tyrant who suppressed it, sabre in hand, but 'weak governments who, under the mask of liberty . . . are unjust to the weak and humble before the strong', by which he clearly meant the government of Louis-Philippe. The Republic that followed the French Revolution had, before its slide into the Reign of Terror, stood for equality and liberty and Napoleon's empire for patriotism, glory and honour but – so he claimed – the restored monarchy of 1815 had only brought the re-establishment of ancient privilege and Louis-Philippe's régime had introduced fear, selfishness and cowardice.

He called for a new régime in France which would no longer be an aristocracy of birth or of wealth but solely of merit. Only in this way could the country follow in the true path of Napoleon, its greatest benefactor.

It was powerful stuff, combining adroitly – and probably sincerely – an appeal to patriotism, French obsession with 'glory' and a kind of benevolent State socialism. The people should rule, argued Louis, but only through a strong leader. That self-contradictory message was to be the basic theme of all his subsequent books, pamphlets and speeches, both before and after assuming power.

But, at this stage, with the Duke of Reichstadt still alive, it was all postulated on the basis of Reichstadt, as Napoleon's only legitimate son, being the sole heir to his father's greatness. 'The son of the great man is the only representative of the greatest glory,' wrote Louis.

Within a few weeks, that view was no longer to be tenable, even in theory.

On a bitterly cold day in January 1832, the Duke of Reichstadt had insisted on taking command of a regiment in Vienna, of which he was second colonel, at the funeral of a distinguished Austrian general. As the procession wound its way with muffled drums slowly through the chill streets, he realised that he had lost his voice. In the following months he made a partial recovery, but he could not fully shake off the illness and by April even his incompetent doctors had to realise that his lungs were seriously affected and that their patient was dying slowly of consumption.

He spent the last few weeks of his life in a suite of rooms at the Schonbrunn summer palace that was normally occupied by Archduchess Sophie, six years his senior and the wife of his uncle, Archduke Franz Karl. Although she was heavily pregnant with her second child, she insisted on being with the dying man for hours on end. They had for some time been close and her constant presence made his misery easier to bear. On 5 July 1832, she gave birth to a boy, Maximilian: court gossips speculated that he was Reichstadt's son. Some thirty years later Louis, as Napoleon III, was to send that same child, then become the Archduke Maximilian, to his death as the ill-starred Emperor of Mexico, in one of Louis' greatest disasters.

On 22 July, in the early hours of the morning, Reichstadt died. 'Between my cradle and my tomb there is a great zero,' he had said (in German) on his deathbed. In his will, he bequeathed Napoleon's favourite sword to his cousin, Louis.

Some months earlier, Metternich had written to his ambassador in Paris to bring to Louis-Philippe's attention 'the character of the man who will succeed the Duke of Reichstadt . . . The young Louis Bonaparte is a man tied up with the plots of the secret societies. He is not formed as the Duke under the safeguard of the principles of our Emperor. The day of the Duke's death, he will look upon himself as called upon to rule France.'

He was quite right. Reichstadt's death had a profound effect upon Louis. It was now that, at last, and with full voice, he heard his call to destiny. Valerie Masuyer was quick to notice the effect upon him. 'Dressed in black and wearing in his cravat a little eagle in diamonds, with a thunderbolt of rubies in its claws,' she wrote later in her memoirs, 'he appeared to me as the man of destiny although, with his serious features that light up with a singularly attractive smile, he is above all the man of mystery.'

Madame Récamier, the great beauty of the First Empire so marvellously captured by David reclining languorously on a chaise-longue, found when she came to stay at Arenenberg later that year that all the household treated Louis as Emperor (*en souverain*) and that he was always the first to walk into a room.

At only twenty-four, the call to destiny had come. The next few years would show how he answered it.

Chapter Seven

Preparing the Response (1832–6)

L OUIS' RESPONSE TO THE call of destiny was far from immediate. He liked the extra trappings that his new status gave
him and the additional deference that he was paid but he
had no appetite for any new military adventures – or any instant
attempt to topple the 'Citizen King' from his recently acquired
throne. His mind did not even think along those lines.

James. F. McMillan states the conventional view in his biography
published in 1991: 'From 1832 Louis Napoleon's life was spent in
preparation for the day when he would exercise power as Emperor
of the French.' That is simply not true. In the summer of 1832 and
for the next three years Louis was content to maintain his earlier
dilettante lifestyle, almost as if his elder brother and the Duke of
Reichstadt were still alive.

The previous year, after Napoleon Louis' death, he had happily
gone back to the Swiss military academy at Thun and resumed his
agreeable role as 'Captain Bonaparte'. A popular and respected
officer sitting trimly upon his horse and looking rather dashing in
his tight, blue uniform and plumed military hat, he had, much to
his delight, been rewarded with honorary citizenship of the canton
of Thurgen – rare achievement for a foreigner. At home, his life
was also enjoyable, having moved his bedroom and study out of
the main house at Arenenberg into an annexe which he shared with
his cousin and close friend, Charles-Henri Bac, the illegitimate son
of ex-King Jerome, Napoleon's brother. Bac's son, Ferdinand, was
later to write: 'The Swiss years are little known in France where
also is unknown the Swiss officer that was Napoleon III at that
time. He was like a fish in water.'

Henri Conneau, the young French–Italian doctor whom he had

met the previous year during the ill-starred Italian adventure, had brought his wife with him to Arenenberg where he was happily ensconced as personal physician to the household. Also resident at the château was a young painter named Felix Cottreau whose romantic good looks, straw hat and Byronesque collar brought a touch of the Latin Quarter to that remote spot on the shores of Lake Constance. His official role was to help Hortense with her artistic endeavours but, in truth, he was the ageing Queen's last lover – and, rightly or wrongly, Louis could not stand him. Pierre de Lacretelle, one of Hortense's better biographers, relates that Louis could not bear to be in the same room as Cottreau and his mother; he so distrusted him that he once hid the key to her jewel box in his pocket and gave the portfolio containing her stocks and shares into the keeping of her comptroller rather than run the risk of Cottreau getting his hands on them.

In fact, there seems no reason to doubt Cottreau's genuine feelings of friendship – if not of romantic love – for Hortense and there is no evidence whatsoever to indicate that he was ever guilty of financial trickery.

Perhaps, as a loving son, Louis could simply not stop himself being jealous of Cottreau, who was almost exactly his own age.

Apart from that, it was a pleasant time for him. As Ferdinand Bac has written, drawing on his father's recollections, 'He bloomed in the two different aspects of his life. At camp, he was always ready to burst into laughter at a good joke or entertaining piece of wit but, when he returned home, he would assume in front of his mother's visitors a serious air, attentive to her comments and keeping a good public face when, for the hundredth time, he heard her recite her verses or read aloud the chapters of her memoirs that he knew by heart.

'Even so, she would rebuke him if, coming in from riding, he threw himself into an armchair, still wearing his muddy boots. She would tell him to go and change them.'

For a while, no one at Arenenberg seems really to have appreciated the major turning point in Louis' life that the deaths of his brother and cousin had brought about. Even Hortense, despite all her long-standing pride in the honour of his family name and her vague notions of the glory that surely awaited him, seems not to have realised what had happened. Like any other old-fashioned mother with a bachelor son of twenty-four, all she now wanted was for him to get married.

In December 1832, she actually wrote to him: 'I no longer have any other wish than to keep you with me, to see you married to a good little woman, young, well brought up whom you could mould to your character and who would look after your little children.'

The one person who *did* appreciate what had happened was Napoleon's elder brother Joseph, ex-King of Spain and for the past seventeen years living in comfortable exile in the United States as the self-styled Comte de Survilliers. He had now become, by Reichstadt's death, the rightful heir to the Imperial throne of France, so he decided that it was time to settle his affairs in America and return to Europe.

He landed at Liverpool on 16 August 1832 and, after having moved in to a large mansion at 23, Park Crescent overlooking London's Regent's Park, he wrote to his three brothers, Louis, Lucien and Jerome, convening a family council for November. Ex-King Louis, lurking in his vast *palazzo* in Florence, pronounced himself, as might have been expected, too ill to travel and his son came in his stead: it is still unclear whether this was by express invitation or on his own accord.

At all events, Louis later wrote to accuse Joseph of a cold and austere welcome: 'You received me as a stranger and not as a nephew, with formality and absolutely no warmth.'

In truth, all three of his ageing uncles shared his own father's view of him: that the disastrous Italian episode had shown him as an uncontrollable youngster who could only do them all harm. Joseph who, in his forties, had been a vigorous King of Spain within the limitations imposed by Napoleon,[1] now, in his sixties, only wanted a quiet life. So did the other three. They remained proud of their family name and wished to be accorded the full respect that they considered due to surviving brothers of the Emperor. But they were more concerned with perhaps being able to persuade Louis-Philippe to abolish or amend the Law of Exile so that their civil rights could be restored and their property in France handed

---

[1] Today the official handbook to the Prado in Madrid acknowledges that this world-famous art museum owes its existence to two royal decrees of 'José I' in 1809 and 1810.

back to them than in trumpeting a theoretical claim to his throne.

As Lucien wrote to a lawyer friend, 'I consider the right of Napoleon as the right of yesterday, that of Louis-Philippe as the right of today.' The uncles wanted prudence not hotheaded gestures of defiance.

It will, therefore, come as no surprise that the family council broke up in disarray. 'For the last fifteen years,' Louis wrote angrily to Hortense, 'the only motive force behind the actions of my entire family has been the fear of compromising themselves.'

But he did not immediately return home. On this his second visit to England, he took the opportunity to see more of the country and its way of life. He cut a splendid figure in London society where the young women considered him darkly handsome and romantically alluring with his grey eyes and touchingly melancholic air. He sat in on the formal opening of Parliament where *The Times* commented on 'the live interest that he appeared to take in the proceedings'. He visited factories in Birmingham and Lancashire and coal mines in South Wales where he was appalled to see children under thirteen working underground. He travelled on one of the early trains from Manchester to Liverpool and afterwards wrote excitedly to Hortense: 'All objects flash by at an incredible pace. Houses, trees, fences and everything else disappear before you can really see them.' (The train was travelling at twenty-seven miles an hour.) It was an exciting time.

But by May 1833 he was back in the calm of Arenenberg and writing to his father: 'I have no ambition but that of returning some day to my country.' Yet he had no illusions about returning as emperor. Blanchard Jerrold has written: 'At that stage, he would have been content with a commission in the French Army.'

But there was also, of course, a philosophical, if not literary, side to his character. In the late summer of 1833, he published his second book, *Considérations politiques et militaires sur la Suisse*, as a follow-up to his *Rêveries politiques* of the previous year. It was supposedly only about politics in Switzerland but he still managed to bring in Napoleon and rhapsodise lyrically about his government that 'offered the world perhaps the first example of a régime in which all classes were welcomed, none rejected and in which institutions were set up equally favourable to all'.

In February 1834 he wrote to his old tutor, Abbé Bertrand, with whom, typically affectionate, he had kept in touch: 'In waiting for France to render justice to my name, I have made myself Swiss. I am loved in this country and they give me proof of that every day.'

But, although generally content to pursue a quiet life, Louis was still capable – at the age of twenty-six – of an impulsive moment of hot-headed stupidity. In April 1834, on hearing that an insurrection against Louis-Philippe had broken out in Lyons and that there was fighting in the streets, he immediately declared his support and departed hurriedly for Geneva, intending to slip over the border and place himself at the insurgents' head. Sadly, the very night that he arrived in Geneva, tired and dusty from the long journey, they told him that the uprising had ingloriously failed. As Adrien Dansette has shrewdly commented: 'The incident reveals the blinkered eyesight of the exiled prince. The insurrection had broken out without any reference to him and without any link whatsoever to the cause of Bonapartism but he imagined that, once there was a popular uprising in his native land, his name alone would suffice to lead it on to victory.'

He returned to calmer matters. Later that year, he published a *Manuel d'artillerie* of some 500 pages. It was a work of genuine military scholarship and was actually used by the Swiss army. It served to enhance his status in Switzerland and the canton of Berne made him an honorary captain of artillery.

Much to Hortense's despair (and despite several of her marriage-making intrigues), he still remained a bachelor, and that seemed his fixed intention. Yet somehow, in August 1834, the rumour spread that he was being considered as a husband for the young and recently widowed Queen Maria of Portugal. At once he wrote to several newspapers in various European countries to deny it. The words that he chose are interesting:

> Convinced that the great name which I bear will not always be a title of exile in the sight of my countrymen, because it recalls to them fifteen years of glory, I wait quietly in a free and and hospitable country till the people shall recall into their midst those who were banished from their native land by twelve hundred thousand foreigners. The hope of one day serving France as a citizen and a soldier fortifies my heart and counterbalances, in my estimation, all the thrones in the world.
>
> Napoleon Louis Bonaparte.

As Blanchard Jerrold, alone among Louis' biographers, has rightly pointed out, 'In this letter there is the pride of the chief of a great house but no indication of the pretender.'

In fact, Louis was simply enjoying himself: 'He had the tastes of a country gentleman, and he indulged them', Jerrold further writes. He paints a picture of the young Louis taking part in 'mild gaieties' at his mother's château and driving over in his cabriolet to spend evenings with 'pleasant, cultivated families in Constance who were glad of his company'.

In fact the truth was far more robust. As he would continue to do throughout his life almost to the very end, Louis devoted a substantial part of his time to sexual pleasures. His approach to women, whether as a young prince or as a middle-aged emperor, left much to be desired. He either made a lunge for them or else he would fall briefly – but passionately – in love with them, a sentiment which often they did not reciprocate.

To illustrate one such instance, his second visit to London in the autumn of 1832 was not only to attend ex-King Joseph's family council following the Duke of Reichstadt's death but also because Hortense thought it wise to put the English Channel between her enamoured son and a certain Mme Saunier, the young widow of a planter from Mauritius who had recently come to live in a château near Arenenberg. According to Charles-Henri Bac's account to his son, Ferdinand, Louis was so besotted that he secretly proposed marriage to the lady who had enough sense to refuse him, which only made him more ardent in his declarations of love. In fact, as Hortense correctly surmised, by the time he returned from London six months later, he had completely forgotten about the charming widow.

Louise de Crenay was another pretty neighbour who, according to the French historian André Castelot, had enough good sense at this time to refuse Louis' offer of marriage. As Prosper Mérimée, the creator of Carmen who knew Louis well in later life as emperor, once said, 'He falls in love with every pretty girl he meets, imagines that it will last forever and then at the end of a fortnight forgets she ever existed.'

Not all the young prince's amorous intentions, even with young women of good family, were so honourable. On one occasion, he followed a young daughter of Baroness de Reding, a friend of the family who had been visiting Arenenberg, on her way home. When she and her party broke their journey for the night at an inn, he made a pretext to join them for dinner. Later, when she had gone to her room, he forced his way in and fell on his knees begging her to sleep with him. She was already undressed and in bed but he pleaded with her to satisfy his great love and surrender into his arms. It was like a scene out of farce. He implored her to make him happy, said that no one would hear her cries or come to her aid as everyone in the inn was sound asleep, and so on.

The young virgin was terrified. She implored him to stop. 'My only asset in life is my honour,' she sobbed. 'Please, please, do not take it away!' Louis was, after all, not only a prince but a gentleman. He quietly left the room.

For the rest, everyone seems to have been fair game. He flirted with almost every attractive woman he met: with businessmen's daughters in Baden where he would go to visit his mother's relations, Customs officers' daughters in Constance just across the lake, flighty young country girls from villages around Arenenberg and barmaids in local inns with whom he would sing love-songs while helping with the washing-up. No pretty girl was safe from his advances: as Ferdinand Bac more delicately puts it, 'his days were peopled with gracious silhouettes, fleeting shadows of a transitory love'.

He would court women with poetry and song in the romantic style of the time but, when it came to the act of sex itself, he was a selfish lovemaker. It was all over very quickly: he smothered them with kisses, devoured their body with his hands and then within minutes had achieved his climax. He was not very concerned about theirs. He was often accused of persuading a girl to go boating alone with him on the lake and then bringing them back at dawn in what Ferdinand Bac calls 'a dishevelled state'. When irate parents complained to Hortense, she would merely smile indulgently. 'Boys will be boys' was her attitude, even if her 'boy' was in his mid-twenties. Her only concern was that he should not be forced into an unsuitable marriage because he had made a girl pregnant.

But that was not Louis' style and never would be. He would never countenance a 'shotgun wedding'; but he would also never leave completely in the lurch any illegitimate child of his who needed protection.

Some forty years later, when the Second Empire was in ruins and Napoleon III languished as an exiled prisoner-of-war in Germany, officials of the Third Republic raking through the ashes of his burnt-out Tuileries Palace found fragments of the *Papiers et correspondance de la Famille Impériale*. In 1871, they were published in two slim, black-covered volumes. One set is now in the Library of the Reform Club in London, and an entry from the Emperor's personal accounts on page 137 of the second volume tells us that in the early 1860s a Mme Knussy, 'daughter of the carpenter Laubly at Ermatingen [a small village near Arenenberg] near the house of Doctor Dobler had married a sculptor but they were not happy and wanted to emigrate to America. She claimed to be the daughter of His Majesty and wrote to the Emperor for help. He handed the letter to Hippenmayer, his confidential assistant, to deal with.' There can be little doubt that she was his illegitimate daughter.

Many different strands went into the making of the man who eventually became Napoleon III. The open warmth and generosity of spirit of his Creole maternal forebears contrasted with the natural caution, tinged with ruthlessness, of his Corsican paternal ancestors; and there was also the trauma of his youthful exile and the devastating memory of his brother dying in his arms and his own desperate escape with sentence of death hanging over his head.

In the early 1830s, he began to keep an exercise book in which he wrote down phrases and thoughts which he found appealing. One, in particular, deserves to be quoted: 'People say to me, "You do not say what you are thinking!" but is not the reply that I know how to defend myself?'

By his mid-twenties, Louis had learned to play the poker-game of life with his cards close to his chest.

In January 1835, he wrote to Narcisse Vieillard, his brother's former tutor who had become something of his own mentor:

> As to my position, please believe that I understand it well, although it is very complicated. I know that I count for a great deal by virtue of my name but nothing by virtue of my own qualities. By birth I

am an aristocrat but by temperament and opinion I am a democrat.
I owe everything to heredity. I am fêted by some because of my
name and by others because of my title. If I take a step outside my
accustomed place in life, I am charged with ambition. If I stay
quietly in my corner, I am accused of apathy and indifference . . .

I have political friends only among those who, accustomed to
the twists of fortune, think that, among the possible events of the
future, I may become a useful tool. That is why I have made it my
rule to follow no guidance but the inspirations of my own heart,
my reason and my conscience, and of not allowing myself to be
diverted by any secondary considerations when I am sure of the
path I have entered upon – in short, to pursue the straight line
ahead, whatever difficulties I may come upon; for only thus may I
succeed in raising myself to a height at which I may still be lit by
one of the dying rays of the sun of St Helena.

It is easy to put such a piece down to flowery rhetoric; and in
its original French it at first read as this, mere bluster. But I now
believe it to be a brilliant piece of self-analysis by a very clever
young man. For Louis realised that, for all his grandiose dreams,
he had, as he approached his twenty-seventh birthday, achieved
very little. Like Prince Hamlet of Denmark he had thought too
much and done too little. He could apply Shakespeare's immortal
words to his own cause:

How all occasions do inform against me,
And sour my dull revenge! What is a man,
If his chief good and market of his time
Be but to sleep and feed? A beast, no more.
Sure he that made us with such large discourse,
Looking before and after, gave us not
That capability and godlike reason
To fust in us unus'd. Now, whether it be
Bestial oblivion or some craven scruple
Of thinking too precisely on the event, –
A thought which, quartered, had but one part wisdom
And ever three parts coward – I do not know
Why yet I live to say, 'This thing's to do.'

The truth is that, as we have already seen with regard to his brother and the Italian adventure, Louis always needed someone else to sharpen his resolve and spur him to decisive action. And within six months of writing that poignant letter to Narcisse Vieillard, such a person entered his life.

Jean Gilbert Victor Fialin was the same age as Louis. Lean, intense and wiry with the face of a handsome weasel, he had sacrificed a career in the French army to join in the Revolution of July 1830. Thereafter earning his living as a journalist, he had soon become disillusioned – like so many others – with the new régime and for a brief while had flirted with Republicanism. But he had then been converted almost in a flash to the cause of Bonapartism.

It was a ridiculously trite incident. As he was being driven along a road in Germany, on a work trip, his coachman suddenly took off his hat and cried out to a young man in military uniform sitting in a passing carriage: '*Vive Napoléon!*'. It was, in fact, Louis' cousin and older son of ex-King Jerome, the teenage Prince Jerome, who was a cadet at a nearby military academy.[1] The encounter had an amazing effect on Fialin. He became engrossed with Napoleon and the Empire. He saw in his mind's eye the massed soldiers of France roaring their loyalty to a new Napoleon, and he returned to Paris with a revivalist faith in the dynasty.

He founded a magazine to the greater glory of his cause and turned it into almost a religious crusade. 'The principle of my devotion is not only dynastic, it is religious,' he wrote. 'I have never been drawn to the Bonaparte princes whom I do not know. If now I express my devotion to them, it is because of my faith. They carry within themselves, independently of their personal qualities, a principle of which they are not the masters but which will have its inevitable consequences, whether they desire them or not.' And, in a reference to the first Jesuit who three centuries earlier had written *Spiritual Exercises*, perhaps the greatest of all post-Biblical Christian works, he declared with typical lack of modesty: 'I want to be the Loyola of the Empire.'

He gave himself aristocratic airs and, resurrecting a somewhat

---

[1] He died, as an unambitious infantry colonel, in 1847, while Louis was still in exile.

dubious old family title, began calling himself Comte de Persigny, the name by which he is known to history.[2]

In April 1835, he travelled, at his own expense, to London to visit ex-King Joseph whom he tried to persuade to put forward his name as head of a new Bonapartist political party in France. But the very thought terrified the old man and courteously he declined the honour.

Back in Paris, a mutual friend suggested that Persigny approach Prince Louis and, in July 1835, he presented himself at Arenenberg. The two men took an instant liking to each other: the dreamer had met his man of action, the man of action had met the living embodiment of his dream. Over the next few years, Persigny had so great an influence over Louis and their relationship was so intense that now it would be fashionable to question if there was a homo-sexual link between them. If so, no evidence of it remains but it is not impossible to conjecture that someone so highly sexually charged as Louis with regard to women would also be capable of feeling sexual attraction for a man. Indeed, the prominent English writer, Philip Guedalla, in his 1922 classic *The Second Empire* cites one woman friend of Louis at this stage (an opera singer, Eleonore Gordon) as saying that she was devoted to him 'but to tell the truth, he gives me the effect of a woman'.

What of Persigny, who later contracted a somewhat unhappy marriage? Four years after meeting Louis, he wrote in his *Lettres de Londres*, a propagandist broadsheet, published when the two were sharing a house in London with other members of Louis' entourage: 'The Prince has an agreeable physiognomy, is of middle height and has a military air. To personal distinction he adds those simple, natural, easy and delicate manners which seem to belong to the superior classes ... The distinctive character of the features of young Napoleon are nobility and severity, and yet, far from being hard, his physiognomy breathes a sentiment of kindness and gentleness ...

'But that which excites interest before all is that indefinable shade of thought and melancholy which covers all his individuality, and reveals the noble sorrows of exile.

'Now, with this portrait you must not figure to yourself a hand-

---

[2] Under the Second Empire, Louis upgraded him to *Duc* de Persigny.

some young man – such an Adonis of romance as would excite the admiration of boudoirs. There is nothing effeminate in the young Napoleon. The sombre shades of his physiognomy indicate an energetic nature; his composed demeanour, his look at once sharp and thoughtful, all indicate in him one of these exceptional natures – one of those strong natures that feed on the contemplation of great things, and that are alone capable of accomplishing them.'

Even allowing for the highly stylised language of the time, this might be construed as being slightly over the top. Does it not perhaps reveal something of Persigny's true feelings for Louis? Whatever the basis, in Freudian terms, of the nature of their relationship, within just over a year of meeting Persigny, Louis made his first military attempt to seize power in France. The days of dalliance and dreaming were at last over.

Chapter Eight

Strasbourg (1836)

O N THE EVENING OF 31 October 1836 a telegram – or rather the beginning of one – arrived at the Ministry of War in Paris. It was from General Voirol, the Military Governor of Strasbourg. In those days, Strasbourg was an important garrison town of some 10,000 soldiers on the Franco-German border on the Rhine guarding access to a major highway leading straight to the French capital. The telegram had been sent the previous day. Its contents were dramatic: 'This morning at about six o'clock Louis Napoleon, son of the Duchesse de St-Leu, who had in his confidence the Colonel of Artillery Vaudrey, traversed the streets of Strasbourg with a party of . . .'

And here it broke off. For this was an early, pre-electric telegram, using a system only recently invented and dependent on clear visibility so that operators stationed at high points across the country could, with telescopes and in fine weather, read messages sent by semaphore (movable arms attached to a wooden pole rather like a modern railway signal post) from as far as ten miles away. On this occasion, however, fog had blanketed from view the rest of the message.

Louis Napoleon? In Strasbourg – and clearly with troops? What could this mean? The French Government's spies in the countryside around Arenenberg had reported nothing untoward: what had happened?

At once, a deeply troubled Minister of War informed the king and the other ministers, and a cabinet meeting was hastily held at the Tuileries Palace. Neither Louis-Philippe nor his Cabinet members slept very much that night. They were too worried. They knew how unpopular they were with the workers and with the army.

For the July Revolution had run out of steam. Brought to power by the Paris mob, the 'Citizen King' had quickly shown that he had no interest in working-class causes or in bettering the lot of the poor. His was a bourgeois government run for the benefit of the bourgeoisie to whom he had given greatly increased opportunity to make money: '*Enrichissez-vous!*' (Enrich yourselves!) was the blatantly materialistic cry of François Guizot, perhaps his most able Prime Minister.

So the workers were unhappy – and susceptible either to re-emergent republicanism or to Louis' brand of benevolent, semi-socialistic Bonapartism.

The army was also unhappy because there had been no foreign wars to earn them glory and because their sovereign looked – and behaved – more like a grocer than a general. They, too, were perhaps susceptible to a revolution led by the Emperor's own nephew, resplendent in uniform and with sword in hand.

Neither Louis-Philippe nor his ministers were fools. They appreciated the appeal of the Napoleonic legend – which was not the same as the reality – to the vast majority of the people of France. In an attempt to win over, if not subvert, the legend's increasingly popular appeal, Louis-Philippe was trying to clothe himself in the mantle of the Emperor. He had ordered Napoleon's statue to be returned to its original place on the central column in the Place Vendôme. He ordered the names of Napoleon's victories to be carved on the walls of the Arc de Triomphe that had stood half-finished since the Emperor's defeat, and which only now did he order to be completed, with himself presiding at the inauguration in July 1836 of the magnificent structure that we see today. He was even negotiating with the British for the return of the Emperor's body from St Helena to a last resting place in Paris.

Thus, on that night of 31 October, neither the king, his ministers, nor indeed the entire royal family,[1] took lightly the news that what sounded suspiciously like a military insurrection led by Prince Napoleon Louis Bonaparte had erupted on to the streets of Strasbourg. Anxiously, they waited for the fog to lift and for the rest of the Military Governor's message to come through.

[1] The Duc d'Orleans, one of the King's sons, wrote to his brother, the Duc de Nemours who was out of town: 'I am happy to think that, far from us, you have not had to submit to the appalling uncertainties which we have endured. All last night was passed waiting without news. If Colonel de Franqueville had not arrived, I would have set out myself for Strasbourg.'

But before that could happen, at six o'clock next morning, the carriage of Colonel de Franqueville, General Voirol's aide-de-camp, clattered into the courtyard of the Tuileries at the end of its long journey from Strasbourg.

Horse-drawn transportation had triumphed over the newfangled science of aerial telegraphy. To their immense relief, the king and his Cabinet learned that Louis' attempt to hoist the flag of rebellion had ended swiftly – and in great humiliation.

The failure had not been for want of planning or lack of boldness. The basic idea hammered out by Louis and Persigny at Arenenberg was modelled on Napoleon's return from Elba. The bloodless return of the Emperor in 1815 was to be repeated by his nephew in 1836. He was to appear suddenly in a frontier town, show himself to the troops with a grand Napoleonic gesture and, as they cried '*Vive l'Empereur!*', march triumphantly at their head on Paris.

Poring over Louis' maps in his annexe at Arenenberg, they chose Strasbourg as the starting-point of this splendid adventure. This was for two reasons: *One*, strategically placed on France's eastern frontier, it was easily accessible from Switzerland and from Louis' home-from-home at Baden in Germany where he frequently visited his mother's cousin, the Grand Duchess Stephanie, and her daughters. *Two*, the 4th Artillery, one of the regiments stationed in Strasbourg, was Napoleon's old regiment and it had spontaneously joined him at Grenoble on his return from Elba and marched with him on Paris.

The two conspirators divided their labour. Because communications were poor, Persigny visited Strasbourg and the surrounding area many times. He talked with soldiers and officers, sounding out those who might or might not answer their call, and reported back to Louis the result of his researches. Louis then picked up the trail and, on his visits to Baden (with its casino and other worldly attractions, it was a popular resort for French officers on leave from garrison duty in Strasbourg), made it his business to strike up a conversation here, offer a glass of wine there, and generally make a number of extremely useful acquaintances. In this way, he enlisted in his enterprise a dozen young men, of whom Lieutenant Armand Laity of the Engineers was the most devoted.

Then, in late August, despite the 1816 Law banishing him (under threat of sentence of death), from France as a Bonaparte, he rode alone – but not in uniform – across the Kehl Bridge into Strasbourg. He had come to address a roomful of officers assembled by Persigny to meet him. It was a small room and his audience was no more than twenty but their response was enthusiastic. 'The nephew of the Emperor is welcome among us,' one officer told him. 'He is under the protection of French honour: what does he have to fear? We will defend him at the risk of our lives.'

Yet these recruits were all in their twenties or thirties. Louis still needed a more senior officer and here, again, Persigny played a decisive role. One evening in Baden he introduced Louis to Colonel Vaudrey of the 4th Artillery Regiment and, at the level of courtesy, the meeting went well. This veteran of Waterloo was in his fifties and an able soldier but, according to garrison rumour, disillusioned with the Government at not having been promoted to general. He also venerated the memory of the Emperor.

At subsequent meetings, however, he held back from committing himself to Louis' cause: he had too much to lose. Yet he had one important weakness: although married, he was known to be an inveterate philanderer. Accordingly, Persigny invited him to dinner one night at Baden when he knew that Louis would be accompanied by his current mistress, the beautiful twenty-eight-year-old Eleonore Gordon, who had quickly overcome her initial impression that Louis 'gave her the effect of a woman'. As intended, Vaudrey was at once attracted and Eleonore agreed to see him again on her own. In truth, she was besotted with Louis and had offered to serve his cause in any way she could.[1]

The result? After several meetings she told Vaudrey that she would sleep with him only if he agreed to help her lover. It was an offer that the gallant colonel could not and did not refuse.

All was now set. It was only a question of working out the final details and setting the actual date. As Louis later wrote to his mother, 'I was so confident that the Napoleonic cause was the only creed that could civilise Europe, and so satisfied as to the nobility and purity of my aims, that I had fully made up my mind to raise

[1] Louis never forgot a service or a friend. The *Papiers et correspondance de la Famille Impérial* show that when later Eleonore, ageing and in failing health, fell upon hard times, the Emperor gave her a pension and, when she died, he paid for a statue on her grave.

the standard of the Imperial eagle and, if necessary, to perish for my political faith.'

One other matter needs to be drawn into the narrative at this point: in April 1836, Louis had become unofficially engaged to be married.

The bride-to-be was his cousin, Princess Mathilde, daughter of ex-King Jerome. From the start, it was a half-hearted affair on both sides. Mathilde was only fifteen and, in her memoirs, she looked back on the episode as merely 'our little flirtation'. As for Louis, although Mathilde was quite pretty with brown eyes and a rose-petal complexion, she did not exactly sweep him off his feet. 'She is charming,' he wrote to his mother, 'but do not think that I am in love with her. Not at all. I have quite a different feeling for her.' To him, she was still just a young cousin and, although he liked her as a person (and later was to accord her a high place of honour in the hierarchy of the Second Empire), he found it difficult to think of her as a potential wife.

Yet Hortense was delighted at the idea and the project, shrewdly suggested by the Emperor's youngest brother, ex-King Jerome, did have some important dynastic arguments in its favour. Louis' elder brother had been married to the daughter of a brother of the Emperor, ex-King Joseph, so there was a certain symmetry in Louis now contemplating marriage to the daughter of another brother, especially when he was planning a bold military adventure to win back Napoleon's throne. But the elder Bonapartes did not see the proposed union in that light. Louis' father expressed his strong disapproval of the match, almost as a matter of principle.[1] Ex-King Jerome was himself not too happy about it: the Comte de Montfort, as he now called himself, lived well beyond his means and would have preferred a more wealthy son-in-law.

All in all, there was no hurry to fix the wedding date.

Valerie Masuyer saw through the charade: '[Mathilde] and the Prince are inseparable,' she wrote in her dairy. 'He sits at her feet

---

[1] Louis was by now used to his father's chronic negativism but it still hurt. The previous year, after ex-King Louis had complained at his publication of the *Manuel d'artillerie* and at his large subscriptions to local charities, he had written: 'I receive harsh words from you so often that I ought to be used to them. Yet each reproach you address to me wounds me as keenly as if it were the first.'

and goes through all the antics of a man in love. He whispers to her a thousand pretty things which she cannot understand because she has not enough heart. I think bitterly that the Princess will never understand him. She is coquettish, frivolous and Heaven knows! he has all the opposite qualities. How much more he deserves!'

One suspects that Mlle Masuyer, by now thirty-nine and contemplating a life without husband or even lover, would have been delighted to have Louis 'whisper a thousand pretty things' in *her* ear.

Shortly before daybreak on 25 October 1836, Louis climbed the stairs to his mother's room where she, awake, was waiting for him. He had told her the previous day that he was going on a hunting expedition in Germany, but she must have guessed that something more substantial was afoot, for now she pushed on to his finger the marriage ring that Napoleon had given Josephine. It was her most precious possession and, for her, a symbol of good luck. He embraced her tenderly and departed. When next he saw her, ten months later, in that very same room, she was dying.

Three days later, Louis and Persigny slipped into Strasbourg just as the city gates were being closed for the night. They hurried to a small house near the centre of the town which Persigny had rented under a false name. Colonel Vaudrey, Eleonore Gordon, the young Lieutenant of Engineers, Armand Laity, and another Napoleonic veteran, Colonel Parquin, the husband of Hortense's old schoolfriend, Louise Cochelet, who had thrown in his cause with Louis, were waiting for them. They spent that evening and most of the next day going over yet again the details of the coup, and decided to bring it forward by twenty-four hours to prevent any possibility of betrayal.

Louis did not have his uncle's famous ability to sleep at will, no matter what the circumstances. He sat up the whole of the night of 29–30 October, partly because he was too nervous to sleep but also because he was drafting three sets of proclamations: to the people of France, the garrison at Strasbourg and the local civilian population. These were to be hurriedly printed early the next morning and plastered on the walls of the town.

To the French people, he proclaimed:

Confident in the sacredness of my cause, I present myself to you, the last will and testament of the Emperor Napoleon in one hand, the sword of Austerlitz in the other. In Rome, when the people saw Caesar's bloodstained corpse, they overthrew their hypocritical oppressors. Frenchmen, Napoleon is greater than Caesar; he is the emblem of the civilisation of the Nineteenth Century . . .

Men of 1789, men of March 20, 1815, men of 1830, arise! See who governs you, and behold the eagle, sublime emblem, the symbol of liberty, and choose! Long live France! Long live Liberty!

(Signed) NAPOLEON

To the army, he was appropriately martial:

Soldiers, – The time has come to recover your ancient renown. Made for glory, you can less than others endure longer the shameful part you are made to play. The Government which betrays our civil interests would tarnish your military honour. The simpletons! Do they think that the race of the heirs of Arcole, of Austerlitz, of Wagram is extinct?

And there was much more in similar vein, ending:

Soldiers of the Republic, soldiers of the Empire, let my name re-awaken the old ardour in you . . . From heaven above the great shade of Napoleon will guide our arms and, satisfied with our efforts, will say, 'They were worthy of their fathers.' Long live France! Long live Liberty!

His third proclamation, to the people of Strasbourg, was in the same over-heated style, even by the overblown standards of the ape.

But governments are not overthrown by words alone, however brilliant or impassioned, and sadly for Louis from the very outset his cause was doomed. 'I intend to arrive in Paris without a shot being fired,' Napoleon had declared on stepping ashore from Elba at Golfe Juan on 1 March 1815 and, indeed, he arrived in Paris nineteen days later without a shot having been fired. But he was, after all, the great Emperor returning from a brief exile: how could Louis have been so unrealistic, and so stupid, as to have put himself in that category?

No one could doubt his bravery. He genuinely thought that his life was at risk in this endeavour, as did Vaudrey, Persigny and the other main conspirators; and it is true that they could either have been killed by Louis-Philippe's troops during the attempted coup itself or, if it failed, executed afterwards for treason. Their courage is not an issue, only young Louis' lack of realism.

At 6.00 am on 30 October, as snow was falling, four uniformed men left the small house on the rue de la Fontaine. They were Louis himself, dressed in the blue uniform of an artillery colonel (Napoleon's favourite uniform) with the gold badge of the Legion of Honour gleaming on his breast; Colonel Parquin, dressed as a general; Persigny, bearing an Imperial eagle; and Laity, holding Louis' draft proclamations. Persigny and Laity were both in captain's uniform: like Parquin, they had been 'promoted' (without any legal authority) by Louis.

The four silent figures walked through the darkness to the nearby Austerlitz Barracks where the 4th Regiment was quartered, and Vaudrey had the entire regiment of 1,000 men out on parade waiting to greet them, complete with military band.

As Louis and his companions appeared, Vaudrey bellowed: 'Men of the 4th Artillery Regiment, today a great revolution is in the making! You see before you the nephew of the Emperor Napoleon. He comes to concern himself with the rights of the people ... Can he count on you?' '*Vive l'Empereur!*' was the reply roared by all the assembled men.

Headed by the regimental band, and with Persigny holding aloft the Imperial eagle, Louis set off at the head of the 4th to march to the city centre. By now, the town was slowly waking up and civilians coming on to the streets cheered as they passed: some crying '*Vive l'Empereur!*' and others '*Vive La Liberté!*'

Watching the soldiers march past and hearing the widespread shouts of support, Charles Thélin, Louis' faithful valet, thought that victory had already been achieved. His master had given him two alternative letters to post to Hortense, one saying that the coup had been successful and the other that it had failed. Now Thélin hastened to post what proved to be the *wrong* letter, the one claiming success. By the time that it arrived and Hortense read it, Louis was already in prison. (Typically, on learning the real news, she immediately set out for Paris to plead with Louis-Philippe for her son's life, a journey that turned out to be unnecessary.)

But Louis also showed himself remarkably naïve. He broke off the march to stop by the house of the Military Governor. General Voirol was, at that hour of the morning, not even dressed. Louis asked him to put on his uniform and accompany them: 'The garrison has declared for me. Make up your mind, and follow me.' Persigny showed him the Imperial eagle but the general, still in his underwear, pushed it aside. 'They have deceived you, Prince,' he said. 'The Army will do its duty.' Louis ordered him to be placed under arrest but, as he later admitted in a letter to Hortense, 'I was deeply affected by this failure, which I had not expected. I had been certain that the mere sight of the eagle would have revived the general's old memories of military fame, and would have brought him to my side.'

But an even worse miscalculation was to follow. Three regiments were housed in the town: the 4th and 3rd Artillery and the 46th Infantry. If Louis had been an out and out man of action and not such an idealistic dreamer, he would then have gone at once to the barracks of the 3rd Artillery Regiment. With the 4th already on his side, these fellow gunners – with their 150 cannons – would almost certainly have joined his cause as well, and he would have had the 46th Infantry and the entire population at his mercy. *But that was exactly what he did not want.* The words of Napoleon at Golfe Juan were ringing in his ears: 'I intend to arrive in Paris without a shot being fired.' He was determined not to rely on brute military force but on what Dr F. A. Simpson has called 'a spontaneous outburst of democratic enthusiasm in which soldier and citizen, infantry and artillery, should join.'

Louis and the 4th Artillery Regiment marched straight to the Finckmatt Barracks where the 46th Infantry were stationed, and here he made his final, grave error.

Instead of leading his men into the barracks and impressing the infantrymen with how well everything was going, he entered the barracks alone with only a few men, announced himself as the nephew of the Emperor and ordered the captain of the guard to parade the regiment. The captain refused. There was an embarrassed shuffling and mumbling. Who was this stranger in an artillery colonel's uniform? Someone shouted that he was an impostor, someone else declared that he was Colonel Vaudrey's nephew, not the Emperor's.

What happened next is best left to Louis himself to narrate, as he did in a long letter written to his mother from prison:

'I suggested to Colonel Vaudrey that we should leave. He advised me to stay, and I took his advice. A few minutes afterwards it was too late. Some infantry officers arrived, shut the gates and strongly reprimanded their men. They hesitated. I tried to arrest these officers but their men released them. This led to general confusion and the space was so restricted that we were all lost in the crowd. Civilians standing on the city wall threw stones at the troops. The gunners wanted to use their guns but we prevented them for we saw at once that we should have caused a number of casualties.

'I saw the Colonel at one moment arrested by the infantry and at another moment rescued by our men. I myself was nearly killed in the middle of a mass of men who, when they recognised me, struck at me with their bayonets. I was parrying their blows with my sword and trying to quieten them down when some gunners came up, rescued me from their muskets and surrounded me.

'Then I dashed with several non-commissioned officers towards the mounted gunners in order to secure a horse but all the infantry followed and I found myself hemmed in between the horses and the wall, unable to move. At that moment, soldiers came up from every direction and seized me, taking me to the guardroom. As I went in, I found M. Parquin there. I grasped his hand. He greeted me with a calm and resigned air, saying: "We shall be shot, Prince, but we will make a good end." – "Yes," I replied. "We have failed but it was a fine and noble attempt."'

In fact it was just the opposite. It was barely 8.00 am and the whole disastrous affair was over in two hours. The press, both in France and throughout Europe, were unanimous in condemning Louis' foolhardiness. In London, *The Times* thought the episode 'contemptible' and 'ridiculous', and the *Frankfurter Journal* quoted Metternich: 'Bonapartism without Bonaparte is an absurdity' and called Louis 'a young fool without genius, talent or fame'.

But not for the first or last time in his life, Louis shut his eyes to reality and saw the world, and himself, only as he wanted to see them. He further wrote to his mother: 'What care I for the cries of the common crowd who will call me mad because I have failed, and who would have exaggerated my merits if I had succeeded?' To ex-King Joseph, he wrote: 'If the Emperor looks down from

Heaven, he will be satisfied with me,' but Joseph did not even answer the letter and told a friend: 'Louis has ignored his father and uncles as though they were already in their graves.' As for ex-King Jerome, he insisted on Mathilde breaking off her engagement and having no further contact whatsoever with her cousin.

Yet Louis could still write to his mother: 'It is a source of moral strength to be able to say, "Tomorrow I shall be the deliverer of my country or else I shall be in my grave."'

Louis-Philippe and his Government reacted with sensible restraint to the episode. They refused to make Louis a martyr and did not put him on trial for any offence. After a short spell in prison in Strasbourg, tended by the loyal valet Thélin, they ignored his urgent request to be put up against a wall and shot, and deported him instead to the United States aboard a French warship, the *Andromède*.

Persigny had managed to escape but Colonel Vaudrey, Parquin, Laity and Eleonore Gordon were put on trial at the Strasbourg assize court as traitors. Louis hated this privileged treatment. 'Against my will, I do not share the fate of those whose existence I have compromised,' he wrote on board ship to Narcisse Vieillard before sailing for America. 'And so all the world will take me for a fool, a self-seeker, a coward. Before ever I set foot in France I expected that, in case of failure, the two first qualities would be applied to me but the third is too cruel!'

Yet he remained charming and generous. 'As Colonel Vaudrey is not rich,' he wrote to Hortense, 'please send his lawyer after the trial the amount of his fees, and take it from what is left at my bank.'

Fortunately for the defendants, in January 1837 the local assize court jury at Strasbourg acquitted them of all charges.

By then, Louis was on the high seas bound for the New World. 'I shall need little in America. I will become a farmer,' he had written to Hortense. But that was just temporary bravado. In truth, he was deeply sad and uncertain as to what exactly he was going to do with the rest of his life.

Yet his faith in his cause was undimmed. To silence him during his fellow conspirators' trial, the *Andromède* took more than four months to sail to the United States, taking a circuitous route of some 10,000 miles via the South Atlantic. It meant that Louis might be able to see St Helena, if only in the distance; but as he later wrote to Colonel Vaudrey, 'Alas! I could never catch sight of the historic rock. Yet it always seemed to me that on the breeze floated the last words of the Emperor to the companions of his exile – "I have sanctioned all the principles of the Revolution; I have infused them into my laws, into my acts".'

Landed at Norfolk, Virginia, on 30 March 1837, within a week he was staying at the Washington Hotel in New York. It was by then already a city of some 300,000 people, and Louis at once proceeded to have an extremely enjoyable time, subsidised by his mother and by a substantial cash sum that Louis-Philippe had secretly – charitably – given him before he left France.

Even then, the Americans loved visiting royalty. Louis was fêted and dined as an alluring, romantic character. As General James Grant Wilson later wrote to Blanchard Jerrold, 'He received a great deal of attention from many of the best New York families.' Being Louis, he also saw a great deal of New York's female population – and not always 'from the best families'. When doing research for his massive four-volumed official biography after Louis' death nearly forty years later, Jerrold wrote to several of New York's more respectable citizens in an attempt to refute the wild stories about Louis' behaviour that were to appear in the American press after he had become emperor. One of these worthy souls was a Rev. C. S. Stewart, who wrote: 'Louis Napoleon may have had some associations in New York of which I was ignorant and he, like Dickens and other distinguished foreigners, may have carried his observations, under the protection of the police, to scenes in which I would not have accompanied him.'

One thing that no one could deny was Louis' intelligence. From New York, he wrote to Narcisse Vieillard an assessment of the young United States as he found it, some sixty years after the Declaration of Independence and less than twenty years before the Civil War:

The United States were originally British colonies. They were detached from their mother-country at an early age. But a minor who declares himself independent at twelve years of age, whatever may be his physical strength, is still only an infant. One only becomes an adult when one attains the full development of one's physical and moral forces. This country has an immense material strength but it lacks totally any moral strength. The United States created itself a nation from the moment that it had an administration elected by itself, a president and two legislative chambers but it has still only reached the stage of being an independent colony. Even so, each day you can see the transition: the caterpillar is shedding its cocoon and freeing its wings to fly ever higher as a magnificent butterfly; but I do not think that this transition will take place without crises and upheavals.

A good assessment from a man who was only in the country for less than eleven weeks.

For the last few years, Hortense, then in her early fifties, had not been in good health and in the aftermath to the Strasbourg adventure her condition had deteriorated. The sudden shock of learning that her son was a prisoner facing a possible death sentence, her hurried and secret journey to Paris where she had not even been allowed to see him, then her sad return to Arenenberg which had been made infinitely worse by the inhumanity of the French Government in not having warned her of Louis' circuitous route to America so that she had been given no explanation of receiving no news from him for so long (none of his letters written on board the *Andromède* was posted until after arrival in Virginia) – all had combined to hasten the progress of her illness. Dr Conneau, in consultation with two Swiss colleagues, now diagnosed cancer and a surgeon from Paris was asked to operate.

On 3 April, she wrote Louis a remarkable letter. It was found after his death thirty-seven years much folded and in his wallet, still bearing the stain of his tears:

My dear son, I have to undergo an operation that is absolutely necessary. If it does not succeed, I send you by this letter my last blessing. We shall meet each other again, shall we not? in a better world where you will come to join me only as late as possible. And you will remember that in leaving this world I regret only you – only your gentle affection which alone has given my life some charm.

It will be a consolation to you, my dear friend, to think that by your care you have made your mother as happy as she could possibly be. You will think of all my love for you and that will give you courage. Believe that we always keep a kindly and clear-sighted eye on those we leave here below and that certainly we will meet again. Hold to that sweet hope, it is too necessary not to be true.

I give you my blessing and press you to my heart, my dear son. I am quite calm and resigned, and I still hope that we may see each other again in this world. Let the will of God be done. Your loving mother, Hortense.

When that letter arrived in New York on 3 June, after the mail-boat had been delayed by bad weather at sea, Louis saw at once on the back of the envelope in Conneau's handwriting: '*Venez! Venez!*' He acted at once. He booked a passage on the next mail-boat bound for England, the *George Washington*, and sailed on 12 June, but not before, as one head of state to another, he had written to President Van Buren, apologising for having to leave the United States without first calling on him at the White House.

As the wind gathered in the sails of the *George Washington* and sent her lurching forward across the waters of the Atlantic, Louis' thoughts concentrated on only one person: the woman who had given him birth. She was still comparatively young and he had thought that for a long time yet she would still be there for him, his best friend[1] and his most unselfish adviser.

Now she was dying and he yearned only to be by her side.

[1] Note that in her letter of 3 April 1837 Hortense had, in the first line of the second paragraph, addressed her son as 'my dear friend'. Blanchard Jerrold, in his Victorian stuffiness, translated that as 'my dear son' and, so far as I can tell, all British biographers have followed suit, but the words in the original French are '*mon cher ami*'. The relationship between Hortense and Louis was, in essence, a very modern one, well ahead of its time. They were friends as well as mother and son.

Chapter Nine

Farewell to Arenenberg (1837–8)

As THE *GEORGE WASHINGTON* lay off the English coast on 9 July 1837 waiting to berth at Liverpool, Louis wrote to his mother: 'On my arrival in London, I intend to ask the Prussian Minister for a passport to Switzerland . . . I dare not think of my happiness at seeing you again so soon. The thought of climbing the hill of Arenenberg makes my heart throb already.'

But it was not going to be so easy. In those days, passports were not given by the country of one's nationality to its citizens for a renewable period of time. They were assigned by governments to people wishing to visit or travel through their territories, irrespective of nationality. They were more akin to visas than modern passports.

Reunited in London with Persigny whom he had not seen since Strasbourg when Persigny had fled into exile, Louis applied at once to the French Ambassador, General Comte Sebastiani, for a French passport, explaining the urgent nature of his request. But Sebastiani kept him waiting for an answer: 'It seems to me improper for any Government to show an interest in this person by meddling with his affairs,' he reported tersely to Louis-Philippe's Government in Paris, and they were in no hurry to give a decision.

While waiting for their response, Louis also tried the Prussian Minister and the Austrian Ambassador but again, although he told them that his mother was dying, neither hastened to reply.

He was in despair. 'I am waiting impatiently for passports,' he wrote to his father, ex-King Louis. 'If they refuse me, I shall not know what to do. The object of my journey is so legitimate that it seems to me impossible that they can put an obstacle in the way of it . . . If you knew, dear father, how sad I am in the midst of this London tumult, with near relatives shunning me[1] and enemies fearing me!

'My mother is dying, and I cannot bring her a son's consolation ... What have I done to be the pariah of Europe and of my family? I have raised the flag of Austerlitz for one moment in a French town and I have offered myself as a sacrifice to the memory of the prisoner of St Helena. Blame my actions if you will but never deny me your affection. It is, alas, all that is left to me.'

Those words may seem exaggerated but there is no doubt about the intensity of their feeling.

Finally, after more than two weeks, all three passport applications were refused. Louis – now under secret surveillance by the Metropolitan Police at the French Ambassador's request – was desperate. 'I write in haste to tell you that our friend, being unable to obtain the papers he needs, has decided to leave without them,' Persigny wrote to Valerie Masuyer, still loyally in service as Hortense's lady-in-waiting.

To this day no one knows how exactly he did it but Louis, almost at the last moment, managed to obtain a passport from the Swiss Minister in London in the name of an American called Robinson. He was free to travel to Switzerland, so long as he avoided France, Prussia or Austria.

On the morning of 31 July, 'Mr Robinson' sailed for the Dutch city of Rotterdam from Gravesend, then a minor cross-Channel port on the Thames just east of London. That same day Ambassador Sebastiani reported to Paris: 'Sir F. Roe, chief of the London police, has just announced that he has lost all trace of Louis Bonaparte ... The English police can give no information as to the port at which he meant to embark.'

Safely arrived two days later at Rotterdam, 'Mr Robinson' travelled up the Rhine by boat to Mannheim where he took the road for Arenenberg.

Late on the evening of 4 August a noise outside the château made Valerie Masuyer look through the slats of the closed shutters of her window and she saw the lights of a carriage appear up the

---

[1] Ex-King Joseph had still not forgiven Louis for the fiasco at Strasbourg and, although now living in England, had refused to see his nephew and written him a sharply unfriendly letter.

drive. Louis had come home across half the world to be by his mother's side.

Despite Louis' entreaties, they would not let him see Hortense that night. She was sleeping and Dr Conneau insisted that she not be disturbed. But the following morning Louis – 'white as a sheet,' as Valerie wrote in her journal – climbed the stairs to Hortense's first-floor bedroom and gently pushed open her door.

He was shocked by the sight of the emaciated, hollow-cheeked woman propped up in her bed that greeted him, but tears of joy were in her eyes as she called his name. All he could do was cry: '*Mama, Mama!*' and throw himself into her arms.

Conneau and Valerie had been terrified that the trauma of seeing Louis again might prove too much for Hortense; that it might be, as Valerie wrote, 'the coup de grâce for the dying woman'. It had the opposite effect. It seemed as if she were reborn. A little colour returned to her cheeks, her eyes regained some of their lustre.

For the next few weeks, at her express request, she was carried out into the gardens of the château and lay there, content in the summer sun, with her son beside her.

It could not last. She had not had the operation which had prompted her letter of 3 April because the doctors had changed their minds and thought it would have been too risky. Desperate, Louis sought a second, and a third, opinion but the medical verdict was unanimous: Hortense did not have long to live.

Slowly again she began to fade and Louis spent many daylight hours sitting beside her bed reading to her or silently holding her hand.[1] Only one other person in the château had anything like the same privileged access, and that was Felix Cottreau, the young painter who was almost certainly Hortense's last lover. Hortense was departing this life as she had lived it, according to her own rules.

Her last few days were painful, as the cancer worked its inexorable way through her body. In scenes of great sadness, one by one the members of her household were called to her bedside to make

[1] But Louis was still, after all, Louis. Despite his genuine grief and concern for his dying mother, he had resumed his earlier relationship with his pretty neighbour, Louise de Crenay. At least, it gave him something to do in the evenings.

their farewells. Dr Conneau in particular, was never to forget the event: lying there on her death-bed, she asked him to swear never to leave Louis but always to care for him as his doctor and his friend. Hardly able to restrain his tears, he gave his word.

Finally, as the first rays of the sun began to lighten the early morning darkness on 5 October, 1837, Louis, a grim-faced Dr Conneau, Felix Cottreau, Valerie and the other ladies silently gathered in Hortense's room for the inevitable end. 'Give me your blessing, Mother,' begged Louis kneeling in tears beside her. '*Mama*, I am here. Can you hear me?' The thin figure in the bed struggled to speak: 'I hear you!' she whispered.

She held out her arms towards him and, at that moment, died. Hopelessly weeping, Louis caught her in his arms.

Later that day, he wrote to his father: 'I have just suffered an irreparable loss. Today, at five o'clock in the morning, my mother died in my arms. She had received all the consolations of the Church and of a son's love. I have not the strength to write to you more about it.' She was only fifty-four.

Biographers still disagree as to the extent of Hortense's wealth or how much of it Louis inherited upon her death, but to my mind the issue was settled in 1961 when Adrien Dansette published his major work, *Louis Napoléon à la conquête du pouvoir*. Based upon his study of Hortense's will and other documents preserved in the Bonaparte archives, his calculations make it clear that Hortense left her son an extremely rich man. After a long list of legacies to friends and servants, she left the rest of her fortune to Louis. Dansette says that it amounted to three million francs in capital, producing an income of 120,000 francs a year. That is the equivalent today of £7 million capital and £278,000 annual income.[1]

Louis was now, in modern terms, a multi-millionaire.

'I have no political advice to give my son,' wrote Hortense in her will. 'I know that he understands his position and all the duties which his name imposes upon him.' For her estranged husband,

---

[1] I owe these estimates of the modern value of Louis' inherited wealth to M. Roland Lemarchand of the French Embassy in London and to Mr Spencer Sturgeon of the St James's private office of the National Westminster Bank.

ex-King Louis, she had only the bitter-sweet words: 'Let my husband give a thought to my memory and let him know that my greatest regret has been that I was not able to make him happy.'

She made no mention of the greatest love of her life, Count Charles de Flahaut, nor of the product of that love, her twenty-six-year-old illegitimate son, Charles Auguste Demorny, registered at birth as the son of a French planter from the Caribbean island of Dominica and his Parisian wife.

Auguste, as the young man was always called, was first brought up by his official parents (although he seems to have been told very early on that he was not really their son) but then went to live with his paternal grandmother, Countess Adelaide de Flahaut. It was she who gave him the more aristocratic version of his surname with Demorny changed to de Morny, by which he is known to history. Unknown to him, his education was paid for by Hortense.

He was told only at the age of nineteen that he was the son of Count Charles de Flahaut in 1830, when the former Napoleonic general returned to France from exile in England following Waterloo and after the July Revolution had sent Charles X, the last of the Bourbon kings, scurrying from the throne.

Another five years then passed before Charles took him aside and told him the true identity of his mother. Astute, ruthless and charming, Auguste was then an officer in the 1st Lancers and immediately appreciated the enhancement in his status of being the former Queen of Holland's son, albeit outside of marriage. He began sporting a hortensia (a variety of hydrangea) in his buttonhole and at once wrote a fawning letter to Hortense. They exchanged a few half-embarrassed letters but they never met. It was a part of her life that Hortense preferred to forget and of which she never told Louis.

But on the day after she died, he learned the truth in the most unexpected and hurtful fashion.

Baroness Salvage de Faverolles was a capable but insensitive busybody of a woman, wealthy in her own right, who had made herself useful to Hortense in the queen's last years as a sort of honorary business manager. Hortense had named her as executor of her will and, on the day after Hortense died, she casually handed

Louis a letter from Auguste which she had found among Hortense's papers. Louis read it and burst into tears.[1]

He had always known that his mother, in her long years of separation from her husband, had not lived the life of a nun: few people at Arenenberg, including Louis himself, believed that handsome young Felix Cottreau was merely the official painter to her household. But Louis was sick at heart to discover that not only had his adored mother been unfaithful all those years ago but she had kept from him all his life the knowledge that he had a younger brother.

It is surely significant that he never tried to make contact with Auguste. He never wrote to him nor tried to arrange a meeting. He showed no interest in him whatsoever.

They did not even set eyes on each other until nine years later, in the summer of 1846, when Auguste and his father were being driven in a taxi down Regent Street on a visit to London and Flahaut raised his hat to someone on the pavement. When Auguste asked who it was, Flahaut replied with a slight smile: 'That is Prince Louis Napoleon!'

They did not actually meet until three years later, in the spring of 1849. Then Auguste, retired from a distinguished career in the army, made a count in his own right by Louis-Philippe and now an extremely rich, if not too scrupulous, businessman, had been elected to the French Parliament. Along with the other new Deputies, he came to the Elysée Palace to present his respects to the Prince-President of the new French Republic. There was no embrace, no warm discussion of their shared parentage: Louis merely shook his hand as he did with all the others.

Nevertheless, they soon became close political associates and Auguste served loyally as one of Louis' most senior aides until his comparatively early death, at the age of fifty-four, in 1865. But emotionally the blood-bond seems to have meant very little to either of them: Auguste perhaps because he felt that he had little cause to love his mother, Louis because he preferred to ignore this one

---

[1] Why did she do it? Was she simply being clumsy or tactless, as Adrien Dansette maintains, or was there a darker significance? Perhaps the answer lies in her own troubled sexuality. The French historian, Jean Savant, claimed in 1971 that she was lesbian but he provided no evidence to support the allegation.

A drawing by Eugéne Isabey in the late 1790s that, rarely among contemporary portraits, shows Josephine de Beauharnais, Napoleon I's future Empress, as the strikingly beautiful woman she was.

Ex-King Joseph of Spain, Napoleon III's uncle and Napoleon I's oldest brother, painted by Robert Lefevre.

Francesco Duca di Reichstadt

François Joseph Charles Bonaparte, Napoleon I's only legitimate son (by his second wife, Marie-Louise, daughter of Emperor Francis I of Austria). He is shown as a young man at his grandfather's Court where he was brought up as the Duke of Reichstadt. He is now also known as Napoleon II, although he never reigned.

The house at Arenenberg on the shore of Lake Constance in Switzerland where Napoleon III spent many formative years. It is now a museum.

Louis-Philippe, the 'Citizen King' of France (1830–48), in a portrait attributed to Pierre-Roch Vigneron.

The future Napoleon III, when a 31-year old exile in London, as drawn by his friend Count Alfred d'Orsay in 1839.

The future Napoleon III in his prison cell in the Château at Ham in about 1841.

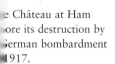
e Château at Ham
ore its destruction by
German bombardment
1917.

The newly-elected Prince-President takes his oath of office in December 1848, swearing to defend the Second Republic's constitution, an oath which he broke almost exactly three years later.

A scene of desolation in Paris during the 'Red Days of June' in 1848.

Dr Henri Conneau in official Court uniform as Napoleon III's principal private physician during the Second Empire.

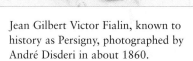

Jean Gilbert Victor Fialin, known to history as Persigny, photographed by André Disderi in about 1860.

Auguste, Duc de Morny, photographed in the early 1860s.

A misleading image of bourgeois marital bliss: Napoleon III and Empress Eugenie photographed in 1861.

A perfect picture of a *femme fatale*: the Countess of Castiglione in her Second Empire heyday.

Marguerite Bellanger, the vivacious young 'actress' who was for two years Napoleon III's mistress, defying the open anger of Empress Eugenie.

Ex-King Jerome, the wily old roué, close to the end of his life in 1860.

Prince Napoleon Joseph Bonaparte ('Plon-Plon').

Princess Mathilde photographed around 1860. She had put on a lot of weight in the fourteen years since, at the age of fifteen, she had nominally been the future Napoleon III's fiancée.

blemish in the behaviour of the woman whose memory he still idolised.

Hortense's funeral took place on 11 October 1837, six days after she died, at the small village church at Ermatingen near Arenenberg but, on her death-bed, she had said that she wanted to be buried at the Church of St Pierre and St Paul at Rueil, near Malmaison, where her mother, the Empress Josephine, had been buried.

On a bitterly cold day in January 1838, her embalmed body was laid to rest in a small chapel on the other side of the high altar from Josephine. Louis was not allowed into France for the ceremony but, standing in the back of the crowded church, were the black-coated figures of Charles de Flahaut and Auguste de Morny.[1]

A few days later Valerie Masuyer came face to face with Flahaut at a reception. Hortense had confided in her the sad tale of her affair with this now ageing, almost bald charmer and she found that she did not much like him. 'For a quarter of an hour and with excruciating courtesy,' she recorded in her journal, 'he asked me about the last moments of the Queen as a gentleman might about the death of a great lady whom he has had the honour to know, nothing more. He showed not the slightest sign of emotion: neither in his look nor his voice.'

As for Auguste de Morny, whom Valerie met at a subsequent reception when he accompanied his father, she wrote that he 'showed unmistakable signs of his maternal origin. He resembles the Queen perhaps even more than the Prince himself [i.e. Louis] – to the point that I could not prevent tears welling in my eyes on seeing him.' When introduced to him as Hortense's lady-in-waiting, she thought that she saw 'an extra tenderness come into his eyes but it was only for a second. He is as much a diplomat as his father.'

* * *

[1] Today a visitor can see the two kneeling marble statues of Josephine and Hortense at prayer on either side of the altar. Josephine's statue dates from 1825 and was commissioned by her two children, Hortense and Eugene. Hortense's was ordered by Louis after he became emperor and there is still displayed a portrait of its solemn inauguration in 1858 with Louis and his wife, Eugenie, on their knees before it.

With Hortense gone, Louis could no longer bear to live at Arenenberg. Two months after her funeral he moved into a smaller château that she had recently bought as a possible second home, at Gottlieben, a few miles further down on the banks of Lake Constance.

Louis had not come simply to brood. He was determined to heed his mother's last counsel, stated in her will: 'I know that my son understands his position and all the duties which his name imposes upon him.' He re-dedicated himself to his cause but now, for the first time, he tried a shrewd, devious approach rather than direct confrontation. This was to be his favoured style in later years.

The background to his plan was that, since his early return from the exile in America to which they thought they had sent him for ever (or, at least, a very long time), the French Government had been rumbling its discontent at his continued presence in Switzerland, so close to France. Now that Hortense was dead, they increased the pressure on the Swiss to order his expulsion and on 30 January 1838 formally demanded it in a diplomatic note to the Swiss Government.

At once, Louis saw a way in which to make himself appear a martyr, set up the pompous ministers of Louis-Philippe's Government as figures of ridicule – and perhaps even achieve a new, strategically preferable base for another attempt at seizing power: namely, England only just across the Channel.

He therefore invited Armand Laity, the young officer who had been with him at Strasbourg and, along with all the other conspirators, acquitted of treason, to visit him at Gottlieben and for several months the two worked on a pamphlet glorifying the failed coup and presenting it almost as a triumph which had seriously threatened Louis-Philippe's throne.

As Louis later wrote to his old mentor, Narcisse Vieillard, in a rare moment of truth: 'I caused the Laity pamphlet to be published not only to defend myself but to afford the French Government an excuse for getting me expelled from Switzerland.'

And so it worked out. Louis-Philippe's ministers walked right into the trap.

Published in Paris in early June 1838, with Laity named as its sole author, *Relation historique des événements du 30 octobre 1836* caused a major political scandal. Ten thousand copies were widely distributed and, as Louis had hoped, the government completely over-reacted. It put Laity on trial for 'an attempt on the security of the State' before the Chamber of Peers, a French version of the British House of Lords which was much more likely to convict than the ordinary sort of jury that had acquitted the Strasbourg conspirators.

On 10 July, Laity was convicted and sentenced to five years' imprisonment, a fine of 10,000 francs and police surveillance for the rest of his life after release from prison. The harshness of the sentence was widely condemned in the Opposition press in France and in many a leading newspaper outside France.

Louis was pleased with the way his plan was working out. Not so his family. His uncle, ex-King Joseph, wrote sadly to his wife, Marie: 'This young man has become crazy with intrigue and ambition: he looks on his father and myself as nonentities! I indeed regret that I have not the Atlantic between me and this old Europe, the scene of so much intrigue, perfidy and ingratitude.' Ex-King Louis was even more angry. 'My son,' he wrote to Louis, 'this is the last letter that I am going to write to you [and he increased the insult by using the formal "vous"]. I can forget everything except what you do against established governments, public order and repose; for that is the distinctive characteristic of dishonest men.'

The French Government would doubtless have agreed. Puffed up with a sense of their own virtue and seemingly having lost all sense of proportion, they stumbled on into the second great error that Louis had envisaged for them. They turned even more angrily against their Swiss neighbours.

On 1 August, the French Ambassador, the Duc de Montebello,[1] presented a new demand to the Federal Government at Berne calling for Louis' immediate expulsion from Switzerland. Several times over the next few weeks they repeated the request, turning it more and more into a command; even threatening to go to war against their much smaller neighbour and massing 25,000 troops at a crucial point along the frontier.

---

[1] Ironically, he had been one of the aristocratic children christened at Fontainebleau in 1810 during the same magnificent ceremony as the infant Louis.

The Swiss stood firm and many people throughout Europe were disgusted at the spectacle of a major power such as France trying to bully a brave little neighbour into expelling a young man from the home where he had lived for twenty years and where his beloved mother had so recently died.

As for Louis, he was delighted at how everything was going according to plan. 'The Government is doing everything it can to increase my importance,' he wrote happily to his sister-in law, Charlotte, the widow of his dead older brother, Napoleon Louis.

Finally, came his master stroke. On 22 September, he wrote to the president of his local canton of Thurgau that he would leave the country of his own free will. Magnanimously, he offered reluctantly to do what he wanted to do anyway and which was the whole point of his well-planned exercise. 'Switzerland has known how to do her duty as an independent state,' he wrote. 'I know how to do mine and to be faithful to my honour. I will leave as soon as I have obtained the necessary passports to travel to a place where I shall find a safe asylum.'

That safe haven was England. As a contemporary French newspaper shrewdly pointed out, France would be much more accessible to Louis across the narrow Straits of Dover than ever it had been from distant Thurgau; and to this one should add that a major power like England was clearly a much more appropriate base from which to mobilise one's forces for a new assault upon power than a quiet, rustic corner of Switzerland.

In his letter of 22 September Louis expressed hope that one day he might be able to return to Switzerland 'where a sojourn of twenty years, and the rights I had acquired, had created for me a new country'. That was sheer hypocrisy. Once his mother was dead, Switzerland no longer had any calls on his affection. Except for one brief visit, he never returned. In recent years he had come to regard it as merely one more staging-post in his long exile, and now he was moving on.

On 14 October, armed with a passport from the British Minister at Berne, he bade farewell to Arenenberg and to his mother's room (which to this day, as any visitor can see, remains as it was on the night that Hortense died)[1] and started the journey to the next stop along the way towards achieving his destiny: London.

It was a triumphal exit. The local people came to cheer and salute him. Even in Constance, the German town through which he passed on the other side of the lake, the streets were full of people, with women waving from every window. *Le Courrier Français*, an Opposition newspaper in France, astutely observed that until then there had been only one Pretender, the Duc de Bordeaux, son of the deposed Charles X, but now, thanks to the stupidity of the French Government, there were two. *L'Europe Indépendante* was even more to the point: 'Louis Napoleon Bonaparte is withdrawing to England. He is is no longer a Swiss citizen, he is Napoleon III.'

The man who walked into the entrance hall of Fenton's Hotel in London's St James's Street on 25 October 1838, accompanied by Persigny, Dr Conneau, Colonel Vaudrey, another colonel and three servants could be forgiven the quiet smile on his face.

[1] During the Second Empire, on his one return visit to Switzerland, Louis came back briefly to Arenenberg with his wife, Empress Eugenie; and after his death she visited the château several times with their son, the Prince Imperial. In fact, convinced that he would never again want to see the place, Louis had sold it in July 1843 to a Saxon industrialist but twelve years later, realising how much her husband still pined for the house where his mother had died, Eugenie bought it back – for less than the industrialist had paid for it! She had it restored to its former condition which is how Louis saw it when he returned the following year with her, and how a visitor can still see it today. In 1906, Eugenie handed over the property to the local canton of Thurgau on condition that the estate buildings were turned into an agricultural college and the château itself into a museum.

Chapter Ten

A New Life in London (1838–40)

T HIS WAS THE FOURTH time that Louis found himself in London but it was totally different from his previous three brief visits in 1831, 1832 and 1837. Then he had been a poor adventurer and a transient refugee: now he was rich, almost a national hero and the capital's most celebrated new resident.

Carlton House Terrace had recently been built by John Nash, the most fashionable architect of the day, as opulent mansions for the aristocracy. Close to Buckingham Palace, it was also on the fringe of what that arrant snob Sir William Fraser called 'the only real world', bounded by St James's Street, the Haymarket, Piccadilly and Pall Mall. So it was both highly appropriate and a shrewd move that Louis now chose to live at one of the gleamingly new houses on Carlton House Terrace.

He took a lease of No. 17 from Lord Cardigan where he lived in great style, moving a year later to an equally grand address a few doors down at 1, Carlton Gardens, in a house rented from Lord Ripon and overlooking the gardens of Marlborough House, where lived Queen Adelaide, widow of William IV, the young Queen Victoria's recently deceased uncle.[1] It was all terribly splendid with a host of servants, a stable full of horses, a box at the opera (always with Persigny and another member of his household standing respectfully on either side behind his chair) and a coach emblazoned with the Imperial eagle.

His cook was one of the most sought after in London and some

[1] Today there has been no lessening in its social status: 1, Carlton Gardens is the official residence of the British Foreign Secretary.

forty years later Benjamin Disraeli gave this description of his life-style, drawing on his memories of Louis for Prince Florestan in his last novel, *Endymion*: 'The Duke of St Angelo [Persigny] controlled the household at Carlton Gardens with skill. The appointments were finished and the cuisine refined. There was a dinner twice a week ... It was an interesting and useful house for a young man, and especially a young politician, to frequent ... The prince encouraged conversation, though himself inclined to taciturnity. When he did speak, his terse remarks and condensed views were striking, and were remembered.'

Louis was just about accepted in society. Some objected to his views: as Sir William Fraser later wrote, 'Sarah, Lady Jersey, at that time the supreme head of London society, absolutely refused to give him any position. With her vigorous appreciation of the monarchical system, the Bonaparte family would not be acknowledged.'

Many doors *were* open to him but they tended to belong to the more enlightened, less 'respectable', houses where writers, politicians and artists were more likely to be encountered than dull members of the peerage up from the country.

In particular, Louis was a frequent guest at Gore House in Kensington, later demolished to make way for the Royal Albert Hall but then the home of the widowed Lady Blessington, an ageing society beauty whom he had met ten years before in Rome, as a friend of his mother. Marguerite Blessington had for years scandalised 'respectable' people by living openly with her tall, handsome, hazel-eyed young French lover, Alfred, Comte d'Orsay, who had during Lord Blessington's lifetime happily been the lover of both husband and wife – at the same time.

A gifted artist and sculptor, with irresistible charm and expensive tastes, d'Orsay was the fashion icon of the day and, having met at Gore House when the newcomer first visited Marguerite, he and Louis quickly became friends. They saw a great deal of each other and liked to ride out together in the two-wheeled carriage that d'Orsay had designed himself and which he drove at breakneck speed through the crowded London streets 'half swinging in the air clinging on to the straps', as one contemporary put it, with an enormous horse champing between the shafts and 'the trimmest of tiny grooms – "tigers" as they were called – half standing on the footboard behind'.[1] D'Orsay always drove in faultless white kid gloves with his shirt-sleeves tucked back over his coat-cuffs in a style which is still smartly casual today.

Louis saw nothing wrong at all with d'Orsay's exotic lifestyle. One of his finest qualities was to take his friends as they came, and not seek to impose his own ideas upon them. Indeed, it was at about this time that some of his new English acquaintances tried to make him drop Persigny by telling him that the man was virtually a confidence trickster and not really a count. His reply was typical: 'I do not sit in judgement on my friends.'

He was himself a good friend and, when in April 1849, d'Orsay had finally to flee to Paris to escape his creditors, followed by the failing Marguerite who died a few weeks later, Louis, then Prince-President, took him under his wing. He helped him obtain work as a sculptor and designer and in April 1852 made him Director of Fine Arts. Sadly, cancer of the spine then struck and d'Orsay died four months later, at the age of fifty-one, with Marguerite's niece softly playing Chopin waltzes on a piano in the background. He died in the style in which he had lived.

Many believe that Louis ordered one of the new quais that Haussmann built along the Seine to be named the Quai d'Orsay. Appropriately, the name also lives on today in the Musée d'Orsay, one of the finest art galleries in the world.

But in 1838, the upper echelons of the British aristocracy treated Louis with that particular form of disdain they habitually keep for foreigners with their strange 'un-British' ways. Although proudly boasting of the ex-Emperor as an old friend when writing his Recollections nearly forty years later. Sir William Fraser could not stop himself observing that his dress at that time 'was not that of a man who knew how to dress. It was distinctly what the French call *apprêté*: represented in some measure by the British term "got up" – but without success. I should say that he was dressed after the fashion books: with considerable tightness; yet not neat: his clothes

---

[1] It is interesting to note the way in which legends grow up. Some biographies of Napoleon III state wrongly that, during this time in London, he would like to walk around the streets with a 'tiger' on a chain. This is almost certainly a corruption of the fact that he liked to drive out in d'Orsay's carriage with a human 'tiger' on the footboard.

invariably of sombre colours; trousers strapped down; a frock coat always buttoned: at that time unusual.'

Yet, as Disraeli wrote, 'Prince Florestan [i.e. Louis], though he was not insensible to the charms of society, and especially of agreeable women, was not much chagrined by the neglect of the *crème de la crème* of society.'

He did not need to be since he was extremely popular with the friends that he did have who treated him fully as one of their own. One summer's day, for instance, Louis was rowing Disraeli, his wife Mary Anne, Persigny and himself up the Thames when, trying to escape the swell of a passing steamer, he manoeuvred the boat on to a mudbank where, despite all his efforts, they remained firmly stuck. Mary Anne Disraeli turned on him: 'You should not undertake things which you cannot accomplish,' she told him sternly. 'You are always, Sir, too adventurous.'

Undoubtedly, Louis was having a perfectly happy time. But the two constants of his life remained: his enjoyment of young women and his lust for power.

No one is certain how many young women Louis knew during the two years that he lived in London as a French version of an English gentleman. Sir William Fraser says that, in the comparatively brief time, he actually proposed twice, and there is no reason to believe that his sexual appetite went unregarded in circumstances where there would not have been even for one moment the slightest question of marriage. Not for nothing did Disraeli write so many years later that Louis was 'not insensible to the charms . . . of agreeable women'.

It is worth looking more closely into the case of Emily Rowles, one of Louis' two would-be fiancées. She was the sixteen-year-old daughter of Henry Rowles, a prosperous builder and magistrate, and his Spanish-born wife. Rowles had a town house in Stratton Street, Mayfair, and a country home at Camden Place in Chislehurst, then a small country town some fifteen miles south of London, in Kent. This was the same house where over thirty years later Louis was to spend his last few years in exile after his fall from power in 1870; as we shall see later, there is good cause to believe that his choice was not at all coincidental, based partly on his memories of the agreeable visits that he made in the late 1830s to Mr and Mrs Rowles and their beautiful young daughter.

This is extremely important for a proper understanding of Louis' final years. I am convinced that it is highly significant that Louis told Sir William Fraser when he visited him at Camden Place in 1872: 'I used to be here frequently in former years.' For some reason, Jasper Ridley, in his exhaustive biography, *Napoleon III and Eugenie*, published in 1979, chooses to pour scorn on this vital statement. He writes that it is not possible because a family named Martin 'were in residence at Camden Place from 1835 to 1862'. He gives no source for this, other factors militate against it (including the fact that Camden Place was sold in 1860 to owner-occupier Nathaniel Strode) and, despite several hours spent in the Local Histories section of the Bromley Central Public Library and elsewhere, I can find nothing to support it. Furthermore, although Fraser was remarkably pompous and no longer young, he was not senile and Louis, who was then only sixty-four, can presumably be counted on to know whether or not he visited 'frequently' thirty years earlier the house where he was then living.

Undoubtedly, Louis and Emily seem to have become at least unofficially engaged and he gave her many valuable presents, including furs that had once belonged to the Empress Josephine. But perhaps because she was too young or because her fortunes changed (her father blew his brains out in 1840 and she and her mother went to live in Florence) or because it was simply one more case of Louis falling madly in love for only a very short time, there never was a wedding. Even so, they remained close friends for the rest of their lives.[1]

Apart from the pursuit of young women, Louis' other continuing passion was his resolute and unshaken belief in his Imperial destiny.

---

[1] When Louis was serving a term of life imprisonment at the Château de Ham in the early 1840s, Emily regularly sent him parcels. She married the wealthy Marquis Giovanni Pietro Campana in Rome and, when Louis needed additional money to fund the coup d'état in December 1851 which set him on the path to becoming emperor the following year, she made him a substantial loan. As ever, Louis never forgot a favour and when Campana was sentenced to twenty years' forced labour in 1858 for fraudulent embezzlement, Louis repaid Emily by gifts and annuities to a far higher value than her loan, and intervened with the Pope to commute Campana's sentence to banishment for life. Emily died in 1876 and Campana in 1880, by when he was poor, forgotten and an early but ardent spiritualist.

Sir Archibald Alison, an early Victorian historian who met him at a shooting-party in Scotland, has written: 'No disasters shook his confidence in his star or in his belief in the ultimate fulfilment of his destiny. This is well known to all who were intimate with him in this country after he returned from America.' 'Nothing can persuade him,' wrote a young friend, the future 11th Earl of Westmoreland, 'that he is not to be Emperor of France. This Strasbourg affair has not in the least shaken him. He is thinking constantly of what he is to do when on the throne.' And the Duke of Newcastle later reminisced to Blanchard Jerrold, 'We frequently went out to shoot together. Neither cared much for sport and we soon sat down and began to speak seriously. He always opened these conferences by discoursing on what he would do when he was Emperor of France ... The idea that he would eventually be the Emperor of the French never for a moment left his mind.'

But he did much more than just talk about it. Almost from the first moment that he came to live in London he began preparing and planning for a new Strasbourg-type coup, only this time one that would really carry him on to victory.

He invested some of his newly inherited wealth in sponsoring two political clubs and two Bonapartist newspapers in Paris. Realising that France lagged far behind Britain in modernising its economy in the aftermath of the Industrial Revolution, he twice toured the factories and workshops of Lancashire and the Midlands, notebook in hand. There was a regular string of different visitors, some from abroad, to his London home and there was much to keep the watching detectives, paid by the French Embassy, busily scribbling notes in *their* notebooks.

But before he could properly launch himself back on to the political stage in France, he needed a manifesto: a clear and compelling statement of his cause.

The 250 pages of *Idées Napoléoniennes*, published in July 1839 in a green paper cover stamped with the Imperial eagle and at a price (50 centimes, only half a franc) that everyone could afford, was aimed over the heads of France's current politicians directly at the mass of the people, middle class and working class alike. It caused an instant sensation; the French Government vilified it but thousands bought it. Within a few months, it had reprinted three times and been translated into six languages. It gave Louis a status that he had never enjoyed before: he was no longer merely a symbol of past glory but now a powerful voice with a programme for the future.

Even though we are primarily concerned with Louis as a human being and not as a political phenomenon, we must pause to examine *Idées Napoléoniennes* because it is a unique statement of what Louis personally and genuinely believed. It was a blueprint for himself as well as for everyone else.

It set out to be an explanatory account of his great uncle's policies. The first Napoleon – his motto: 'Everything for the French people' – had already left a highly idealised account of his achievements and aims in his outpourings on St Helena during his last bitter six years of remote exile. He had always been a brilliant propagandist in his own cause: 'I will lead you into the most fertile plains of the world ... There you will reap honour and glory and wealth,' he had told his soldiers during his first Italian campaign in 1796.[1] Twenty years later, on St Helena, he made the somewhat improbable claim: 'I always believed that true sovereignty resides in the people. The Imperial government was a sort of republic.'

Now his nephew took up the same theme, seeking to reconcile what can never be reconciled: the concept of a strong central government with liberty and democracy. 'The Napoleonic idea', he wrote, 'is based on principles of eternal justice ... It replaces the hereditary system of the old aristocracies by a hierarchical system which, while it ensures equality, rewards merit and guarantees order. It finds an element of strength and stability in democracy because it regulates democracy. It follows neither the unsure steps of a party nor the passions of the mob. It regards Frenchmen as brothers who need to be reconciled and the various nations of Europe as members of one great family. It does not seek to overturn society but to reorganise it.

'By its very nature, it is an idea of peace not of war, an idea of order and reconstruction not of upheaval. It appeals to reason not to force; but, if driven too far by persecution, it will once more take up its helmet and lance.'

---

[1] Historians differ as to whether Napoleon actually said this at the time or 'invented' it later when re-writing his personal history on St Helena but, either way, it confirms him as an inspired self-propagandist.

There was, perhaps inevitably, a high degree of hyperbole. 'The Emperor is no more ... but his soul is not dead. Deprived of the possibility of defending his watchful authority by force of arms, I can at least try to defend his memory by my writings ... I am not bound to any party, to any sect or any government. My voice is free like my thoughts ... and I love liberty. Government is not a necessary ulcer but the beneficent driving force of every social organism. The Emperor must be considered as the Messiah of new ideas.'

Louis claimed that Napoleon I was the heir of the Revolution and the champion of liberty, but it was the Revolution purified. Liberty did not mean mere licence that had dragged down the original revolutionary movement into the dirt. Napoleonic ideas were a synthesis of progress since the old ruling system in France was swept away in the Revolution of 1789: without Napoleon's great achievements, the whole work of the Revolution would have perished.

The Emperor had known what was wanted because he was in harmony with his time and understood the needs of France and of her people. This was the first necessity of any government and, sure in this knowledge, he had gone forward triumphantly. The mystical union between ruler and people was a basic article of his faith, and that of his nephew. (Hence, the use both made of what were then called plebiscites but are now better known as referendums.)

Anxious to refute the charge that the Emperor's rule had been, in reality, a military dictatorship, Louis maintained: 'Under the Imperial system no post in the civil administration was occupied by soldiers. The man who created civil honours to counterbalance military decorations, who by instituting the Legion of Honour wished to reward equally the services of the citizen and the soldier, who from his coming to power busied himself with the condition of the civil servants, who always gave precedence to the latter, who both at home and even in conquered countries sent Councillors of State armed with a civil authority superior to that of the generals, is the man whom the spirit of faction wants to portray as the partisan of a military regime.

'When the Emperor appointed an administrative head, he did not consult the man's political inclinations but his capacity as a civil servant.'

He pointed out, not without reason, that only the administrative system devised by Napoleon (and still substantially in place today) had saved France from collapse over the last twenty-five years. 'Under the Empire all the best brains and the talent of France worked to one end: the prosperity of the country. Since then the most intelligent have been busy fighting amongst themselves, arguing about the way to go rather than moving on. Political discipline has been broken so that, instead of marching ahead in a straight line, everybody sets up his own line of march and has drifted away from the main body.'

After many more pages in similar vein, he ended by putting into the old Emperor's mouth these triumphant words: 'All that I did for the prosperity of France, I had to do between battles but you who blame me, what have you done in twenty-four years of peace?'

According to Robert Sencourt, a British writer in the early 1930s also much respected in France, the central idea of the book is the free instinct of the people accepting the 'guidance' of authority. Louis wanted, in effect, a benevolent despotism, founded on frequent referendums and guided by ability, whose aim would be to make the masses of the people prosperous. Such a régime, he wrote, 'gives work to all hands and capacities: it enters the cottage, not making empty declarations about the rights of men but providing means to quench the poor man's thirst, to satisfy his hunger and, with a glorious story, to awaken his patriotism.'

But he claimed that the Napoleonic ideas were not only of value for France but for the whole of Europe, if not the world. They would make France a centre of harmony among nations. Hers was a sacred cause and it was for her to spread throughout Europe those principles of justice, freedom and authority of which she would be the prime example. France would thus become the arbiter of Europe.

Louis gave a copy of his book to his friend Edward Bulwer-Lytton, later the first Lord Lytton and a leading novelist of the time. His judgement, written on a piece of paper still kept inside his copy, is worth quoting:

'It is the book of a very able mind with few ideas but those ideas bold, large and reducible to vigorous action ... Prince Louis Napoleon has qualities that may render him a remarkable man if he ever return to France. Dogged, daring, yet somewhat reserved and close, he can conceive with secrecy and act with promptitude. His faults would comprise conceit and rashness but, akin with those characteristics, are will and enthusiasm. He has these in a high degree. Above all, he has that intense faith in his own destiny with which men rarely fail of achieving something great.'

But when was he actually going to *do* something positive about 'achieving something great'?

In early 1840, Louis had paid to be published in France an anonymous pamphlet (written by Persigny) called *Lettres de Londres* which purported to describe his working day. It reads like something put out by a contemporary PR agency . . .

> The Prince is a working, active man, severe towards himself, indulgent towards others. At 6.00 am, he is in his study, where he works until noon, his luncheon hour. After this repast, which never lasts longer then ten minutes, he reads the newspapers and has notes taken of the more important events or opinions of the day.
>
> At 2.00 pm he receives visitors, at 4 he goes out on private business; he rides at 5 and dines at 7; then generally he finds time to work again for some hours in the course of the evening.
>
> As to his tastes and habits, they are those of a man who looks only at the serious side of life. He does not understand luxury for himself. In the morning he dresses for the entire day; he is the simplest-dressed man of his household, although there is always a certain military elegance in his appearance.

But still there was no 'new' Strasbourg. Although professing to the outside world that the fiasco of October 1836 had had no effect upon him, in reality Louis was desperate not to repeat the same mistake. The next attempt to seize power would have to be better planned, better researched. As early as March 1839, within five months of his coming to live in London, he had been in contact through an intermediary with the Comte Bertrand Clauzel, then one of France's most famous soldiers. Clauzel was one of Napoleon's generals who had fled into exile in the United States after Waterloo but had returned to France following the July Revolution in 1830, when Louis-Philippe promoted him to the rank of Marshal and gave him several leading military appointments. But in November 1836 the King had turned against him after defeat at the Battle of Constantine, in Algeria, and forced him into retirement. Yet, at the age of sixty-seven, he remained a formidable and influential figure and Louis invited him to London for talks at Carlton House Terrace. He offered to put at Clauzel's disposal 20,000 francs for a ten-day visit and to rent for him 'a beautiful apartment in a fine part of town'.

As Adrien Dansette has commented, 'It is not known if Marshal Clauzel in fact visited London but it seems not impossible that the Prince had good reason to count upon his co-operation in any adventure he might launch against the King's authority.'

From the end of 1839, London society began to see less of the one-time playboy prince. He continued to give small dinner-parties at Carlton Gardens and to enjoy reciprocal hospitality from a small circle of truly intimate friends, such as Marguerite Blessington and Alfred d'Orsay, but increasingly his time was spent in planning the new Strasbourg. One evening, Lord Fitzharris his old friend from the carefree days in Rome, seeing him standing on the steps of Gore House, wrapped in his cloak, with Persigny by his side, laughingly remarked, 'You look like two conspirators!' 'You may be nearer right than you think,' replied Louis.

The plot was basically the same as before: he would present himself at a garrison town, win over the soldiers and local inhabitants then march triumphantly upon Paris gathering increasing support along the way. It would be his version of his uncle's return from Elba, and hopefully similarly bloodless. It was not an impossible dream but it had to be properly prepared.

And the timing had to be right.

It was more than three years since the Strasbourg fiasco and Louis-Philippe had become even less popular. A reactionary and corrupt administration at home had been accompanied by a servile timidity in foreign affairs; the working classes wanted an escape from their poverty, the middle classes wanted France to be great again. There had been several attempts to assassinate the King and uprisings by Socialist or Republican militants had been vigorously repressed.

Yet despite the temptations, Louis still held back.

It was not through personal cowardice. When, in the autumn of

1839, pro-Government newspapers in Paris accused him of having instigated an unsuccessful revolt in Paris by Armand Barbès, a fiery Socialist agitator, and then leaving Barbès and his supporters to face alone the fury of the law, Louis wrote angrily to the editor of *The Times*: 'Sir, I see with pain that it is wished to cast upon me the responsibility of the late insurrection. I rely upon your kindness to refute in the most distinct manner this insinuation. The news of the bloody scenes that took place caused me as much surprise as grief. If I were the moving spirit of a conspiracy, I would also be the chief actor in it on the day of danger and would not skulk away after defeat.'

This refusal to accept a coward's role led him within a few months into the near-farce of a duel on Wimbledon Common with the worthless Comte Léon, his cousin and an illegitimate son of Napoleon I.

In January 1840, Léon, an unsavoury character with none of his father's immense ability nor even the good looks of his mother, Eleonore Denvelle, a pretty young lady-in-waiting of Napoleon's sister, Caroline, arrived in London after being released from imprisonment for debt in France. In an insolent letter to *mon petit cousin*, he demanded an interview with Louis, which was peremptorily refused. Louis realised that he was a troublemaker in the pay of the French Government. So, in accordance with the spirit of the age, Léon challenged him to a duel and Louis accepted the challenge: no gentleman could have done less.

Duelling, however, remained technically unlawful. It was, at the very least, a breach of the peace.[1] That is why, shortly after 7 o'clock on the morning of 3 March 1840 when Louis and Léon had loaded their pistols for their encounter on Wimbledon Common in south-west London, the portly Inspector Pierce of the Metropolitan Police intervened. Tipped off by the French Embassy, he arrested the duellists and their seconds (in Louis' case, old Colonel Parquin, his accomplice at Strasbourg, and Alfred d'Orsay) before a shot could be fired.

Later that morning, the future Emperor of France and the son of an earlier Emperor stood day side by side in the dock at Bow

---

[1] That is still the legal position today. There is no statute specifically saying that duelling is a crime.

Street Police Court charged with attempting to commit a breach of the peace.

Louis tried to speak up for himself and explain what had happened but Mr Jardine, the Bow Street magistrate renowned for his bad temper, brusquely said that he was not interested and bound over all six defendants to keep the peace. That evening, in a rare show of family solidarity, Louis appeared in his box at the opera flanked on either side by his two uncles, Joseph and Jerome.

But the time was now fast approaching when there would be an end to play-acting. At last, Louis-Philippe gave Louis the opportunity for which he had been waiting to mount a new attempt to seize power, this time in the northern French seaport of Boulogne just across the Channel from England. The tragedy was that it was to prove an even more abject failure than the abortive coup at Strasbourg.

Chapter Eleven

Boulogne – Not Such a Fiasco (1840)

L OUIS WAS A BORN and devious conspirator. 'If only I could stop him conspiring with himself against himself!' the exasperated Princess Mathilde, his cousin and erstwhile fiancée, once said. And there are many instances in later years of how his adroit manoeuvring could save him from disaster – at least, for a while.

But in his earlier years it is remarkable how a man given so naturally to plots could have sometimes seemed to be so inept at bringing them to fruition. It was certainly not for lack of confidence. In July 1840, James Planche, the dramatist, commented to another guest as they left a dinner-party at Gore House which Louis had also attended: 'What could the Prince have meant by asking us to dine with him this day twelve-months at the Tuileries?'

The story begins in the early spring of 1840, when London was buzzing with the news that the French Ambassador, François Guizot, had obtained from the British Government permission to bring back to France the body of Napoleon I, then dead some nineteen years. Why? Because Louis-Philippe, forever anxious to wrap his non-military figure in the glorious mantle of the dead Emperor and now desperate for some new ploy to bolster his shrinking national regard, had decided to honour the emperor's last wish, stated in his will, that he should be buried in Paris: 'on the banks of the Seine, amidst the French people whom I have loved so well'.[1]

---

[1] In fact, the idea was not that of Louis-Philippe himself but that of Adolphe Thiers, then his Prime Minister, but the king was quick to appreciate its obvious advantages. Thiers appears again. An astute lawyer-politician and one of the most enduring figures in French nineteenth-century history, thirty years later, at the age of seventy-three, he became the ruler of France as the first President of the Third Republic which followed the collapse of Louis' Second Empire.

For Louis, this was like a red rag to a bull. He could not stand the thought that the great Emperor was returning to his capital – and that he would not be there to greet him. The *Idées Napoléoniennes* of the previous year was reissued with a new foreword stating defiantly: 'It is not only the Emperor's remains but also his ideas which must be brought back to France.' As the Comte Charles François de Rémusat, the astute French Minister of the Interior, wrote to Ambassador Guizot: 'I have very little doubt but that Prince Louis Bonaparte's head will be excited, and that he will try some adventure.'

How right he was. As *Le Moniteur*, the official newspaper of the French Government, later reported after Louis' 'adventure' at Boulogne had disastrously failed in August 1840: 'The Government have known for some time that Louis Bonaparte and his agents had a plan for bringing themselves before the public, through some sudden attempt, before the arrival of the ashes of the Emperor Napoleon. Emissaries had been constantly travelling between Paris and London, between London and our fortified places, to study the spirit of our garrisons.'

Louis has received a bad press in the annals of history for the abortive coup at Boulogne. 'Fiasco', 'ridiculous', 'miserable', 'absurd', 'extraordinary' are typical of the words used by French and English historians and biographers alike.

But that is not entirely fair. They give him too little credit for the depth, and cost, of his preparation. Indeed, to finance the coup, he sold jewels and works of art for 100,000 francs, land in Italy for 300,000 francs and 1,400,000 francs' worth of stock in the Bank of Vienna: a total of 1,800,000 francs (a staggering £4,194,000 by today's values).

He also raised £20,000 (more than £1 million today) in London by way of a loan from an Italian-born banker in London, Count Joseph Orsi, whom he had known since they fought side by side against the Pope in 1831.

Boulogne was not the original point first chosen for the coup, but Lille, a major industrial town in northern France with a large garrison and headquarters of the powerful Army of the North. In March 1840, shortly after his aborted duel with the Comte Léon, Louis sent one of his two seconds to Lille, the widely respected Colonel Parquin, and a Dr Jules Lombard, a former military surgeon to the

Army of the North. They were well received by some of the officers who talked freely about their warm feelings for the great Emperor's nephew. Encouraged by their reaction, Louis then sent a former army officer named Séverin Le Duff de Mésonan, angry (as Marshal Clauzel had been) at having been retired against his will, to have discussions with no less a person than Bernard Magnan, the Commander-in-Chief of the Army of the North.

Rarely for a French general at that time, Magnan was not an aristocrat but had worked his way up through the ranks and, it was suspected, not averse to a little discreet bribery. The operative word was 'discreet'. When Mésonan clumsily showed him a letter in which Louis described Magnan as one of his future marshals, and wrote that Mésonan should offer him 100,000 francs down for an immediate promise of support and deposit 300,000 more at his bankers, in case the coup failed and he lost his command, Magnan told him to go and get himself hanged. Covering his own back, and playing a double game, Magnan then secretly reported the conversation to the French Government – but did not take the elementary step, as he might if he had been genuinely shocked or insulted, of putting Mésonan under immediate arrest.

Nor did he arrest Mésonan when he returned in early July to repeat the offer in more discreet terms. He merely muttered ambiguous words about his 'great regard' for the memory of the late Emperor. To Louis, the implication was clear: Magnan would not declare for him in the first instance but if he managed to win over at least one regiment to his cause, the general would come to his aid. It would obviously be too risky to attempt a coup in Lille itself but somewhere not too far away – and also nearer to England – might well do.

The question was: which regiment – and where?

The answer was the 42nd Infantry Regiment which Louis had nearly won over at Strasbourg and of which two detachments were now based at the major ports of Calais and Boulogne, directly approachable by sea across the English Channel. The second-in-command of the detachment at Boulogne was a young lieutenant named Jean Aladenize who secretly pledged his support to Louis and thereby settled the issue.

The coup would be at Boulogne.

*   *   *

By now the Prince de Joinville, one of Louis-Philippe's sons, was several hundred miles out to sea aboard the frigate *Belle Poule* bound for St Helena to bring back Napoleon's body, and Louis needed to intensify his preparations. The aim was clear: when the vessel returned with its illustrious cargo, it should be a slim new Emperor and not the fat old king waiting to receive it.

Rifles had been bought from a firm in Birmingham, a cousin of Persigny was in Paris buying uniforms and orders had been placed with several London firms for buttons bearing the number '40' which Dr Conneau himself was to sew on to the uniforms as soon as they were delivered. (Why '40'? Because the scheme was that Louis and his men, dressed in what looked the uniforms of the 40th Infantry Regiment, which was stationed at Dunkirk further up the coast, were to land on the beach at Wimereux, a small village some three miles from Boulogne, march along the coast road to the port and, if stopped, were to say that they were soldiers of the 40th Regiment who had sailed from Dunkirk to Cherbourg but had been forced to land, owing to an accident to their steamer.)

Louis and Persigny recruited fifty-five men, some household servants, others French supporters and Italian or Polish romantics, to go with them to Boulogne. They included Colonel Parquin and Dr Conneau but also General Comte Charles de Montholon, a highly distinguished soldier who had been with Napoleon on St Helena, Count Joseph Orsi, Louis' banker and former Italian revolutionary, and Pierre Bure, his foster-brother and the son of his old nanny 'Madame Bure' who had fed them both at her breast when they were babies.

A pleasure steamer, the *Edinburgh Castle*, was chartered with the ostensible aim of taking a party of tourists on a pleasure cruise to Hamburg, the German port.

Dr Conneau also had charge of a small hand press which, as in Strasbourg, was busily printing proclamations written by Louis to the French army, the local inhabitants and the people of France. It is not without significance that, in his proclamation to the local population, Louis stated positively: 'I have powerful friends outside as well as inside France who have promised me their support.'

Although insufficiently acknowledged by many subsequent commentators, this is undoubtedly true. Louis was not embarking on a scatter-brained scheme without reasonable hope of back-up.

Among his papers, later seized by the French authorities, were maps of northern France with minute particulars of the situation of different regiments on the way to Paris and written instructions to Persigny and others detailing whom they might find helpful at each garrison. But it has to be said that none of the generals and other high-ranking officers who had talked warmly but vaguely of coming to Louis' aid (all of which, of course, they later denied) could be expected to honour their somewhat ambiguous words unless he himself managed to achieve an inspiring victory at Boulogne. That is something he failed to do.

The coup was set for 5 August 1840 when Captain Col-Puygélier, the commanding officer of the detachment of the 42nd Infantry at Boulogne, was due to be away on leave for a day's shooting and Lieutenant Aladenize would be in charge.

Early on the previous morning, 4 August, Louis' men loaded on to the *Edinburgh Castle* moored on the Thames at London Bridge two carriages, nine horses and many crates labelled 'Hamburg' which contained sixty rifles, ammunition, sixty fake uniforms of the French 40th Infantry Regiment, three sets of printed proclamations – and £20,000 in gold and British banknotes.

The ship sailed down the river, picking up members of the expedition at landing-stages along the way, to Gravesend where Louis was due to come aboard at 3.00 pm, in plenty of time to reach Wimereux by daybreak on the 5th. But he did not arrive until 8.00 pm because agents of the French Government, who seem to have known that something was afoot but not exactly where or what form it would take, had been keeping watch upon his house in Carlton Gardens, and he had had to travel around London to throw them off the scent. With hindsight, one can say that this delay of five hours doomed the enterprise to failure from the very start, because, with the state of the tides, it made it impossible to reach Boulogne by daybreak the next day, which meant that disembarkation had to be put back twenty-four hours to dawn on 7 August. By that time Captain Col-Puygélier, known to be fiercely loyal to Louis-Philippe, would be back in command and Lieutenant Aladenize's effectiveness much reduced.

Louis felt that they could not turn back because they ran the risk that British customs officers might find the arms and ammunition on board and the scheme would become public knowledge, with disastrous political and diplomatic consequences for France and Britain. At the very least, he would almost certainly be expelled from Britain. So they pressed on with the unlikely, if not slightly ridiculous, 'mascot' of a tame eagle tied to the masthead.[1] While waiting for Louis at Gravesend, Colonel Parquin had gone ashore to buy some cigars and seen a boy feeding the bird. He bought it for £1.

Shortly before dawn on Friday 7 August, Louis and his men landed on the darkened beach at Wimereux, a boat-load at a time. Two customs officers saw them and were instantly suspicious of the story that they had concocted. They were then forced to accompany them as guides into Boulogne. Arrived at the outskirts of the town, Persigny wanted Louis to shoot them on the spot or at least take them prisoner but the gentle Louis, who had not yet learned to be ruthless, merely asked them to promise not to warn the authorities – which, of course, they ignored.

It was now close on 5 o'clock and broad daylight as the little army entered the still sleeping town. Lieutenant Aladenize was at its head, next came Jules Lombard, the ex-army surgeon, carrying a huge, gold-fringed flag, emblazoned with the names of Napoleon's victories and surmounted by an Imperial eagle. Louis and his brilliantly uniformed staff of officers marched behind, with the 'soldiers of the 40th Regiment' bringing up the rear.

As they advanced through the silent town, they met a sub-lieutenant of the 42nd Regiment named Maussion hurrying back late – very late – to his barracks.[2] That was where Louis and his men were also heading and, as they strode along side by side, Louis said to Maussion amiably as if he were a fellow guest at Gore House: 'I hope that you will be one of ours . . . I have come to

---

[1] Some accounts say that it was a vulture that looked like an eagle but the majority view seems to be that it was indeed an eagle. Writing in 1909, André Lebey insisted that it *was* an eagle and stated that it escaped from the local abattoir where the Boulogne authorities later sent it to be destroyed and ended up quite happily as a household pet in the nearby town of Arras, first at a restaurant and later at a coal merchant's.

[2] The barracks have long disappeared. On their site today stands the squat, ugly, modern building of the Banque de France. British visitors coming off the cross-Channel catamaran from Dover pass it on the left as they leave the docks and enter the town.

restore to our humiliated France the rank which she deserves to hold.' Maussion's answer was to run off down a side-turning and when Aladenize said they should send someone after him and capture him, Louis refused. 'No, let him go,' he said airily. Sadly, he still seems to have been playing games in a half-world of his own.

Of course, what happened was that Maussion immediately ran round to Captain Col-Puygélier's quarters, roused the sleeping officer who, hastily pulling on his clothes, hurried down to the barracks.

He found Louis and his men already in the barrack-square, the guards on sentry duty having obeyed Aladenize's orders to open the gates. Col-Puygélier advanced upon the intruders, sword in hand, Persigny tried to grab the sword and push him away, and there was a general tumult. in the confusion, Louis did what he had specifically ordered his men *not* to do: he fired his pistol, and a soldier fell wounded – mercifully, only slightly – in the face.[1]

That was it. The men of the 42nd, seeing one of their number fallen, turned angrily upon Louis and, in as good an order as they could, the intruders left the barracks and the gates were slammed fast behind them.

The next move was uncertain. Some of Louis' men wanted to hasten back to the *Edinburgh Castle* and get clean away but Louis would not hear of it. He marched his men up through the streets towards the Upper Town, contained, then as now, within its mediaeval stone walls; but, alerted by the Customs officers whom Louis had allowed to go free, the sub-Prefect denied him entry. All three gates were impenetrably barred against him.

Louis then embarked on a course the rationale of which historians still debate. Many of his men had by now deserted and run off down the narrow streets, tearing off the false insignia on their regimental tunics, but he ordered the remnants to march to the giant Column of the Grand Army which still exists today and was erected some two miles out of the town to commemorate Napo-

---

[1] This is Louis' explanation at his subsequent trial: 'There are moments when one cannot account for one's actions. When the tumult began, I drew my pistol; it went off without my having wanted to aim it at any one.' How many times have defendants charged with murder told some such story in the witness box – with varying results from their jury!

leon's attempt to invade England in 1805 from the wide, sandy beaches below.

It was then, as now, a somewhat remote spot of little or no strategic value. Some writers claim that Louis had decided, despite his earlier insistence on no bloodshed, to stand there and fight to the death; others say that he had determined to kill himself there or else wait dramatically for a government soldier's bullet to end his life. I believe that neither claim is correct. Jules Lombard forced the solitary sentry on duty to hand over the keys at pistol-point, then he ran up the stairs inside the column and planted the Imperial flag at its summit. That flag could have been seen for many miles around: is it too fanciful to believe that it was hoisted as a pre-arranged signal in case of success to call upon reinforcements that Louis had been promised – or perhaps half-promised – and that he now desperately hoped might still come?

There was no time to find the answer. Within a short while, troops and armed members of the National Guard (amateur soldiers on the lines of Britain's modern Territorial Army) came running up the hill from Boulogne. Louis drew his sword and wanted to stand and fight but Persigny, Dr Conneau and others pulled him away. Protesting, he was dragged down towards the beaches where, now that their quarry had thrown down their weapons in their flight, the brave bourgeoisie of the National Guard – *but not the soldiers* – fired into the sea as Louis and five others waded out through the bullet-peppered waters and tried to clamber aboard a lifeboat to make good their escape to the *Edinburgh Castle*. One fugitive was shot dead, two others severely wounded, a fourth drowned, Louis himself was slightly wounded – and the boat capsized. The four bedraggled survivors, including Louis, were dragged from the water and taken prisoner.

They and any other stragglers who could be found were marched under armed guard to the prison at Boulogne, and Louis' humiliation was complete.

The news travelled fast. The next day, Disraeli wrote to his wife: 'Louis Napoleon who last year nearly drowned us by his bad rowing has now upset himself at Boulogne. Never was anything so rash and crude.' The pro-government French newspapers ridiculed him, contrasting his abysmal failure with the magnificent triumphs of the great Napoleon, whose body was about to be brought back to France thanks to the strenuous efforts of their own noble king. *Punch* went even further and printed a cartoon showing a dripping wet Louis being fished out of the water on a boat-hook.

In the Boulogne of today, few people have even heard of the events of August 1840. The Tourist Office's guide to the town speaks glowingly of 'Boulogne and Napoleon', and proudly boasts: 'Several monuments celebrating the glory of the Emperor or witnessing his stay in Boulogne still exist.' But of his nephew, the third Emperor, there is not a word. A young assistant in the Tourist Office does not know that there was an abortive coup in the town by the future Napoleon III and his older female colleague says: 'He did not have a very illustrious career, did he?'

It is much the same with modern historians. In 1991, James F. McMillan wrote in his book, *Napoleon III:* 'The comic opera element was present from the start, and the expedition quickly degenerated into a débâcle even more complete than that of Strasbourg.' Few writers are prepared to give Louis the benefit of the doubt. As a modern French academic, Frédéric Bluche, has written in his standard work *Le Bonapartisme*, 'The piteous collapse of the Boulogne adventure has made people forget too quickly its meticulous preparation.'

But no one could be harder on himself than Louis: 'Boulogne was an overwhelming catastrophe for me,' he wrote two years later to Narcisse Vieillard. Yet, in a sense, he only has himself to blame for the harsh verdict of his contemporaries and of history, for he never uttered in public or even, it would seem, in private, one word of rebuke against the army officers who had let him down. One can surely be too forgiving.

For its part, the French Government was determined not to deal so leniently with Louis and his supporters as they had after Strasbourg. This time, the conspirators, including Louis himself, were all put on trial for treason, not before a jury of local citizens at an ordinary assize court but before the much more forbidding Court of Peers in Paris, consisting exclusively of dignitaries who owed their high position in the State to the benevolence of the king. Acquittals on any major scale were not to be expected.

One can understand why Louis-Philippe's ministers did not want to repeat the mistake of giving Louis the soft option of discreet exile in the United States. But although he was almost certain to be convicted, this inevitably high-profile trial gave him a marvellous opportunity to state his case to the French nation – and on French soil. He seized his chance magnificently.

The proceedings began on 28 September 1840 and, almost at once, Louis told the presiding judge, Baron Etienne Pasquier, who twenty years earlier had been proud to be his uncle's Prefect of Police: 'For the first time in my life, I am at last permitted to raise my voice in France and to speak freely to Frenchmen. Despite the guards who surround me, despite the charges that I have just heard read out, as I stand here within the walls of the Senate, so full of memories of my early childhood . . . I cannot believe that I have to justify myself here and that you can be my judges.'

He ended his opening address with similar defiance: 'One final word, gentlemen. I stand before you representing a principle, a cause, a defeat. The principle is the sovereignty of the people; the cause is the Empire; the defeat is Waterloo. You have acknowledged the principle; you have served the cause; you wish to avenge the defeat.'

He then started his evidence with the same air of calm dignity:

'What is your profession?' asked Pasquier.

'French prince in exile.'

'By what right do you wear the badge of the Legion of Honour?'

'I found it in my cradle.'

He would not admit that anyone else bore the blame for the failed insurrection. He steadfastly refused to incriminate anyone else, he insisted that he alone was responsible and that his friends in the dock beside him should be forgiven for following him.

He further claimed: 'Motives of honour and prudence forbid me to reveal how far-reaching and overwhelming were my reasons for counting on a success.' His sense of honour – perhaps aided subconsciously by feelings of shame at his own bungling on the day of the coup itself[1] – prevented him from raising a proper defence

---

[1] Namely, letting the two customs officers and Sub-Lieutenant Maussion go free to raise the alarm and losing control during the tumult at the barracks when he shot, however inadvertently, one of the soldiers.

to what has been the overwhelming, if unfair, verdict of history: that he had been foolhardy in the extreme.

In recent years, at least in France, attempts have been made to paint a fuller picture. In 1972, Jeanne Henri-Pajot claimed that she had found evidence that Louis suspected that his secret had been sold to Louis-Philippe's chief of police, Zangiacomi, and she asserted that, when he came to power, Louis called for the file and saw for himself that his suspicions were well-founded. 'He then had the generosity,' writes Jeanne Henri-Pajot, 'to destroy the letters which compromised three of his former companions. Not only did he not hold a grudge against them but they all benefited from the kindness of their former victim and they were all promoted to higher positions during his reign.'

But it was surely not just generosity of spirit on Louis' part, it was also a cynically shrewd assessment of the value of those who were useful to him. Almost certainly one of the three men referred to by Jeanne Henri-Pajot was General Bernard Magnan, one-time Commander-in-Chief of the Army of the North, whose role in the Boulogne episode is profoundly dubious, to say the least.[1] But once Louis had become Prince-President in 1848, there was nothing dubious whatsoever about Magnan's open sympathy for the new ruler's cause. He became one of Louis' strongest military supporters and in 1851 was rewarded with command of the troops in Paris. As such, he would play a vital part in the successful coup of 2 December 1852 which transformed overnight France's Second Republic into its Second Empire.

On 6 October 1840, the Court of Peers brought in its verdict. It was much as expected: Pierre Bure, Louis' foster-brother, was acquitted for lack of evidence but all the other main conspirators were found guilty. Lieutenant Aladenize was sentenced to deportation. General Montholon, Colonel Parquin, Jules Lombard and

---

[1] Ronald Zins, in his *Les Maréchaux de Napoléon III* published in 1996, writes that Magnan was 'gravely compromised by the evidence that he gave at the Court of Peers', despite his denials under oath that he had ever, in any way, encouraged Louis' endeavour.

Persigny were each sent to prison for twenty years,[1] Le Duff de Mésonan (who had clumsily tried to bribe General Magnan) got fifteen years, Joseph Orsi, the Italian banker, and the ever-faithful Dr Conneau were gaoled for five years.

The most severely treated was Louis. He was sentenced to 'perpetual imprisonment' in a fortress within the French frontiers. As the sentence was read out to him in his cell, he asked wryly: 'Is anything in France "perpetual"?'

Even at that lowest stage in his life, he still had sublime confidence in his destiny. He still believed that one day – somehow – he would govern France. He knew how many governments the country had seen since the Revolution of 1789, how many different rulers, how many amnesties, how many failed attempts to seize power. He also knew that Louis-Philippe was an old man, with an uncertain grip on power. He did not allow himself to lose hope.

They told him that within a few hours he would start the journey to the Château de Ham, a 400-year-old fortress in north-eastern France some eighty miles from Paris that was both a military garrison and a prison for the country's most important State prisoners. At the moment, it was empty of inmates: the last prisoners, the Prince de Polignac and other members of Charles X's government who had been thrown into gaol after their master was deposed, had left some time ago. But Louis knew the place, and its frightening reputation, set on the outskirts of the small town of Ham in the middle of the damp, cold and foggy marshes of the Somme. He had briefly spent some time there after the failed coup at Boulogne on his way to prison in Paris to await the trial at which he had just been sentenced.

Now he was returning and he knew that he was coming back to a grim, remorseless building where nothing had been spent on maintenance or repair for years. Where there were holes in the ceiling, the barred windows of the prison cells looked out only onto the thick surrounding wall, the tiled floors were broken and damp and, in winter, the icy chillness of the air outside crept

[1] As ever, Persigny seems to have been remarkably lucky – or adroit. He went straight into a military hospital at Versailles and at the end of a mysterious 'illness', of which we know no details and from which he never suffered in later life, he was set free under the care of a local doctor, promising not to leave the area.

through the ancient stones and into the very marrow of one's bones.

He knew that he was going to a living hell but he was still sure that one day his time would come.

Chapter Twelve

'Perpetual Imprisonment' (1840–46)

T HE CHATEAU DE HAM no longer exists. A present-day visitor
to Ham, a rather dull town of some 5,000 inhabitants,
will find only a few battered ruins. The forbidding stone
building on its outskirts that had stood for nearly 500 years was
dynamited by the retreating German army during World War One
in 1917.[1]

In recent years, a local organisation named *Les Amis du Château
de Ham* has done its best to clean and preserve the ruins which had
become overgrown and dilapidated and used as a rubbish dump.
Nowadays it is a quiet, charming curiosity, one more souvenir from
France's turbulent history.

But when, at about midday on 7 October 1840, the carriage
carrying Louis and a solitary police colonel arrived from Paris with
a mounted police escort, it must have seemed like an outpost of
hell. As the creaking drawbridge of the solid-walled gate tower was
lowered to receive him, one cannot believe that Louis did not feel,
for all his defiant hopes for the future, serious moments of anguish
and despair. The dark, vaulted passage beneath the gate tower led
out into a flagstoned courtyard lined on either side by the barracks
of the soldiers who were to guard him night and day while, in the

[1] Ironically, this was in delayed revenge for the fact that in 1870, during the Franco-
Prussian War that brought about Napoleon III's fall and the end of the Second Empire, the
château's garrison was the only one in all of France to receive the surrender of any German
soldiers.

middle, a half-decaying, two-storey prison building awaited him, its windows heavily barred. The sombre setting was ringed by a massively thick wall with giant corner towers and topped by ramparts lined with battlements from which, centuries earlier, defending archers had loosed their arrows.

By a strange quirk of history, on that very same day 5,000 miles away the frigate *Belle Poule* was casting anchor off St Helena and the Prince de Joinville was nervously preparing to receive with great ceremony the remains of Napoleon I.

By contrast, the dead Emperor's nephew found himself being led by armed soldiers up a crumbling stone staircase in the low-lying prison building, along a grubby, whitewashed passage and into a small, barely furnished room with holes in the ceiling through which the bare rafters were visible above. The paper curtains he was supposed to pull to cover the two windows were in shreds and the brick floor cracked and broken. This was to be his sitting-room and the cell on the other side of the passage his bedroom. It was in a similarly depressing state of disrepair and furnished with only a narrow bed, chairs, a white wooden wash-stand, a commode and an earthenware stove for heating. There was no bathroom.

In a few days, Louis was to be joined by three of his followers who had volunteered to be with him at the château. Two had preferred to serve their own prison terms in the same tough military prison as their friend rather than in the more relaxed régime of the civil gaol at Doullens where most of the other Boulogne conspirators were to serve their time. They were the old general, the Comte Montholon, and Dr Henri Conneau, the most loyal of all Louis' associates. But his third voluntary companion had not even been convicted of any offence: he was his valet, Charles Thélin, who, of his own free will, chose to continue looking after his master, even in prison.

Montholon was given two rooms on the ground floor, Dr Conneau was assigned a small bedroom adjoining Louis', and Thélin had another room on the same floor.

All three assembled three times a day for their meals in a fourth small room on Louis' floor. As might perhaps be expected of the French and almost certainly because of Louis' rank, the food, especially provided by the prison canteen, was both good and ample. Breakfast, served at 8.00 am, was only the classic *café au lait* and bread, and lunch at 11.30 was a plate of vegetables or meat, depending on choice but dinner at 5.30 was quite grand: consommé with boiled beef and a choice of two first courses followed by roast poultry, a salad and then dessert. The prison cook, Madame Quentin, was somewhat mean with the wine – only one bottle a day for the three of them – but she always insisted that it should be of the best Burgundy vintage.

The food was the only thing even halfway pleasant about Louis' incarceration.

The very setting of his prison was insanitary as well as depressing. Dr F. A. Simpson, who actually visited the château in the early years of the twentieth century as part of the research for his book *The Rise of Louis Napoleon*, saw it in much the same condition as when Louis was there. His description is graphic:

'[The château] still found its sombre reflection in the sluggish waters of a little-used canal running part of the way around its outer wall. From the marshy bank would steal up in the evening a white mist, halfway to greet the dark low-lying clouds which generally overhung the place by day. If the building itself was picturesque, the surrounding landscape was desolate and monotonous to a degree; while an unhealthy site combined with an inhospitable climate to render it a far from desirable dwelling-place.'

The first winter had a damaging and lasting effect upon Louis' health: the doors and windows of his rooms were ill-fitted and the brick floor was damp and uneven. For the first time in his life, he was afflicted with rheumatism from which he afterwards always suffered. Dr Conneau did not cease in his complaints to Henri Girardet, the army major in command of the château, who sent them on to Charles de Rémusat, Louis-Philippe's Minister of the Interior. Finally, Rémusat gave grudging permission for 600 francs to be spent on renovating the rooms. It was barely enough for the most obvious repairs but at least Louis acquired a new floor. Girardet told him that he might make further alterations at his own expense but Louis refused to spend his own money on 'putting a State prison into repair'.

Yet he did make certain additions to his furniture. In the bedroom, he set planks against the wall for a dressing-table and bought himself a more comfortable bed and a small mirror; for the sitting-room, he bought a small table with a desk lamp and a clock, and built with his own hands as many bookshelves as the narrow walls would take. He also installed a portrait of his mother (but not of his father) and marble busts of Napoleon and Josephine. He converted a small spare room on the first-floor passage into a make-shift laboratory while Dr Conneau, copying his example, built himself an aviary in the window at the end of the passage.

But life remained dour. Of the 400 soldiers stationed in the fortress, sixty were always on duty as sentries. Outside his own rooms, Louis was always followed by a police superintendent, Commissaire Leras, summoned from Paris the day after his arrival to keep him under constant surveillance and supply daily reports.[1] When he was allowed to walk on the ramparts (his only permitted exercise), sentinels watched his movements at every point, even including the far bank of the canal and if, as occasionally happened, townsfolk from Ham waved their hats in greeting, Louis was forbidden to acknowledge them, an order he studiously ignored, always raising his general's red kepi in reply. The authorities were taking no chances: four times a day Major Girardet had to satisfy himself personally of his prisoners' continued presence. All letters to and from Louis were opened and, if written in English, first sent to Paris for examination. Visits were strictly limited and all soldiers were forbidden to salute him, although he was invariably dressed in general's uniform, or even, except for his immediate guards, to acknowledge his existence.

General Montholon, with his memories of St Helena, wrote to a friend: 'The Emperor was not so badly treated by the English in an English prison as his nephew is by the French in a French prison.'

It took time for Louis to adjust to prison life. Nor was the process helped by the news given him in early December 1840 by his first visitor, a lawyer friend named Ferdinand Barrot, that his cousin, Princess Mathilde, whom he had never completely given up hope of marrying one day, had married a rich Russian prince – with the full blessing of her father, ex-King Jerome, a blessing that had been hurtfully withdrawn from him after the Strasbourg fiasco. 'This is

[1] Ironically, Commissaire Leras' first name was Napoleon. Like many youngish men in France at that time, he had been named after the Emperor.

the last and heaviest blow that fortune has in store for me,' Louis told Barrot.[1]

But at that stage of his life it was not yet in his nature to allow melancholy thoughts to warp his mind or blunt his actions. Years later, he was to tell his son, Louis, the Prince Imperial, when reading the boy's reports by his tutor, that he had himself been educated 'at the University of Ham'. In fact, it was self-education for he set himself to take advantage of his years of enforced isolation by reading an enormous number of books on every subject that interested him. They were readily supplied by the inner circle of friends who regularly kept in touch. Of these, the two closest were Narcisse Vieillard and Hortense Cornu, to whom in the five-and-a-half years that he was in prison he wrote no less than 232 letters. He told Narcisse Vieillard, 'To pass the time I occupy myself with 36,000 different things at the same time.'

He turned the first-floor passage dividing his sitting-room from his bedroom into, of all things, a miniature firing range where he experimented with firing bullets, later writing a detailed memorandum on a proposed new method of adjusting the percussion caps of military rifles, that he sent to the War Ministry in Paris for the personal attention of the Minister. He read voraciously about the English revolution of 1688 which drove the authoritarian monarch James II from the throne, bringing over in his place as joint sovereigns his liberal daughter, Queen Mary of Holland, and her husband, William of Orange. This was later to serve as the basis of a short book, *Fragments historiques 1688–1830*, published in May 1841, in which he compared the revolution in England with the revolution in France that had brought Louis-Philippe to the throne, the clear implication being that Louis-Philippe was nothing like so

[1] Ironically, the marriage was a disaster. Prince Anatole Demidoff proved a violent drunkard and womaniser who had bought the extravagant and always hard-up Jerome's consent with lavish gifts of money and jewellery. After four unhappy years, the resourceful Mathilde secured the Russian Tsar's consent to their legal separation by attending the court in St Petersburg in a low-cut, off-the-shoulder dress that clearly showed the scars and bruises of her husband's latest attack. She then formed a long-lasting relationship with Count Emilien Nieuwerkerke, a talented sculptor whom Louis, as emperor, made Superintendent of the Imperial Museums. She always retained a soft spot for her outspoken cousin, even though she quickly fattened in middle age and soon looked like Queen Victoria.

able a king as Dutch William. For our own purposes in seeking to understand Louis' own way of thinking, the book remains memorable for the one observation: 'March in the vanguard of the ideas of your time, and they will follow and support you. March behind them, and they will drag you down. March against them, and they will destroy you.'

Given that he had lost his liberty, life was not really too bad in those early months.

Yet Louis was never slow to make political capital out of any misfortune which befell him, including being in gaol. 15 December 1840 was the day on which the coffin bearing Napoleon I's remains was borne in triumph for reburial in the chapel of the Invalides. Louis-Philippe and the entire Court rose to their feet in salute as the Court Chamberlain bellowed: 'L'Empereur!' It was a great and emotional day throughout France and on that very morning there appeared in the streets of Paris a tribute written by Louis from his prison cell in which he hailed the dead spirit of his uncle in his own somewhat overblown style. 'Sire,' he wrote, 'you return to your capital and the people in their masses salute you but I, from the depths of my dungeon, can only see the rays of the sun which light up your funeral. Yet from the midst of your funereal pomp you have cast a glance on my sombre prison and you who caressed me when I was a child have said to me, "Friend, I am content with you. You suffer for me."'

After six months, that 'suffering' became less acute. The prison commandant, Major Girardet, whom Louis had charmed by inviting him to join the prisoners every evening for a convivial game of whist, battled on his behalf with the Minister of the Interior, Rémusat, and extracted some notable concessions. Louis was permitted to fit out a small laboratory in an unused room on his first-floor passage and a local chemist was allowed into the prison to spend many hours with Louis on experiments in electromagnetism, which later formed the basis of a treatise that Louis sent to the Academy of Sciences. He had loved gardens ever since his first visit to England more ten years earlier, and now he was authorised to dig up a few square metres of ground on the lower edges of a slope at one end of the ramparts, where he planted a few seeds and shrubs. Their growth, although stunted by the absence of sunlight blocked out by the high retaining wall, gave him real satisfaction. Furthermore, the local priest (whom he later made a bishop) was even allowed in to celebrate Mass once a fortnight for the three newly privileged prisoners.

But he still resented what he considered the personal indignities of his position. In mid-May 1841, he wrote to Charles de Rémusat: 'The sovereignty of the people made my uncle an Emperor, my father a king and myself a prince by birth.' He demanded to be treated more in accordance with his royal status. It worked. He was immediately granted three major further concessions, one that he be permitted to exercise on horseback; sadly, that soon proved a privilege not worth having. After a few weeks of riding solemnly round the courtyard on his own, with the walls lined with a doubled post of sentries and Major Girardet standing woodenly in the middle, he gave it up.

The other two concessions proved much more valuable. The first was that Thelin, his valet, was allowed to come and go as he liked and, although often still choosing to sleep in the prison so as to be near his master, he was allowed to take rooms in Ham, thereby giving Louis much easier access to the outside world. The second major concession was that Louis was allowed much greater freedom to receive visitors. From now on, Louise de Crenay, his pretty neighbour at Arenenberg, Baroness Salvage de Faverolles, his mother's executrix, his old friend Narcisse Vieillard and, of course, Hortense Cornu and her painter husband, Sebastien, came to see him frequently. In the summer of 1841, Hortense and Sebastian actually spent two whole days with him, spending the night at a nearby inn.

He also started writing again to his nineteen-year-old cousin, Prince Napoleon, ex-King Jerome's second son with whom he had become close after the younger man had been orphaned at the age of thirteen but with whom he had severed all contact after Jerome had broken off his engagement to Prince Napoleon's sister, Mathilde. This other nephew of the great Napoleon, nicknamed 'Plon-Plon' because of his childish attempts to pronounce the name 'Napoleon', was later to be almost pathologically jealous of Louis because he wanted to be the senior nephew. Erratic and pugnacious, resembling the great Napoleon more than Louis ever did, he was, after Napoleon's two surviving brothers, Joseph and Louis, next in line of succession to the Bonaparte throne. So, in November 1841, with characteristic sense of duty, Louis wrote to his estranged cousin to tell him that the night before he set sail for Boulogne he had drawn up a will naming him as his heir and, as such, he would always regard him. Thereafter, they resumed an outwardly cordial but not over-warm correspondence.

Adapting to life in prison, Louis now began writing a great deal of popular journalism on current political matters that was published in the newspapers and journals of northern France and sometimes even in Paris itself. He even considered undertaking a definitive biography of Charlemagne, creator of the Holy Roman Empire that had lasted for over a thousand years before being finally destroyed by Napoleon in 1806: its aim, of course, would have been to compare the great empire-maker with Napoleon himself. In the end, that proved too daunting a task: besides, Louis convinced himself, the great Charlemagne was only an all-conquering soldier and not also a philosopher and legislator like his uncle.

And so life went on: more articles, another short historical book and an updated artillery manual. His mind remained fertile even though his physical health continued to deteriorate in the unsalubrious conditions of his imprisonment and he never ceased to regret the loss of his liberty. In April, there was one bright spot: a bathroom was installed. We do not know if the other two prisoners were also allowed to use it.

Then on 10 June 1842, Louis sat down in his prison cell to write a long, impassioned letter to Narcisse Vieillard. Already briefly quoted from in Chapter 11 (his frank confession: 'Boulogne was an overwhelming catastrophe for me') but hidden away in its original French in an appendix to Blanchard Jerrold's official biography in 1874, it has not before been translated at length into English. Yet it gives a revealing insight into the deep roots of Louis' almost demonic faith in himself and in his cause at that dark stage in his life, a faith that later, once fame had been achieved and illness had weakened his resolve, he was sadly for him – and for France – to lose:

> You rely on method and calculation. With me, it is faith – a faith which makes one bear everything with resignation, a faith which makes one kick aside domestic joys, the envy of so many people,

a faith which, on its own, can move mountains. Certainly, they appeared truly blind, those men who, locked up in the prisons of Rome, believed that with a few humanitarian precepts they could overthrow the worldly power of Caesar, and yet they were able ultimately to do so.

You saddened me in your last letter by maintaining that I have committed error after error and I concede that Boulogne was an overwhelming catastrophe for me, even though I am at last managing to come to terms with it.

What have I achieved with what you call 'this series of little deeds and cruel troubles'?

An immense thing for me. In 1833, the Emperor and his son were dead: there were no longer any heirs to the Imperial cause in France. Some Bonapartes appeared, it is true, here and there on the backstage of the world like bodies without life, petrified mummies or imponderable phantoms; but for the people the line was broken; *all the Bonapartes were dead* [Louis' own italics]. I have restored the thread; I have resuscitated my fortunes by myself and by my own efforts and I am today at a distance of twenty leagues from Paris, a Sword of Damocles for the government. In a word, I have made my dinghy with the bark of trees I have myself cut down, I have fashioned my own sails, I have raised my oar and I do not demand more of the Gods than a wind to lead to me to victory.

. . . The Napoleonic cause goes to my soul; it stirs and rouses exciting memories, and it is always by appealing to the heart that one moves the masses, never by cold reason.

But with Louis one never remains long at the highest plains of human endeavour. During that very same month of June 1842 when he was pouring out his heart to Narcisse Vieillard on his grandiose certainties of achieving his political destiny, his mistress became pregnant. One could be forgiven for asking how this had come about.

A year earlier Louis had asked to have a mistress – and he already knew whom he had in mind. The story has a uniquely French charm. Eleonore Vergeot, whom everyone called Alexandrine, was a pretty twenty-year-old country girl with a full figure and vivacious eyes who, since January 1841, had been coming into the prison regularly to act as chambermaid to the Irish-born Caroline O'Hara, the mistress of General Montholon. Montholon, then fifty-eight, had, soon after arriving at the prison in mid-October 1840 within days of Louis and Dr Conneau, asked Major Girardet for Caroline to be allowed to accompany him, even though he was still married to his first wife.[1] It seemed a perfectly reasonable request to Girardet who duly passed it on to Rémusat in Paris and – *voilà* – the general's mistress was installed on the ground floor of the prison in two rooms adjoining his.

Caroline (who styled herself Comtesse Lee) could not possibly be expected to clean out her own quarters, so Alexandrine, who was well-known in the area as *La Belle Sabotière*, after the *sabots* or wooden clogs she was wont to wear, got the job.

According to local legend recounted to me by Eric Salandre of the present-day organisation *Les Amis du Château de Ham*, Louis soon spotted Alexandrine crossing the courtyard of the château and, in effect, decided that what was good enough for an ageing general was certainly good enough for him. He began pestering the commandant for Alexandrine to be allowed to visit him 'to clean and repair his linen'. At first, Girardet – who must have understood perfectly what Louis had in mind – put him off with one pretext after another but finally, on 25 May 1841, he wrote to Rémusat asking what formal reply he should make to these repeated requests. 'I have until now avoided giving him a direct answer which seems to have annoyed him a great deal and made him difficult to deal with,' he explained. The result: Louis' request was formally and immediately granted.

The further result was, as we have seen, that over a year later, in June 1842, Alexandrine became pregnant and by late autumn it was impossible not to recognise her condition. By then a new commandant, Major Gaston Demarle, had taken over from Henri Girardet. He too had been charmed by Louis, and was equally happy to join his distinguished prisoners for an agreeable game of whist in the evenings. But, with the best will in the world, there was a limit to how helpful or understanding he could be. Louis assured him that he would arrange for Alexandrine to have her

---

[1] Later, after the general had been widowed, Caroline became the second Comtesse Montholon.

child in Paris but, as the weeks ticked by and Alexandrine, filling out by the day, remained obstinately at the château, Demarle became more and more concerned. On 4 December, he wrote to Rémusat: 'I ask you to tell me, *Monsieur le Ministre*, what I am to do in this case where there is such long delay in ridding me of this young person.'

In the end, Alexandrine took the coach early in the New Year to the home of Hortense and Sebastien Cornu in Paris where, on 25 February 1843, she gave birth to a baby boy named Alexandre Louis Eugene. In accordance with Bonapartist tradition, he was given his father's Christian name but he was always known as 'Eugene'. Everyone seemed to be happy: the Cornus agreed to look after the child for the immediately foreseeable future; Louis was delighted to have had a son and wrote asking Sebastian to send him a sketch of mother and child; and, after satisfying herself that her baby was in good hands, Alexandrine was content to return to Ham where she seems to have been genuinely fond of her princely lover.[1] Two years later the story repeated itself and, on 18 March 1845, Alexandrine gave birth to Louis, her lover's second illegitimate son – or at least, the second one whom he actually acknowledged. He was named Alexandre Louis Ernest but was always known as 'Louis'. Again, the birth took place in Paris at the home of the Cornus who undertook to look after him. As before, Alexandrine then returned happily to Ham to fulfil her double role as mistress and mender of linen.

(Much later, in 1870, during the last days of the Second Empire, Louis made both boys counts. The younger of the two, Louis,

---

[1] According to local legend, again recounted by Eric Salandre, Eugene was not the only illegitimate son born to Louis in 1843. In October of that year, the Comtesse Lee, General Montholon's much younger mistress, also gave birth to a baby boy. Says M. Salandre: 'It is said that there was a love affair between the Comtesse and Napoleon III. Alexandrine and the Comtesse fell pregnant together and they both left for Paris during the same year to give birth.' Tittle-tattle or truth? We shall probably never know but what *is* known is that in 1870, shortly before leaving for the campaign that ended in defeat at Sedan, Louis asked the young man to come and see him at the Palace of St Cloud to bid him farewell. Of course, in all four volumes of his official biography, Blanchard Jerrold does not mention even one illegitimate son and refers not at all to *la Belle Sabotière* – but would one expect him to?

Comte de Labenne, has no living descendants: he died in 1882, at the early age of thirty-seven, his only child following him two years later aged four. But there are several living descendants of Eugene, Comte D'Orx who died in 1910 at the age of sixty-seven. Among them are his great-granddaughter Mlle Marie-Hélène Gémain D'Orx, an elegant and charming senior press officer with Radio France in Paris. When asked today whether she is proud to have the blood of Napoleon III, however diluted, flowing through her veins, she replies: 'Of course, but I am not so enthusiastic about having in my veins the blood of a chambermaid.')

The routine of life at the château continued. On 23 September 1843, Louis wrote to his cousin 'Plon-Plon': 'I am not unhappy because I believe that my sufferings are useful and I have the conviction of having done my duty, and of being the only member of my family to have done so, for I have sacrificed my youth, my fortune and my life to the triumph of the cause which we cannot desert without dishonour.' The reference to his lost fortune was perfectly true. During his mother's lifetime he had been totally dependent on her financially and, although he had inherited her considerable estate six years earlier upon her death in October 1837, it had by now nearly all slipped through his fingers. It was not only because of the high cost of his extravagant lifestyle in London but also because he had poured a great deal of his own money into the Boulogne adventure.

Adrien Dansette has calculated that by the end of 1843 Louis' expenses, although he was shut up in his prison cells at Ham, amounted to 200,000 francs a year and he was running an annual deficit in the region of 100,000 francs a year. He could not go on like that indefinitely.

Needless to say that did not prevent him, throughout his time at the Château de Ham, sending bottles of champagne to his fellow post-Boulogne prisoners in their civil gaol at Doullens.

1844, Louis' fourth year in captivity, began well enough. He continued to rise every morning at six to work with great zeal and concentration on two new projects. One was an update of his *Manuel d'artillerie* which later that year had a limited but prestigious success, and the other was an extended political pamphlet, *L'Extinction du paupérisme*, which was published that April. Indeed, it had a wide and immediate success bringing over many workers, and even some professional and middle-class republicans, to his cause. 'Speak to us often, noble captive, of deliverance and emancipation,' George Sand wrote to him in prison. 'The people are in irons, as you are; and the Napoleon of today [Louis himself] is he who personifies the sorrows of the people as the other Napoleon personified their glory.'

Although some British writers tend to underestimate the importance of this pamphlet, that has never been the case in France. 'It is probably his master work and expresses best his political philosophy,' Philippe Séguin, the leading French politician, wrote in 1990. Even to modern eyes, it is an effective combination of Napoleon-like generalities about the wondrous qualities of 'the people' and a persuasive exercise in vote-catching socialism for the working class.[1] Many people today regard socialism as a uniquely modern phenomenon but, in fact, over the past twenty years it had already become well-established in France as a powerful new philosophy not only among the workers themselves but also among an increasing number of left-wing intellectuals.

So, taking his cue from current socialist literature and, in particular, the highly influential book *Organisation du travail*, published five years earlier by Louis Blanc, a leading left-wing writer and politician, in which Blanc had asserted a 'right to work' that should be guaranteed by the State, Louis put his own paternalistic, Bonapartist gloss upon the idea. He directed his arguments not only to the working class but to all sections of society: 'Today, the reign of individual classes is finished. One can only govern with the support of the masses.'

He called for universal manhood suffrage, instead of the existing system based only on property, where every Frenchman – but not yet any Frenchwoman – should have the right to vote, irrespective of wealth or how much property they did, or did not, own. He showed clearly that he understood the grim realities of life: 'It is

---

[1] 'The best piece of propaganda that Louis could have produced,' according to J. M. Thompson. 'It would be to misunderstand the psychology of Louis Napoleon to see in it merely a piece of propaganda to rally to his cause the working class. Whatever may be the borrowings from other writers, it carries the unmistakable mark of his own ideas,' according to Adrien Dansette. The truth, as so often, is probably a mixture of the two: they *were* his own ideas but he knew full well the strong impact they would have.

with financial reality that one must find the supporting pillar of any system which has for its goal the relief of the working class.'

This combination of 'one nation-ism' plus a seemingly genuine concern for the under-privileged informs the entire work:

> The working class possesses nothing. It must be given property. It has no wealth except in its strength. This strength must be given work which will benefit everyone. It must be given a place in society and its interests attached to those in the land. It lacks organisation and is without roots, without rights and without a future. It must be given rights and a future, and it must be given self-respect by partnership, education and discipline.
>
> Without organisation the masses are nothing, disciplined they are everything. Without organisation, they can neither speak nor be understood.

To provide this 'organisation', Louis advocated setting up military-style associations of working men under leaders who were like army officers. These associations would have the right to compulsory purchase of the nine million hectares of wasteland in France. The state would then lend these associations the money with which to attract unemployed workers from the cities who would till the land for a decent wage and make it pay its way by selling their products on the open market. Out of these proceeds, the associations would pay their workers, repay their loans to the State – and pay an annual rent to the original owners for the use of their land.

It was socialism but with a neat capitalist twist, for Louis did not argue that the landowners should suffer the enforced appropriation of their property without compensation and, as Frédéric Bluche has pointed out, he was careful to preserve the right of private property. The pamphlet, therefore, had powerful resonance for a France where the middle class, though prosperous, was stifling in bourgeois boredom while the working class, for the most part desperately poor, yearned for someone in authority who would speak directly to them.[1] It is little wonder that the pamphlet went into six

---

[1] Thierry Lentz makes the point that few workers actually read the pamphlet in its entirety but its message was widely known by word of mouth.

editions between 1844 and 1848 and within months of its original publication Louis Blanc himself, the arch-socialist and committed republican, came to visit Louis in prison.

Later he wrote: 'I shall never forget our stroll on the narrow rampart assigned to his melancholy walks and overlooked on all sides by sentinels. I think I see him yet, walking with slow steps, his head bent; I think I still hear his voice, speaking low, lest the wind should carry his words to the gaoler.'

It is perhaps sad to record that when eventually Louis governed France and had ample opportunity to create the workers' associations of which he had written so passionately in *L'Extinction du paupérisme*, he almost totally failed to do so, except on a very small scale in the marshy south-west region of France called the Landes, where he bought some land himself and instituted for himself and other landowners a State-subsidised system of land reclamation. For the rest, the ideas in the pamphlet remained unfulfilled.

Why is this so? An earlier generation of French writers was quick to accuse Louis of blatant opportunism, cynically writing politically correct ideas that he had no intention of putting into effect. That would seem to be too harsh. As Philippe Séguin has written, defending Louis' sincerity, 'There are impressive examples of the realisation of his social ideals during his years in power.'[1] These are, among other precedent-setting innovations, a free health service for the poor (1849); State pensions for the elderly and poor (1850); an early version of free legal aid for poor workers (1851); legal holidays on Sunday and religious festivals (1851) and the right to strike (1864).

One thing has to be said for Louis: many other European countries – including Britain – had to wait many years, if not decades, for such far-reaching and beneficial reforms.

In July 1844, ex-King Joseph, Napoleon I's oldest surviving brother, died at the age of seventy-six in Florence. Louis had for some years been reconciled with his uncle and genuinely mourned his passing but he was acutely conscious that now only his sixty-six-year-old father, ex-King Louis, stood between him and his just entitlement

[1] In Jean Tulard's *Dictionnaire du Second Empire* in 1995.

to the Imperial throne of France.[1] The former King of Holland, with whom Louis had had no contact since going to prison (he had taken it as almost an affront to his own personal dignity that his son was a prisoner of state), was by now genuinely – and not only in his imagination – in failing health and it could be only a matter of time before Louis would, at least in theory, 'inherit' the throne.

He seems, for a while, to have lost his overwhelming confidence in his destiny. His health weakened by four long years shut up in an ancient prison set amid damp marshes, he grew uncharacteristically melancholy. 'I say a prayer every day for you and your husband,' he wrote to Hortense Cornu. 'You will smile, I dare say; but I pray every evening for those I love. There are not more than fifteen of them, so it is a very short prayer.'

There was only one answer: he must get out of prison. He must be free.

In January 1845, he wrote to his English friend Lord Malmesbury, whom he had known ever since they were young men together in Rome in the late 1820s, asking him to visit him 'on a matter of vital importance'. Malmesbury, who was already prominent in British politics (seven years later he was to be Foreign Secretary), readily agreed but warned Louis that it might take some time to gain official French approval. The months of waiting passed heavily. 'Being in prison is like waiting for death,' Louis wrote to Hortense Cornu on 14 February. 'Nobody writes to me now, they have all forgotten me.'

But on 20 April 1845 Lord Malmesbury strode into Louis' room with outstretched hand. 'I found him little changed,' he later wrote in his memoirs, 'although he had been imprisoned five years, and very much pleased to see an old friend fresh from the outer world, and that world London. As I had only half a day allowed me for the interview, he confessed that, although his confidence and courage remained unabated, he was weary of his prison, from which he saw no chance of escaping, as he knew that if the French Government

---

[1] At this stage, Napoleon I had only one surviving brother, his fourth and youngest, ex-King Jerome. His third brother, Lucien, had died in 1840 but he had not been in line of succession because he had married a divorcee against Napoleon's wishes. He was the Emperor's only brother not to have been made a puppet king but merely given the title of Prince of Canino.

gave him an opportunity of doing so they might shoot him in the act.

'He stated that a deputation had arrived from Ecuador offering him the Presidency of that Republic if Louis-Philippe would release him, and in that case he would give the King his word never to return to Europe. He had therefore sent for me as a supporter and friend of Sir Robert Peel, at that time our Prime Minister, to urge Sir Robert to intercede with Louis-Philippe to comply with his wishes, promising every possible guarantee for his good faith.

'. . . "My power is in an immortal name," he told me, "and in that only; but I have waited long enough, and I cannot endure imprisonment any longer." '

Malmesbury promised to do his best but held out no great hope of success.

In fact, he underestimated his abilities because within less than a month an emissary came from Louis-Philippe offering Louis immediate release from prison – if he gave a formal undertaking to take no further action against his Government and to renounce all claims to the throne. Louis had not lost his pride: he refused the undertaking.

He did not, however, give up his efforts to gain his freedom. Instead, he fell back on his old skills as a manipulator. It was well known within the Bonaparte family that the health of his father, ex-King Louis, had begun seriously to deteriorate: real illness was now taking over from the one-time hypochrondia. Louis was never slow to try and turn any situation to his own advantage. Seven years earlier, after his mother's death, he co-operated in writing a self-glorifying pamphlet about his failed coup at Strasbourg in a deliberate, and successful, attempt to force the French Government into asking Switzerland to expel him, and so brand him to the world as an unfairly hounded political martyr. Now he used his surviving parent in much the same kind of ploy.

On 20 August 1845, he wrote out of the blue a fulsomely affectionate letter to his ageing father on his forthcoming Saint's Day, his first letter to ex-King Louis during the entire five years of his captivity. 'The Feast of St Louis approaches,' he wrote. 'In writing to you, dear father, I cannot repeat the banalities common on such occasions. But I will tell you that every evening I address to God fervent prayers for those I love; and in them my first thought is to ask for the lengthening of your days and the realisation of my dearest wish – that of seeing you again, and being able once more to embrace you.'

The letter had the desired effect. Louis must have realised that, even in the unlikely event of the French authorities permitting him to leave prison on some kind of compassionate leave to visit his dying father, it was perhaps even more unlikely that the authorities in Florence would have allowed him entry into the Grand Duchy of Tuscany, with its close links to the Austrian Empire. The Grand Duke, Leopold II, was the nephew of Francis II, the Austrian Emperor from whose troops Louis had fled, under sentence of death, for his part in the abortive Italian uprising fourteen years earlier. Yet it achieved its immediately desired effect. The failing ex-King Louis wrote back almost at once saying that his own 'dearest wish' was to see one more time his only surviving son before it was too late. 'Yesterday,' Louis replied on 19 September 1845, 'I had the first real joy I have experienced for five years when I received the kind letter you were so good to write . . . Till then I was resolved to do nothing at all to leave my prison.[1] For I had nowhere to go, nothing to do . . . But now a new hope dawns on my horizon, a new object presents itself for my efforts.'

Louis realised that it would be better for the first official approach to the French authorities not to come from him, so he asked his father to write formally to the French Government requesting a special dispensation for him to visit Florence. Ex-King Louis went one better than this and sent his personal secretary to Paris, armed with letters to two leading Ministers.

But this intervention from the late Emperor's brother cut no ice. The Ministers did not even condescend to reply.

Louis persevered. On 23 December 1845 he wrote himself to General Duchatel, the new French Minister of the Interior, promising on his honour that, if he were permitted to travel to Florence, he would return and 'place himself at the disposal of the Government'. Duchatel replied, but only to reject the offer.

By now, Louis was desperate. He wrote again to Paris, this time

---

[1] The bizarre invitation to become President of Ecuador and Lord Malmesbury's efforts only a few months earlier to obtain Louis' release show this to be a cynical – but emotionally useful – lie.

to Louis-Philippe personally, 'appealing to his humanity' to overrule his Government's decision. The only reply – in the form of a second letter from Duchatel – was an insistence that Louis must first sign a renunciation of his claim to the throne and a request for pardon for his 'offences' at Strasbourg and Boulogne. Louis valued his honour even more than his freedom (or a desire to see his father): his own response this time was, as one might perhaps have expected, an equally firm refusal.

But that only masked a new determination to leave prison. While he would still continue to maintain that his immediate aim was only to see his father one last time before he died, he was now resolved on the only possible course that remained to him: escape. And this was so even though he knew that, as he had told Lord Malmesbury, the French Government would be only too happy to have him shot in the attempt.

On 23 January 1846 he wrote to Hortense Cornu: 'The whole thing has broken down. I shall not leave Ham now unless it is to go to the Tuileries or to the graveyard.'

Chapter Thirteen

The Great Escape
(1846)

D ECIDING TO ESCAPE WAS one thing but Louis soon found
that waiting for the right opportunity was another.

First, there was the question of finance: not so much the
cost of the escape itself but the expense of living in appropriate
style thereafter. This was a problem that Louis had had to face
towards the end of the previous year before he had begun seriously
to think of escape but when there was still a reasonable chance of
Louis-Philippe giving him his freedom on one pretext or another.
His father was slowly dying and, as the only surviving son reconciled to a one-time hostile parent, he could expect to benefit
substantially from ex-King Louis's will, as proved to be the case.
But his inheritance from his mother had almost gone and his father
was, after all, not yet dead; apart from that, with the irascible
ex-King Louis one could never be sure of anything, least of all his
continued benevolence.

So, if Louis was, as a free man, to have a lifestyle worthy of his
royal dignity, a substantial loan was needed.

It came from a most unusual source: the eccentric Duke Charles
II of Brunswick, a small, independent duchy in Germany. Charles
had been driven from his throne some years earlier in favour of his
younger brother because of popular discontent with his chaotic,
half-mad rule. But, extremely wealthy in his own right, he had
never given up hopes of a triumphant return. He was therefore easy
plunder for Louis' astute Italian banker friend Count Joseph Orsi
who, in the autumn of 1845 and recently released from a French
gaol for his part in the Boulogne adventure, was once again living
in some splendour in London.

In December 1845, by a combination of lies and flattery, Orsi

successfully negotiated with Charles a loan at only 5 per cent interest of 150,000 francs' worth of bonds. The loan was rather grandly
called a 'treaty of alliance' in which the would-be emperor and the
deposed duke agreed to help each other gain power in their respective countries.[1]

But Louis had to sign both documents, the bonds and the 'treaty'.
How was that to be possible? The problem was solved in an appropriately conspiratorial way.

On a specially requested visit to Ham in early January 1846,
which was only allowed to take place in the presence of Major
Demarle because the château commandant was suspicious of these
two former plotters meeting so soon after Orsi's release, Orsi shook
hands warmly with Louis and slipped into his palm the bonds and
the 'treaty', written on satin. When the time came for Orsi to leave,
the two men once again cordially shook hands with Demarle again
looking on, and this time it was Louis who slipped into the departing
banker's hand the two documents, newly signed. Two days later,
back in London, the bonds were safely in the possession of Baring
Brothers, Louis' English bankers.

But ensuring sufficient funds for survival when freedom was at
last achieved was only a preliminary matter. The really essential
question was how to escape from an impregnable stone fortress
with a garrison of 400 of whom sixty were always on duty as
sentries.

As the early months of 1846 passed, even Louis' nimble mind could
not come up with a practical solution. For days on end he discussed
the problem with Dr Conneau who, ironically, did not have the
same problem. His own five-year gaol term had ended in October
1845, when he could have returned home to his wife and family,
a free man. But, in a remarkable display of loyalty and love, he
had refused to leave Louis and insisted on remaining with him as
a voluntary prisoner.

In vain the two men tried desperately to think of a foolproof
plan for Louis to escape but the task seemed impossible. (Louis did
not bring the other remaining prisoner, General Montholon, into

[1] In fact, Charles never regained power and died in embittered exile in 1873, ironically,
the same year as Louis.

the discussions because he did not entirely trust the ageing soldier. Montholon had a fearsome reputation for always looking after himself first, and might well have won his own freedom by betraying Louis' intentions to Major Demarle.)

Then, in the third week of April 1846, a new development dramatically changed the situation: workmen arrived at the château to carry out long overdue maintenance and repairs to the centuries-old building. For the first time since Louis had entered the château nearly six years earlier there were strangers milling around, coming and going daily.

The schemers did not have much time to come up with a viable plan: the workmen's job was only due to take, at the very most, a month.

It did not take long for Louis and Dr Conneau, studying intently how the workmen went about their task, to notice something extraordinary. It was this: when the workmen arrived at 5.00 am the guards at the main gate would carefully scrutinise them and check their passes, and the process was repeated even more carefully, with Major Demarle looking on, when the workmen left in the late afternoon. But if a workman should happen to walk out on his own during the day to throw some rubbish on a dump set up outside the château walls, no one looked at his pass at all! He simply walked out and came back in at his leisure, also with no one asking to see his pass.

There were other apparent lapses in security. Normally, two soldiers always guarded the foot of Louis' staircase inside the prison building itself but now he and Dr Conneau noticed that, on a Saturday morning, one of these guards went to fetch the weekly newspapers from the town at about 6.00 am. While he was away, for as long as fifteen to twenty minutes, only one guard was left on duty and, if Charles Thélin, Louis' valet, came down just ahead of him on some innocuous journey, such as taking Louis' dog, Ham, for a walk, it would obviously be much easier for him to distract one man's attention than two.

So Louis came up with this bold but simple plan: shortly after 6 o'clock on a Saturday morning, the workmen having arrived as usual about an hour earlier and with only one guard on duty downstairs, he would put on a workman's clothes, shave off his moustache, carry a plank of wood[1] over his shoulder so as to hide one side of his face, allow Thélin to go downstairs first with the dog and then follow him past the solitary guard below. Thélin would take the dog out for a walk, as he often did; Louis, in his workman's disguise, would follow him across the château's inner courtyard and stroll out through the main gate to freedom, as if to throw the wooden plank on the dump outside – with no one asking for his pass. He would have to walk past the windows of the commandant's house that overlooked the courtyard, but at that time Demarle was suffering from an attack of rheumatism brought on by the damp conditions of the château and was not getting up for the day until some two hours later, at about 8.00 am.

Louis was enthusiastic about the idea and was sure that it would work, but Dr Conneau thought it was far too risky. Louis insisted that it was his only chance, assuring his friend that it was now or never. Conneau gave way and, with typical loyalty, agreed to help by giving him valuable cover by telling the authorities, if they wanted to see Louis, that he was ill in bed.

At that point, the two conspirators brought Thélin and Pierre Bure (closer to Louis than many a blood brother, he had come to live in Ham specifically to be near him) into the plot. Bure had handled Louis' personal household accounts ever since Queen Hortense's death and now, with normal princely disdain for getting himself involved in money matters, Louis asked Dr Conneau and Bure to handle the financial side of his escape.

Conneau therefore duly asked Bure for some money in cash which he promptly handed to Thélin and told him to go into Ham and buy a set of workman's clothes, dye to darken the prison pallor of Louis' face, a wig to cover his head and a pair of wooden clogs to give him added height. One can read in *Papiers et correspondance de la Famille Impériale*, in Bure's scrupulously kept accounts, the details of this expenditure totalling the grand sum of 25 francs and 25 centimes.[2]

---

[1] In fact, a bookshelf taken from Louis' cell.

[2] Throughout the Second Empire the legend persisted that Louis had escaped from Ham, not with workman's clothes bought for him by his valet but wearing clothes loaned to him by a workman at the château named Badinguet. The name was a derogatory nickname in colloquial nineteenth-century French and many anti-Establishment pamphlets referred to

The expenses may have been small but the risks were great. As Louis himself later wrote to his friend, Frédéric Degeorge, editor of a local newspaper, it was 'the boldest undertaking I have ever attempted for which more resolution and courage were necessary than at either Strasbourg or Boulogne, for I had determined not to endure the ridicule which is the lot of persons arrested under a disguise and failure would have been insupportable.' What he did not tell Degeorge was that, to guard against the 'ridicule' which failure would have brought, he had decided to slip into his pocket a dagger with which to kill himself, if caught.

As so often in his life, Louis was not lacking in physical courage.

The day fixed for the escape was Saturday, 23 May, but before that, one more matter had to be resolved: what would happen to Eleonore Vergeot, Louis' mistress who practically lived in the château? Louis had never pretended that he loved her with any great passion and had never made any promises about any possible future life together, but he was fond of her and it was not in his nature simply to leave and make no provision whatsoever for her.

So on Wednesday 20 May, three days before Louis' planned departure, a carriage trundled out of the main gate of the château taking a weeping Eleonore to Paris where she was to join her two sons at the home of Hortense and Sebastien Cornu. Pierre Bure sat beside her, vainly trying to console her. Louis had asked Bure to look after Eleonore and that is exactly what he did: perhaps more than Louis intended. He took her over as his own mistress and, after a short stay with the Cornus, she went with her boys to live with him in his new home in Paris, and eventually they had a son of their own.

In 1858, by which time Louis, then Emperor, had made Pierre Treasurer-General to the Crown, they were married and Pierre formally acknowledged all three boys as his own. The couple lived

Louis contemptuously as Badinguet and even to his wife, the Empress Eugenie, as Badinguette, the feminine version of the name. After the publication of *Papiers et correspondance de la Famille Impériale* in 1871, this practice should have stopped but amazingly even such reputable contemporary French biographers as André Castelot (1973) and Philippe Séguin (1990) still write about Louis having made his escape in clothes borrowed 'from a mason named Badinguet'. Some myths are stronger than facts.

together in perfect harmony until his death in 1882, Eleonore's following four years later.

In the event, Louis did not try to escape on 23 May, 1846. On the day before, Major Demarle came to see him to say that two English friends who had several months earlier asked to visit him had at last received their permits, and would be coming the next day. Louis did his best to appear delighted but it can easily be imagined how he really felt: apart from anything else, the workmen were due to finish within the next few days and there would not be another Saturday morning when only one guard was on duty downstairs in that vital gap shortly after 6.00 am.

There was no alternative: the escape attempt would have to take place on a weekday, even though that meant two guards would be on duty downstairs. Louis decided to make his escape on the very next possible day: Monday 25 May.[1]

Despite his disappointment at the delay, Louis was able to squeeze some kind of benefit out of it. The original plan had been for Thélin to hire a cabriolet in Ham the night before, collect it after leaving the château with Louis' dog and, after handing the animal over to a friend, join Louis on the outskirts of the town and drive him to St-Quentin, a nearby town. There they could easily hire a larger post-chaise, which would take them fifty miles to Valenciennes, only nine miles from Belgium on a new railway. The two men would part at Valenciennes and Louis would take the train on his own, armed with a false passport obtained for him by Thélin a few days earlier from Bonapartist supporters in Paris.

Now, because of his friends' visit, Louis was able to have the pleasure – and extra comfort – of taking Thélin along with him, for he was able to persuade Lady Crawford, one of his two visitors, to hand over one of her servants' passport by telling her that he wanted to send Thélin on an errand to Belgium. She readily agreed because she knew she could easily claim that the passport had been lost and obtain a replacement from the British Ambassador in Paris.

On the Sunday evening, 24 May, Louis sat down and wrote three farewell letters to be handed over only after he had gone. The first was to General Montholon, confined to bed with the rheumatism,

[1] Sunday was not appropriate since no workmen came to work that day.

the curse of many at the château. Louis explained that he had told him nothing of his plans because he wanted to protect him from possible reprisals by the authorities. He also wrote that he hoped his escape would lead to the general's own speedy release, which, in fact, happened within a few months. But part of the letter deserves to be quoted in full to show, yet again, his charm and his generosity:

> Believe me, General, I was very sorry not to have shaken your hand before I left. But I could not have done it; my emotion would have betrayed the secret I wished to keep from you. I have taken steps to ensure the payment of your pension. As you may have need of money in advance, I have given Conneau two thousand francs which he will give to you.

The two other letters were more mundane: one to thank the local chemist who had helped him pass his time with scientific experiments, the other to the local priest who had regularly visited the prisoners to celebrate Mass.

Then, with his moustache still not yet shaven off in case something else went wrong and he had again to postpone, at the last moment, his departure, he and his colleagues went to bed.

At 6.30 on the Monday morning, looking out from behind the curtains of their rooms, Louis and his two companions saw the workmen arriving to start their new week's work.[1]

Louis was already prepared for the day's events. At daybreak, he had, with Thélin's help, shaved off his moustache and put on his ordinary clothes, slipping into an inside pocket two letters that were never to leave him and would be found, tear-stained in his wallet, twenty-seven years later upon his death. These were a letter that the Emperor Napoleon had written to Queen Hortense, when Louis was very young, saying that he 'hoped he would grow up to be worthy of the destinies that await him' and Hortense's own letter to him of April 1837 when she faced the prospect of an

---

[1] This account of the day of Louis' escape is taken from several sources, some of which differ in detail between themselves (as often, sadly, happens with historical research), but I am primarily indebted to Louis' own account to Frédéric Degeorge, and Dr Conneau's evidence in the witness box when tried two months later for his part in the affair.

operation from which she knew she might never recover: 'If it does not succeed, I send you . . . my last blessing. We shall meet each other again, . . . in a better world where you will come to join me only as late as possible. And you will remember that in leaving this world I regret only you – only your gentle affection which alone has given my life some charm.'

Then he slipped a sheathed dagger into the same pocket and put on top of his ordinary wear the workman's clothes that were to aid his disguise: a coarse undershirt, blue trousers, a blue blouse and a workman's apron. He added a dash of rouge to his cheeks to disguise their prison pallor and carefully placed a full black wig on his head, then a peasant's country hat. A pair of wooden clogs for extra height and he was ready. Dr Conneau reassured him: 'Don't worry. No one will recognise you!'

At 6.45, Charles Thélin strolled out into the first-floor passage where workmen were already busy painting the top of the stairway and asked if they would like an early morning drink on that fine, chilly day. Readily they agreed and all trooped downstairs to the ground-floor room used by Louis as a laboratory. As the men happily drank each other's health in rather good brandy, Thélin slipped out, hastened up to his master and told him the moment had come.

Louis took the plank that was lying in readiness, put a clay pipe in his mouth (a somewhat pathetic attempt to heighten the working-class image) and stepped out into the passage a few paces behind Thélin who had caught hold of Louis' dog, and had already started to carry him downstairs.

Louis was hardly out of the door of his cell when a lone workman suddenly appeared in the passage, as if from nowhere. Instinctively, Louis half-stepped back but Dr Conneau, hard behind him, muttered: 'Go on then!' and gently pushed him forward. With the plank over one shoulder and the clay pipe clenched firmly between his teeth, Louis carried on; the workman ignored him and Louis, his heart pounding, walked slowly down the stairs.

At the entrance to the prison building, Thélin, still slightly ahead of Louis, engaged the attention of one of the two guards with some trite remark about the weather and Louis walked past the other, his face hidden from the guard by the plank on his shoulder.

Then came potential disaster. Louis, who smoked only cigarettes, was not used to walking with a pipe in his mouth. As he crossed the open courtyard with several soldiers and workmen milling around, the clay pipe fell from his lips and shattered. But he did not panic. He stopped, knelt down and carefully picked up all the pieces.

He then passed the officer commanding the guard who was – perhaps fortunately – reading a letter and, when he reached the soldiers on duty at the gate, gruffly asked leave to pass. These soldiers – especially a certain drummer, as Louis later wrote to Degeorge – looked curiously at this peculiar workman who wore clogs on a fine day (usually they were only worn in bad weather as protection against mud underfoot) but again Thélin came to his master's aid with a bit of comic 'business' involving the dog. The gate-keeper opened the gate and Louis walked out on to the lowered drawbridge.

But he was still not out of danger. As he crossed the bridge, he saw two workmen coming towards him. Hastily he transferred the plank to his other shoulder to mask his face from this other direction. As he passed them, he heard them say: 'Oh, it's Berthoud.'

After that all went well. Louis walked slowly on. Thélin passed him without any sign of recognition and hurried on towards Ham to collect the hired cabriolet while Louis hastened as fast as plank and clogs would allow him along the main road towards St-Quentin. A cemetery on the outskirts of Ham, about a mile and a half from the château, was the arranged meeting-point. Arrived there, Louis hid his plank and the clogs in a cornfield and sat down to wait for Thélin. But first he fell on his knees before a cross in the graveyard and thanked God for his deliverance. He had not lost his sense of humour. 'Don't laugh,' he wrote a week later to Narcisse Vieillard. 'There are instincts which are stronger than all philosophical arguments but God preserve you from ever feeling them under similar circumstances.'

They must have looked an odd pair travelling on the road to St-Quentin in their single-horse cabriolet: Thélin, dressed like a valet, and Louis, still wearing his crude wig but dressed again like a gentleman, his workman's clothes thrown into a nearby ditch. Arrived at the outskirts of St-Quentin, Louis stepped down from the cabriolet while Thélin went into town to hire the post-chaise to take them on the next stage of their journey. Louis skirted half the the town on foot and, as agreed, waited for Thélin at the start of the road to Cambrai leading on to Valenciennes. After a while, with no sign of Thélin, he grew anxious. Seeing a man coming along in a carriage from the centre of the town, he asked him if he had seen a post-chaise he was waiting for. 'No, sir,' replied the man and it was only later that Louis discovered that he had been talking to the Public Prospector of St-Quentin.

They reached Valenciennes in good time at 2.15 pm, arriving at its new railway station an hour and three-quarters before the 4.00 pm train to Brussels. At first, Louis wanted to hire another cabriolet and drive the nine miles across the frontier to Belgium and safety but, since the building of the railway, few people crossed the frontier by road and, on further consideration, he realised it might have attracted too much attention.

They had a long, anxious wait at Valenciennes station. At one point, their hearts were in their mouths as an off-duty gendarme in civilian clothes from Ham who knew Thélin, came up to him, ignored his bewigged companion, and asked him what he was doing there and enquired after Prince Louis Napoleon's health. Thélin replied that he was no longer in the Prince's service but had taken a job with the railway company.

That seemed to satisfy the gendarme. He wandered off and left Louis and his valet waiting nervously for their train. Thélin could not stop looking back from time to time along the road from Cambrai in case he saw a posse of policemen coming after them.

But he need not have worried. No one at the château yet knew that Louis was missing. Dr Conneau had played his role superbly and had convinced the guards that Louis was ill in bed and could not be disturbed.

He told the commandant the same story when Demarle came to see Louis for his usual afternoon visit and Demarle duly went away; but when he returned later that evening for his usual game of whist, Demarle was not so easily dismissed. He insisted on seeing his prisoner with his own eyes, strode into his bedroom, pulled down the sheets – and found a home-made dummy with its face turned towards the wall. 'The Prince has escaped!' he said.

'*Mais oui*,' smiled the doctor.

By then Louis had been safely in Belgium for several hours.

Dr Conneau was promptly handcuffed and put under arrest. Two months later, he was put on trial at the nearest assize town of Péronne, convicted of aiding a prisoner to escape and gaoled for three months. Thélin, similarly charged and convicted – but in his absence – was sentenced to six months' imprisonment which he never served.

In the early evening of Wednesday 27 May Louis and Thélin arrived in London from the Belgian port of Ostend and went straight to the Brunswick Hotel in Jermyn Street, off Piccadilly. As Louis alighted from the carriage and entered the hotel (to register as the Count of Arenenberg), he saw his old friend Lord Malmesbury riding by on his way to dinner with the Duke of Beaufort. He ran over to him and they greeted each other warmly. Later, as the Duke's guests were sitting down to dinner, Lord Malmesbury found himself face to face with the Comte Louis de Noailles, who was an attaché at the French Embassy. 'Have you seen him?' he asked.

'Who?' said de Noailles.

'Louis Napoleon,' replied Malmesbury with a smile. 'He is in London. He has just escaped.'

Malmesbury later recorded in his diary: 'De Noailles dropped the lady who was on his arm and made but one jump out of the room. I never saw a man look more frightened.'

Chapter Fourteen

Enter Miss Howard
(1846–8)

'MISS HOWARD', AS FRENCH biographers of Napoleon III still call her to this day,[1] was born Elizabeth Ann Harryet in August 1823 in Brighton. The daughter of a bootmaker who made shoes for the town's fashionable women and granddaughter of a prosperous local hotel owner, she was brought up as a respectable middle-class girl who presumably would eventually marry a respectable middle-class young man and have the appropriate number of children.

But from a very young age 'Lizzie', as her friends called her, wanted to be an actress, in those days a profession regarded in solid English middle-class circles as only one degree removed from prostitution. Her parents forbade her even to think of such a career, but Lizzie was headstrong as well as pretty. At the age of fifteen, she ran off with Jem Mason, a famous jockey of the day, who had many useful contacts in the theatre and promised to help her follow her chosen profession.

The break with her parents was absolute. Lizzie changed her surname to 'Howard' and described herself as an orphan. Helped by Mason's contacts and her own shining young beauty, she landed her first part, in a comedy called *The Love Chase* – at London's Haymarket Theatre in January 1840, at the age of sixteen. To tell the truth, she did not have very much talent and subsequent parts were few and far between.

[1] For example, Philippe Séguin (1990) and Thierry Lentz (1995). In fact, 'Miss Howard' has had no English biographer but an excellent French one, Simone André Maurois (1956), whose work, partly based on family research with her twentieth-century descendants, is far more helpful and reliable than the passing references to her in Louis' English biographers.

She did not like living with a man who was not her husband and, although she did not love Mason, was forever asking him to marry him. After three years he became fed up with the continual nagging and looked around for someone to pass her on to. Eton-educated Francis Mountjoy Martyn, a major in the 2nd Life Guards whom Mason knew through racing circles, seemed the ideal choice. Very rich, with a wife conveniently both ailing and living in the country, the thirty-eight-year-old Martyn – without the outlet of modern divorce laws – was looking around for a woman to settle down with, but stopping short of matrimony.

In 1841, Mason introduced Martyn to Lizzie, by then eighteen, and the major was bowled over. A description of her at this time may help us understand why: 'An exquisite apparition, full of grace and dignity. A face worthy to inspire the sculptors of Ancient Greece.'

A handsome figure in his fine Life Guards' uniform, Mason made Lizzie an unrefusable offer – which she was sensible enough not to refuse. He set her up in her own splendid house in St John's Wood, then a charming, wooded area being developed as a pleasant inner London suburb where, among others, wealthy men were building comfortable homes for their mistresses. He also established a sub-stantial trust fund in her name and appointed an astute financier and landowner friend of his, Nathaniel William John Strode, as her trustee.[1] This guaranteed her a substantial income for life, no matter what might happen to their relationship.

For the next five years they would live together in all respects as man and wife, save that Lizzie remained 'Miss Howard' and offici-ally she was only Martyn's 'hostess'. Yet they were happy enough. They both loved horses, dancing, hunting and the theatre and, when in August 1842, Lizzie bore Martyn a son, albeit illegitimate, he was so delighted that he settled even more money on her together with a considerable amount of land, and re-appointed Strode to look after her.

And so they jogged along in an unmarried version of what an English divorce judge[2] has called 'the ordinary wear and tear of

---

[1] Strode was later to have at least as great an importance in Napoleon III's life as in that of Lizzie Howard.

[2] Lord Justice Asquith in *Buchler v. Buchler* in the Appeal Court, reported in (1947) 1 All England Law Reports at page 319.

conjugal life' until an evening in June 1846 when Martyn took Lizzie along with him to a reception at Gore House given by Lady Blessington, his cousin by marriage. It was intended to be just another social evening, its purpose being to honour the hostess's close friend, Prince Louis Napoleon Bonaparte, recently escaped from prison in his native land.

Lizzie had never met him before, but as she curtseyed before him and Louis courteously brushed his lips across her hand in salutation, she raised her eyes and found herself looking into the face of a man with whom she instantly fell in love. The meeting changed both their lives.

This was the first time that Lizzie had ever experienced such an emotion and, despite all Louis' later unkindnesses to her, she remained in love with him until the day she died. 'Miss Howard' was that figure usually found only in fiction: a courtesan with a heart of gold.

When Louis had arrived in London from Ham only a few weeks earlier, he had at first been worried about how long he might be allowed to stay in Britain. He had, after all, escaped from a lawfully imposed sentence of imprisonment in a country with which Britain had diplomatic relations and, although Britain had a noble tradition of granting asylum to political refugees so long as they did not use their time in Britain to plot insurrection against a friendly foreign government, France could still have asked for extradition with some faint possibility of success.

So, on the day after he booked into the Brunswick Hotel, Louis wrote to Sir Robert Peel, the British Prime Minister, and Lord Aberdeen, the British Foreign Secretary, assuring them that he had escaped only to visit his dying father and stating that he had no intention of indulging in any political activity while in their country, nor in disturbing the peace and tranquillity of Europe. He wrote a similar letter to Count St-Aulaire, then the French Ambassador to the Court of St James. After taking instructions from Louis-Philippe's Government in Paris, St Aulaire replied that, on the basis of Louis' assurances, they would not apply for extradition. In truth, they were probably extremely glad to be rid of him.

As we have seen in the previous chapter, it may be doubtful to what extent Louis was sincere in claiming that he had 'only' escaped from the Château de Ham to pay one last visit to his dying father but, at that stage in his life, he genuinely seems to have lost his taste for further military adventure.

After six years in gaol, and with his health impaired, he still believed passionately in his destiny one day to rule over France.[1] But Strasbourg and Boulogne – and the years at Ham – had taken their toll: he no longer thought in terms of achieving that destiny by further military excursions against the French King. 'I wait upon events,' he said to his American friend, Thomas Winkoff, who visited him at the Brunswick Hotel in December 1846. 'I await my hour,' he told his cousin, the former Princess Marie of Baden, who had married the Marquis of Douglas and now lived in London, when she asked him what were his intentions for the future.[2]

As for seeing his dying parent, he did his best to try and obtain permission to visit ex-King Louis in Florence. But, as Louis must surely have foreseen from the outset, Grand Duke Leopold II of Tuscany, with his close political and family ties to the Austrian Government (he was grandson and nephew of two earlier Austrian emperors and the reigning Emperor Ferdinand's first cousin), would not grant him permission to enter his grand duchy and the Belgian and Austrian Governments denied him transit visas to pass through their territories en route. The Austrians, under the long-serving chancellor Prince Metternich, were old enemies, but the reason for the Belgian refusal was more personal: Queen Louise of Belgium was a loyal daughter of Louis-Philippe of France.[3]

[1] For instance, after attending a Society wedding in the country in March 1847, he sat up into the early hours of the morning smoking cigarettes, sipping brandy and talking at great length to Lord Alvanley, one of Wellington's former generals, about his future. 'It is written ere long I shall become Emperor of France, avenge the defeat of Waterloo and drive the Austrians out of Italy,' he told the somewhat startled old soldier. 'On the subject of politics, he is as mad as a hatter!' commented their mutual host and father of the bride, a retired colonel.

[2] This was the same Marie who, as a child of six, had told the fifteen-year-old Louis to dive fully clothed into a river and rescue a flower from the hat of one of her sisters that had fallen into the water.

[3] The Belgian royal family's prejudice against the Bonapartes continued even into the twentieth century. Princess Clementine, Louise's granddaughter, was not allowed to marry Prince Victor Bonaparte, Louis's second cousin and then head of the Bonaparte family, until after Leopold II of Belgium, Louise's son, had died in 1909.

Within two months, the need to travel to Tuscany had vanished. On 25 July 1846, ex-King Louis died at the age of sixty-seven. Although he had not seen his son for fifteen years, they were at the end totally reconciled. In his will, he tried to stifle any remaining doubts as to Louis' legitimacy by declaring him to be 'the only son who remains to me' and, in more practical measure, appointed Louis his sole heir, leaving him all his considerable wealth. This included not only his personal mementos of 'the Emperor Napoleon' but also his *palazzo* in Florence, his money in the bank (then equal to 1,200,000 French francs) and his Italian landed estates bringing in a yearly income equivalent to 60,000 French francs. Allied to what was left of Louis' inheritance from his mother – investments bringing in an annual income of 100,000 French francs – this should have been enough to end all Louis' financial problems.

But, of course, it did not.

According to his own lights, he did his best to curb his expenditure. In early February 1847 he moved out of the Brunswick Hotel and rented a house at 3, King Street. 'For the first time in seven years,' he wrote to Narcisse Vieillard, 'I am enjoying the pleasure of being at home. I am collecting all my books, papers and family portraits; in fact, everything of value which has escaped the shipwreck.' The house, which still exists in King Street and bears to this day a wall plaque indicating that the future Napoleon III lived there, was much smaller and cheaper (at only £300 a year) than his former splendid residence at 1, Carlton Gardens. But it was still within that wealthy, tight little area that Sir William Fraser had earlier identified as 'the only real world'.

There was, in fact, no substantial change in Louis' expensive lifestyle. After a short visit to Bath in the summer of 1846 to try and restore his health – he actually put on four pounds in weight in a few weeks – he returned to his pre-Boulogne social life of frequent visits to theatres and the opera (but now without his own box), to the racetrack where he bet on horses with more enjoyment than success, to lavish receptions and hunt balls, to Society weddings and country house weekends; and he joined – or rejoined – several leading gentleman's clubs.

Ex-King Louis' death had left him, in the eyes of all true Bonapartists, the legitimate Emperor of France. Joseph, Napoleon's oldest brother, had died in 1844 and, according to the Law of Succession of 1804, ex-King Louis, as next in line, had 'succeeded' to the title. Sixty-four-year-old Jerome, Napoleon's youngest brother, lived on but he was six years ex-King Louis' junior and Louis took precedence in the order of succession. 'It is sad, indeed, to think that neither you nor I have any children. So I should be very glad to marry,' wrote Louis to his cousin 'Plon-Plon', ex-King Jerome's son. Although still childless, this dynastically ambitious prince had already taken the precaution three years earlier of finding himself a wife, albeit a remarkably plain Italian princess.

Over the next two years, Louis, now himself free to marry but still without any great enthusiasm to do so sought to follow his cousin's example and paid court to various rich young women of good class and background as possible brides. But it was only a half-hearted exercise and he had little luck with any of them or their fathers.

It was much more to his taste to enjoy, in the summer of 1846, a brief but passionate affair with Rachel, the most famous French actress of the time. She was on a visit to London and playing, to ecstatic reviews, the title role of Phèdre in Racine's classic tragedy at the St James's Theatre. Short, slim and no great physical beauty, she nonetheless had such radiance and so wonderful a voice that at seventeen she had made her successful debut at the Comédie Française. Now she so 'enchanted' Louis that he wrote to Narcisse Vieillard asking him if he would, on her return to Paris, look after this 'young and inexperienced girl, threatened with many dangers and beset by innumerable temptations'.

He must have been besotted. Rachel was by then, at the age of twenty-five, a highly experienced sexual creature. One of her previous lovers had been the Duc de Joinville, and among her many future lovers were to be Louis' cousin, 'Plon-Plon', seeking solace from his plain Italian wife, and Count Alexandre de Walewski, Napoleon I's illegitimate son, whose wife was later to be one of Louis' own many mistresses. In these people's lives, sexual probity played very little part.

The following year, when Rachel was once again touring in Britain and their affair had long since lost its sparkle, she and Louis, then aged thirty-nine, were travelling with 'Plon-Plon' up to Manchester for her farewell performance in that city when, lulled by the slow jogging of the train, Louis fell asleep. After a while, he woke up and, opening his eyes, saw Rachel and his twenty-seven-year-old cousin making love on the opposite seat of their reserved first-class compartment. He quickly closed his eyes and pretended to be still asleep but the next day he caught an early train back to London. Many years later, he recounted this incident to his wife Eugenie who, in turn, told it to Augustin Filon, their son's tutor. She clearly knew her husband well. 'That sounds just like him, doesn't it?' she commented with a smile.[1]

Through all this, Louis remained as generous as ever to his friends and supporters, pouring out gifts and paying their pensions out of his own pocket. When Dr Conneau came out of prison in October 1846 at the end of his three-months' gaol term for helping him escape from the Château de Ham, Louis bought him a medical practice for £900 in London.

So it was not long before, despite his father's ample inheritance, Louis was once again living well beyond his means and even Blanchard Jerrold has to admit that these were 'his days of comparative poverty'. He had a perpetual overdraft of £2,000 from Baring Brothers and had to borrow quite large sums of money from other finance houses, including the Rothschilds, to keep his princely head above water.

Yet he was enjoying his life and enjoying his freedom, while still not missing any possible occasion to proclaim to the world his continuing dream of eventual power. In his will, ex-King Louis had asked the French Government to allow him to be buried in the small church at St Leu, the village near Paris from which, forty years earlier, he had taken the title of the Comte de Leu. His eldest son, Charles Louis, who had died in childhood during the First Empire, was already buried there and Louis begged that his second son, Napoleon Louis, who had died in Italy at the age of twenty-seven, should be brought from his foreign grave and the two finally interred beside their son and brother in French soil.

After a year's delay, Louis-Philippe's Government gave its somewhat grudging consent and, on 29 September 1847, the bodies of ex-King Louis and Prince Napoleon Louis were returned together

---

[1] In his reply to her remark: 'Comme c'est bien lui, n'est-ce pas?' Filon replied: 'Oui, comme c'est bien *eux*!' (Yes, it sounds just like *them*!) referring also to 'Plon-Plon', always ready to betray his cousin of whom he was perpetually jealous.

to St-Leu. An ageing guard of honour of veterans of Napoleon's army, proudly wearing their old uniforms, saluted the coffins. It was a moving spectacle and Louis wrote from London to thank the officer in command for 'this act of homage and of reparation', an act which 'has softened my own bitter grief at my inability to kneel before the tomb of my family and, for a moment, has even made me forget that I am condemned to be separated, apparently for ever, from the men I love best and the objects I most cherish'.

Those were, no doubt, noble sentiments but Louis sent copies of this letter to the editors of many leading newspapers in Europe. Louis had not lost his touch. He was still expert at turning the most private events in his life to the maximum public advantage. He had used the death of his beloved mother as an excuse to work up a politically acceptable reason for leaving Arenenberg and finding sanctuary in Britain. He had used the fact that his not quite so beloved father was dying as a pretext for trying to persuade the French King to allow him to leave prison and, when that failed, as an honourable reason for breaking the law and escaping.

Now he was using the reburial in France of that same father and the brother who had died in his arms as a means of reminding the world of his own continued suffering and enforced exile.

How did Miss Howard fit into all this? At Lady Blessington's reception in June 1846, when they had first met and she had fallen instantly in love, Louis had also been much moved. They had managed to speak briefly to each other. Lizzie had told him that she was always alone at the end of the afternoon and that she hoped His Imperial Highness would do her the honour of visiting her, which he said he would be happy to do. She confessed that she had an illegitimate son and he replied that he had two: 'The fruits of my captivity!' he said with a slight smile and a typical shrug of his shoulders.

They did not immediately become lovers. For a start, Major Martyn would not have tolerated it and, besides, Lizzie regarded him as her husband in all but name. She had not once been unfaithful to him in their five years together, and she had no intention of starting now. In fact, so anxious had she always been to preserve at least the semblance of bourgeois respectability that she had not registered their son, Martin, in his father's name or even in hers. She had passed him off to the local parish priest as Martin Constantine Harryet, her newly born *brother*, and her own mother's youngest child.

It took several months for the new relationship between Lizzie and Louis to be physically consummated. He had nothing to lose but she most certainly had; she took her time about coming to a decision. Finally, in January 1847, the same month that Louis moved out of the Brunswick Hotel and into his rented home in King Street, she left Major Martyn and her large house in St John's Wood and moved, with her four-year-old son, into a newly built, rented house at 9, Berkeley Street.[1] This was on the other side of Piccadilly – and therefore out of the 'real world' – but still only a five-minutes' journey by carriage or on horseback from King Street.

In fact, although 3, King Street was Louis' official address, to all intents and purposes, they lived together at Lizzie's house in Berkeley Street. She insisted on paying all the outgoings and he called her 'my landlady' and 'my beautiful hostess'. But her generosity went further. In early 1847, Louis' financial position became really acute: even with Lizzie bearing so much of their ordinary, everyday expenses, his debts were piling up and his creditors were pressing hard upon him. He did not know where to turn. Lizzie came to his rescue and bought his estate at Città Nova near Rome that his father had given him in his will. She did not need the property and never even went there but it was a way of subsidising him without compromising too much his dignity or self-respect.

It was the opposite of the normal situation. For once, the beautiful rich young woman was keeping the poorer, older man, not the other way round.

As usual, tongues wagged in 'respectable' society and they were not welcome as a couple in the very best houses although, with typical English hypocrisy, on his own Louis was still accepted. No matter. Lizzie and he held court in their own home to their own circle of friends. A young French prude named Alexis de Vallon wrote to his mother, on a visit to London: 'Prince Louis lives publicly, to the great scandal of English propriety, with a tenth-rate

[1] Neither the house in St John's Wood at 23, Circus Road nor the property at 9, Berkeley Street still exists. The site of the former is now occupied by part of the St John & St Elizabeth Hospital and on the latter stands a modern office block.

actress, who is however extremely beautiful, called Miss Howard.'
But Emile Fleury, a somewhat high-minded young French officer
introduced into Louis' circle by Persigny, who in his memoirs written thirty years later when he was both a general and a count,
insisted pompously on calling Lizzie 'the Courtesan', had grudgingly
to admit: 'Whether from devotion or ambition, this charming young
Englishwoman had declared to her lover that she wanted nothing
better than to serve him and that, for him, she would give up all
her luxury, her success and her triumphs . . . One cannot but deny
that this behaviour lacked generosity or disinterest.'

In this happy, uncomplicated style, Lizzie and Louis lived almost
idyllically for well over a year. He had the best of both worlds: a
loving, beautiful companion who gave him financial support and
allowed him a great deal of freedom to live his own life in his own
fashion. She had all that she wanted: the man whom she loved –
on whatever terms were acceptable to him.

There is no doubt as to the depth of Lizzie's feelings for Louis,
but what about him? Did he love her or was he merely using her?
There are no extracts of autobiography available to give an authoritative answer; no memoirs or letters to friends on the subject have
survived. He wrote many letters to Lizzie herself but when he finally
dropped her five years later – cruelly and deliberately – in order to be
free, as emperor, to marry suitably, his secret police broke into her
house in Paris and stole them all, from their place in a secret drawer
beside her bed. Not one has since resurfaced to the world's gaze.

But one important letter does survive, written to a third party in
August 1849, when he had become Prince-President and she was
openly his mistress in Paris. It gives an insight into the depth of his
feelings for her.

While on a formal visit to Tours, as part of his campaign as
newly elected head of state to show himself to the nation, he stayed
at the home of the local Prefect and Lizzie was lodged in the mansion
of a certain M. André, a prominent local citizen who was away at the
time. On his return, this worthy and devout person was so enraged
that the Prince-President had dared to place his mistress under his
roof that he sent an indignant letter of protest to Odilon Barrot, an
austere politician, 'always dressed in black, neat and tightly
buttoned', as Victor Hugo, then Louis' Prime Minister, put it.

'Have we returned to that epoch when the king's mistresses

proclaimed the scandal of their lives throughout the cities of France?' demanded M. André in his letter to the Prime Minister, who was only too happy to send it on at once to Louis himself.

Louis responded immediately and with uncharacteristic heat:

> How many women, a hundred times less pure, a hundred times less devoted, a hundred times less excusable than the one who lodged at M. André's, would have been received with every possible honour by this M. André, because they would have had the name of their husband to cover their guilty liaisons? I loath this pedantic severity, which disguises a withered heart, is indulgent towards oneself but inexorable where others are concerned. True religion is not intolerant . . .
>
> As for myself, I admit myself capable of seeking, in an illegitimate liaison, the love that my heart needs . . . Since, up to the present, my position has prevented my marrying; since, surrounded by the cares of government, I have in my country, alas, no intimate friends, no childhood acquaintances, no relations who can give me the sweetness of family life, I may well, I believe, be pardoned an affection which causes no harm to anyone and which I do not seek to proclaim to the world.
>
> If M. André really believes, as he says, that his house has been *soiled* by the presence of a woman who is not married, then I pray you to inform him that, for my part, I sincerely regret that a person of such pure devotion and of such high character should have happened by chance to visit a house where the ostentation of bombastic virtue without any Christian spirit reigns under the mask of religion.

In many ways it was a magnificent, and certainly a heartfelt, reply.

There can be little doubt that, in their years together in London and beyond, they both got what they wanted out of their arrangement, albeit perhaps in their own different ways. In a perfect world, Lizzie would have been happy for it to go on for ever.

Meanwhile, in France the ageing Louis-Philippe, now in his seventies, looked as secure upon his throne as ever. He shrewdly wore the mask of the 'Citizen King' to disguise the fact that, in essence, he was as authoritarian a ruler as any of his Bourbon cousins or predecessors. In an early photograph dating from 1839 he is dressed in civilian clothes with a large, stove-pipe hat on the table beside him, but his pose is awesomely regal and his stern, arrogant expression would have done credit to any of the kings of France before the Revolution.

He ruled with parliamentary support but that parliament was grievously unrepresentative of the nation at large. The Upper House, the Chamber of Peers, was hand-picked, consisting only of men nominated by Louis-Philippe himself, and the Lower House, the Chamber of Deputies, was elected by less than a quarter of a million out of a total population of over thirty million. No working-class man had the vote and it was even too expensive for many of the ordinary middle classes: one had to pay a tax to the State of 200 francs to be entitled to vote and another 500 francs to stand as Deputy.

For the past eight years since October 1840, François Guizot, the former French Ambassador to London, had been Louis-Philippe's Prime Minister.[1] A slim, steely man, his attitude to life, and to power, exactly complemented that of the king: conservative, cautious and dedicated to the acquisition of wealth and the mainten-ance of the established order.

In August 1846, both Louis-Philippe and Guizot were delighted with an election result that returned 291 pro-Government deputies to power with only 168 for the Opposition. Their delight was short-lived. The corn harvest for that year was bad, floods ravaged the region of the Loire and a disease transported on the air from the potato famines in Ireland destroyed much of the potato crop. An industrial crisis also brought widespread unemployment. Corn had to be bought from abroad, the gold reserves of the Bank of France dropped perilously and the nation slipped into an economic depression from which there seemed little prospect of speedy emerg-ence. Alexis de Tocqueville, an Opposition deputy and contempor-

---

[1] Technically, for most of that time Guizot was only Foreign Secretary with old Marshal Soult, to whom Napoleon had said before Waterloo that the seven-year-old Louis Napoleon might one day be the hope of the French nation, as Prime Minister, but Guizot was the only minister in whom the king had total confidence and to whom he would go, occasionally, for advice.

ary French historian, had earlier compared the régime to 'a joint stock company all of whose activities are designed to benefit only the shareholders' but now, for the first time, some of those shareholders, in particular, the poorer members of the middle classes, began to lose confidence in the chairman of the board and his managing director.

In July 1847, the parliamentary Opposition, seeing how hopeless the situation was in the Chamber of Deputies and responding to calls for action from an increasingly worried middle class, began a series of political banquets – called Reform Banquets – at which speeches were made denouncing the incompetence and corruption of the Government and calling for electoral and parliamentary reform. These banquets, held first in Paris and then in many major provincial cities, were a run-away success. But it was a middle-class campaign. One had to pay to attend the banquets and the electoral reform demanded was only to allow greater middle-class representation in Parliament. The working classes, though suffering even more from the economic effects of the Government's mismanagement and increasingly pro-republican and anti-monarchist in mood, were not a party to this discreet bourgeois form of protest combining food and wine with eloquent speeches.

The Government remained impervious to this groundswell of unhappiness. Old age had made the king even more authoritarian and determined to pursue his own path. In November 1847, one of his sons, the Duc de Nemours, wrote to his brother, the Duc de Joinville: 'Ministers no longer exist; their responsibility is gone; all centres on the King. He has arrived at an age at which a man no longer accepts criticism. He is accustomed to govern, and likes to show that he governs. With his immense experience, his courage and his fine qualities, he knows how to face danger boldly; but the danger exists all the same.'

Those words were to prove to be prophetic. A 'Monster Reform Banquet' was announced to take place in Paris on 22 February 1848 and, at last, both Louis-Philippe and Guizot realised that something had to be done. But it was not to grant reform. On the contrary, it was to ban the banquet. 'The question of who rules the country,' Guizot told the Chamber of Deputies, 'has passed out of the Chamber into that vague, obscure, turbulent outside world which blunderers and idlers call the people.'

How Louis, reading that speech in his exile in London, must have smiled to himself. It was the absolute opposite of his own political creed where the people, albeit under a suitable leader – namely himself – were the supreme arbiters of the French nation's fate.

On 22 February 1848, the day of the by now banned banquet, thousands of Parisians, not only members of the middle class but also ominously for the first time the workers, took to the streets of Paris to demonstrate in favour of electoral reform, a reform which, in theory, would only benefit the middle classes. There were several small clashes with soldiers, some buses were overturned, a few barricades were erected, but by nightfall all was quiet. 'The Parisians will not make a revolution in winter,' muttered Louis-Philippe complacently.

The following day it was a different story. The crowds were bigger, their mood more dangerous. 'À bas Guizot!' (Down with Guizot!) they cried as they marched through the streets. Louis-Philippe called in the National Guard to control them but these part-time soldiers simply cried 'Vive la réforme!' (Long live reform!) and even some regular soldiers openly sided with the crowds. The old king lost his nerve. He dismissed Guizot and tried desperately to find someone else prepared to take over his task.

As Professor Alfred Cobban has shrewdly observed, 'The whole system disintegrated when the man who had been the key-stone of the arch fell.' That evening, a working-class mob collected outside the fallen Prime Minister's home on the Boulevard des Capucines. It was guarded by a detachment of infantry but the mob tried to force their way in. One of the soldiers, accidentally or otherwise, fired a shot, the crowd panicked, the soldiers lost their heads and in the next few minutes sixteen people were either shot or trampled to death and many more injured. The corpses of the victims, men and women, were piled high upon a cart and trundled round the city for all to see. A comparatively minor incident had turned into a revolution.

That night gunsmiths' shops were broken into and their weapons seized, barricades sprang up all over central Paris and the mob took over.

By morning they were masters of the city. They had captured the Hôtel de Ville and were marching on the Tuileries Palace. Adolphe Thiers, the new Prime Minister who had served Louis-Philippe in that capacity in the 1830s and been sacked for his pains because he had refused to accept the absolutism of the king, now begged Louis-Philippe and his family to flee to the comparative safety of St Cloud on the outskirts of the city and let the army, many of whose soldiers still remained loyal, deal with the situation in the capital. But Louis-Philippe to his great credit refused, and in his own grand style: 'I will not allow the blood of my subjects to be spilled,' he said.

At 1.00 pm on the afternoon of 24 February, he abdicated in favour of his ten-year-old grandson, the Comte de Paris,[1] and, under the protection of a squadron of soldiers, left the palace by a back door with Queen Marie-Amelie, clambered into a carriage and trundled out of history.[2] Two hours later the mob burst into the Chamber of Deputies, where Louis-Philippe's daughter-in-law was trying to have her infant son proclaimed king by the deputies, all middle class to a man, and, amid wild scenes of exultation, forced the child 'King Philippe' and his mother to flee and triumphantly proclaimed the Second Republic of France.[3] It had all happened within twenty-four hours. Louis-Philippe admitted: 'When I woke up in the Tuileries that morning, I thought I would go to sleep in the Tuileries that night.' Instead, the mob looted his palace, desecrated his bedsheets and clambered jubilantly upon his red and gold throne before hacking it to pieces with their swords.

Strasbourg had failed, Boulogne too. But now Louis-Philippe, determinedly ignorant of his people's real desires, had played into Louis' hands. Two days later, Louis Napoleon Bonaparte, accompanied by his valet, Charles Thélin, and his banker friend, Count Joseph Orsi, left London for Paris. His long exile and Lizzie Howard's eighteen months' idyll with her lover were about to end. For both of them, nothing was ever to be the same again.

---

[1] This child was the son of Louis-Philippe's oldest son, the Duc d'Orléans, who had died six years earlier when, his horse having bolted out of control, he tried to save himself by jumping to the ground only to break his neck on landing.

[2] After hiding for a week near Honfleur, they crossed the Channel to England and settled in a large country house in Claremont, Surrey, where Louis-Philippe died two years later.

[3] The First was the republic that ruled France after the Revolution from the imprisonment of Louis XVI in August 1792 to the creation of the Consulate in December 1799.

PART THREE

POWER AT
LAST

Chapter Fifteen

Return to France (1848)

Louis' THIRD AND FINAL thrust for power began badly but, thanks to a combination of his shrewdness and Lizzie Howard's wealth, it ended less than ten months later in triumph.

He arrived in Paris at the home of his old friend, Narcisse Vieillard, on the evening of 28 February 1848. Persigny was already there waiting for him. At midnight Persigny, quickly resuming his role as Louis' most devoted aide, hurried round to the Hôtel de Ville to hand over this brief note to Alphonse Lamartine, the Romantic poet and statesman who had coined the famous phrase 'France is bored' for life under Louis-Philippe and was now a leading member of the Provisional Government:

'Gentlemen, I hurry from exile to place myself under the banner of the newly proclaimed Republic. Without any ambition other than to serve my country, I report my arrival to the members of the Provisional Government, and to assure them of my devotion to the cause they represent. L. N. Bonaparte.'

But Lamartine and his colleagues were understandably wary of these newly found republican sentiments in a man who until then had stood for exactly the opposite kind of government. Within hours, he wrote back commenting on 'the difficult situation' in which the Provisional Government found itself and requesting that Louis return to England at once and not return until France was 'in a calmer state'.

Persigny, hot-headed as ever, wanted Louis to ignore this and stay but Louis was both more cautious and more astute. 'Gentlemen,' he replied. 'after 33 years of exile and persecution, I believed I had acquired the right to find again a home on the soil of my native land. You think that my presence in Paris at this moment is a matter for embarrassment; I therefore withdraw for the time being. You will see in this sacrifice the purity of my intentions and of my patriotism.'

And he took the next available cross-Channel steamer back to England – but not before he had sent a copy of this letter to the press in both Paris and London.

Lamartine's suspicions were well-founded. From the very beginning, despite all his present and subsequent public avowals of support and respect for the new Republic, Louis had not lost sight of his eventual Imperial ambitions: this leopard had not changed its spots. Back in London, he told a friend: 'I have wagered the Princess Mathilde that I shall sign myself Emperor of the French in four years.'

From the very beginning, the new Republic was like a ship with two captains, each wanting to go in a different direction. The Provisional Government consisted of seven nominees of the right and three of the left, and they were constantly in disagreement with each other. They had come to power so suddenly and unexpectedly that they had no coherent idea of where exactly they were going. They could easily agree on broad intellectual principles: abolition of capital punishment, end of slavery in the colonies, freedom of public assembly meetings, liberty of the press and election by all adult Frenchmen of a Constituent Assembly to take the place of the old Chamber of Deputies and draft a new Constitution, but when it came to the mechanics of everyday government and how to secure the basic requirements of financial and economic stability, they were in hopeless turmoil. Louis was content to sit back in London and watch from a distance how they would fare, biding his time and, for practically the first time in his political life, doing nothing rash.

'After Strasbourg and Boulogne,' he wrote to Persigny, 'the poor and the republicans showed their sympathy for me while the rich and the monarchists laughed at me as a mere Pretender. The revolution has not changed these opinions but it has altered the interests of the two parties. The republicans have no further need of me and have become my enemies . . . We must look at things more philosophically. At present the people believe in all the fine words they hear . . . They are drunk with victory and hope. There must be an end of these illusions before a man who can bring order (*un homme d'ordre*) can make himself heard.'

On 23 April 1848 general parliamentary elections for the new Constituent Assembly were held and three nephews of Napoleon were returned as Deputies.[1] But Louis refused all Persigny's entreaties to stand. As he wrote to Narcisse Vieillard on 11 May, 'So long as the social condition of France remains unsettled, and so long as the Constitution remains to be written, I feel my position in France must be very difficult, tiresome and even dangerous.'

Persigny, joined now by by another enthusiast, Armand Laity, familiar now for his part in the Strasbourg adventure, was champing at the bit for more action. In June, a round of by-elections for the Constituent Assembly gave them the chance. Laity, without even asking for Louis' approval, announced his candidature in posters all over Paris. Louis was forced into agreeing to stand but he warned Persigny not to commit him to any particular policy. 'I want to be outside it all,' he wrote. 'I want to go my own way and play the part that suits me – that or nothing at all.'

Despite this, Louis was elected a Deputy in no less than four departments, including Paris. But he still did not rush to take up his posts. In letters also distributed to the press, he wrote to his supporters in each department thanking them for their votes and indicating that he would, 'as a child of Paris', in due course be happy and honoured to take up his role 'as a representative of the people working with my colleagues to reestablish order, confidence and employment', but he did not give a date. The mere possibility of such an event was enough for Alphonse Lamartine to announce that the Law of 1832 banning Louis from setting foot in France was still in effect and ordering his arrest, if he dared to appear in any of the departments for which he had been elected. Meanwhile, Persigny and Laity were promptly arrested.

Even so, Louis had been legally elected and it would have been highly embarrassing to the government to try and prevent him taking his seat. But he shied away from physical confrontation. That was no longer his tactic: the days of Strasbourg and Boulogne

---

[1] They were Prince Napoleon ('Plon-Plon'), son of ex-King Jerome, Pierre Bonaparte, son of Napoleon's third brother, Lucien, the only one whom he did not make a king, and Lucien, son of Napoleon's sister, Caroline, whom he made Queen of Naples.

were long over. Instead, on 14 June he wrote to the President of the Constituent Assembly declining to take his seat. 'I was starting to take up my post,' he wrote, 'when I heard that my election had become the pretext for deplorable disorders and misunderstandings. I did not ask for the honour of being a representative of the people . . . still less did I seek power. If the people were to impose duties upon me, I should know how to carry them out. But I disavow those who attribute to me ambitious aims which are not mine. My name is a symbol of national glory and I should be sincerely grieved if it were used to worsen the disorders and divisions of the nation.'

Note that sentence: 'If the people were to impose duties upon me, I should know how to carry them out.' It was a Freudian slip of profound significance. For all his protestations of loyalty to the Republic, it had an unmistakably autocratic, if not Imperial, ring to it. There were angry speeches of protest in the Assembly and Louis at once wrote again, reaffirming his allegiance to the Republic – but resigning his seat.

Again, his caution paid off. Within a few days the Republic itself almost disappeared, toppling over the edge of re-emerging normality into ungovernable anarchy. In May, the Provisional Government had been replaced, after the Assembly elections of the previous month, by a predominantly middle-class Executive Committee. Now, on 21 June, this new Committee announced the closing down of the National Workshops, a left-wing innovation dating back to the early days of the Republic which gave physical shelter and a small weekly hand-out to some of the unemployed. All men between seventeen and twenty-five were now to be evicted and conscripted into the army and older workers sent to work in the provinces.

Working-class disillusionment with the euphoria of February was complete. On 23 June, a new revolution erupted as poor, workless and starving Parisians, led by extremists with no clear idea of what they wanted to achieve except to destroy the middle-class Government that had betrayed 'their' revolution, again took to the streets of Paris. In time-honoured tradition, they rioted, looted and erected barricades. The politicians were terrified. On 24 June, the Executive Committee resigned and the National Assembly declared a State of Emergency and surrendered full military and executive powers to the outgoing War Minister, General Louis Cavaignac. Victorious leader of a ruthless North African campaign which had only a few years earlier conquered Algeria and brought it under French rule, he had a reputation for sternness and swiftness. In three blood-soaked days, soldiers under his command crushed the ill-armed Parisian workers as they had crushed the ill-armed Algerians. As in North Africa, he showed no pity and gave no quarter. Three thousand civilians were killed and twice that number were rounded up for exile and paraded through the streets like cattle. In the words of Victor Hugo, 'Civilisation defended itself with the weapons of barbarism.'

What was to be Louis' attitude to this appalling event? If he supported it, he would have forfeited his carefully built reputation as a friend of the workers. If he sided with the rioters, he would have lost the respect of the army and of politicians. Astutely, he chose neither. He made no public pronouncements one way or the other. But he was not slow to appreciate the beneficial consequences for himself: 'That man [Cavaignac] is clearing the way for me,' he told a friend at a Gore House dinner-party.

Two months earlier he had shown his true attitude towards working-class revolt: despite his oft-proclaimed views, for propaganda purposes, of 'the people' as the ultimate source of political sovereignty.

The outcrop of national unrest erupting through western Europe in 1848, the 'Year of Revolutions', had not left Britain totally unscathed. Chartism, a largely northern-based, working-class movement for political reform, had been building up over the past ten years. Among its most persistent demands were universal male suffrage, voting by ballot and abolition of property qualifications for MPs, who should, for the first time, be paid on a professional basis instead of being merely rich dilettantes.

Later, by Acts of 1867 and 1884, these aims were achieved peacefully but the scent of conflict from across the Channel was heady stuff. The Chartist leaders announced that a monster petition, signed by six million people, would be presented to Parliament in central London on 10 April 1848 by a great procession marching from Kennington Common, some five miles away.

Lord John Russell's Whig Government took the threat to established law and order very seriously. The Duke of Wellington, still the country's outstanding soldier at seventy-nine, was placed in command of the army to defend the capital. As Lord Malmesbury recorded in his diary on 9 April: 'The alarm today is very general all over the town. The Government have made great preparations.' But the task was not left only to the military. Gentlemen, in great numbers, volunteered for service as special constables to support the troops.

One of them was Louis.

On 10 April itself, he patrolled the area around Trafalgar Square with three other recruits. Other special constables brandished heavy wooden staffs but Louis had rather more style. His only weapon was a light, gold-headed cane. But even that proved unnecessary. His only arrest was a drunken old woman, whom he duly handed over to the regular police.

In fact, the day turned out a fiasco for the Chartists. As Lord Malmesbury recorded: 'The mob was not very considerable and the best behaved I ever saw.' (The street protests in central London in the mid-1980s against the Thatcher Government's controversial Poll Tax were far more violent, and far more unpleasant.) Faced with massive deployment of armed soldiers, supported by local constables, the Chartist leaders discreetly abandoned their procession and meekly delivered their petition to Parliament by cab. Chartism, as a political force, was dead.

The relevance for our purposes is shown by Louis' response to a remark made to him by a friend, George Palmer Putnam, the American publisher, who came across him on his beat. 'What the hell is Monsieur Napoleon doing here?' he asked. 'Sir,' replied Louis. 'London must be preserved.'

The 'Red Days of June', as they were called, marked the turning-point in Louis' fortunes. Further by-elections to the Assembly were due in September. Now, at last, he saw the way clear: election to the Assembly followed by election to the Presidency. The one would be a stepping-stone to the other. The middle classes had shown that they were too weak and faint-hearted to govern. The working classes had taken the route of anarchy and violence. Only *un homme d'ordre* could save the day for France and, unless Louis acted resolutely and swiftly, that 'man of order' would be General Cavaignac, at forty-six, only six years older than Louis, and already preening himself as a candidate for the Presidency.

Even in those days electioneering cost a great deal of money, especially for serial campaigns, one after the other. Lizzie Howard was now to make her financial presence felt. She had earlier bought from Louis his father's old estate at Città Nova, near Rome, as a discreet way of subsidising his lifestyle. Now, with her help, that same estate was pressed again into service to yield a double benefit. She 'sold' it back to Louis on long-term credit with no money actually changing hands, and he promptly mortgaged it to an Italian nobleman for 60,000 Roman *écus*, the equivalent of 324,000 French francs.[1]

He was therefore able, on 10 August, to write to Persigny, by then released from prison following his arrest by Lamartine, to say that he had decided to stand in the new elections planned for the following month. 'I have arranged all my affairs accordingly and nothing can any longer retain me in England, if events demand my departure,' he declared.

Within two weeks, Persigny had flooded France with manifestos, posters and pamphlets extolling Louis' virtues. 'I should consider myself wanting in my duty if I did not respond to the call of my fellow-citizens,' humbly declared the candidate. He warned Persigny not even to hint at any aspirations to the Presidency at that stage but to concentrate on the simple message that there was one name alone which symbolised order, glory and patriotism, and that only the bearer of that name could obtain an amnesty for the gaoled victims of June, bring economic prosperity and deliver the country from unemployment, destitution and anarchy.

It was a powerful package. Despite the obvious disadvantage of being an absentee candidate, Louis' victory was sensational: he stormed to the lead in no less than five departments with a massive poll of 300,000 votes.

This time, he showed no hesitation. On 24 September, as soon as the results were known in London, he and Charles Thelin left for Paris. They departed so quickly that next day, when Charles Phillips, the Old Bailey barrister who owned the house in King Street, came to take back his property, he found Louis' bed unmade and the water still in his bath.

Two days later, Louis took his oath as Deputy before a crowded

---

[1] Louis paid this back in 1851, when he was Prince-President.

Assembly. His speech on the printed page reads extremely well, despite the florid oratory of the time:

'*Citoyens représentants*. It would be impossible for me to keep silent after the slanders to which I have been subjected. I must in this place, and on the first day that I am allowed to take my seat amongst you, make a public statement of the opinions which I really hold and which I have always held.

'I have at last regained my country and my citizenship after thirty-three years of proscription and exile.

'It is to the Republic that I owe this happiness. It is to the Republic that I give this pledge of my gratitude and devotion. I want to certify to those generous fellow-countrymen who have returned me to this House that I shall do all I can to justify their confidence by working with you for the preservation of tranquillity, for that is the primary need of the country – and for the development of those democratic institutions which the people rightly demands.'

And there was much more to similar effect. The words were fine but Louis' delivery was mediocre. He was no orator, and never would be. But, in that Assembly of talking heads, oratory and a strong declamatory style were considered as at least as important, if not more so, than one's policies or the wishes of the people that one was supposed to represent. His fellow Parliamentarians noticed his nervousness at public speaking (he had very little previous experience), his foreign-sounding accent derived from his schoolboy years in German-speaking Switzerland (for instance, he said '*Ripiblique*' instead of '*République*') and his unassuming appearance – and they were not impressed. 'He's unintelligent. He's a fool whom we shall be able to lead,' commented one Deputy. 'What an idiot!' another said tersely. Victor Hugo, then a moderate Deputy, was one of the few to understand his true significance and appreciate his strength. 'He is not a Prince but an idea,' he said. 'The people have not elected the blunderer of Boulogne but the victor of Iena ... His candidature dates from Austerlitz,' naming two of the Emperor's greatest triumphs.

But this was only the first stage in Louis' electoral campaign. On 4 November, the Assembly approved by an overwhelming majority the new Constitution: a President with full cxccutive powers and an Assembly, both to be elected by the entire male population. The Assembly was to have a three-year term and could be re-elected; the President had a four-year term but could *not* be re-elected. The message was clear: the politicians of the Second Republic only wanted a single-term President. They were already sufficiently frightened by Louis and the magical appeal of his name and all it stood for to wish to limit any long-lasting power he might enjoy. In Victor Hugo's biographer Graham Robb's telling words, 'There was a great yearning for a passionless, peace-loving Napoleon who would restore order without trying to conquer the world.'

Of the five main candidates who stood for the Presidency, Louis' only rival of any consequence was General Cavaignac himself who still ruled as temporary head of state. But from the start Louis was the favourite to win. Persigny, with the ample funds provided by Lizzie Howard, fought a presidential campaign that, in its use of the contemporary media, was positively modern in its tone and intensity. The streets of Paris and all the major cities of France were flooded with posters, leaflets and placards, match boxes adorned with Louis' portrait were distributed, medals on red ribbons bearing his effigy in yellow, red or silver copper were handed out together with miniature flags inscribed: '*Vive prince Louis!*' Persigny bribed journalists to insert articles favourable to Louis in newspapers whose owners were often hostile to his cause and paid street singers to sing newly composed songs extolling his virtues. He was a master of his craft – and well ahead of his time.

But it was not just propaganda. Louis proved a highly popular candidate in his own right. He may not have been very good at making formal, set speeches in the Assembly – of which, indeed, he made very few – but he was friendly and approachable on the hustings. Unlike the aloof Cavaignac, supremely aware of his high military status, Louis had his uncle's knack of making instant contact with ordinary people. His easy charm was a powerful weapon. Accompanied by Persigny and other stalwarts, he would ride through Paris on horseback, greeting the crowds in the streets and talking happily to the soldiers in the barracks. He was a modern-style candidate in a modern-style election.

Always discreetly in the background was Elizabeth Howard. She had followed him to Paris a few days after he had left London on 24 September to take his oath as a newly elected Deputy.[1] On

---

[1] A friend had spotted her on the train to Dover, with her jewel case on her lap and ready cash in her handbag, prepared to do all she could to aid her lover.

arrival, she had checked into the Hôtel Meurice in the rue de Rivoli, just round the corner from Louis at the Hôtel du Rhin on the Place Vendôme. Thereafter she was openly his constant companion in a way that, in England even today, would be impossible for the lover of a leading political figure. When he interviewed his political agents to discuss the campaign for which she had done so much to help provide the resources, she was always at his side.

But she seemed to know her place: remarkably beautiful and exquisitely dressed, she would sit quietly listening but would never ask a question. People looked upon her as an enigma, for she never spoke a word. Occasionally she would smile her approval or nod her head in agreement but that was all. Everyone was very impressed. They thought she was a model of discretion. She probably was; but the truth also is that, at that stage of her life, she could hardly understand or speak a word of French.

She and Louis never actually lived together in Paris under the same roof but they made no effort to keep the nature of their relationship a secret. They went for long rides on horseback together in the forests of St Germain or Meudon to the west of Paris, with Louis riding on a thoroughbred mare that Lizzie had given him, and it was not long before a clubman was heard to say: 'Who said that Prince Louis Napoleon lacks intelligence? He has brought from London the most beautiful woman and the most beautiful horse in the world!'

On 10 December 1848, Louis was elected President by an overwhelming majority. He received 5,434,226 votes as against Cavaignac's 1,448,107, with the other three candidates capturing less than half a million votes between them. He had polled about 75 per cent of the total votes cast and over 60 per cent of the total electorate had voted him into power. The victory was sensational.

Ten days later, dressed simply in black and with the same star of the Legion of Honour pinned to his jacket that he had worn when sentenced at his trial eight years earlier to prison in perpetuity, Louis took the oath of office as President.

Hand raised, he declared: 'In the presence of God and before the French people represented by the National Assembly, I swear to remain faithful to the democratic Republic, one and indivisible, and to fulfil all the duties imposed upon me by the Constitution.' He then read a short speech in which he extolled the many virtues of the Republic and promised it again his total loyalty.

That was not all. Stepping down from the rostrum, he walked over to where Cavaignac was grimly sitting and, in a spontaneous and typical gesture, extended his hand in friendship. Cavaignac was so surprised that he hardly had time to proffer his whole hand in reply and Louis found himself shaking only one or two of his fingers.

He then left the building to a standing ovation from the Deputies amid loud cries of: '*Vive la République*!' Thirty-three years after Waterloo, a Bonaparte was once again head of state in France.

It would only be a matter of time before he would also be Emperor.

Chapter Sixteen

Prince-President
(1848–52)

L OUIS WAS NOT SWORN in as Prince-President, although that
is how he is known to history. He was quite simply 'President' and Armand Marrast, the President of the National
Assembly, had pointedly called him to the tribune to take his oath
of office as 'Citizen Charles Louis Napoleon Bonaparte'. From the
very beginning, Louis adopted a semi-Imperial style. Louis-Philippe,
even in his days of greatest power, had always been careful to wear
the mask of a 'Citizen King' but Louis made it clear that he was
not going to be a 'Citizen President'. He chose as his official dress
the deep-blue uniform of a general-in-chief of the National Guard,
complete with two-cornered hat topped with ostrich feathers, and
made it known that he was to be addressed, not as 'Excellency' or
even 'Monsieur', but as 'Highness' or 'Monseigneur'.

There had been isolated cries of '*Vive Napoléon!*' or, even more
encouraging, '*Vive l'Empereur!*', during the election campaign but,
as ever, Louis did not overplay his hand. He did not set up home in
the Tuileries, traditionally the palace of the kings of France, but in the
Elysée Palace, which had been one of Napoleon's homes and where he
had signed his abdication after Waterloo. The significance of Louis'
choice was not lost upon Parisians. The Elysée has ever since been the
official residence of the Presidents of France and for everyone today
symbolises the Republic but, in 1848, its connotation was very different. It represented the First Empire. By choosing to live there, Louis
was, in his own quiet, astute way, telling the world of the continuum
of power: after the uncle now came the nephew.[1]

---

[1] Even on that very first day, there were those who realised where his ambitions would
ultimately lead him. 'Suppose I were to take him to the Tuileries instead of the Elysée?'

And for the discerning, there was another more intimate indication of his desires and lifestyle. Louis rented for Lizzie Howard a magnificent house at 23, rue du Cirque, with its gardens backing on to the avenue de Marigny which ran (and still runs) alongside the walled grounds of his presidential palace. Louis had two doors, facing each other, built into the walls of Lizzie's garden and the Elysée grounds through which at night he would pass to make love to his mistress.[1]

Louis did not go through those doors only for purposes of sexual gratification. Just as during his last years in London, his official residence had been in King Street but his real home was at Lizzie's house in nearby Berkeley Street, so in Paris his presidential palace was at the Elysée but where he really relaxed was at 23, rue du Cirque.

Dr Thomas W. Evans, a young American living in Paris, was the new President's dentist and Louis was delighted to have someone to whom he could talk in confidence in English without anyone else understanding. They soon became friends and remained on good terms for the rest of Louis' life. In his memoirs written nearly forty years later, Evans gives this revealing pen-picture of Louis' pleasant evenings under Lizzie's roof with a few close friends:

> There, free from the restraint of official surroundings, the Prince-President loved to take a cup of tea or to sit during the whole evening sipping a cup of coffee or smoking a cigarette, his black dog, a great favourite with him, sometimes at his feet and sometimes on his knee . . . He talked with the utmost freedom of his past life in exile but spoke rarely and with great reserve about the French politics of the day.

General Nicolas Changarnier, who was in command of the troops escorting the new President to his official residence, said to Count Molé, Louis-Philippe's ex-Foreign Secretary. 'Be sure you don't,' was the reply. 'He will go there soon enough of his own accord.'

[1] You can no longer see the door in the wall of Lizzie's garden because a building now stands at 23, avenue de Marigny where the end of her garden used to be but you can still see Louis' door. It has not been blocked in. One day I went to photograph it for this book and, conscious of security, a young policeman wanted to know what I was doing. I told him the story of the door: 'That is where the President of France went through to make love' – and he held up the traffic for me so that I could stand in the middle of the avenue de Marigny and get a better shot. It could only have happened in Paris!

He liked to hear others talk of their own lives, of the subjects that personally interested them, of their occupations and amusements during the day, and to have the conversation go on as if in a family circle, without the restraints of etiquette. He also liked, on these occasions, to listen to simple music – at the same time admitting that music in general he did not like. He seemed to seek the satisfactions of á home and the pleasure of being with a few but intimate friends ... Here I met MM. Fleury, Persigny, Mocquard, Edgar Ney and some others.[1] But only a very few persons were ever invited into this little society.

But, although everyone in the upper levels of Parisian society knew that Lizzie was the *maîtresse en titre*, that lovely French phrase for 'official mistress', and Louis soon developed the habit of riding with her in the fashionable Bois de Boulogne in the early evening whenever possible, Lizzie never set foot in the Elysée Palace, nor was she invited to do so.

Louis' first cousin and his former fiancée, Princess Mathilde, was his official hostess and some of his supporters wanted her to divorce her husband from whom she had been estranged for several years and become re-engaged to Louis. In her memoirs, written nearly fifty years later, she claimed that this was actually suggested to her but she refused 'without hesitation and without the least regret. I was not going to give up my independence for someone I did not love.'

Louis himself was more basic. When his old friend, Ferdinand Bac, who knew of his preference for slim young women, mentioned the possibility to him, he traced in the air a large circle to indicate Mathilde's plump and, to him, utterly unattractive figure. For her part, she later told Edmond and Jules Goncourt, the two famous brothers and critics of the arts who recorded the conversation in their celebrated *Journal*: 'What do you want? This man ... he is neither open nor impressionable! Nothing moves him! A man who never loses his temper and whose angriest phrase is to say: "It's

---

[1] Jean-Francois Mocquard was Louis'.Principal Private Secretary and Edgar Ney was the son of Michel Ney, Napoleon's only marshal to be shot after the Emperor's defeat, and one of Louis' favourite young aides-de-camp.

absurd!" If I had married him, I would have broken open his head to discover what was inside it.'

In fact, Marguerite Castillon du Perron, a recent biographer of Mathilde, claims that Mathilde was convinced the forty-year-old Louis was a confirmed bachelor and would never marry anyone. Content to be his confidante and, to her mind, his most valued adviser but at the same time jealous of Lizzie Howard, she went out of her way to introduce Louis to some of the most beautiful young women in Paris. As François Guizot wrote tartly to a friend in the country: 'They say that Mme Howard wants to marry the President. He has not married her but he loves her more than many others, though he has many others too.'

Louis's quickly acquired reputation as a womaniser was so great that Adolphe Thiers, now a prominent opponent of the new President, advocated a simple method of limiting his impact upon the nation. 'We'll see that he gets plenty of women,' he said contemptuously, 'and in that way we'll keep him under our thumb.'

But both Mathilde and Thiers underrated Louis, as others were to do later. Despite the many agreeable evenings spent with Lizzie, and in frequent encounters with the other young women who found their way to his bed, he was never distracted from his self-imposed task of using the Second Republic as a stepping-stone towards the creation of the Second Empire.

But first Louis had to form a Government. As Persigny wrote to a friend, Louis 'did not know one man of importance who could serve him and had not a friend whom he could suitably make a minister'. He was virtually a foreigner, or at least a stranger, in his native land. But, astute as ever, he asked Odilon Barrot, who had been the last leader of the parliamentary opposition under Louis-Philippe, to be his first Prime Minister.[1] It was his way of reinforcing the message that his policies and manner of government would be diametrically opposed to those of the deposed monarch. However, apart from Barrot, Louis' first Ministry consisted almost entirely of mediocrities. Thiers and the other leading politicians of Louis-Philippe's régime refused to accept office – few people would

---

[1] In fact, he first approached Barrot during the presidential campaign before he had even been elected.

anyway have welcomed the discredited figures of the departed Provisional Government – and, at that early stage, Louis simply did not know of any better qualified candidates.

But the loyal supporters of his long years in exile were not forgotten. Persigny was immediately made a presidential equerry and within a few months, having been elected Deputy, was appointed Ambassador to Berlin; Armand Laity and Emile Fleury, the latter the young officer who had visited Louis' home with Lizzie in London, were both made aides-de-camp; Colonel Charles Vaudrey was promoted to general and also made aide-de-camp; Pierre Bure was made treasurer to the presidential (and later Imperial) household; Charles Thélin was given added status as the President's head servant (later promoted to treasurer of the Imperial privy purse) and Dr Henri Conneau was appointed Louis' principal personal physician, a post which he maintained to the end of Louis' life. Though hardly an entirely consistent supporter in the past, ex-King Jerome, the Emperor's youngest (and only surviving) brother, was made Governor of the Invalides, given a suite of rooms there and a substantial incomes.[1] No one was left out.

On 16 February 1849, Louis held the first of a fortnightly series of Friday evening balls at the Elysée. Every general in the army was there but, in a touch worthy of a modern public relations consultant, Louis also invited eight young privates from the Polytechnic and the École Militaire whose simple uniforms contrasted with the ornate, full-fig splendour of the generals.

So started a succession of splendid balls, receptions and galas that continued throughout the Second Republic and into the Second Empire and became a hallmark of Louis' personal style as ruler of France. Even at this very early stage, they made a profound impression. 'Fêtes, concerts, banquets and balls are becoming so numerous, are given on so large a scale and attract such crowds as almost to require the daily labours of a minister for that department alone,' reported the Paris correspondent of *The Times* on 17 March 1849.

But it was not only in Paris that the new President vaunted his new power and prestige. He was determined to show himself to the people of France throughout the country in a way that no

[1] At sixty-five, having recently squandered the fortune of his third wife, the woefully extravagant and lazy Jerome was, as often, in need of financial assistance.

previous ruler had ever done or, indeed, *could* have done, even if he had wanted to, before the building of the fast-expanding network of new railway lines that was beginning to traverse the country. In one day alone in April 1849, Louis left Paris by train at 5.00 am and endured official visits to Champagne, Morel (where he reviewed the National Guard), Ornes, Romilly, Montereau and Troyes (where he attended a banquet) before returning exhausted but content to the Elysée at 8.30 that same evening.

Over the next two years, he seems to have travelled stoically to almost every town in France where there was a new stretch of railway line to be formally opened, a new hospital to visit, an exhibition on which to bestow his patronage or military colours to be presented, and always he made well-considered and well-received speeches covering both major questions of national policy and local issues of importance. On one such visit in July 1849 to Amiens in northern France, where he gave new colours to the local National Guard, he took the opportunity to visit Ham, only twenty miles away, only three years earlier his home 'in perpetuity'. He attended an official banquet in the town and, accompanied by his fellow ex-prisoner, Dr Conneau, visited the château where the entire garrison was drawn up to salute him. In his old cell, where he noticed wryly that they still had not replaced the bookshelf he had employed during his escape, he found the rebel Arab chief, Bou-Maza, captured when fighting against the French in Algeria. He ordered his immediate release.

As he travelled from district to district and town to town, his popularity blossomed. At first, he was often greeted only with cries of '*Vive Napoléon!*' or '*Vive le Président!*' but later '*Vive l'Empereur!*' came increasingly to be heard. Always he showed his natural flair for making easy contact with ordinary people. At Rouen, when an old soldier tried to kneel before him, he lifted him up, saying: 'A soldier should kneel only to God or to fire at the enemy.' At San Quentin, when handing out 20,000 francs to distressed workers and hospital patients, he proclaimed, 'My sincerest and most devoted friends are not to be found in palaces but in cottages, not in rooms with gilded ceilings but in the workshops and fields.' At Lyons, after opening a shelter for retired silk workers, he wrote in the visitors' book: 'No more poverty for the sick worker nor for him whose age demands repose.'

But he did not lose sight of the high standing of his new position.

At Tours, where he had earlier incurred the displeasure of the stuffy high-minded local official, M. André, over Lizzie Howard's presence in his home, he said: 'Put faith in the National Assembly and in your First Magistrate who are the elect of the nation and, above all, rely on the protection of the Supreme Being who still guards France.' Claiming God as an ally hardly showed great modesty. Although Louis was nominally Roman Catholic, God seems to have paid little part in his life except as an entity whose supportive mystique he could use to good effect in political rhetoric.

But that was at the core of the ambivalent nature of Louis' approach to government: he was both one of the people and at the same time divine-appointed spokesman for the people.

It will perhaps come as no surprise that, on 31 October 1849, after less than a year in office, he dismissed Odilon Barrot and announced that, at least for a while, he proposed to rule directly through Ministers with no Prime Minister. 'An entire system triumphed on 10 December of last year,' he wrote in a message to the National Assembly, 'for the name of Napoleon is in itself a programme. It means, at home, order, authority, religion and the welfare of the people; abroad, national dignity.'

France already had an Emperor, even if that was not his official title.

The slide towards Imperial rule did not go unnoticed by Opposition politicians. They were suspicious of Louis' motives and wary of his ambitions. His oath on taking office to uphold the Republic and the Constitution became ever more suspect. During one of his provincial tours, he was widely reported as having said: 'To me order is the maintenance of that which has been freely elected and consented to by the people; it is the national will triumphing over all factions.' For 'all factions', it was very easy to read 'Opposition parties'. With Louis' track record of two previous attempts to seize power by military force, the possibility of a third – and successful – coup d'état was already in the air. Indeed, as early as July 1849, in a speech during his controversial visit to Tours, Louis had specifically denied rumours 'that the Government meditates some surprise like that of the 18 Brumaire'. (This was a reference to his uncle's successful coup d'état in November 1799 when he overthrew

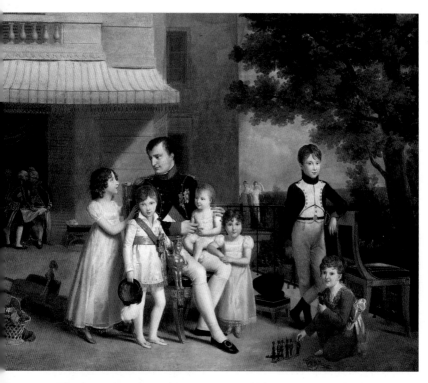

The future Napoleon III, as a two-year-old baby, sitting on the
lap of Napoleon I, his uncle, surrounded by other nieces and a nephew.
Painted by Louis Ducis in 1810.

Letizia Bonaparte, Napoleon I's mother, painted by François Gérard in 1804, the year of Napoleon's Coronation.

One of the best portraits of Queen Hortense, Napoleon III's mother, painted by Jean-Baptiste Regnault in 1810.

Louis Bonaparte and his favourite son Napoleon Louis (Napoleon III's father and older brother, who was later to die in his arms), painted by Jean-Baptiste Regnault in 1810, the year Louis abdicated as King of Holland.

The official portrait in 1853 of Napoleon III as the newly crowned Emperor of the French, accredited to the studio of Franz Winterhalter.

A rare portrait of Napoleon III's longstanding English mistress Lizzie Howard, painted by Henriette Cappelaere in the mid-1840s. Today it hangs on the wall beside Napoleon III's desk at the Château de Compiègne, which would have been impossible during their lifetime.

The Empress Eugenie and her ladies painted in 1855 by Franz Winterhalter at his flamboyant best.

In 1853, the architect Louis Visconti proudly shows Napoleon III his plans for the remodelling of the Louvre as we know it today, under the baleful gaze of Georges Haussmann, newly appointed to mastermind the rebuilding of Paris.

A scene that sums up the imperial splendour of Napoleon III's court: Jean Léon Gérôme's magnificent painting of the Emperor and Empress receiving the Ambassadors of Siam at the Château de Fontainebleau in June 1861.

The last Great Hurrah: Napoleon III surrounded in 1867 at the Universal Exhibition in Paris by visiting sovereigns, including King Wilhelm of Prussia (second from left), to whom three years later he will surrender his sword at Sedan.

Napoleon III and his generals at the Battle of Solferino in June 1859. French troops vanquished the Austrian Army but with losses of 6,000 dead and 30,000 injured. 'What a terrible thing war is!' he said, and rode off to make peace, to the dismay of his ally, Count Cavour, Prime Minister of Piedmont. Painting by Ernest Meissonier.

The scene outside a cottage on 2 September 1870, the morning after Napoleon III's surrender at Sedan, when he and Bismarck sat briefly talking.

Napoleon III and his beloved son Loulou, the Prince Imperial, in the early 1860s.

The widowed Empress Eugenie with the Prince Imperial, in the uniform of a gentleman cadet at Woolwich Military Academy, in the grounds of Camden Place. Painting by James Tissot.

the Directory and proclaimed himself First Consul en route to becoming Emperor five years later.) The Opposition politicians listened to Louis' denials but many did not believe them. In André Maurois' memorable words, 'Already the rattle of bayonets could be heard at the doors of the Palais Bourbon, home of the National Assembly.'

Accordingly, the Opposition tried to limit Louis' power. On 31 May 1850, they pushed through a new law, abolishing universal manhood suffrage[1] and reinstating a residence qualification (three years' residence) to vote. At a stroke, over two million Frenchmen were deprived of the vote. Primarily, this was designed to damage the Socialists and other left-wingers whose voters were mostly working-class, often with no permanent home – *la vile canaille* (the vile rabble), as Adolphe Thiers unpleasantly called them – but also aimed at many of Louis' supporters.

Yet Louis did not want a confrontation. Since the catastophes of Strasbourg and Boulogne, that was no longer his style and, in a sense, it never really had been. He preferred manoeuvre and intrigue, the smooth word not the naked sword. For their part, many Opposition politicians were also wary of a fight. Many were former supporters of Louis-Philippe anxious to maintain their comfortable bourgeois lifestyle. They did not want to risk a repeat of the Revolution of February 1848 or the subsequent months of turmoil and occasional bloodshed.

For a while, they tried to humour Louis and keep him reasonably contented by voting him increasingly large sums of money with which to maintain his lavish entertaining and his penchant for making large gifts. His annual salary was 600,000 francs but within eighteen months of his taking office, the National Assembly, at his urgent request, had voted him a total of 3,360,000 extra francs.

But that still was not enough for Louis. In February 1851, he asked the National Assembly for a further 1,800,000 francs but this time they turned him down. In effect, they told him to live within his income, like any other elected Head of State.

The trouble was that Louis simply could not – or would not –

---

[1] All the books talk about 'universal suffrage', and that is the expression I shall use, but, of course, it was only universal *manhood* suffrage. Women did not get the vote in France until 1944.

adjust to a lower standard. He obtained private loans from various sources: these included Baring Brothers, the ever loyal Lizzie Howard, who lent him 800,000 francs and – intriguingly – Emily Rowles, to whom as a sixteen-year-old living at Camden Place, Chislehurst, he had some ten years earlier been unofficially engaged. Now married to an Italian nobleman, she loaned him 33,000 francs.

As the year progressed, there was a growing feeling on all sides that France was moving into crisis. Louis' time as legal ruler of the country was running out. Next year, 1852, unless something happened to prevent it, there would have to be a change of President. As we have already seen, the Constitution of the Second Republic allowed Louis only one four-year term as President. Most commentators overlook the fact that technically the Constitution allowed him to stand again for a second term but only after someone else had taken over for an intervening four years. But that was no use to Louis. He wanted his power to be continuous.

Only two courses were available to him, and the possibilities were discussed with increasing openness in the corridors of power, the press and in the country generally. One was a successful coup d'état. This would not be fully to establish immediately Louis as Emperor but, on the style of 18 Brumaire and Napoleon's emergence as First Consul, to extend his term of office during which time it would be easy for him to make the transition to Imperial rule.

The alternative was to ask the National Assembly to amend the Constitution to allow Louis to stand for a second successive term as President. If legally able to do so, there was very little doubt that he would romp home to victory. But no one knew for certain what was going to happen. One observer, the snobbish Comte Horace de Viel-Castel, wrote in his diary on 23 June 1851, 'Goodness knows where we shall be this time next year!'

Louis' own preference was, as might be expected, to eschew a possible coup d'état and try to negotiate an extension of his term of office as President. This was against the combined view of the six men who were at that time, in the summer of 1851, his principal advisers. Doubting that the National Assembly would ever agree to the proposed amendment to the Constitution, they were united in urging Louis to stage a military coup as soon as possible.

These six men were: Persigny, now returned from the Berlin Embassy; Jean Mocquard, Louis' Principal Private Secretary; General Bernard Magnan, who had let him down at Boulogne but had now repledged his loyalty and, in return, been made commander of the army in Paris: Eugene Rouher, an able politician-lawyer who was Minister of Justice; Pierre Carlier, the Prefect of Police; and a recent addition to Louis' inner circle, Auguste de Morny, his half-brother.

Louis had never met Auguste until January 1849 although, as we know, he had first heard of him back in 1838 soon after the death of their mother, Queen Hortense. Thirty-eight years old, ruthless and charming, almost as great a womaniser as Louis but with a far better commercial head, he had fought with great distinction in North Africa and, after resigning from the army, had become a successful businessman of sometimes doubtful morality, investing in all kinds of speculative ventures and making a vast fortune with the help of his mistress, the Comtesse Le Hon, wife of the Belgian Ambassador.

Auguste had been a deputy and loyal supporter of Louis-Philippe but throughout his life he knew where his own best interests lay. Within weeks of Louis' election as President, he requested a private interview and, late on the evening of 23 January 1849, he was ushered into Louis' study at the Elysée.

Auguste later described the meeting in his memoirs, and it seems to have been a somewhat frosty encounter, both brothers calculating exactly how much they could be worth to the other. Louis advanced towards him with both hands outstretched and neither said a word as they stood silently contemplating each other, Auguste's hands clasped in those of Louis. In accordance with protocol, the President was the first to speak and his words had a formal tone: 'You have a great future to play in the future of France. That future is charged with storms and men of goodwill are not too numerous. I will have need of you.'

Auguste protested his devotion, and soon the conversation moved to a more intimate – but still material – terrain. He mentioned that he had heard that their mother had left him a secret legacy but he had never seen any of it. Louis replied that he knew nothing about it but promised he would look into it and right any wrong that might have been done. The conversation lasted for over three hours and it was not until 1.00 am that Louis walked with his guest to the front steps of the Elysée and, as they parted, assured him: 'I hope to arrive at a better fortune, and I shall repay the past with interest.'

The two never warmed to each other as human beings and it used to grate on Louis when Auguste boasted rather too much about their close blood relationship. But, as working colleagues, they were made for each other. Auguste swiftly became a key member of Louis' inner team, to some extent putting Persigny's nose out of joint and replacing him as Louis' most important adviser. Persigny was ideal for Louis' long years in exile as a manipulator of public opinion but, once he had achieved power, the flair, toughness and hard-nosed organising ability of Auguste were of greater value.

On 19 July 1851, after a heated debate in which Victor Hugo uttered the classic line: 'Because we have had a Napoleon the Great must we now have a Napoleon the Little?', the National Assembly rejected the proposed revision of the Constitution. Technically speaking, the motion was carried by 446 votes to 278 but since this was ninety-seven short of the three-fourths majority required by the Constitution for such a major change, the motion was lost.

The future was clear. By their own action, the politicians had sealed their own fate. They had made up Louis' mind for him. The only possible course left to him was a coup d'état. Reluctantly, he told Auguste and Persigny to complete the contingency plans on which they had been working for the past several months. The only question was the date.

It was first fixed for 17 September, but the splendidly named General Achille Le Roy de Saint-Arnaud, Auguste's protégé brought over from the French army in North Africa to command a Division near Paris and soon to be promoted to War Minister, shrewdly pointed out that the National Assembly would then be in summer recess and, with the Deputies back in their constituencies, they could more easily organise armed resistance around the country. It would be much more sensible to wait until after 4 November when the Assembly would be back in session and the Deputies would all have returned to Paris. Those hostile to Louis could then much more easily be rounded up and arrested. The logic was perfect.

The second of December was the date agreed upon. This had immense historical significance: it was both the anniversary of Napoleon I's coronation in 1804 and of perhaps his greatest victory in battle, at Austerlitz in 1805. There could be no greater omen of success.

Chapter Seventeen

Coup d'État and Almost Emperor (1851–2)

O N 1 DECEMBER 1851, the eve of the proposed coup d'état, Louis held his usual Monday evening reception at the Elysée. Wine flowed, canapés were served, the ladies were beautifully dressed, a small orchestra played in the background, the uniformed courtiers, generals and ambassadors made the usual polite small talk, trying to remember interesting tit-bits of information to be dictated to their secretaries the following morning. And the Prince-President made his usual urbane progress through the throng: a gracious smile here, a few words of polite conversation there, an occasional glint of pleasure in his eyes at the sight of a particularly pretty woman. All seemed absolutely normal.[1]

Dr Thomas Evans recalled in his memoirs many years later in his uniquely sycophantic fashion, 'He knew that great events were about to happen but the knowledge did not ruffle his serenity or change in the least the suavity of his voice or the complaisance of his address.' But Evans saw one tell-tale indication that perhaps all was not as straightforward as it seemed. Louis' cousin, the former Princess Marie of Baden-Baden, now married to the Scottish Duke of Hamilton, was one of the guests and Evans noticed that, as she

---

[1] In fact, a few days earlier there had been a last-minute hitch in the conspirators' plans when a shortage of liquid cash, essential for the final stages of preparation, was revealed. But the problem was immediately solved by Lizzie Howard who handed over to Louis 200,000 gold francs (worth much more than ordinary francs).

was leaving and Louis took her hand in farewell, he said to her quietly: 'Marie, think of me tonight.'

Shortly before 10 o'clock the reception was almost over and Louis excused himself for a moment to visit briefly Jean Mocquard, his Principal Private Secretary, who was still working in his office. 'Do you know what's happened?' he said with a laugh. 'There's a great deal of talk about a coup d'état the Assembly is preparing against me!' And he returned, still with a smile on his face, to bid farewell to his last departing guests.

That talk about a coup was not entirely frivolous, nor was it something new. Eight months earlier, Louis had told Lord Malmesbury, whom he had invited for breakfast at the Elysée on a visit to Paris: 'I have tried to consolidate all political parties but I can conciliate none. There is now a conspiracy to seize me and send me to [the prison at] Vincennes, and General Changarnier and Thiers are at its head. The Chamber is unmanageable. I stand perfectly alone but the army and the people are with me, and I don't despair.'

The hour for positive action had now arrived. By 10.15, the reception was finally over; but Persigny, General Saint-Arnaud and General Magnan did not leave with the other guests. They joined Louis and Jean Mocquard in Louis' private office, a room still called today *le Salon d'Argent* because its walls and most of its furniture are decorated in silver. Also present were Auguste de Morny, who had preferred to go to the theatre than attend his half-brother's reception,[1] and a new figure on the scene, Emile de Maupas, a burly lawyer-policeman (then as now in France a frequent combination) whom Louis had recently appointed Prefect of Police. He was a replacement for Pierre Carlier, one of the original conspirators who, losing his courage, had resigned a few weeks earlier. 'I need some men to help me cross this ditch,' Louis had told Maupas. 'Will you be one of them?' Ambitious and ruthless, Maupas had at once accepted and from then on was to prove a devoted aide, serving as Minister of Police throughout the Second Empire.

---

[1] At the Opéra-Comique, Auguste ran into General Cavaignac, the temporary ruler of France in the summer of 1848. They greeted each other cordially, Cavaignac not knowing that Auguste had already given orders for him to be arrested within the next twenty-four hours.

With the others gathered around him, Louis unlocked a secret drawer in his desk and took out a file on which he had written the one dramatic word 'Rubicon'. He opened this file and spread three sealed envelopes on the Roman mosaic table upon which his uncle had signed his abdication after Waterloo.[1] Each contained a different proclamation drawn up by Louis himself to be pasted on the walls of Paris during the night. Then Louis read the final orders for the coup from notes written by his brother. There was no great need for discussion. Their detailed plans had been hammered out in many tense, secret meetings over the previous few months. No provisions had been made for failure. It was make or break. Shortly before the meeting broke, Auguste said grimly: 'It's well understood, gentlemen, that each one of us is risking his skin over this.' 'Mine,' replied Mocquard, 'is old and well-used. I haven't got all that much to lose.'

They all shook hands and the four others departed, leaving Louis alone with his thoughts. As Auguste left, he pointed at the presidential guard on duty outside Louis' door and, thinking of the possibility that they all might end up in prison, commented wryly: 'In one form or another, you'll still have a guard outside your door tomorrow night.' Louis gave orders that he should be awakened at five in the morning and retired to bed.

Auguste and Mocquard also went to bed; but Auguste only after spending nearly five hours happily gambling at the Jockey Club en route.

No such delights for Saint-Arnaud, Maupas and Colonel de Béville, Louis' orderly officer. They had work to do. Saint-Arnaud went to visit General Magnan, the Military Governor of Paris, to tell him personally that the coup d'état was now about to take place. They had already discussed many times in detail their plans for military intervention in the coup but, because of Louis' lingering doubts about Magnan's reliability, he had never been told its exact date. Now Magnan issued immediate orders to his troops and throughout the night those orders were transmitted down the

---

[1] After the coup d'état, Elysée officials wanted to remove Napoleon's abdication table from Louis' private office but he would not hear of it. 'It might serve again,' he said.

various lines of command. Emile Maupas returned to the *Préfecture de Police* where he was to spend the night and Colonel de Béville, with Louis' three proclamations in his hands, hurried to the State printing works in the Marais, where the workers had been told to stay behind for a special night shift. While the police kept guard outside with orders to shoot anyone who tried to leave, many copies of the proclamations were swiftly run off the presses and then handed to the waiting Colonel who hastened with them in his carriage over to Maupas at the *Préfecture*. After checking they were all in order, Maupas handed them over to be distributed by bill-posters throughout the capital. By 7.30 on the morning of 2 December, the first workmen appearing in the streets found them posted up at every corner of the city.

Before then, at 5 o'clock, in the pre-dawn darkness, Magnan's soldiers had occupied the Palais Bourbon, home of the National Assembly, while others had marched to a dozen key points, followed later by regiments of light and heavy cavalry. They even took over church belfries to prevent bells being rung as a warning and occupied National Guard barracks where they commandeered the drums that might have been sounded to muster guardsmen to defend the Republic. Nothing was left to chance.

Between 6.15 and 6.45, sixteen Deputies (despite their parliamentary immunity) and some seventy other persons who might have organised resistance to the coup were simultaneously arrested in their homes by Maupas' policemen and taken off to the *Mazas* Prison (nowadays rebuilt and modernised as La Santé. Each responded in their own way. General Changarnier, whose troops had three years earlier escorted the newly elected Louis to the Elysée, met the armed police officers in his nightshirt with a pistol in his hand. Thiers panicked and pleaded with them not to kill him.[1] A Deputy named Roger, awakened in his bed, had rather more style: 'Oh, so I'm arrested! Well, Joseph, serve some sherry to these gentlemen then help me to get dressed.'

By then, Parisians stumbling sleepy-eyed to work had had time to read Louis' three proclamations. The first, called 'Appeal to the People', declared: 'The present situation cannot continue ... The Assembly ... is attempting to seize the power which I hold directly

---

[1] In fact, he ended up, for a short while, in Louis' old prison at Ham.

from the people. I have dissolved it and I have appointed the people to judge between the Assembly and me.' He announced that he had re-established universal manhood suffrage by abrogating the property qualifications of the Law of 31 May and that within a fortnight he would be holding a plebiscite so that the people could vote on whether or not to accept his plans for carrying on the government of the country.

It then continued in Louis' typical proclamatory style:

'You know that the Constitution was expressly framed to limit in advance the power which you were about to confer on me. Six million votes were a striking protest against it, and yet I observed it faithfully. Provocations, slanders, outrages have not stirred me.

'But now that the fundamental pact is no longer respected, even by those who continually invoke it and when the men who have already destroyed two monarchies wish to tie my hands in order to overthrow the Republic, it becomes my duty to thwart their treacherous schemes, to maintain the Republic and to save the country by invoking the solemn judgement of the only sovereign I recognise in France – the people.'

He went on to give an outline of the new Constitution under which he proposed to govern. It was a constitution identical in all its essentials with that laid down for France by his uncle in 1799 when Napoleon seized power as First Consul. It would entail:

(1) A Head of State elected for ten years by universal manhood suffrage.

(2) Ministers responsible only to the Head of State and not to any Assembly.

(3) A Council of State, 'composed of distinguished men', who would prepare laws, and support them in debate before the Legislative Body.

(4) A Legislative Body (i.e. Assembly) debating and voting the laws, elected by universal suffrage.

(5) A Senate, 'composed of illustrious men', which would act as 'the guardian of the fundamental pact (with the people) and public liberties'.

There was also an Edict by which 'in the name of the French people', the President of the Republic decreed, as a matter of law, that the National Assembly was dissolved, universal manhood suffrage re-established, a State of Siege proclaimed in the Paris region and Auguste de Morny appointed Interior Minister.

The third proclamation was – as earlier at Strasbourg and Boulogne – addressed directly to the army. As might have been expected, it played the Bonapartist card for all it was worth. 'Soldiers,' Louis declared, 'I do not speak to you of the recollections attached to my name. They are engraved on your hearts. We are united by indissoluble ties.' And there was much in similar vein.

On that first day, there was virtually no resistance to the coup. At 7.00 am some thirty Deputies entered the Palais Bourbon by a back door but were quickly dispersed by Magnan's troops. At about 10.00 am, an estimated 300 Deputies, finding the building closed, met in a local town hall and made long and impassioned speeches of protest until the police broke down the doors and carted them all off to gaol. A bloodless victory seemed assured and at 11.00 am Louis rode out from the Elysée into the streets of Paris.

His uncle, ex-King Jerome, who, of all Napoleon's brothers, had always looked most like the Emperor, had caused a stir on arriving at the Palace to join in the parade, resplendent in a marshal's uniform with his hand stuck into his jacket as Napoleon always used to. 'It was as if the old Emperor himself had come to join us', an impressionable member of Louis' staff later said.

As the gates of the Elysée Palace were thrown open, Louis rode out on a strikingly handsome black stallion, with Jerome on horseback beside him, a living embodiment of his link with the history and glory of France. They were followed by an entourage of generals and other senior officers, clattering along with swords clanging noisily against hard leather saddles and the hooves of the horses singing out as they clip-clopped along the highway. Some of the crowds watching their progress were muted, perhaps not fully realising what had happened or even not caring all that much. They cried simply: '*Vive la République!*' But the soldiers along the route had immediately realised the significance of events: '*Vive l'Empereur!*' many of them cried.

Riding proudly behind Louis, among the other high-ranking officers, was Count Charles de Flahaut in general's uniform, the hair surrounding his bald pate now silvery grey. He was the man whom Louis' mother, Hortense, had loved more deeply than any other, and he was there at Louis' express invitation. In a very real sense, Hortense was also present: sharing in her son's celebration and triumph.[1]

But the triumph was not yet absolutely complete. French historians often refer to Louis' coup d'état simply as *le Deux-Décembre* but there was much more to it than the events of 2 December alone.

On the following day, all started quietly in Paris. The shops and cafés opened as usual and in many parts of the capital normal life resumed as if nothing untoward had happened on the previous day. That was not to last for long.

Soon after daylight a group of intellectuals opposed to the President and led by Victor Hugo formed a grandly entitled 'Committee of Resistance' to organise opposition to the new régime and Hugo, with typical flamboyance, signed and issued a poster *Au Peuple!* saying that Louis was an outlaw and calling them *Aux Armes!* But there was little popular response. A few barricades sprang up in time-honoured Parisian fashion but there was little raw enthusiasm among the population as a whole: neither with the ordinary middle classes nor with most of the working classes.

An incident that occurred shortly before 10 o'clock on the Faubourg St Antoine in a working-class district around the Place de la Bastille was a typical, if tragic, example. A small group of middle-class militants, including a dozen Radical deputies proudly wearing their tricoloured ceremonial sashes of office, threw up a barricade and began haranguing the crowd that quickly gathered. They wanted them to clamber with them over the barricade, on the other side of which had hurriedly assembled a troop of armed soldiers, and join in a march of protest on the *grands boulevards* in the centre of the city.

But the crowd did not respond to this call to action. All over Paris that day, the workers were to prove apathetic to the cause of protest led by the middle and professional classes. Why should they be so opposed to a President, one of whose first actions had been to arrest and throw into prison the hated General Cavaignac who had slaughtered, imprisoned and sent into exile so many thousands of their comrades in the 'Red Days of June' only three years before?

---

[1] Neither Persigny nor Morny was in the cavalcade. They were schemers and planners, not ceremonial dignitaries.

So far as many Parisian workers were concerned, this was a struggle between two contending sections of the middle and professional classes. It had little to do with them.

Exasperated by the lack of response on the Faubourg St Antoine, one of the Radical deputies, named Baudin, passionately urged the crowd to join in the fight to defend the Republic. But someone shouted out: 'Why should we fight to defend your Deputy's salary of 25 francs a day?' Whereupon Baudin, a brave but foolish man, cried: 'You will see how a man is prepared to die for 25 francs a day!' and mounted the barricade – only to fall back dead a few seconds later, his brains blown out by a soldier's bullet.

But the crowd did not react by swarming angrily over the barricade, screaming for revenge. They quietly dispersed while, in hushed silence, the Deputies carried away the body of their fallen comrade.[1]

There were a few other minor disturbances that day, including an incident near the Town Hall where two civilians were killed. But when Gustave Flaubert's hero Frédéric Moreau in his epic novel *L'Education sentimentale* asked a worker if they were going to join in the fight, he replied contemptuously: 'We're not such fools to get ourselves killed for the bourgeois! Let them sort it out between themselves.'

That afternoon posters went up in the streets, signed by General Saint-Arnaud, announcing that anyone found carrying arms or helping to build a barricade would be shot on the spot. In truth, such a warning was hardly necessary.

But Louis and his advisers could not leave anything to chance. In the volatile situation that ensued, anything still might happen. General Saint-Arnaud, backed by Morny, wanted their troops to withdraw from Paris, allowing the militants to come out into the open and strengthen their ramshackle barricades, breathing the

---

[1] Some historians on both sides of the Channel (Simpson, Dansette, Ridley) doubt the full melodramatic version of Baudin's death, although that is how it is usually recounted. But it almost does not matter. The apathy of the crowd and the reckless bravery of the Deputy are a perfect replica of the reality. An Englishman in Paris, writing two days later in the British newspaper the *Morning Chronicle*, makes this observation of the scene in the streets of the French capital on 3 December, the day that Baudin died: 'The workmen and artisans are calm and do not seem by any means so much enraged as the bourgeoisie and the upper classes.'

heady whiff of impending victory – but then, on the next day, the troops would counterattack in force, slaughtering all opposition with their vastly superior manpower and gunpower. Maupas, the police chief, preferred a different tactic: he did not want to seem to be giving way. He wanted to attack in strength that very same day. He thought the workers who had rallied to the call of the bourgeois intellectuals were too few to constitute a real problem.

The only one to decide was Louis and, perhaps typically, he opted for the more devious resource. He gave orders for the troops to withdraw and a massive counterattack to be mounted on the morrow.

And so it worked out. The next day, 4 December, 30,000 troops descended upon Paris and within six hours all opposition was crushed. The barricades were smashed by artillery and the men behind them, hopelessly outnumbered, were overwhelmed by the hail of bullets and the cold steel of bayonets. Some threw down their arms and fled but the soldiers showed no mercy and many prisoners were shot out of hand.

According to official figures at the time, only 215 civilians were killed but the modern French estimate is 'between 300 and 400'.[1] Ironically, around fifty of these were not directly involved in the fighting but were innocent individuals, caring little for politics, shot down indiscriminately in the middle of the afternoon in a 'Massacre on the Boulevards' in the heart of Paris.

At around 3.00 pm the Café Anglais on the boulevard des Italiens and the nearby Café Cardinal on the corner of the boulevard and the rue de Richelieu were crowded with their normal fashionable clientele when a shot rang out in the boulevard outside. To this day, no one knows who fired it, but the soldiers and artillery on duty in the streets as a show of armed strength panicked, and began firing in every direction. They ransacked the two cafés, destroyed at least one entire building and left nearly a hundred people dead or dying before their outraged brigadier dashed to the scene and ordered an immediate ceasefire.

There was very little, if any, further violence that day. As the sun set on Paris on 4 December, it looked as if the new dimension

---

[1] See Professor Georges Pradalié's *Le Second Empire* whose ninth edition was published in 1996.

of Louis' presidential power had been achieved with comparatively little loss of life. After all, 3,000 civilians alone had been killed in the streets of Paris in the three 'Red Days of June' in 1848.

Sadly, however, the 'Massacre on the Boulevards' was not an end to the loss of life and suffering of many thousands of Frenchmen.

In Paris and in all the other major cities of France, the vast majority of the workers had not answered the call of the intellectuals to rise against the coup d'état but, in country districts, the peasants were, as always, much more ready to follow those whom they considered their social superiors. For a week between 4 and 10 December, in central, southern and south-eastern France, bands of peasants, led by middle-class extremists and working-class rabble-rousers, rampaged through the countryside, pillaging, looting and in some cases committing appalling atrocities: in one town, a priest was tortured, in others a child was killed in its mother's arms or a policeman slowly put to death. Morny, as Minister of the Interior, and General Saint-Arnaud, as Minister of War, assured Louis, horri-fied as ever by untrammelled violence, that they knew how to deal with it: swiftly and conclusively.

He gave them a free hand and, in so doing, earned for himself the hatred of many subsequent French generations. For not only were the actual insurgents themselves put down with great cruelty but 27,000 alleged supporters were arrested on mere suspicion and tried in their absence by local committees without witnesses or right of appeal. Many had probably committed no crime whatsoever except to have acquired a reputation with their neighbours for holding 'dangerous' opinions.

In this way, 9,500 men were transported as prisoners to Algeria and 239 to Cayenne in French Guinea, 1,500 expelled from France and 3,000 given forced residence away from their homes.

Later, Louis, appreciating something of the horror committed in his name, had the sentences revised and 3,500 people were eventu-ally set free. But in 1859, when a near-total amnesty was finally given, 1,800 people were still serving their sentences. His many detractors have accused him of ruthlessly sacrificing human life and liberty on the altar of his own ambition. As recently as 1995, his French biographer, Thierry Lentz, was writing of 'the black legend of the coup d'etat'.

It was all very well for the aged Empress Eugenie to claim over fifty years later: 'Moral considerations apart, *le Deux-Décembre* was a masterpiece ... Machiavelli himself ... would have had nothing but praise for it.'[1] The fact remains that one must still ask how Louis could have brought himself, not only to break his solemn oath to maintain and defend the Constitution of the Republic which he had made on becoming President three years earlier, but also pay heed to Adrien Dansette's penetrating question in 1961 in his discerning study of Louis' long struggle for power, 'How could he have taken the responsibility for a repression at once so brutal and also so blind?'

Undoubtedly Louis felt guilty for the rest of his life.

In January 1853, when George Sand, a staunch supporter during his imprisonment at Ham, wrote to him to express her sorrow at the tragic events perpetrated in his name, he invited her to come and see him. Then, with a tear in his eye which she was sure was genuine, he pleaded: 'It was not my fault.' In 1870, when discussing the coup with Napoleon Daru, a godson of Napoleon I who had fled the country at the time but later returned to serve as one of his last Ministers, he commented soberly: 'You did your duty then just as I did. I could have done nothing else.' More intimately, when one day Eugenie saw him in a dark and gloomy mood and said knowingly: 'You wear *le Deux-Décembre* like a hair-shirt,' he replied: 'I think of it constantly.'

Adrien Dansette's answer to his own question is probably as close to the truth as one can now get: 'It is possible that, following a manner of proceeding very much in his style, he felt himself forced to follow the path dictated to him by events while reserving to himself the right to make triumph later his own personal point of view.' This might be translated as saying that Louis' style was to go with the flow and then later, when practicable, try to right at least part of the wrong that had been done.

The verdict of subsequent generations of the French nation on the coup d'état may be somewhat critical but there is no doubt that the contemporary verdict was entirely in its favour.

---

[1] This was in December 1903 when answering questions on her husband's régime put to her by Maurice Paléologue, a retired diplomat, which he published in *Les Entretiens de l'impératrice Eugenie* in 1928, after her death.

On 31 December 1851, the final figures in the plebiscite that Louis had called for the 21 and 22 December were announced. The approximately eight million male voters in France had been asked to reply yes or no to the proposition, 'The French people wishes to maintain the authority of Louis Napoleon Bonaparte and delegates to him the powers necessary to establish a Constitution on the basis set out in the Proclamation of 2 December.' The result was a landslide for Louis: 7,145,000 voted yes and only 592,000 voted no. As F. A. Simpson has put it, 'If the coup d'état was a crime, France was less its victim than its accomplice.'

On the following day, the first day of the New Year 1852, a solemn Te Deum mass celebrating Louis' victory – prepared long in advance – was held at Notre Dame. As Louis entered the ancient cathedral in solemn procession, the opening chords of the Triumphal March written by Jean-François Le Sueur for Napoleon I's coronation some fifty years earlier thundered out, supported by the massed voices of a choir of 500 singers. It was the ultimate accolade.

Louis had come to Notre Dame from the President's palace at the Elysée. He was driven back afterwards to the Tuileries, the old royal palace of the kings of France since the days of Louis XIV, the 'Sun King'.

It was not a snap decision. Confident of victory, Louis had visited the building a few days earlier and selected the suite of rooms he wished to occupy. His choice was typically astute, for they had a special significance that was both immensely personal and at the same time deeply symbolic. They had once been the private apartments of the adoring grandmother whom he still recalled from his early childhood: Josephine, wife of Napoleon I and the first Empress of France.

His choice was one more positive indication of the direction in which the fulfilment of his destiny would shortly take him.

Everyone knew it was only a matter of time before the President became Emperor. The new Constitution promulgated on 24 January 1852, and based on the outline contained in his proclamation at the time of the coup d'état, was much more fitting a despotic Empire than a democratic Republic. 'The President of the Republic is responsible to the French people to whom he always has a right of appeal,' it stated. He commanded the land and sea forces and had the right to declare war and peace. He alone appointed and dismissed all Ministers. He initiated all laws. Justice was done in his name and he alone had the right of pardon. It was a blueprint for dictatorship.

The Second Empire, substantially based on this Constitution, was to be throughout its life a police state, paying lip-service to democracy and the wishes of the people, as so many police states have done before and since. But not even his most eloquent modern apologist would seek to deny that Louis was anything other than a despot – with the best of intentions, of course.

But no one was to be allowed to question too strongly those intentions. On 17 February 1852, Louis brought out the notorious Press Decree which was to curb public debate and freedom of expression for the next eighteen years. It set up a system of three official warnings (*avertissements*) which treated editors as if they were naughty schoolboys who needed to be disciplined or punished. If the Minister of the Interior thought that a newspaper or magazine article was insulting to the President (later the Emperor) or harmful to public order or good morals, he could issue a first warning which brought the offending passages to the editor's attention and urged him to take greater care in future. A second warning entailed automatic suspension of the publication for a given period, and a third warning closed it down completely. In the fourteen years from 1852 to 1866, 109 *avertissements* were served in Paris alone, although only six publications were permanently closed down.

A sort of self-imposed censorship soon grew up with editors realising exactly how far they could go in criticism of the régime without incurring too great a manifestation of its wrath.

It was not only the press that was muzzled in this way. Books too could be banned at the will – or whim – of the Government. Victor Hugo's vitriolic minor masterpiece, *Napoléon le Petit*, written in the comfort of exile in Belgium (before he moved on to Guernsey in the Channel Islands), was published in Brussels and in London. Few people in France were able to read it. It was not on sale in the shops and had to be smuggled into the country by such ingenious devices as floating it across the Belgian border hanging from balloons or encasing it in plaster busts of Louis arriving by train at Paris's Gare du Nord.

Few French people, therefore, knew of Hugo's sneering reference to Louis as: 'a man of middle height, cold, pale, slow, who looks as if he were not quite awake ... with no resemblance to the Emperor ... esteemed by women who want to be become prostitutes and men who want to become Prefects.'

But what would have hurt Louis much more was that, at least for a while, Hortense Cornu broke with him. When Princess Mathilde visited her a few days after the coup d'état, Hortense denounced Louis as a traitor who had betrayed the Republic, shed the blood of innocent Frenchmen and himself deserved to die at the hands of an assassin. In her normal forthright manner, she instructed Mathilde to make sure that she told Louis every word she had said. Mathilde did so, and Louis' not untypical reply was to say that he hoped Hortense would not play Charlotte Corday to his Marat.[1]

Louis' rule had always been in style semi-Imperial. Now increasingly one could drop the 'semi'. As Sir William Fraser commented in his memoirs, 'Immediately a monarchical change took place. I observed that on the State box at the Théâtre Français, instead of the initials R. F. (République Française) were placed at once the letters L. N.' He was called "Imperial Highness" and no longer "Prince" or "*M. le Président*". He signed himself the imperious "Louis Napoleon" and no longer the more timid "L. N. Bonaparte".[2] In February, Lord Cowley, the newly appointed British Ambassador to France, attended a ball at the Tuileries and reported back to London: 'The same etiquette was observed towards the President as would be towards royalty. A chair of state was placed for him and he occasionally paraded the rooms, way being made for him as for a Sovereign ... I saw no difference between his treatment and that of a Sovereign.' Lord Malmesbury, by then the British Foreign Secretary, wrote to Sir Hamilton Seymour, the British Ambassador to Russia, in March 1852: 'There is good reason for supposing that his (Imperial) mantle is in the hands of the *brodeuses* (embroiderers).'

[1] An ironic reference to the young ex-Revolutionary woman who stabbed to death the Revolutionary leader Jean-Paul Marat, in his bath in July 1793 because she thought he had betrayed the original 'purity' of the French Revolution.

[2] Later, as Emperor, he was to sign himself simply 'Napoleon'.

There were many other indications of Louis' new grandeur. The nation's legal code was once again called the Code Napoléon. Imperial eagles replaced the pikes which had until then topped official flag poles. New coins struck by the Mint still bore on one side the words *République Française* but on the other, for the first time, was his own bearded profile.

Already Louis was all but Emperor.

Someone less cautious might, in the early summer of 1852, have made the translation to full Imperial splendour that everyone knew was his intention. But he still hung back. He wanted to make absolutely sure, despite the massive vote in his favour in the plebiscite following the coup d'état, that the overwhelming majority of the people in the country as a whole were still behind him.

So, in the autumn of 1852, he set out on a triumphal progress through the provinces: from Lyons on to Grenoble and Marseilles, then by Montpellier right across the south-west of France to Bordeaux, finally returning to Paris by way of La Rochelle and Tours. The zealous Persigny, who had by now succeeded Morny as Minister of the Interior,[1] used all his influence, financial and persuasive, to ensure that wherever possible Louis was greeted with cries of '*Vive l'Empereur!*' or '*Vive Napoléon III!*'[2]

Of course, at times, Louis would modestly – and hypocritically – decline the title, as in Lyons where he had the considerable nerve to say: 'The cry *Vive l'Empereur!* is a heart-touching reminder rather than a hope that flatters my pride . . . If the modest title of President makes it easier for me to carry out the mission entrusted to me, then I am not the man to let personal interest exchange that

[1] His mission accomplished (i.e. the success of the coup d'état), Morny had resigned in January 1852 to devote himself to his lucrative, if sometimes questionable, business affairs. But he remained close to his half-brother, who made him a Duke and in 1854 appointed him to the prestigious but not too demanding post of President of the Legislative Body, formerly the National Assembly, which he retained until his death in 1865.

[2] In his memoirs Lord Malmesbury tells a charming story of an incident on the first night of Louis' grand tour when the local Prefect had given written instructions that the people were to shout '*Vive Napoléon!*' but, in fact, wrote '*Vive Napoléon!!!*' The people took the three exclamation marks as a numeral. On hearing their cries, Louis sent an aide to the Prefect asking what had happened. When explained to him, he said: 'I didn't know I had a Machiavellian Prefect.'

title for the name of Emperor.' At Bordeaux on 9 October, in the most famous speech of this grand tour, he was equally inexact with the truth. 'France', he said, 'seems to want the return of the Empire. But there are people who say, "The Empire is war." I say, "The Empire is peace."' Those words echoed around Europe and quite a few ageing rulers and politicians who remembered that his uncle's Empire had stood for the very opposite of peace doubted the sincerity with which they were uttered.

For Louis was not only talking to the surrounding nations. He was primarily addressing himself to his own countrymen with their love of national fame and glory. 'The Empire is peace,' he continued, 'because France desires it, and when France is satisfied, the world is peaceful.' Nothing could be more appealing to the French soul. To this day, any visitor to Versailles can see written on the stone high up on the walls of the 'Sun King's' Palace dating back over two centuries the bombastic claim, twice repeated: *A Toutes Les Gloires De La France* (To All The Glories of France). No one has ever lost popular support in France by reminding the people of their eternal glory.

On 7 November, within three weeks of Louis' return to Paris, the Senate, manned solely by his appointees, passed – subject to the inevitable subsequent plebiscite – a solemn resolution (*sénatus-consulte*) constituting him Emperor and his heirs after him. Only one senator voted against the proposal: Narcisse Vieillard. The old man wrote a personal letter of apology regretting that his conscience would permit him to do nothing else. As might perhaps have been expected, Louis' reply was to tell him that it made no difference to their long friendship and to invite him to lunch.

On 21 November, a national plebiscite approved the Senate's resolution by an overwhelming majority: 7,824,189 for with only 253,145 against.

On the evening of 1 December 1852, 200 coaches in solemn procession, lit by torches held aloft by riders on horseback, headed from central Paris to the Palace at St Cloud on the outskirts of the city where Louis, flanked by his uncle Jerome, other members of his family and all the senior officers of State, was waiting for them. 'Sire,' declared Adolphe Billaut, the President of the Legislative Assembly, 'the whole of France delivers herself into your hands.' In his emotional but, as always, carefully scripted reply, the new

Emperor said: 'I assume from today, with the Crown, the name of Napoleon III . . . But that title is not one of those effete dynastic pretensions which look like an insult to reason and to truth: it is a homage rendered to a Government that was legitimate, and to which we owe the grandest pages of our modern history. Even so, my reign dates not from 1815 [when Napoleon I had finally abdicated]. It dates from the moment when you have just made known to me the wishes of the nation.'

And he ended: 'Help me, *Messieurs*, to establish a stable Government which will have for its basis religion, probity, justice and' – a nice touch – 'a love of the suffering classes.'

The very next day, another fateful 2 December, Louis signed the decree that juridically proclaimed the Empire and declared him to be 'Napoleon III, Emperor of the French by the Grace of God and the Will of the People.' At the age of forty-four 'the other Napoleon' had at last fulfilled his dream and achieved his destiny.

PART FOUR

THE SECOND EMPIRE

Chapter Eighteen

Choosing an Empress (1852–3)

AN EMPEROR NEEDS AN Empress. A mistress, however beautiful or loyal, is not enough. Louis already had at least two illegitimate sons but he now needed not only a lawful spouse but also lawful male children – or, at the very least, one. The Imperial succession had to be guaranteed and, although one of Louis' first official acts as Emperor had been to designate his sixty-eight-year-old, sole surviving uncle ex-King Jerome as next in line of succession and, after him, Jerome's only son Prince Napoleon ('Plon-Plon'), that clearly was only a stop-gap measure.[1] 'Plon-Plon' was far too self-centred, erratic and unpopular to be a serious candidate for the throne.

There was only one course open to Louis: marriage. It was inevitable and, at forty-four, had to happen as soon as possible. In fact, having become Emperor on 2 December 1852, his wedding to the beautiful, auburn-haired twenty-six-year-old Spanish countess, Eugenia de Montijo, took place less than two months later, on 29 January 1853. Many, if not most, biographers on both sides of the Channel portray Louis as ruthlessly casting aside the loyal, generous

---

[1] The sexual niceties of the matter are quite intriguing. The Senate's resolution of 7 November 1852, which had started the legal process of elevating Louis to the throne, had left it to him to choose for himself his heirs. But it specified that, as with the First Empire's Succession Law in 1804, they all had to be male. It then broke down the sexual barriers by saying that, of all the many existing Bonaparte princes and princesses, the only ones to rank as members of the new Imperial family and be styled 'Your Highness' were those male heirs and their descendants – of either sex. So Princess Mathilde, as the legitimate daughter of the No. 1 male heir, ex-King Jerome, and her brother, 'Plon-Plon' as the No. 2 male heir, were the only two of Louis' numerous cousins to have this honour.

and devoted but clearly unsuitable Lizzie Howard in easy preference for an aristocratic young woman, three years younger than Lizzie and of impeccable family background. That does Louis far less than justice. As so often with him, the truth is much more complex.

Although outwardly still Louis' *maîtresse en titre*, Lizzie had during the years of his Presidency become, in reality, much closer to the modern concept of an 'unmarried partner', and this had continued after the coup d'état. In early 1852, Louis had given her a new home in addition to her charming house on the rue du Cirque across the road from the Elysée Palace. He gave her a ground-floor apartment at the Château of St Cloud on the western outskirts of Paris, a magnificent building standing in spacious grounds some eight miles from the centre of the capital. He was in the process of turning it into a sort of country palace where he could unwind and spend much of his leisure time not too far from the Elysée. He wanted Lizzie near him, not only during normal 'working days' in central Paris but also when relaxing at the weekends and during other rest periods.

Perhaps to cement her position but also out of genuine concern that Louis should see more of his two young sons, Eugene and Louis, she prevailed upon their mother, Eleonore Vergeot, and foster-father, Pierre Bure, to let them come and live with her and her own young illegitimate son, Martin. In fact, they were so often seen together that the story quickly spread around Paris that Louis was the father of all three boys, which would have been a physical impossibility. Martin was born in 1842 when Lizzie was still living happily in London with her previous lover, Major Francis Mountjoy Martyn, four years before she had even met Louis who was then still languishing in prison at Ham.[1]

The reality is that Louis did not want to marry, and fought as hard as he could against it. By that stage of his life, he was genuinely that somewhat rare creature for a heterosexual man: a confirmed bachelor. He had all that he needed in his private and emotional life without getting married: he had the love and companionship (when the mood took him) of an outstandingly beautiful woman;

---

[1] Yet, for reasons now impossible to determine, Lizzie told Martin that he was Louis' son and he believed it, in all good faith, for the rest of his life. So did his own children after him. His present descendants have no such delusions.

he could also enjoy unrestricted sexual adventures with as many other attractive women as he liked and he could see his young sons whenever he wanted. At a personal level, why should he get married? That was the last thing he desired.[1]

So, with his typical deviousness, he squirmed and manoeuvred to try and avoid it.

There was never any question of his being able to marry into any of the leading royal houses in Europe: the Saxe-Coburg-Gothas in Britain, the Habsburgs in Austria, the Romanovs in Russia or the Hohenzollerns in Prussia. Those old allies against Napoleon I would never have tolerated for one moment his nephew as a member of their families.[2]

Only minor or even exiled royal houses were a practical possibility. In July 1852, while Louis was still Prince-President, his cousin Marie, the Duchess of Hamilton, of whom he had always been fond, talked him into visiting her mother, Stephanie, by then the Dowager Grand Duchess of Baden-Baden, and discussing with the old lady the possibility of his marrying Stephanie's granddaughter (and Marie's own niece), the eighteen-year-old Princess Caroline of Wasa, a member of the exiled Royal House of Sweden. But, even apart from Louis' lack of enthusiasm, the project was doomed: Caroline was Protestant while he was Roman Catholic and, rather more important, she was already romantically interested in the Prot-

---

[1] Almost alone among Louis' contemporaries, Baron Hübner, the worldly Austrian Ambassador to France, appreciated this essential truth. 'Projects of marriage have never been happy in the case of Louis Napoleon,' he wrote from Paris to Count Buol, his Foreign Secretary in Vienna. 'Habits contracted in the obscurity of exile or of prison and kept up later among his intimates within the Elysée, a distinct taste for independence, relations with a woman whose intimacy might be excused, if one may so, by a devotion rare in persons of this kind and proved in adverse fortune ... were among the many obstacles in the way of those of his friends who sought in marriage the strongest guarantee of consolidating the new throne.' The kind words about Lizzie Howard are both charming and revealing.

[2] The existing sovereigns of Europe, including Queen Victoria, were reluctantly prepared to address the new Emperor as 'Monsieur mon frère' in their official correspondence, according to then common practice between crowned heads of state, but Tsar Nicholas I of Russia balked at even that courtesy. He was only prepared to write to 'Mon cher ami'. Louis' comment was typical: 'I don't really mind. One can choose one's friends but not one's brothers.'

estant, Crown Prince Albert of Saxony, whom she later married and whose queen she became.

News of the abortive marriage negotiations swiftly became common knowledge in well-informed circles in Paris and Louis found himself having a lot of explaining to do to a deeply worried and unhappy Lizzie Howard. The position was made worse for him by the fact that she had somehow persuaded herself that there was perhaps some chance, however remote, of his marrying *her*. She was not the first, and certainly not the last, mistress to cling stubbornly to the belief that somehow, despite all the odds, her lover would one day become her husband. She had one immense advantage: Louis was still not only genuinely fond of her but also very much in her sexual thrall. Comte Horace de Viel-Castel made this entry in his diary for 18 August 1852:

> At the ball at St Cloud, the President was preoccupied. Miss Howard, his mistress, had been in the house since morning and, as she had been absent because of the marriage negotiations, her return was in a sense a reconciliation. At about half-past ten, the Prince went with her to rest [*se reposer*] for half an hour. He finally retired [*retiré*] at one o'clock.

Nothing could be clearer. Lizzie decided to try and make the most of her position of power. As General Fleury wrote later in his *Souvenirs*, 'A woman like her, of quite exceptional beauty, beloved, intelligent, might well aspire to the highest position. Although our relations with Miss Howard were extremely pleasant and she never departed from a manner of almost deferential politeness towards us, her attitude had slightly changed ... If military reviews took place at Versailles, she no longer stood some distance off, lost in the crowd. A special place had to be found for her, well in the public view.'

During that summer of 1852, she began to nag Louis about marrying her. Not every monarch's wife in Europe was of royal birth, so why not she?

Finally, one night at St Cloud, in an outburst of passion, he took what she always afterwards called 'the Holy Oath'. To the end of her life, she maintained that it was a promise of marriage, but she did not reckon on his Machiavellian thought processes. When he wrote to her, as he did soon afterwards, that he 'would ensure her happiness' (*faire le bonheur*), he later explained that he meant he would restore her finances after her over-generous contributions towards the cost of the coup d'état. By writing that he intended 'at last to raise you to the position you deserved' (*te mettre enfin à ta vraie place*), he claimed he would ennoble her by Imperial decree. And so on, and so on. Louis was a past master at the art of deception.

In truth, he did not want to marry anyone and, even if he were to marry Lizzie, he realised that she probably could not give him an heir. Although still only in her late twenties, she was almost certainly no longer fertile: in those days long before modern contraception, unmarried liaisons often produced illegitimate offspring but she had not given birth in all the six years of their relationship.

All he could do was prevaricate and fudge, neither of which was anathema to his soul.

So, in October 1852, he invited to dinner his uncle, ex-King Jerome, and his son, 'Plon-Plon', and told them both in the presence of two Ministers also seated at the table: 'I have no intention of marrying.'

Nevertheless, the charade continued. On 13 December 1852, Comte Walewski, Louis' first cousin and then Ambassador in London, paid a formal visit to Louis' old friend Lord Malmesbury, the outgoing British Foreign Secretary. He came to tell him officially that the new French Emperor wished to ask for the hand in marriage of the seventeen-year-old Princess Adelaide, daughter of the Prince of Hohenlohe-Langenburg, a minor German principality. She was also a niece of Queen Victoria, since her mother was the queen's half-sister, being the daughter by her first marriage of Victoria's own mother – which put a wholly different complexion on the matter.

In fact, it was a cynical but typically well-calculated move on Louis' part. Adelaide and her parents, being sincere Protestants, would probably be reluctant to agree but there was just a chance that, perpetually strapped for money in their tiny little realm and tempted by prospects of Imperial glory, they might do so – in which case, Louis would have, as his aunt, the most powerful sovereign in Europe, Victoria herself.

Fully aware of this, Victoria astutely told Malmesbury that she would leave the decision to the girl and her parents – but not without alluding, as he records in his memoirs, 'to the fate of all the wives of the rulers of France since 1789'. For his part, the Prince of Hohenlohe-Langenburg replied that 'there were objections of religion and morals' but he would let his daughter decide.

It would have been a triumph for Walewski to have brought about this illustrious union so, as the year drew to its close, he hurriedly left London for Paris, intending to go on to Langenburg to intervene personally with the prince and his young daughter.

But, as he entered Louis' study at the Tuileries on December 31, the Emperor seized his hands enthusiastically and said: '*Mon cher, je suis pris!*' ('My dear, I am taken!') and told him delightedly that he was in love and thinking of marrying someone else. Appalled, Walewski replied that it would be politically impossible to jilt Queen Victoria's niece and that Louis should, at least, wait until he received Princess Adelaide's formal reply before doing anything rash. Reluctantly, Louis agreed: the very next morning, on New Year's Day 1853, a letter arrived from Adelaide rejecting the honour of being his wife.

Who had 'taken' the ageing philanderer? Over a century and a half later, the French still cannot make up their minds about Maria Eugenia Ignacia Augustina de Guzman y Palafox y Portocarrero, daughter of the late Count of Montijo, Countess of Teba in her own right and soon to be Empress Eugenie of France.

Throughout the second half of the nineteenth century and most of the twentieth, they were almost unanimous in their view: she was a scheming foreign adventuress who brought tragedy and despair to her adopted country. Only in recent years has a new, perhaps fairer, more rounded appreciation of her character begun to emerge: in 1990, Philippe Séguin wrote: 'The reproaches addressed to her are not totally without foundation. But her personality was at the same time more complex and more worthy of affection than one believed.' In 1995 Professor William Smith, in his contribution to Jean Tulard's *Dictionnaire du Second Empire*, quoted Eugenie herself as saying in extreme old age: 'My legend is made. At the beginning of the reign, I was a frivolous woman occupying myself only with chiffons; towards the end of the Empire, I became *la femme fatale* held responsible for all its faults and all its sadnesses. And legend always triumphs over history!'

Strangely, perhaps the most discerning judgement was that made by a young French writer whom she befriended in exile in the early years of the twentieth century. In 1911, Lucien Alphonse Daudet, son of the famous author of *Lettres de mon moulin*, wrote in his biography of Eugenie:

> Because of a somewhat sombre childhood – she saw little of her father whom she hero-worshipped while knowing that her mother preferred her elder sister – she became accustomed to existing within a world of her own creation, fortifying her soul – her Spanish soul – hardening it so feverishly, taking human weakness so little into account, spurning compromise to such an extent that this soul, indomitable to the point of obduracy, became frank to the point of blindness. Lucky for her that she forged her own armour at so tender an age, for in the future she would need all her courage to bear her up through adversity; not to die of grief.

Yet, of course, all this lay undiscovered in the future when on an evening in early October 1852, Eugenie[1] and her mother, the widowed Maria Manuela, Countess of Montijo, entered the room at a reception in the Tuileries Palace. The two women were both strikingly beautiful: Eugenie, with her blue eyes, auburn hair, fine complexion and exquisite neck and shoulders; her mother, dark-haired, vivacious, with a figure still slim and eyes that told their own tale of years of warmth and passion.

Louis inclined his head low to both, but he saw only Eugenie. He remembered her from their first meeting more than three years before when, on an earlier visit to Paris, she and her mother had been presented to him at a reception at the Elysée. He had then been so overwhelmed by the young Spaniard's beauty that he had invited them both to dine at his new country home, the Palace at St Cloud. The evening had ended in embarrassment. The two women had expected a formal dinner-party with a large number of guests at the Palace itself. Instead, they were conducted to a small house in the grounds for what they quickly realised was a

---

[1] Henceforth Eugenie, the French name by which she is known to history.

private supper for four: Louis, Comte Felix Bacciochi, his cousin and First Chamberlain – and them. It was a warm summer's evening, and after they had dined, Louis suggested that they stroll in the grounds. He offered his arm to Eugenie, while Bacciochi approached Maria Manuela to render her a similar service. Eugenie realised at once the notorious womaniser's intentions alone with her in the semi-darkness of the grounds. She said coolly: '*Monseigneur*, my mother is there!' and stepped back to allow Maria Manuela to have the honour of walking on the Prince-President's arm.

There had been no second invitation to a private supper party.

Now she stood in front of him again. If anything, she was more beautiful than before, but with a suggestion of melancholy in her eyes. Louis was enraptured for the second time.

Born in Granada, southern Spain, on 5 May 1826 in a tent set up for safety's sake in the aftermath of an earthquake, Eugenie's life had been as dramatic as her birth. Her father, Don Cipriano, Count of Teba and afterwards also of Montijo, born in 1786, was a dashing soldier who had fought and been wounded on the French side in the Peninsular War, and had taken part in the defence of Paris in 1814. In 1817, he had married Maria Manuela Kirkpatrick y Grévignée, the half-Scots, half-Belgian daughter, born in 1794, of a Scottish landowner who had emigrated to Spain and established a flourishing fruit and wine business in Malaga.

Despite his aristocratic blood, Don Cipriano was a fierce opponent of the repressive Spanish kings restored to power after Napoleon's brother, 'José I', had been forced to flee. As such, he spent many years under house arrest in Granada, where both his daughters were born. But that was not the life for Maria Manuela. She took off with the two girls for Madrid where she was to spend most of her time, soon becoming notorious for the freedom of her ways. She was reputed to have taken many lovers, including Prosper Mérimée, who remained a lifetime friend. One can most easily get her measure by her reply, when her daughter was about to become Empress of the French and she was asked about the scurrilous rumour that Eugenie was really the daughter of Lord Clarendon, British Ambassador in Madrid at the time: 'The dates don't fit.'

In 1839, Don Cipriano died and Maria Manuela devoted herself to finding a 'good' marriage for her two beautiful, Paris-educated daughters.[1] After nearly four years, she met with singular success, in February 1844, when the older girl, nineteen-year-old Francisca (known in the family as 'Paca') married the richest man in Spain: Jacobo Luis Fitz-James, 15th Duke of Alba.

That made Maria Manuela all the more determined to find a really splendid match for Eugenie who was, if anything, prettier and certainly more intelligent than the new Duchess of Alba. As a child of eight, she had sat on Stendhal's knee and listened to his stories of the great Napoleon and for her he had written the description of Waterloo at the opening of *La Chartreuse de Parme*, one of the greatest novels in the French language. She was also a brilliant horsewoman, highly sociable, with a lively wit and a habit of falling – chastely – in love with only the richest and most handsome young men.

Yet despite Maria Manuela spending eight expensive years trailing Eugenie around Europe's principal spas, always during High Season, with frequent visits to London, Paris and Madrid, she remained obstinately unmarried; and, by the time they returned to Paris in September 1852, she was getting possibly a little too old to find a really top-drawer Society husband.

Perhaps that was why Louis thought it might be worthwhile having a second try at seduction. Comte Bacciochi was therefore instructed to invite the two Spanish ladies to several more receptions and balls.

As part of this plan for sustained further contact, Eugenie and her mother were invited to a four-days' hunting party at Fontainebleau in mid-November. This was to occupy everyone's mind in the interval between the Senate's nomination of Louis as Emperor and the holding of the referendum on which he had insisted and which everyone knew would confirm the Senate's proposal. It was a tense time and, amid the added excitement of the chase, Louis 'suddenly and impulsively fell in love' with Eugenie. At least, that is the phrase used by Jasper Ridley. But, for once, the French are more prosaic. 'It was lust,' Adrien Dansette has bluntly written. 'The Prince-President was mad with desire,' is the comment of Jean Autin, Eugenie's recent biographer.

---

[1] Both girls were brought up completely bilingual: their sisterly letters to each other often mixed both languages.

As a fine horsewoman, she was first in at the kill at the end of one day's hunting and, in accordance with custom, Louis handed her the slaughtered stag's foot in tribute. This meant she had to ride back alongside him to Fontainebleau Palace. As she grimly recalled over half a century later, 'That triumphal return earned me an outburst of jealousies and calumnies.' For the word quickly got around Paris that she was Louis' latest sexual conquest.

Nor was that all. A few days later Louis gave her the superb chestnut horse she had ridden at the hunt. The stir that caused was even greater than the ride together back to the Palace. 'Dear Enrique, you cannot believe what is said of me for having accepted this damned horse!', she wrote to Don Enrique, Count of Galve and younger brother of her sister's husband, the Duke of Alba.

On 21 November, Eugenie and her mother attended another presidential ball, this time at St Cloud, and the young Spanish woman's notoriety had by now become so great that the Austrian Ambassador, Baron Hübner, reported to his Foreign Secretary in Vienna: 'The young and beautiful Mlle de Montijo[1] was much singled out by the President.' In a later dispatch, he wrote that people 'whispered at table and wrote to their friends about her. They made guesses when the breach would open and the fortress surrender.'

The surrender did not occur and Louis kept up the pressure. He had decided to spend his first Christmas as Emperor at Compiègne in the large château where the kings of France and his own uncle had often stayed and held extravagant hunting parties. So, among the 101 guests, were Eugenie and her mother, and all eyes were upon the new Emperor and the young Spanish beauty. 'Always hoping,' Hübner reported to his Foreign Secretary, 'and always disappointed, the stay at Compiègne, which was planned for only a few days, was prolonged to nearly a fortnight.'

Exasperatingly for Louis, it was at Compiègne that he finally realised there was only one way to breach the walls of 'the fortress'. While riding beside Eugenie, and thinking they were alone – but

---

[1] She was always called this in France at the time, although, after her father's death, she had, in fact, become the Countess of Teba while her widowed mother was the Countess of Montijo.

were, in fact, seen and overheard by several people – he made what Hübner called 'a new and pressing proposal'. Eugenie was seen to pull her horse up short and looking Louis straight in the eye, heard to say: 'Yes, when I am Empress, yes!' An alternative version of the same conversation that swiftly went the rounds was Louis asking, 'What is the way to your heart?' and getting the reply, 'By the church, Sire.'

Whichever form of words was used, the meaning was clear. Henceforth, Louis – and half of Paris – knew that, if he wanted to go to bed with her, he would first have to marry her.

But would he do so? Old habits die hard and none more so than the habits of one's entire adult lifetime. So many years of dedicated bachelordom were not lightly to be brought to an end. It was all very well for his uncle, ex-King Jerome, to have said some years earlier: 'He will marry the first woman who turns his head and refuses him', he still did not rush into matrimony, even after Princess Adelaide's letter arrived on 1 January 1853 rejecting his formal proposal.

That very same evening, Louis was nearly provoked into proposing to Eugenie but he still held back.

The occasion was at a grand reception and ball at the Tuileries to celebrate the New Year. Eugenie and her mother were there and, as Eugenie was about to pass into the room where supper was to be served, Madame Fortoul, the wife of the Minister of Education, complained in a loud voice that, in breach of protocol, she was entering the room ahead of her. '*Passez, Madame!*' said Eugenie at once and drew back to allow the Minister's wife to pass, but everyone could see her distress, including the Emperor. He came over and asked what was wrong. 'Sire, I have been insulted and will not be insulted a second time,' she replied, almost in tears. 'Tomorrow,' said Louis in a voice that everyone around could hear, 'no one will dare to insult you.'

And that was that. Many people, including Eugenie and her mother, assumed that a formal proposal of marriage must surely follow, if not the very next day, at least the day after.

Yet, at that very last moment, Eugenie seems suddenly to have asked herself if marriage to Louis was what she really wanted. Out of the blue, she sent a telegram to a handsome young Spanish nobleman named José, Marquis of Alcanices,[1] with whom a few years earlier she had fallen passionately in love. It had been the first, and some say, the only true love of her life and she had tried to poison herself after discovering that his only reason for paying court to her was to gain access to her married sister, Paca, whom he had hopes (unfulfilled) of seducing. Eugenie had not lost touch with him because he was also the girls' cousin and she still retained, like many a woman wronged by a man, feelings of tenderness for him. So now she wrote: 'The Emperor is asking to marry me. What should I reply?' Unknown to her, Louis' secret police were keeping her under surveillance and they brought the telegram to him asking if they should allow it to go on its way. 'It is none of my business,' said Louis. 'Send the telegram.'

Alcanices' only reply was to give Eugenie his congratulations.

Meanwhile, day followed day without any message from the Tuileries. Not since Louis had first seen Eugenie at the ball in October had so long a time gone by without any communication from the Palace. The truth is that Louis was having to cope with the objections of his Ministers who were, almost to a man, opposed to the match, as unworthy of his new Imperial dignity. Most of his close associates agreed. 'If he couldn't find a royal princess, why couldn't he at least have chosen a French countess not a Spanish one!' said Morny. 'We've not made the Empire for the Emperor to marry a flower-girl,' exclaimed Persigny. 'One sleeps with Mlle de Montijo, one does not marry her,' sniffed Louis' cousin, 'Plon-Plon', conveniently forgetting that Eugenie had refused to sleep with him during her visit to Paris three years earlier.

As for Princess Mathilde, who saw her privileged position as the Emperor's official hostess fast disappearing, she is alleged to have thrown herself at Louis' feet begging him not to make such a grievous error. (Her objection was not only self-serving. With one woman's insight into another, she realised that Eugenie was too cerebral for Louis, too coldly calculating, too uninterested in sexual matters, to make him really happy. Never one to mince her words, she said to friends: 'She has neither heart nor cunt.')

---

[1] In this small world, where everybody seems to have known everyone else, Alcanices, later Duke of Sesto, married the widow of Auguste de Morny, Louis' half-brother.

Persigny did not restrict his opposition to angry words. With an intensity bordering on jealousy, he whipped up even greater popular clamour against '*l'Espagnole*', circulating scurrilous pamphlets against Eugenie and her mother. 'To hear the way in which men and women talk of their future Empress is astonishing,' Lord Cowley reported to the Foreign Office in London. 'Things have been repeated to me ... which it would be impossible to commit to paper.'

It was all very well for Lord Cowley to refer to Eugenie as 'the future Empress' but she – and her mother – were by no means so sure. Why had they not heard from the Palace? On 7 January, a council of war took place in their apartment on the Place Vendôme involving the two women, their cousin, Ferdinand de Lesseps, future builder of the Suez Canal, Prosper Mérimée and the Count of Galve, on a visit to Paris. What should they do? How were they to bring Louis to a decision, preferably the right one?

It was Prosper Mérimée's cool advice that won the day: the two ladies were to announce that they were leaving Paris at once for Italy.

Then, almost at that moment, there arrived an envelope from the palace. But it was not a proposal of marriage, merely an invitation to Eugenie and her mother to yet another Court ball, this time on 12 January. 'Go to the ball,' Mérimée told Eugenie, 'and tell the Emperor to his face that you are leaving.' With some embellishments of her own making, that is what Eugenie agreed to do.

On the evening of 12 January, Eugenie entered the ballroom at the Tuileries dressed in a flamboyant gown of ivory brocade trimmed with silver tassels, a wreath of orange blossoms in her hair. The significance of the blossoms was not lost on anyone: they were usually worn by a bride on her wedding day.

After curtseying to the Emperor on his dais, with Princess Mathilde beside him, Eugenie, on the arm of the Baron James de Rothschild, and Maria Manuela, escorted by the Baron's son, moved to a table reserved – as they surely would have known – for Ministers' wives. The Baron and his son bowed and left them. But they had nowhere to sit. The Baroness Drouyn de Lhuys, wife of the Foreign Secretary, angrily rose to her feet and said there was nowhere at the table for 'a foreign adventuress'. This really was too much. Louis at once went over and invited Eugenie and her mother to join him on the Imperial dais.

Then, when the orchestra struck up a quadrille, he led her on to the floor. As they danced, she demanded to speak to him in private. They finished the set and then, watched by the hundreds of guests, left the room. Alone in Louis' study, she tearfully declared, her eyes flashing with anger, that she was no longer prepared to stay at Court to be insulted again in such appalling fashion. She and her mother would leave for Italy the next day. 'I am willing to live dangerously by your side,' she said, 'but I am not prepared to remain here and be insulted.' That did it. Taking her hand in his, Louis promised that he would write to her mother formally requesting permission to marry her.

When they returned to the ballroom, with a gentle smile upon Eugenie's lips, everyone knew – or guessed – what had happened. 'One can say that the marriage was announced at that ball,' Baron Hübner reported to Vienna.

On 15 January, Maria Manuela received this letter at her apartment on the Place Vendôme:

Madame la Comtesse

For a long time I have been in love with Mademoiselle your daughter and have wished to make her my wife. I am today therefore asking you for her hand, for there is no one so capable of making my happiness or more worthy to wear a crown.

I pray if you consent to this proposal not to reveal it until we have been able to make our arrangements.

Believe me, Madame la Comtesse, when I assure you of my sincere friendship.

Napoleon.

Maria Manuela immediately replied giving her consent and later that very same day Eugenie sat down and wrote to her beloved sister, Paca: 'My dear and good sister. I wish to be the first to announce to you my marriage with the Emperor. He has been so noble, so generous with me, he has shown me so much affection that I am still overcome. He has struggled with the Ministers and conquered.' She enclosed a handwritten copy of 'His Majesty's' formal letter of proposal received that morning but, slipping into their native Spanish, assures her sister that, no matter what the future may hold, she will always turn her eyes towards her and that 'the Destiny that has held them so close together since their childhood' will never change. It is a poignant and patently sincere letter.

On 22 January, when the 'arrangements' mentioned by Louis had been finalised, he announced his decision to the entire Senate, the Council of State and the Legislative Body assembled at the Tuileries.

In a brilliantly written, but (it has to be said) not brilliantly read, speech, he told them of their new Empress. 'When, facing the old Europe,' he said, 'a man is carried by the force of a new principle to the height of the old dynasties, it is not by making his coat-of-arms look older and by trying at all costs to introduce himself into the family of kings that he wins acceptance but by frankly taking up before Europe the position of a *parvenu* – a glorious title when it is obtained through the free vote of a great people . . .[1]

'The lady whom I have preferred is of lofty birth. A Catholic and a devout one, she will join me in my prayers for the happiness of France. I have chosen a woman I love and respect rather than one unknown to me or an alliance which would involve sacrifices as well as advantages. In a word, I put independence of mind, a warm heart and domestic happiness above dynastic interests: I shall be the freer and therefore the stronger for it.'

That same day, Eugenie and her mother moved into the Elysée. 'Today,' she wrote to Paca, 'was the first time I heard the cry of *Vive l'Impératrice*! God grant that may never change but adversity will find me firmer and more courageous than prosperity.'

The thirtieth of January was the date fixed for the wedding at Notre Dame. On the previous day, Eugenie wrote again to Paca a revealing letter, in which, although writing with great affection of her husband-to-be, she never once, even in the full text, says that she loves him:

Dear Sister,
This is a sad time for me. I am saying farewell to my family and

---

[1] Queen Victoria, in particular, disliked his defiant use of this word. She wrote in her journal that it was 'in bad taste'.

my country in order to devote myself exclusively to the man who has loved me sufficiently to raise me up to one of Europe's greatest thrones ... I cannot defend myself against a certain terror. The responsibility is immense. Good and evil will be attributed to me. I have never been ambitious and yet my destiny has raised me to the summit of a slope down from which one could be hurled for the most slight of reasons ...

I look upon my future as a Divine mission, at the same time thanking God for having placed a heart so noble and so devoted as that of the Emperor in my path. I have suffered so much in my life that I had almost ceased believing in happiness yet now once more I do believe in it ...

This man has an irresistible strength of will without being obstinate; capable of the greatest and smallest sacrifices, he would go into the woods to gather a flower on a winter's night, tearing himself from his fireside to get soaked in order to satisfy a woman's whim. The day after he will risk his crown rather than not share it with me. He does not count the cost. He will risk his fortune on a throw, and that is why he always wins.

Soon after midday on 30 January 1853, amid the fanfare of trumpets and the salute of guns, Eugenie, in a dress of white velvet with a diamond crown on her head, walked down the aisle of Notre Dame, on her husband's arm, as Empress of the French. The crowd outside, to whom she had curtseyed low upon her arrival – we will never know whether it was her own idea or Louis' shrewd suggestion – cheered as they emerged from the great West Door of the cathedral.

But there were still many discordant voices. 'We are living in a society of adventurers. The great one of all has been captured by an adventuress,' Lord Cowley, the British Ambassador, reported to London.

Chapter Nineteen

Consolidating His Throne (1853–6)

L OUIS NOW HAD AN Empress; but what about his mistress? Throughout the entire period of his courtship, despite all the intensity of his desire for Eugenie, he had never ceased to visit Lizzie Howard either in her apartment at the Palace of St Cloud or in her town house on the rue du Cirque. The chaste Eugenie may well have ruled his heart but the exciting and accomplished Lizzie still ruled his more basic sexual impulses. Of course, during December 1852 and the first three weeks of January 1853 she had heard the rumours about Louis' impending marriage but she was a realist: if she was not to be Louis' wife – for practical reasons which she now reluctantly accepted[1] – she saw no reason why she could not happily continue as his mistress.

And, as throughout his life, Louis was content to have the best of both worlds for as long as he safely could.

The operative word was 'safely'. He knew that Lizzie was unpredictable. She was a passionate, highly jealous woman who, in a torment of rage at rejection, might do almost anything to harm him. And she had a very powerful weapon with which to do so: scores, perhaps hundreds, of his letters written to her during the six long years of their liaison, in which he had poured out his innermost hopes and despairs. He knew she had kept them all, in neat bundles tied with silk ribbon. If published, they could be highly embarrassing, if not dangerous.

Louis resorted to a typically Machiavellian manoeuvre. He asked her to perform a highly secret and personal service, the need for which had suddenly arisen. He explained that he was being black-

---

[1] As she wrote to an English friend, 'If the fair Infanta has not yielded, marry he may.'

mailed by an Englishman who was threatening to reveal secrets of his political activities during his exile in London between his escape from Ham and his successful return to Paris. He had to be bought off, but it could not be through normal channels. He could not ask Walewski, his ambassador in London, to get involved in such a highly confidential matter. He begged Lizzie to go swiftly to London as his special envoy, accompanied only by Jean Mocquard, his Private Secretary, and do all that was necessary to rid him of the perils of this blackmail.

The date chosen for her cross-Channel voyage? 22 January, the day on which he knew that he was going formally to announce his forthcoming marriage to Eugenie before the entire Senate, Council of State and Legislative Body assembled at the Tuileries Palace.

But his plans went awry. Early on the morning of 22 January, Lizzie and Mocquard left Paris to catch the overnight boat from Le Havre to Southampton. The boat did not sail. A storm in the English Channel kept it in harbour so that Lizzie and Mocquard had to spend the night in a local hotel. So it was at breakfast the next morning in Le Havre – and not safely in England – that she read the official news that His Imperial Majesty was about to marry Eugenie 'to consolidate his government . . . and to assure the future of the dynasty'. Furious, she turned on Mocquard who bleated his excuses. Angrily, she insisted that they return at once to Paris, and when she stormed into her house on the rue du Cirque she realised at once the true reason for her so-called 'secret mission' to London. The place had been ransacked: the furniture overturned, the wardrobes opened and their contents scattered on the floor; but nothing of value had been stolen. Her silver, her jewels, her paintings, her rare china, all were intact. The only thing missing was her letters from Louis, the secret drawer in her desk in her bedroom, where she kept them, lying empty on the floor, its lock broken. On the personal orders of the Emperor, Charlemagne-Emile de Maupas, Louis' chief of police, had instructed his men and they had efficiently carried out their task.[1]

Lizzie was beside herself with anger. She demanded that Louis come to see her at once, no matter what else he was doing; and, to

---

[1] The letters were never to be seen again. Almost certainly, they were destroyed.

give him grudging credit, he did so. Despite his almost pathological dislike of personal confrontation, he came round that evening to the rue du Cirque and a 'deal' was hammered out. But it does not seem to have been a very edifying scene. 'His Majesty was here last night offering to pay me off,' Lizzie wrote to an English friend. 'An earldom in my own right, a castle and a decent ... husband into the bargain ... Oh, the pity of it all! I could put up with a dose of laundanum ... The Lord Almighty spent two hours arguing with me ... Later he fell asleep on the crimson sofa and snored while I wept ...'

Even so, the 'pay-off' was quite reasonable. Since Louis wished it, she agreed to get married to someone else, but she insisted that it would have to be to an Englishman, not a Frenchman. She was to become a countess, with her son, Martin, eventually succeeding to the title and given French nationality. She would be allowed to live at the magnificent Château de Beauregard she had recently bought on the south-western outskirts of Paris[1] and Louis' two illegitimate sons, Eugene and Louis, would continue to live with her and Martin until they had grown up. (Their natural mother was rightly expected not to oppose this plan. She had lost much interest in the two boys since her third son had been born nearly three years earlier, the offspring of her marriage to Pierre Bure.) Finally, Louis agreed to pay back the five million gold francs that he owed Lizzie for her financial help over the years.[2]

Yet money and a title were not enough. Lizzie's distress was real and compelling. Before leaving her apartment at St Cloud she wrote him a letter which must have moved him, for he kept it until the end of his reign. After the collapse of the Second Empire in September 1870, it was found among his personal effects at the Tuileries. Why did he keep it? Was it as a souvenir of the only woman who had ever really loved him, and whom alone he had ever truly loved?

[1] Nowadays only one wall of the château remains and the 400 acres of its grounds have been converted into a vast modern housing estate. But Lizzie is not forgotten: one of the roads is called 'Avenue Miss Howard'.

[2] He paid one million gold francs within two months and the balance of 4,449,000 gold francs over the next two years. Generously, he gave her – from State coffers – nearly half a million gold francs in interest. A formal record of the transactions was found among the papers of the Imperial household after the fall of the Second Empire, as verified by pages 157–60 of Volume I of *Papiers et correspondance de la Famille Impériale*.

'Sire, I am leaving,' she wrote. 'I could easily have sacrificed myself to political necessity but I cannot forgive you for sacrificing me for a whim. I am taking your children with me and, like another Josephine, your star.

'I ask only for one last interview to say an eternal goodbye. I hope you will not refuse me . . .'

It is sad to report that he *did* refuse her. There was no tear-stained 'eternal goodbye'. But it also has to be said that Louis, being the man that he was – and Eugenie being the frigid lover that he soon discovered her to be – was back in Lizzie's bed within six months. For the truth was that his bride, although performing grimly her matrimonial duty and duly becoming pregnant inside two months, disliked the physical act of love so much that she used to describe it to her ladies-in-waiting as 'disgusting'. Nor was this disgust helped by the fact that in April 1853 she had a painful miscarriage. The following month, she wrote to her sister, Paca: 'I have been in bed for twenty-two days . . . I am beginning to become extremely depressed . . . Today, I wanted to try to stand but I could not, so great is my weakness, the result doubtless of loss of blood . . .'

In those circumstances, it is easy to understand how even more unwelcome any sexual advances by Louis would have been.

The result was inevitable. By early July 1853 it was public knowledge in Court circles that Louis had resumed frequent sexual encounters with the newly styled Comtesse de Beauregard. But it was not to last for long. In late September, Eugenie, hearing what had happened, gave her husband a simple choice: his ex-mistress or his wife. As a secret police agent reported to de Maupas, who kept secret files on his Emperor: 'Something of a scene took place . . . Her Majesty the Empress told the Emperor that she did not care for the throne but only for her husband; that she had not married the Sovereign but the man; and that the first wrong he committed towards her would be decisive . . . The Emperor, always calm and gentle, even when he is in the wrong, ultimately succeeded in calming her anger by promising to break off all contact with the person in question.'

Louis was as good as his word. He wrote to Lizzie saying that, with regret, they could not meet any more but that Jean Mocquard would always be available for a 'verbal message'.

For all his one-time feelings of love and great passion, Louis thereafter effectively cut Lizzie out of his life. He had an Empire to build, an Imperial future to secure. He could not allow himself the luxury of pondering his ex-mistress's fate. As for Lizzie, although still only just thirty, she was never again to know full happiness.

In May 1854, she married in London Clarence Trelawny, the handsome son of an army captain and three years her junior. He was very much in debt and there seems little doubt that he married her primarily for her money. They were together for only a few years before he departed and she was left alone in quiet semi-contentment with her 'three sons', as she called Martin, her only true son, and Louis' two boys, Eugene and Louis.

She was soon to lose the last two.

In August 1858 their mother, Eleonore Vergeot, once again pregnant, married her long-time partner Pierre Bure and, in so doing, automatically legitimised Louis' two illegitimate children. Now promoted to French upper middle-class respectability, she demanded that Eugene and Louis be returned to her. In vain, Lizzie protested that the boys had been given into her hands by their father and that, for ten long years, she had cherished them. But that provided no legal answer. The two boys, then aged fifteen and thirteen, were taken away from her and sadly, with the callousness of youth, soon forgot her.

She wrote to an English friend: 'I am in sorrow. The terrible ordeal of parting from my beloved boys shall be my undoing ... Unfortunately I have not met His Majesty for years and now Mme Bure wants her whole family to look respectable ... Anyhow, let us all do as he pleases. His will be done in Beauregard as it is in Paris. God bless the Emperor! He that can do no wrong probably knows best. Whatever he enforces, I shall love him till I die.'

The rest of her story was a long, sad farewell to life. She shut herself up in her sumptuous château and became known as 'the hermit of Beauregard' with Martin, by then living an adult life in Paris, as her only – infrequent – visitor. Then in 1861 she was diagnosed as suffering from cancer. She calmly made her will, leaving everything to Martin, and prepared to die.

But she was still only in her late thirties and her body remained strong. She lingered for three years until in the winter of 1864–5 the doctors told her that the cancer was spreading and the end was near. In one last flourish of independence, she returned to Paris and took up again something of her old life. She was often to be seen on the Champs Elysées and in the Bois de Boulogne, driving her phaeton speedily behind a superb pair of bays.

Then came her final, personal gesture of defiance. She booked a box opposite the Imperial box at a leading Parisian theatre for a first night which she knew Louis and Eugenie would be attending. Long before the curtain went up, she took her place dressed magnificently in a silk gown, trimmed with sable. During the whole evening, leaning upon the edge of her box, she gazed remorselessly at the Imperial couple through her opera glasses. The audience had more regard for the drama being enacted within the auditorium than that being played out upon the stage.

Then, having made her point, she returned to Beauregard and gave orders that a suite of rooms should be made ready in case the Emperor came to bid his farewell.

But it did not happen. Louis never came to Beauregard and on 19 August 1864 Lizzie slipped quietly into the comfort of death. She was entirely alone. Not even her own son was present.

If Louis felt any remorse or sadness, he did not show it. The only indication that, deep down in his complicated nature, he preserved some special feeling for her is the fact that he kept, locked away among his personal effects, the note she had written him eleven years earlier begging him for one last meeting: 'to say an eternal goodbye'. In fact, I believe that he loved her very much and that she was the one woman who, apart from his mother, meant most to him in life.

But, in the ultimate, she stood between him and his destiny and there was no question that she must be sacrificed.

The new reign and Louis' marriage had not started off well. Lord John Russell, the new British Foreign Secretary, had written to Lord Cowley: '[The marriage] is a very false step. A marriage with a well-behaved young Frenchwoman would, I think, have been very politic, but to put this "intrigante" on the throne is a lowering of the Imperial dignity with a vengeance!' That was a view shared by many people on both sides of the English Channel.

And there were those in Paris who had noticed with dismay that, as the state coach bearing Louis and Eugenie left the Tuileries for

Notre Dame on the day of their wedding, the gilt crown on its roof fell to the ground. It had done this twice before: in 1804, when Napoleon I went with Josephine to his coronation and, in 1810, when he went with the Austrian princess, Marie Louise, to his second wedding. Neither were good omens.

Yet for the next four years all that Louis touched seemed to turn to gold. In June 1853, he appointed a Frenchman with a German-sounding name, Georges Haussmann (his family's origins were in southern Germany), to be the new Prefect of Paris and to carry out the Emperor's plans for the creation of a new capital that would be worthy of the new Empire. That entailed the destruction of much of the old city, with its narrow alleyways and insanitary, tightly packed tenements, changing it into the wonderfully expansive Paris that we know today. And Haussmann very much worked to Louis' blueprint: within minutes of the new Prefect taking his formal oath of office, Louis presented him with a map of Paris on which he had already marked the new boulevards that he wanted built.

Louis' interest was direct and detailed. Four years earlier, when driving with Persigny through the Bois de Boulogne, he had seen the huge clouds of dust thrown up by their carriage and said: 'We need here a river as in Hyde Park to revive this arid terrain.' He placed a remodelled Bois, complete with two man-made lakes, high on Haussmann's list of priorities.

The images that everyone recognises today – the Place de l'Étoile, the large squares, the splendid parks, the broad, straight streets and tall ornate buildings – all are Haussmann's creation, inspired and supported by Louis. That support was to last until that day seventeen years later, in January 1870, when the Prefect's unpopularity, generated by his personal arrogance and the unhappiness of so many Parisians evicted with little compensation from their homes to make way for the changed city, forced Louis to ask for his resignation and, when refused, to dismiss him with typically reluctant but very real ruthlessness.

But that was in the future. In the early years of the Second Empire, Haussmann could do little wrong in Louis' eyes. In November 1853, for instance, the Prefect announced plans for a magnificent new avenue leading up from the rue de Rivoli to where a new Opera House was to be erected. The thoroughfare was to be called the avenue Napoléon III and for a while proudly bore that name: now we know it only as the avenue de l'Opéra.

The legend has grown up that Haussmann's grand boulevards and avenues, often punched through crowded working-class districts, were primarily designed to make it harder for insurgents to throw barricades across and easier for soldiers to be moved fast along to cope with outbreaks of trouble; and Haussmann himself admitted there was some truth in that. But it was only a minor consideration: it was his – and Louis' – overwhelming desire to create, in Louis' words, 'The capital of capitals.'

But the embellishment of Paris did not stand on its own. It was part of a general upsurge in economic and industrial growth that characterised the Second Empire. It was as if Paris was leading the entire nation into a new and exciting future. 'When building booms, everything booms,' was the current saying. In 1852, the powerful Crédit Mobilier, a bank offering for the first time credit facilities to the emerging lower middle classes, had opened its doors. Swiftly it was followed by a banking revolution that changed for ever the French financial landscape and afforded the easy provision of working capital for industry and commerce.

During his years of exile in London, Louis had seen the rapid growth of the British railway system and, realising that the easy transportation of people and goods was essential to an emergent and viable economy, was determined to create such a structure in France. Fuelled by a powerful combination of State financing and private enterprise, French railways in the 1850s began to forge their way across the country. The figures are eloquent in themselves. In 1851, there were only 3,910 kilometres of operational track; in 1856, the number had risen to 6,500; in 1870, the national network extended to 17,000 kilometres. This led promptly to the progressive creation of broader, national markets and the beginning of specialisation for the most advanced agricultural regions.

At the same time, new forms of retail shops blossomed everywhere, starting with the opening in June 1853 by Aristide Boucicaut, a Parisian entrepreneur, of the first French department store: Au Bon Marché.

Certainly there were similar developments in the mid-nineteenth century in industrial and commercial power in all leading European countries, but Louis gave his a more personal, if not paternalistic,

Napoleon III, Queen Victoria, Empress Eugenie and Prince Albert at the Crystal Palace during the French couple's hugely successful State visit to Britain in April 1855.

Napoleon III (right) watches proudly as his two-year-old son Loulou, the Prince Imperial, is photographed sitting on a tightly held horse in 1858.

The Prince Imperial as a young man.

Napoleon III photographed by André Disderi in 1865.

The Archduke Maximilian of Austria and his wife Charlotte, photographed in 1865 in Mexico where a year earlier they had been installed by French troops as Emperor and Empress. In two years, Maximilian would be executed, while Charlotte would live on for sixty more years, mad with grief.

The unglamorous face of defeat: French prisoners-of-war cooking their meal in a German PoW camp near Cologne after the Franco-Prussian War.

The manuscript (detail) of the famous Ems Telegram of 13 July 1870, as written by King Wilhelm of Prussia's personal secretary. Bismarck did not alter a single word but achieved his desired effect by putting a line through the parts he did not like.

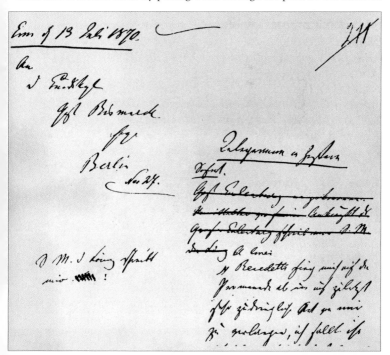

Eugenie photographed in 1880, still in mourning for the Prince Imperial's death the year before.

The last photograph of Napoleon III taken at Camden Place in December 1872
within weeks of his death.

Exterior of Camden Place: engraving in the *Illustrated London News*.

The exiled Napoleon III's small, cluttered study at Camden Place, Chislehurst.

nuance. He had not lost his notions of a vague sort of State socialism of which he had written in *L'Extinction de paupérisme*. As Prince-President, he had ordered that people should not work in public enterprises on Sundays and holidays. Now, as Emperor, in the summer of 1853, when food shortages drove prices up in Paris, he asked the railway companies' directors to carry food to the capital at a nominal cost in return for a free holiday at a château near Dieppe where he and Eugenie had spent their delayed honeymoon. The response was positive and immediate. In November 1853, he asked the authorities to set up a scheme so that doctors in Paris could give free medical treatment to the poor in their homes and relieve overcrowding in the hospitals. In March 1855, he established the National Hospital at Vincennes to care for workers injured at work, on similar lines to the existing Invalides Hospital caring for soldiers wounded in battle. Politically, he was a despot but it was a despotism tinged with humanity.

At home, all was going remarkably well. However, what he needed fully to cement his power and his prestige was, quite bluntly, success in war.

'The Empire is peace,' he had promised at Bordeaux in October 1852. The promise was quickly to prove as cynical as his oath of loyalty to the Second Republic on becoming Prince-President in December 1848. For within two years, France was at war, in one of the most senseless, unnecessary shedding of blood in modern history.

Even as he spoke those words at Bordeaux, Louis knew they were a lie. He knew that, seeking as he was to follow in the steps of the great Napoleon, he would need a great victory in war to seal his bond with the French nation; above all, with the army, eager to achieve new glory on the field of battle. Within weeks of his speech at Bordeaux, he was far more honest in a private letter to Eugenie, his bride-to-be, warning her of the risks she was taking in agreeing to share his throne: '. . . I must tell you too that serious plots are afoot in the Army. I am keeping my eye on all this, and I reckon that by one means or another, I can prevent any outbreak: perhaps by means of a war.'

The chance came soon enough, and from an extremely remote source. For centuries, the Holy Places in Jerusalem had been cared for by both Roman Catholic and Greek Orthodox monks and, for over a century, the Roman Catholics had been regarded as under French protection and given special privileges. During the atheistical days of the French Revolution and in the subsequent turbulent years, France's interest in the everlasting quarrels of the two contending groups of clerics had lapsed, and the Greek monks had been allowed to encroach upon the rights of their Roman rivals. Now suddenly the new French Emperor found this an intolerable stain upon the honour of his nation; he was supported not only by the army but also by the French Roman Catholic Church.

Basically, the dispute boiled down to which monks should have the keys to which doors in the Church of the Holy Sepulchre but Louis purported to take the matter very seriously and demanded full restoration of the Roman Catholic monks' rights. Palestine was then part of the vast but decaying Turkish Empire, 'the sick man of Europe', as Tsar Nicholas I called it, and the Sultan of Turkey, fearing a confrontation with France, readily granted Louis' demands. Tsar Nicholas, whose country had long wanted to have a foothold in the eastern Mediterranean and whose eventual aim was the dismemberment of the Turkish Empire with Russia grabbing Constantinople for itself, supported the Greek monks and insisted that the Sultan withdraw his concession to Louis.

In truth, there was a hidden agenda to Louis' demands. It was not merely because he wanted an excuse to be seen flexing his muscles on the world stage; it was also because, ever since his uncle's abortive conquest of Egypt in the late 1790s, French rulers had dreamed of extending their influence throughout the Mediterranean. Even the boringly non-warlike Louis-Philippe had sent French troops to conquer Algeria in the early 1830s and ten years later supported the pro-French Mehemet Ali as Pasha of a newly independent Egypt, torn from the entrails of impotent and corrupt Turkish rule. For at least half a century France had dreamed of acquiring a paramount influence in the eastern Mediterranean not only for its own sake but also to enable her to cut a canal through the isthmus of Suez, opening up a new and faster route to India and the Far East instead of the long, arduous journey around the tip of southern Africa.

The Sultan dithered between the two conflicting postures of Louis and Nicholas I; in July 1853 Nicholas lost patience and sent his troops across the border into the principalities of Moldavia and Wallachia. Later, these two countries were to constitute the modern state of Romania but then they formed part of the Turkish Empire. Diplomatic efforts to persuade the Russians to withdraw failed and, on 23 October 1853, the Sultan declared war on Russia.

The Turks were no match for Russian might. Within six weeks the Sultan's navy was destroyed by the Russian Black Sea fleet at the Battle of Sinope, and both France and, indeed, Britain, realised that the unappealing prospect of Russian emergence into the eastern Mediterranean was an almost imminent reality. In January 1854, combined British and French naval fleets entered the Black Sea. In early February, a joint ultimatum was dispatched to Russia, demanding its evacuation of the two Balkan principalities. On 30 March 1854, Britain and France declared war.

The war fell into two unequal parts. The first was short, lasting only four months until July 1854, by which time the Russians had been forced to withdraw from the Balkan principalities and retreat into their own territory. But remembering all too well that Napoleon I's undoing had been his disastrous expedition into the Russian heartland, the Allies chose to invade the Crimea where problems of supplies and the difficulties of transport in a vast country without railways and only few roads would – at least, in theory – give the British and French forces, supplied by sea, a tremendous advantage.

The landing of the Allies in the Crimea was secured by the Battle of the Alma in September 1854 but thereafter things did not go well. The war degenerated into a bitter, year-long siege of Sebastopol, the Crimea's main port, and the Russian efforts to relieve it.

It was halfway through this morass of bungling and human suffering that, in April 1855, Louis suddenly announced that he intended to sail for the Crimea to assume control of the French Expeditionary Force. Eugenie, at her own insistence, would accompany him, at least as far as Constantinople. His reasons were basically practical. To begin with, his cousin 'Plon-Plon' (the effective heir to the throne being next in line after his father, the ageing ex-King Jerome) had gone to the Crimea and returned unexpectedly with ill-health as his excuse. But nobody had been deceived. He had quite simply proved a coward under fire. It was not long before the nickname 'Plon-Plon' had been turned into '*Craint-Plomb*' (lead-fearer). Louis felt that the family name had to be vindicated.[1]

The news terrified the British Government: how could they allow the nephew of Napoleon to lead his troops into battle, let alone alongside British soldiers? They invited the French Emperor and his wife to pay a five-day state visit to Britain, knowing that the man who had described himself as a 'parvenu' among Europe's monarchs would find the invitation irresistible.

And so it turned out. On 16 April 1855, roughly the date the Imperial couple had expected to be embarking for the eastern Mediterranean, they landed at Dover and travelled by train to Windsor. The visit was an outstanding success. At the political level, Louis accepted the British Government's discreet advice that he should not go to the Crimea and, at the personal level, both the British people and their queen took Louis and Eugenie to their heart. The sight of the former exile showing his wife the house in King Street where he had once lived, as they drove past in their carriage, brought cheers from the crowd; and everywhere Eugenie's charm and beauty overcame any remaining prejudice against her.

Not only Victoria and her husband, Prince Albert, but also their young children were won over by the visiting couple. Fleury, who was in attendance, noted: 'The Queen had tears in her eyes when she said goodbye to her august guests, and Princess Victoria [later Empress of Germany] was sobbing as she threw herself into the arms of the Empress Eugenie. As for Prince Albert, he seemed to have been charmed by the Emperor and taken a great liking to him.'

Disraeli viewed the events with a more cynical eye. 'There was immense embracing at the departure and many tears,' he wrote to a friend. 'When the carriage door was at length closed, and all seemed over, the Emperor reopened it himself, jumped out, pressed Victoria to his heart and kissed her on each cheek, with streaming eyes. What do you think of that?'

But there seems little doubt about the warmth of the bond that was forged between both families. *'Enfin je suis gentilhomme!'*, Louis had said to the Queen in a remark she found charming, after

---

[1] During the course of one of the many quarrels between the cousins, 'Plon-Plon' shouted, 'You, you've inherited nothing from the Emperor!' 'You're mistaken,' said Napoleon, smiling, 'I've inherited his family.'

she had made him a Knight of the Garter. Writing later to thank her for the generosity of her hospitality, Louis admitted: 'Political interests were originally the source of our *rapprochement*,' but continued: 'Now after becoming personally acquainted with Your Majesty, it is by a sympathy at the same time active and respectful that I find myself bound to Your Majesty for ever . . . The truth is that it is impossible to live a few days within your family circle without falling a victim to the charm of the spectacle before one's eyes of the qualities of greatness and happiness united in the bosom of the happiest of families . . .'

For her part, Victoria was strongly taken with her male visitor. 'He is evidently possessed,' she wrote in a long memorandum with her customary prodigious use of emphasis, '*of indomitable courage, unflinching firmness of purpose, self-reliance, perseverance, and great secrecy*; to this should be added great reliance on what he calls his *Star*.' As for Eugenie, this first encounter laid the foundations of a life-long friendship between Victoria and herself despite the fact that temperamentally they were poles apart.[1]

Victoria's and her family's reciprocal visit to France in August of that year was equally successful. Louis did everything possible to make his guests feel at home: on one occasion, he himself drove the queen and her young daughter round the streets of Paris showing off his city to them, as if they were friends on an ordinary visit. There were the usual reviews of brilliantly uniformed soldiers, dinners at St Cloud, a ball at Versailles and, the highlight, a solemn pilgrimage in a violent summer thunderstorm to Napoleon I's tomb. 'It was touching and pleasing in the extreme,' Victoria later wrote to her former tutor, Baron Stockmar, 'to see the alliance sealed so completely . . . and to see old enmities wiped out over the tomb of Napoleon I, before whose coffin I stood (by torchlight) at the arm of Napoleon III, now my nearest and dearest ally.'

By the end, the queen was almost indiscreet in her written admiration for the Emperor of the French. 'He is so calm, so unspoilt, so naïve even, so happy if you tell him something he didn't know,

---

[1] 'She [Eugenie] is so nice,' the queen is supposed to have said, 'that she might be really royal . . .' Others noted that when the Emperor and Empress sat down, they always looked behind them to make sure that the chairs were in position. Victoria and Albert never did so: they knew that they would be there.

so gentle, with such tact, dignity and modesty, so full of respect and goodwill towards us ... never saying a word, or doing the least little thing that could have put me out or embarrassed me. I know very few people in whom I feel so ready to confide or to speak to so frankly. I felt, I can't quite explain it, so safe with him.'

The old charmer had conquered again. 'Isn't it odd, Lord Clarendon,' she said to her Foreign Secretary. 'The Emperor remembers every dress he has seen me in.'

The Crimean War dragged on, seemingly without end, until on 8 September 1855 French troops under General Patrice MacMahon, future Marshal of France and a President under the Third Republic, stormed the almost impregnable Malakoff fortifications guarding the land approach to Sebastopol. *'J'y suis, j'y reste!'* ('Here I am, here I stay!) cried MacMahon clambering over the battlements at the head of his troops in one of the great cries of French military history. The fortress fell and, on the following day, the Russians evacuated Sebastopol.

The Russians struggled on for a few more months but, on 1 February 1856, they sued for peace. Later that month, representatives of the five warring states, Russia, Turkey, Britain, France and the small north Italian kingdom of Piedmont-Sardinia, which had sent 15,000 men to join in the fight, assembled in Paris under the chairmanship of Comte Walewski, then Louis' Foreign Secretary, to hammer out a peace treaty.

It was a tremendous coup for Louis that the negotiations were to take place in his capital. For the first time in decades, a ruler of France was hosting an international conference, the Congress of Paris. At last, the Tsar wrote to him: 'Your Majesty and my brother.'

The War had been a disaster in human terms[1] and achieved little of lasting value in the volatile cockpit of the Balkans and the eastern Mediterranean, but it gave Louis the high-profile international recognition that he craved and brought back military glory to France. To this very day, French victories are perpetuated in three of the best known street names in Paris: Alma, Sebastopol and Malakoff.

* * *

---

[1] The siege of Sebastopol was said alone to have cost 115,000 Allied soldiers' lives with Russian losses estimated at a quarter of a million.

1856 was also a marvellous year for Louis for a more personal reason. At 3.30 on the morning of 16 March, after a labour lasting twenty-two hours (which made Eugenie even less interested in sex thereafter), she gave birth to a healthy boy weighing four kilos. The child was later christened Napoleon Eugene Louis Jean Joseph but he was at once given the title of Prince Imperial.[1] His parents always called him either Louis or, especially when young, Loulou.

The new father, who had spent the whole of Eugenie's labour in the room with her, was beside himself with happiness. 'When the child was born,' wrote Lord Malmesbury in his journal, quoting from a letter from Persigny, 'the Emperor, in a transport of joy, embraced the first five people he saw in the neighbouring room; then, realising that he was not behaving in a very dignified manner, said, "I cannot embrace all of you!"'

When the hundred and one gun salute to announce the birth of a boy was fired, the whole of Paris was illuminated, even back streets and dark alleys. The boulevards were one line of light from the Madeleine to near the Bastille.

It is no wonder that Louis was so happy. With his dynastic future now assured, he seemed set for a long and glorious reign.

[1] 'The Empress has given birth to a prince,' announced *Le Moniteur* that morning. 'Her Majesty and the Prince Imperial are in good health.'

Chapter Twenty

Fulfilment (1856–60)

S OON AFTER THE BIRTH of his son, Louis made a proclamation to the nation: 'France breathes more freely by the birth of this child. She associates her future with his destinies when he will reign over this Empire.' Then, after recalling for a moment the dismal fate of recent heirs to the throne, he continued with apparent supreme confidence:

'If I hope that my son will be fortunate in the future, it is mainly because I rely on God whose protection I cannot doubt when I see how, by a combination of extraordinary circumstances, He has restored all that was overthrown forty years ago as though, in spite of former sorrow and misfortune, He would bless this new dynasty chosen of the people . . .

'We must not abuse the favour of fortune, a dynasty has only the possibility of continuing if it remains loyal to its origin and protects the public interests for which it was founded.

'This child, whose cradle is consecrated by Peace, by the blessing of the Holy Father which arrived by telegram an hour after his birth, by the unanimous cheers of the people whom the "Great Emperor" loved so dearly, will I trust prove worthy of the high vocation which awaits him.'

It is probably true that Louis was seeking to persuade not only the nation but himself. This was, after all, the same man who, when announcing to the French people only three years earlier his decision to marry 'Mlle de Montijo' had described himself as a *parvenu*, an upstart. He knew that he had created by his own efforts a new Empire and a new force in Europe but he also knew that what the gods give they can take away.[1]

---

[1] As Professor Alfred Cobban has written in his *A History of Modern France*: 'Napoleon III never forgot that he had been brought to power by the masses of the people. His authority had not been created by, nor did it depend on, the army. There was no great party machine,

Six months later, in July 1856, having left Eugenie and Loulou, to take the waters at Plombières, a small spa town in the Vosges in eastern France, he wrote his wife a poignant letter: 'You and the little one, you are everything for me ... I see with happiness approach the moment when I shall see you both again and I am so happy at the prospect that I torment myself fearing that, at this distance, you or he might become ill. During your walks, do not go too near the pool. Do not tire yourself either. All these recommendations are perhaps stupid, *but when I am happy, I am frightened*.' The last phrase is emphasised because I think that it is vital to a proper understanding of Louis' character and of the fact that, despite all his apparent self-confidence and the intense belief in his destiny, deep down inside his inner soul he realised that his days of glory and power might not last. 'When I am happy, I am frightened': it has an ominous ring.

Nor was he alone in his fundamental pessimism. It was shared by Eugenie. Nearly fifty years later, when looking back in exile on her life and talking to the French diplomat, Maurice Paléologue, she recalled the joyous day in June 1856 when she rode in the Imperial coach to Notre Dame to her son's christening. Her husband was next to her silently saluting the cheering crowds, the baby Prince Imperial was travelling behind with his suite in his own coach and the Marshals of France in their splendid uniforms clattered on their horses alongside. But she could not stop a deep sense of melancholy rising within her. 'A secret voice inside me whispered that the same official pomp, the same acclamations of the crowd, the same salvoes of artillery, the same ringings of the bells had celebrated the baptisms of the dauphin Louis XVII, the King of Rome, the Duke of Bordeaux, the Count of Paris.[1] And what had become of those poor children? Prison, death, exile! ...'

As we shall see later, this grim attitude, shared by husband and wife, was to have profound and, until now, unappreciated consequences.

---

as in modern fascist and communist dictatorships, to hold the people down. His was a personal and plebiscitary dictatorship, and what the people had given the people might take away.' This was a fundamental truth that Louis appreciated only too well.

[1] These were respectively the heirs of Louis XVI, Napoleon I, Charles X and Louis-Philippe respectively. None ever succeeded to the throne.

For the moment, however, Louis cast such sad thoughts aside and threw himself back into the wholehearted enjoyment of the pleasures of his life. And, as so often with him, this had a strong sexual resonance.

In fact, instead of the usual succession of brief encounters, he was now enjoying a sustained relationship with his first long-term mistress since Lizzie Howard had disappeared from the scene. She was the nineteen-year-old Virginia, Countess of Castiglione, wife of Count Francisco Castiglione, the newly appointed Ambassador from the small mountain Kingdom of Piedmont in northern Italy.

Their meeting had been somewhat matter-of-fact; they had just crossed each other's path on the staircase at the Palais Royal, ex-King Jerome's home in Paris, on 26 January 1856 when, at around midnight, Louis was leaving a party given by his uncle and Virginia was just arriving. Her beauty was not to be ignored. 'You're arriving rather late!' said Louis ruefully and she is alleged to have replied, with a ravishing smile: 'No, Sire, it is you who are leaving early!' Three days later she went with her husband to a ball at the Tuileries, and this time Louis talked to her for much longer, which everyone else in the room observed. Before long they were lovers. Count Castiglione did not mind: he was the archetypal complaisant husband, weak and besotted both with his wife and his totally unexpected ambassadorship which he knew he owed entirely to her.

Virginia Castiglione was undoubtedly a woman of quite outstanding beauty. Princess Pauline Metternich, wife of the future Austrian Ambassador to Paris, described her in her diary: 'The Countess was clad in a white tulle gown covered with huge long-stemmed roses, her head unadorned, her beautiful hair plaited in the form of a diadem. Her waist was that of a nymph. Her shoulders, neck, arms, hands – she was carrying her gloves – as though sculpted in pink marble. Her *décolleté* though exaggerated did not appear indecent, so much did this superb creature resemble a classical statue. Her face was striking. A perfect oval, a complexion of unrivalled freshness, dark green cloudy eyes crowned by brows that could have been traced by a miniature brush, a little nose, definite yet of absolute regularity, teeth like pearls. In a word, Venus come down from Olympus. I've never seen such beauty as hers, and never will again . . .'

Louis, his wife heavily pregnant and almost certainly denying him sex with even more than her usual vehemence, can perhaps be excused for falling hopelessly in love with her. It was a physical love and not a true meeting of minds; but the affair lasted some eighteen months and there seems to have been, at least initially, genuine feeling between them. They almost certainly had an illegitimate son, known only to history as 'Dr Hugenschmidt' who was apprenticed to Dr Evans, Louis' dentist, who brought him up and who, when he retired, gave him his highly prosperous practice.[1] When Louis was briefly a prisoner-of-war in Germany after his defeat at Sedan, Virginia, grown fat and almost unrecognisable, visited him for a tearful reunion. Upon her death in 1899, she was buried, as she had directed in her will, in the lace-trimmed night-dress in which she and the Emperor had last made love together at Compiègne.

Yet, for all that, theirs had not been a chance encounter on Jerome's stairs. Louis did not know that there was a hidden agenda to their romance: Count Camillo Cavour, the stocky, pugnacious Prime Minister of Piedmont, whose dream it was to unite the Italian peninsula as one country and throw out the Austrians who still ruled a large part of the north, had primed the exquisite Virginia, who happened to be his cousin, to sleep with Louis and 'do something' for her native country.

Virginia had not been the proverbial blushing bride who, until her recent marriage, had been a chaste virgin. Only a few months earlier, at the age of eighteen, she had been seduced by Victor-Emmanuel, the uncouth King of Piedmont of whom it was said that 'no monarch ever succeeded in becoming so much the father of his subjects in that he dispensed his paternity so liberally'.[2] It

---

[1] Eugenie actually met Hugenschmidt when she asked him to visit her in exile after Louis' death. She accepted him at once as her late husband's son: 'How you resemble the Emperor!' she said. They got on well together and he came to see her every year. He died without children.

[2] There is a story that, when visiting Paris and obliged, bored to tears, to attend a performance at the Opéra, he whispered in Napoleon's ear, indicating a young member of the *corps de ballet*, 'How much would that little girl cost?' 'I've no idea,' replied Napoleon, 'ask Bacciochi.' 'Sire,' said Bacciochi promptly, 'for Your Majesty, five thousand francs.' 'That's damn dear,' said the King. 'Never mind,' said Napoleon turning to Bacciochi, 'put it down on my account.'

was at a garden party, and the Countess noted casually in her diary: 'I went for a stroll in the garden with the King. He penetrated me. After that I went into the *toilettes* to tidy up.'

With Virginia's sexual track record, one can understand why, in early February 1856, Cavour wrote gleefully to his deputy foreign minister: 'I have enrolled the beautiful countess in the service of Piedmont. I have told her to flirt with and, if necessary seduce, the Emperor. I have promised that, if she succeeds, her brother will get the post of secretary in our Embassy at St Petersburg. She has already begun to play her part discreetly yesterday at the Tuileries!'

Soon Virginia was able to report complete success. Indeed, she was so delighted with her quick triumph that she confided to a friend: 'My mother was a fool. If, instead of tying us up, Castiglione and me, she would have had the brainwave of taking me to Paris a few years earlier, it would not be a Spaniard but an Italian that was now installed in the Tuileries.'

In June 1856 came an incident which scandalised even Louis' gossip-hardened Court. It was during a *fête champêtre* in the grounds of Villeneuve l'Étang, a small château near the Palace at St Cloud to which only a select few had been invited. In front of everyone, Louis invited Virginia to come with him alone in a small boat, which he himself rowed, and they disappeared, in the semi-darkness of moonlight, onto a small island in the middle of a large pond from which they did not return for well over half an hour. Hearing of this, Eugenie, with false jollity, got up to dance but she was still weak from childbirth and, after a few steps, fell heavily to the ground. As Lord Cowley reported dutifully to London: 'All this is very sad. It does the Emperor an infinity of harm politically speaking and certainly can be of no benefit to him either morally or physically.'

The affair, and much of its details, became such public knowledge in certain quarters in Paris that nearly a year later, in April 1857, it almost cost Louis his life. He was boarding his carriage outside Virginia's home at 28, avenue Marceau in the early hours of the morning to return home to the Tuileries when three armed men lunged out at him from the shadows. They were hired Italian assassins but his quick-witted driver lashed out angrily with his whip, the horses leapt forward and the men were sent flying, one of them falling under the wheels of the carriage. Captured and put on trial, they were duly gaoled.

Yet Louis would not stop his nocturnal visits. Virginia still held him in sexual thrall until finally one night in June 1857, during a glittering reception and ball which spread out over three floors at the Tuileries, his cousin, Princess Mathilde, noticed that he looked more than usually preoccupied. She asked what was wrong: 'I have a bad headache,' he said, 'and I am being pursued by three women who are here tonight.' – 'Three women, that's madness!' said Mathilde. – 'How did you get yourself into such a situation?' – 'It's not really my fault,' replied Louis. 'Over there, you can see the blonde on the ground floor, Mme de la Bédoyère, whom I am trying to untangle myself from.[1] Then there is that woman on the first floor, the Comtesse de Castiglione, who is undoubtedly very beautiful but she means nothing to me, is completely light-weight, and bores me. And there is another blonde on the second floor, Mme Waleswka, who has me in her sights and is in full pursuit of me'.[2] – 'But what about the Empress?' asked Mathilde. 'I was faithful to her for the first six months after our wedding,' Louis replied, 'but I have need of little distractions and I always come back to her with pleasure.'

In truth, Virginia was an empty-headed little chatterbox, insufferably vain about her beauty and, when she eventually realised that Louis was finally beginning to tire of her, she foolishly overplayed her hand by spreading gossip about their relationship, and making out that it was still as strong as ever it had been. That only made Louis more determined to rid himself of her. When a friend, Prince Poniatowski, asked him why, he replied: 'Her need to have everyone talking about herself was the reason for the break-up. I have said nothing about it to anybody but if people have talked, it is because her friends found her many times lying in bed with highly

[1] Later, when Louis made her husband a senator, the waspish Viel-Castel commented, 'Reason: his father was shot in 1815 and his wife is not without attraction in the Emperor's eyes.' He dismissed him as 'the most foolish, obtuse and incapable man in the world'.

[2] This was the Comtesse Marianne de Walewska, another Italian and – not that it mattered to Louis – the wife of his cousin, Comte Walewski, then still his Foreign Minister. She was nothing like so pretty as Virginia but far more intelligent and sparkling company. She soon took over from her more glamorous rival.

expensive bedlinen and lace – which she claimed I had given her!'

The importance of Virginia Castiglione in the unfolding history of nineteenth-century Europe has been exaggerated by many writers. It was for long believed that the mission entrusted to her by Count Cavour was to win over Louis to the cause of a United Italy by a sort of sustained mid-nineteenth-century 'pillow talk', forever dwelling rhapsodically on the subject. In fact, the discovery some years ago of some of her hitherto unpublished correspondence shows that was not her true role. It was more the other way round: she was not so much supposed to influence Louis as to report back to Cavour in which way Louis' mind was going and, if possible, discreetly prod him in the right direction. But, in essence, she was to be more of a listener than a talker.

This new concept of her role, first suggested by the French historian, Alain Decaux, in his biography of Virginia in 1964, is much more likely to be true, and for two reasons. Firstly, she did not have the brains to talk anyone into anything. We know that Louis was not very impressed by her intelligence. We have already seen what he said to Princess Mathilde: 'She is undoubtedly very beautiful but she means nothing to me, is completely light-weight, and bores me'; secondly, he was in any event, emotionally and temperamentally, sympathetic to the cause of Italian unity. Had he not, in the early 1830s, fought as a *Carbonaro* against the Austrians and held his dying brother in his arms?

In fact, Louis *did* substantially assist Italian ambitions but not until nearly a year after he broke off the affair with Virginia Castiglione.

In May 1858, Dr Conneau, whose role as Louis' intimate friend and associate as well as his doctor has tended to be played down, arrived in Turin, then the capital of Piedmont. During the course of a meeting with Count Cavour, he happened to remark that his Emperor would soon be spending some time taking the waters at Plombières, 'quite close,' as he helpfully put it, 'to your Excellency's frontier'. It was a ploy typical of Louis' style of diplomacy. Cavour responded in kind: he promptly decided to take a holiday in Switzerland from where, using a false passport, he travelled by way of Strasbourg to Plombières.

There, on 20 July 1858, in circumstances of absolute secrecy, the two men met over a period of four hours and planned between them a war with Austria that would carry Italy inexorably along the path to full unification.

The Austrians, who ruled most of the northern part of the country, directly in Lombardy and Venetia and indirectly through local puppet princelings in the central Italian grand duchy of Tuscany and the duchies of Lucca, Parma and Modena, would be driven out. Lombardy, Venetia, Lucca, Parma and Modena would be incorporated into Piedmont which would 'stretch to the Adriatic' and be called the Kingdom of Northern Italy. The Pope's temporal power would be cut right back to Rome itself, losing the Papal States of Romagna and the Marches to the new Kingdom of Northern Italy and the third Papal State of Umbria to a new Kingdom of Central Italy which would also take in Tuscany. In compensation for losing so much land, the Pope would become President of a vague 'Italian Confederation' and, for the time being, the corrupt little Kingdom of Naples would be allowed to continue in the south. Four states would, thus, take the place of the existing patchwork of nine, with Piedmont clearly the leading power. As Cavour reported back in triumph to Victor Emmanuel: 'Your Majesty would be legal sovereign of the richest and most powerful half of Italy, and hence would in practice dominate the whole Peninsula.'[1]

But what was Louis to get out of all this, apart from the glory of being part-author of modern Italy? He struck a shrewd bargain. Piedmont was to hand over Savoy and Nice to France and the two Royal Houses of France and Piedmont were to be linked with the marriage of his cousin, Prince Napoleon ('Plon-Plon') to Princess Clotilde, Victor Emmanuel's daughter.

The question at once arises as to why Louis, almost out of the

[1] It is one of the ironies of history that Victor-Emmanuel, later famous as the first king of a United Italy, should have been such a pig of a man. For instance, when the name of a high-ranking woman in French Society was mentioned during a visit to Paris, he bellowed in a loud voice that he had slept with both her and her daughters. Lord Malmesbury, who was in the capital at the time, noted in his diary that he was 'as vulgar and coarse as possible' and recounts how the king told Eugenie that he understood that in France women dancers did not wear knickers. If so, that would be 'heaven on earth for me'. The Empress was not amused.

blue, set up this meeting at Plombières and embarked on this new territorial adventure. Most modern commentators link it vaguely to the still-persisting influence of Virginia Castiglione, although she had by then long gone on to other things.[1] I believe that Louis' old friend, Lord Malmesbury, then again British Foreign Secretary, was closer to the mark. He linked it to Louis' fear of a further attempt at assassination by Italian extremists. 'The truth is,' wrote Malmesbury in his diary on 16 February 1859, 'that Louis Napoleon is determined to go to war with Austria to propitiate the Italians and to save his own life from assassination, since the *attentat* of January 1858. Cavour worked upon this at their interview at Plombières and persuaded him that taking up the cause of Italy will save his life, forfeited according to the laws of the *Carbonari*.' But Austrian domination of the north was not the only major obstacle to Italian unity. The second was the Papal States, lying like a huge cancer across the middle of the peninsula, corrupt and repressive. Yet despite his own earlier participation in the fight against Papal rule, Louis, as Prince-President, had, in the summer of 1849, sent French troops to overthrow the Republic that had then briefly driven the Pope from Rome. Thereafter the Supreme Pontiff was only able to maintain his authority over the Papal States with the help of a permanent garrison of French troops. That policy had been forced upon Louis by the need to keep the powerful Roman Catholic Church in France on his side in French internal politics. It was opposed to his own natural instincts.

Ironically, Louis' politically motivated support for the Pope against his own natural impulses had in the past three years led to no less than three attempts to kill him by Italian extremists. Apart from the attempt outside Virginia's house in April 1857, there were two much more serious incidents, in April 1855 and in January 1858.

In the first incident in April, Louis and Eugenie were enjoying a pleasant evening in the Bois de Boulogne when a man ran up, produced a pistol and fired at Louis at almost point-blank range.

---

[1] Including earning one million francs in one night from the eccentric British libertine, Richard Wallace, 4th Marquis of Hertford, whose every sexual desire she satisfied in a twelve-hour orgy from which she had to spend three whole days in bed to recover – but from which she emerged, according to Viel-Castel, 'more radiant than ever'.

The shot went wide and the assailant, Giovanni Pianori, was grabbed by the police and thrown to the ground. An angry crowd wanted to lynch him but Louis ordered the police to hold them back. He was put on trial and guillotined. Louis' comment was urbane: 'Attempts of this nature will never succeed. To strike home, you need a dagger.'

The second incident was much more dangerous. On 14 January 1858, as the Imperial carriage, with its mounted escort, drew up outside the old opera house for a performance of Auber's *Gustave III*, three bombs were thrown by a small group of Italian revolutionaries. The street was plunged into darkness as a bomb fragment put out all the gas lamps. Pandemonium reigned. The carriage was shattered, a general sitting in front was wounded in the neck and his blood spurted out over Eugenie's white evening gown; horses and men were thrown to the ground. By little short of a miracle, Louis and Eugenie were unhurt, apart from a few scratches, and after pausing to show themselves to the crowd and rally help for the wounded, they proceeded slowly into the opera house where they were greeted with a standing ovation. 'It's our business to be shot at!' said Eugenie to an anxious official.

The ringleader of the would-be assassins was a handsome, bearded count named Felice Orsini whose father had fought alongside Louis in 1831 in the cause of Italian freedom. In fact, Louis wanted to pardon him, and it was only the strongest opposition of his Ministers that blocked him. Nonetheless, he allowed Orsini to turn his trial into a platform for the cause they both had at heart by allowing Orsini's lawyer to read in court a letter written to him by Orsini from prison. In this, the defendant stated that he had no personal hatred for Louis or for the people of France but that, after Louis had, in 1849, destroyed the Roman Republic and restored the Pope, he had come to realise that he was the chief enemy of Italian freedom, and must be removed.

Orsini's letter ended with the stirring words: 'May your Majesty not reject the last prayer of a patriot on the steps of the scaffold! Let him liberate my country, and the blessings of its twenty-five million citizens will follow him through the ages!' On 13 March 1858, Orsini died bravely on the guillotine.

Two months later, Dr Conneau was in Turin talking to Count Cavour.

Louis and Cavour had agreed at Plombières that the war against Austria should be planned as soon as possible: Louis was to send 200,000 men, Cavour 100,000. 'Not only shall we make war at the first opportunity but we will seek a pretext,' Cavour had reported to his king.

So it was that, at the New Year's Day reception at the Tuileries on 1 January 1859, Louis startled the inoffensive Baron Hübner by telling him in a voice that everyone could hear: 'I regret that our relations with your Government are not so good as in the past; but I ask you to tell the Emperor that my personal sentiments for him have not changed.' There was a nervous scurry among Europe's leaders, and Prince Albert, who had never been quite so bowled over by the Emperor's charm as his wife, warned that Louis 'has been born and bred a conspirator, and at his present age will never get out of this turn of mind, scheming himself and suspicious of others'.[1]

A few days later, Victor-Emmanuel opened the Piedmontese Parliament with the words: 'We are not insensitive to the cry of pain which arises to us from so many parts of Italy.' A pretext for war was duly cobbled together. Piedmont mobilised its troops, Austria sent an ultimatum demanding instant demobilisation or war and the French Ambassador in Vienna told the Austrian Government that, if their troops invaded Piedmont, France would consider it a declaration of war on France. Two days later, on 27 April 1859, the Austrians crossed the border and both Piedmont and France were at war.

In June French troops with Louis attempting to command his armies in the field as his uncle had done but with little of his flair, managed to win two blood-soaked victories at Magenta and Solferino – and two more foreign place-names were added to the streets of Paris. But after Solferino, Louis suddenly called a halt. Looking out over the battlefield where more than 6,000 men lay dead and 30,000 more lay wounded, he muttered: 'The poor fellows. The poor fellows. What a terrible thing war is!' Then he rode off to make a separate peace a few days later with Franz Joseph II, the young Austrian Emperor: two men of fifty-one and

---

[1] That was undoubtedly Louis' somewhat unfortunate reputation. As Princess Mathilde told the Goncourt brothers: 'Oh, if only I could stop him conspiring against himself!'

twenty-eight, alone together in a room in a house at Villafranca, with no advisers or anyone else present, deciding the fate of scores of millions of people.

'I look forward with dread to meeting that scoundrel,' Franz Joseph had said at the prospect of their encounter but, in fact, he forged the better bargain. He realised that all Louis really wanted was to get home as quickly as possible, having first made sure that Piedmont got Lombardy so that he could claim his prize of Nice and Savoy. So he readily ceded Lombardy but refused to hand over Venetia. As for the central Italian duchies, the most he was prepared to do was offer plebiscites to decide their future status. The Papal States were left as before: under the control of the Pope but protected by Louis' troops.

When the Villafranca agreement was converted into the formal Treaty of Zurich four months later, Cavour was furious at what he considered a monstrous betrayal. Angrily he resigned, then shrewdly returned to make sure that the plebiscites held the following year in the central Italian duchies resulted in a vote for their inclusion in Piedmont.[1]

The horror of the battlefield at Solferino remained in Louis' memory and four years later, in August 1864, he was a sponsor of the first Geneva Convention on the treatment of war wounded and of the establishment of the Red Cross, both inspired by Henri Dunant, a Swiss businessman who had witnessed the battle. It must be said that it was not only humanitarian considerations that had caused Louis' sudden change of heart. Prussia was becoming restless at the humbling of her fellow German-speaking nation by two upstart Latin countries and he also belatedly realised that he was helping to create a new and powerful neighbour that might one day prove a menace to France.[2]

---

[1] Two years later, plebiscites in the Kingdom of Naples and in the Papal States led to their incorporation into the enlarged Piedmont which had by then become the Kingdom of Italy. Rome remained a separate small state, still supported by Louis' soldiers, until the collapse of the Second Empire in 1870 when all papal temporal power ceased except in the Vatican itself.

[2] Nearly a hundred years later, Benito Mussolini, Italy's Fascist dictator and henchman of Adolf Hitler, showed his support for Hitler by claiming back Nice and Savoy from France.

Yet victories are victories. In August 1859, looking as handsome as ever in uniform on horseback, Louis led his conquering army in a magnificent parade down the Champs Elysées.

In his private life nothing much had changed. For instance, when the Court went to Compiègne in October 1857 he actually made love to his current mistress, Comtesse Marianne de Walewska, on the train.

The Imperial railway carriage was divided into two compartments; Louis was travelling alone in one of them with Marianne while his wife, Marianne's husband, Princess Mathilde and other members of the party were in the other compartment. The jogging of the train made the door between the two compartments fly open, and Princess Mathilde saw 'my very dear cousin sitting astride Marianne's knees as if on horseback, kissing her on the mouth and thrusting his hand down her bosom'. Eugenie was no doubt shocked and angry but Walewski would not have been too concerned. All the Court knew him to be a complaisant husband: in one famous incident, Eugenie's chamberlain saw him strolling in the grounds of the Palace at St Cloud and literally turn his head and go back the way he had come when he spotted the Emperor and his wife in an intimate embrace.

Louis and Eugenie spent less than half the year at the Tuileries in central Paris. They were there from about the beginning of December to May, but in May every year they moved to St Cloud, which was their main residence throughout the early summer, although they would usually also spend a week or so in Fontainebleau. In July they would go to Biarritz, then in its early days as a fashionable resort on the French Atlantic coast. Eugenie liked the place very much and had built there a small château called Villa Eugenie, set on a little promontory a short distance from the town. Far from Paris, it was the only one of the Imperial residences where she could live an almost private life.

In July 1856, there was an innovation in the schedule. Eugenie went on her own to Biarritz for three weeks while Louis went to take the waters at Plombières and later at Vichy. His doctors had advised him that annual visits to a spa would be good for his rheumatism, a legacy of six years in his dank prison cell at the Château de Ham.

This then became their accepted practice, after which Louis would join Eugenie at Biarritz where they would stay until the beginning of October when they would return to St Cloud. But that was not the end of their travels. After a couple of weeks they would leave for Compiègne, where they stayed until their return to the Tuileries in December.[1]

Life at Compiègne was much more formal than at Biarritz. There was room for more than a hundred guests at the château but usually there were about seventy at any one time. They came for a week, with five different sets of guests during each of the five or six weeks that Louis and Eugenie were usually there. Stag-hunts and shooting would take place in the surrounding forest on several days in the week, and a torchlight ceremony every evening when the hounds devoured their share of the stags killed that day before a local crowd. There were balls, plays or some other amusement every night. There was hardly a dull, or even spare, moment.

In November 1857, an exhausted Lord Cowley wrote to Lord Clarendon, his Foreign Secretary, from Compiègne: 'The Empress, instead of letting people alone, torments herself and them by thinking it necessary to furnish constant amusement for them; such amusement generally suiting some people and not others; but they are both so natural and unaffected, and there is so little ceremony and etiquette, that the life is not disagreeable for a short time. Breakfast is at half-past eleven, then there is either hunting or shooting or some expedition to go to. Horses and carriages are found for everybody who wants them and nothing can be prettier than one of their cavalcades. Dinner about eight o'clock which never lasts more than an hour. In the evening there is dancing to a *hand organ* (a dreadful trial to one's auricular nerves) or charades or cards. Now and then the Company of one of the Theatres from Paris is brought down to act.'

But Prosper Mérimée, who was invited many more times than the dour Cowley to the soirées of Louis' peripatetic Court, was not amused by the slightly drunken charades and thought them unfitting pastimes for the Emperor's guests. 'Our hosts,' he wrote

[1] The only variant on this somewhat awesome schedule was that in 1857 Louis established a great military camp near Châlons-sur-Marne, and in future years always spent the last fortnight of August there.

to a friend, 'often allow those whom they invite to enjoy themselves to excess.'

The Second Empire was schizoid when it came to morals. The truth about the Emperor's sex-life, and that of many members of Society, was never known to the people. There was no tabloid press in nineteenth-century France. The Emperor, his wife and their young son often used to pose in pseudo middle-class domestic bliss for official photographs; the reality, however, was very different. Louis was not alone. For many people in authority, adultery was a way of life, but the Church and the bourgeoisie remained grimly dour and puritanical.

It was because of this that, in January 1857, an ambitious young state prosecutor named Pierre Ernest Pinard charged Gustave Flaubert and his publishers with 'outrage to public morality' in publishing *Madame Bovary*. Nowadays this story of a provincial housewife's adulterous life and eventual suicide is considered one of the finest in nineteenth-century French literature but its serialisation in a popular magazine, *La Revue de Hans*, had sparked public outrage, especially from the provincial middle classes scandalised by the book's sub-title: 'Provincial Morals'. The judges acquitted the defendants but not without commenting that the novel 'deserved severe censure'.

One wonders what Louis thought of the affair. The best indication is that some years later he invited Flaubert to Compiègne and made him Chevalier of the Legion of Honour.

The zealous Pinard was not deterred by his defeat. A few months later he returned to the attack on 'obscenity' with a prosecution against arguably the greatest French poet of the century, Charles Baudelaire, for his volume of poetry, *Les Fleurs du Mal* (*The Flowers of Evil*). Pinard alleged that six of the poems, which sang of the 'joyous flesh' of women's bodies and described love-making and women's beauty in considerable, if overtly poetic, detail, 'outraged public decency'. This time the defendant was convicted and the six poems were expurgated from his book; almost unbelievably, they were not restored until 1949. Baudelaire was also fined 300 francs (the equivalent of about £600 today, quite a lot for a penniless poet), but he wrote to Eugenie asking her to intercede on his behalf with the Minister of Justice because the amount of the fine 'exceeded the proverbial poverty of poets'. Despite her deep Catholicism, she showed that, like her husband, she was no prude and at her request the fine was reduced to 50 francs.

1860 was Louis' golden year. All went well for him. In the previous year, Ferdinand de Lesseps had, despite strong British opposition, begun to carve the Suez Canal out of the inhospitable desert and, further afield, French naval and military forces had begun an arduous campaign that was to lead to a new French colony in Cochin-China (now Vietnam) and a French protectorate in Cambodia. In this year itself, Paris reached its modern limits with the twenty arrondissements of today formally delineated. Louis signed a Commercial Treaty with Britain which, nearly a century before the Common Market, cut back heavily on customs duties between the two countries and made each a vastly improved market for the other's goods. In the summer, an Expeditionary Force of French troops was sent to Syria to defend the local Christian community and curb the power of the neighbouring Turkish Empire, so establishing a major French influence in the Middle East which survives to this day. In December, during the Second Opium War with China, combined units of the French and British armies pillaged and burned the Summer Palace in Peking, overtly as a lesson to the 'barbarous' Chinese but really so that their Governments could exact special trading concessions and increase their hold over the highly remunerative opium trade.

Frédéric Loliée, one of the most important of earlier French historians of the period, has written: 'It was the golden age of the Second Empire, at the height of its prosperity, a honeymoon for speculation ... Foreigners flocked to the capital dazzled by the gaiety of Parisian life.'

But the Empress herself was not entirely happy. 'More than ever,' Loliée has written, 'she was overwhelmed by adulation and fulsome compliments. Yet she was no longer satisfied to be just a decorative sovereign, still spared from time's ravages. To look in the mirror pleased her but that did not suffice.

'She was beginning to realise that she had other gifts more serious: those of a politician. She became more and more determined, as with passing years her taste for pleasure diminished, that her life would be devoted to the serious side of reigning rather than to the frivolities and dissipations of the Court.'

For five months in 1859, she had been Regent while Louis was away leading his armies against Austria in northern Italy, and she had acquitted herself well. In the French National Archives in Paris there is preserved a letter written by her uncle-in-law, ex-King Jerome; not one of her most ardent admirers, nonetheless he concedes: 'She shows in every instance and on every question a judgement that is clear, solid and nobly French.'[1]

This new side of Eugenie's nature was not to Louis' liking but he grew to accept it fatalistically. He could not face angry domestic scenes. Robert Sencourt has written of Eugenie: 'Talented, capricious and indulged, she was one of those women who pine for lack of sympathy and whose nerves never allow them to charm except when they have their own way.'

Loliée states the problem astutely: 'The Emperor loved his wife, although, in a manner of which everyone was fully aware, he neglected her. Deeply attached to his son, fidelity was not the most pronounced of his virtues. Too many temptations, which any man would have found difficult to resist, passed continuously before his roving eye. He let himself slide downhill when he should have resisted for, in addition, he was beginning to exhaust himself physically and be drained of his moral energy.'

The strain on Eugenie eventually showed. In the middle of November 1860, she shocked the Court and surprised the nation by suddenly leaving the country without warning or explanation.

Travelling semi-incognito[2] as the Countess of Pierrefonds, she went as far as Scotland where she stayed for several weeks. Not only had she had enough of her husband's compulsive promiscuity but she was beside herself with grief at the sudden death of her beloved sister, Paca, the Duchess of Alba, at the young age of thirty-five 'Cher James,' she wrote to the Duke from the Palace at St Cloud. 'I am leaving for London tomorrow. My health which grows worse daily obliges me to get away. I told *Maman* that I was a little unwell but to you I confess that I feel very weak and sometimes really ill ... Goodbye, my dear James,

---

[1] The reference at the Archives Nationales is 400 AP 126.
[2] But she was still travelled in the style of an empress: accompanied by two ladies-in-waiting, two gentlemen courtiers and ten servants.

you know how much your sister loves you. *Besos a los niños.* Eugenie.'[1]

She returned after a month and Louis was at Boulogne to welcome her back. Outwardly they were reconciled, but Eugenie had done a lot of thinking while she was away. She had decided how she would handle Louis in future. She would, of course, continue as his wife but thenceforth she was to be more of an empress – and a mother – than a spouse. She would dedicate herself to doing all she could to ensure that her son would have an Empire to succeed to. While she was in Scotland – perhaps taking advantage of her absence – Louis had, largely at Morny's instigation, introduced three important changes to his régime, softening its authoritarian nature.

For the first time, Deputies were to be allowed at the start of each parliamentary session to state their own views on the Government's legislative programme as outlined in the Emperor's opening speech. Three Cabinet Ministers were to deal exclusively with the Deputies, and press censorship was to be relaxed. The Liberals were delighted but Eugenie was appalled. She saw these 'reforms' as symptoms of weakness, heralding the end of Imperial power. She feared that they would endanger her son's position when he was called to the throne.

For the past two years, she had insisted on attending Louis' twice-weekly Cabinet meetings: now she was resolved to play more than primarily a spectator's role. She would make her own substantial contributions to the debates around the table. In the words of Jean Autin, a recent French biographer: 'The mother had totally taken the place of the wife and, from then on, only the reign of Napoleon IV would interest her. It was to the preservation of the throne of the young Louis that she now dedicated herself.'[2]

---

[1] 'Kisses to the children' in Spanish. Throughout her long life, Eugenie always kept her deep, typically Spanish, love for her family and would habitually end her letters with this homely greeting to her nephews and nieces, and later to her great-nieces and great-nephews.

[2] Céleste Baroche, wife of Jules Baroche, one of Louis' longest serving ministers, once asked her husband who was the Minister with most influence over the Emperor. 'The Empress,' was his immediate reply.

Chapter Twenty-One

Marking Time
(1860–65)

N APOLEON I SAID TO a friend after the retreat from Moscow in 1812: 'There is only one step from the sublime to the ridiculous.' Furthermore, his carriage had had diamonds concealed in its lining in case of hurried flight.[1] The oft-quoted remark and the little-known fact about the diamonds both stemmed from his own basic uncertainty that, despite all his vast success, his hard-won triumphs might not endure. His mother, Letizia, despite the proud title that he gave her of 'Madame Mère', shared the same inner doubts. She was wont, as she looked around her son's court, full of gold and splendour, to murmur, 'Pourvu que ça dure!' (May it last!)

In the late 1850s and early 1860s, Louis himself began to harbour such pessimistic thoughts. Unknown to the world outside, with the fulfilment of his dreams of power, his confidence in his star, his belief in his destiny, began to fail. For twenty years, he had schemed and plotted and three times (in Italy, Strasbourg and Boulogne) risked his life in seemingly never-ending exile. These events had left their mark. In François Guizot, Louis-Philippe's former Prime Minister's telling phrase, he was 'a political refugee'. Ferdinand Bac, whose father, Charles-Henri Bac, was the illegitimate son of ex-King Jerome and close friend of his cousin Louis, from their days together in Arenenberg, has written in his *Napoléon III*

---

[1] Professor Alfred Cobban states of Napoleon I in volume two of *A History of Modern France*: 'For fifteen years France and Europe were to be at the mercy of a gambler to whom fate and his own genius gave for a time all the aces. He always cheated at cards and his carriage had diamonds concealed in its lining in case of hurried flight.' Except for cheating at cards, the spirit of those words was also true of his nephew.

inconnu[1]: 'In full glory after Solferino the Emperor had a strange presentiment that things would not last. In 1859 he told Prince Napoleon ["Plon-Plon"] *that nothing lasts for ever and he does not believe in the future*' (Bac's italics).

Furthermore, Bac quotes Prosper Mérimée as saying that when the young Prince Imperial, Louis' only heir – and 'his adoration' – got down one day from Louis' lap after lunch to go and play, Louis watched him bound happily out of the room, let fall the ash from his inevitable cigarette and said: 'Will he ever reign?'[2]

These comments, coming from such a source, must be treated with respect for they give a unique insight into the working of Louis' mind at that time. This was, after all, the same man who only a few years earlier had told his wife that when he was happy he was afraid.

Furthermore, there is good reason to believe that, in the early 1860s, Louis actually did something about his personal misgivings. It is surely very significant that, at that time, mysterious entries began to appear in the accounts of the Imperial Household revealing that Louis gave an Englishman named Nathaniel William John Strode the remarkably large sum of 900,000 francs (today about £1,800,000) not in one lump sum but spread over the years 1862 to 1864 in individual payments of 50,000 (about £100,000) francs each. These are not to be confused with the payments totalling 5,449,000 francs (about £10,898,000) that Louis had made to Lizzie Howard between 1853 and 1855 to reimburse her, with generous interest, for the large sums of money she had spent in subsidising his return to France in 1848 and the coup d'état in 1851. The two matters are not connected. The money paid in the 1860s to Strode had nothing to do with the money paid to Lizzie in the 1850s.

What was the purpose of these 'gifts', as they were described? Over sixteen years later, within days of Louis' defeat at the Battle

---

[1] This book was published as recently as 1932 and has singular authority. Born in 1859, Bac did not die until 1952, when he was one of the last living links with the Second Empire.

[2] Louis' deep, if not excessive, love of his son is shown by an incident when he caught Loulou choking on a mandarin. Instead of snatching it away at once himself, he asked a courtier to do it. 'I could not do so,' he explained. 'He would not have loved me, if I had done it.'

of Sedan and the fall of the Second Empire with Eugenie's hurried
flight from Paris on 4 September 1870, officials of the newly proclaimed Third Republic came to look through the accounts of the
Imperial household stored in the Tuileries. Among the books and
papers, they found the records of both Lizzie's and Strode's
payments.

In the two volumes of *Papiers et correspondance de la Famille
Impériale* that the Republican Government ordered to be published
in the following year, the details of the payments to Lizzie are dealt
with at some length on pages 157 to 160 of volume I but those to
Strode are set out under the bare entry 'Strode' on page 156 of
volume II with no initials or Christian name, no indication as to
why or for what purpose they had been made and only the cryptic
expression *à titre inconnu*. What does that phrase mean? 'The best
explanation we can produce,' says Laurent Lemarchand of the
French Embassy in London, 'is that the accountant who entered
the figure in the book didn't have any knowledge of the precise
reason why such payments were made.'[1] Why the mystery? It is
impossible today to seek an official explanation but this was around
the time that Strode bought and refurbished in the French style a
country house called Camden Place at Chislehurst in Kent, to which
Eugenie and Louis were to flee as a safe haven after the debacle of
the Second Empire.

Strode has already been introduced as a link with Lizzie Howard,
Louis' discarded lover, and as the man appointed by the besotted
Major Martyn in the early 1840s to establish a trust fund in her
name. Strode was the trustee of the large estate that Martyn settled
upon her and he was to be her executor.

We shall return later to this gift *à titre inconnu*.

Having consolidated his power as Emperor, Louis seems in the
1860s to have lost all sense of strategy on the broader European
scene. He became almost solely a tactician, like a modern politician,
instinctively going for the 'quick fix' without regard to the larger
consequences – or difficulties – of his actions. He became the Artful
Dodger of European politics, always looking to further his own

---

[1] In a letter to the author dated 3 December 1997.

or France's own best interests, seemingly regardless of any other consideration.

Queen Victoria, though still impressed by Louis' personal charm, came to regard him as untrustworthy and unreliable. Lord Cowley, who remained Britain's Ambassador in Paris from 1852 right through to 1867, reported to London in the mid-1860s: 'He must be a bold man who speculates upon the Emperor's intentions. I am quite sure that he has never revealed them to man, woman or child and I must doubt whether he knows them himself.'

Other diplomats were equally displeased by what increasingly came to be thought of as the French Emperor's shiftlessness. 'He continues to mystify each and all by his sphinx-like attitude,' wrote Prince Richard Metternich, Baron Hubner's successor as Austrian Ambassador in Paris, to his Foreign Secretary, Count Mensdorff. 'He seems like an augur who resists the encroachments of the inquisitive populace by saying: "Keep calm! I know what is going to happen, and you will be satisfied."

'To the most concise, the most logical arguments, he answers nothing. He sticks to his original theme: "Liberty of action."

'If you say to him: "After all, if you want peace, you have only to say a word to Italy and a word to Prussia, and order will be restored," his manner suggests the answer: "But peace is exactly what I do not want."

'If you insinuate that by allying himself with Italy and with Prussia he might recover the Rhine, he answers: "I am not troubling about the Rhine."

'If I whisper in his ear: "Keep Italy quiet and it is more than likely that you will have Venetia," he replies: "I have no influence nowadays in Florence [then capital of an Italy newly united but still lacking Venetia and Rome]."

'I believe that the fact is that, in Florence as in Berlin, in Vienna as in Paris, everyone distrusts him without knowing why, and tries to bribe him without knowing how!'

Louis had only himself to blame. The man always conspiring against himself had become caught up in the internal meshes of his own psyche. Perhaps because of his own inner doubts about how long it would all last, he could not stop himself plotting and counter-plotting. During his last ten years as Emperor, he seems to have become incapable of straightforward action, of being honest with himself, or with others. For instance, in November 1863, when France was ostensibly Austria's friend, he secretly offered Prussia an anti-British and anti-Austrian alliance and was promptly exposed as duplicitous when Bismarck, then only recently appointed as Prussia's Minister-President and Prime Minister, immediately told the Austrian Government.

He was as bad with his own wife. We have already seen how in 1860 Eugenie had resolved to become much more politically active so as to help ensure her young son's succession to the throne. In fact, within a very short time she became virtually co-ruler of France, not merely attending Cabinet meetings but having constant and powerful influence over what passed for her husband's decision-making. The memoirs of foreign ambassadors to Paris during the 1860s are full of references to the Empress and how she conducted her own discussions with them, independent of Louis: they would formally have an audience with the Emperor then go on to a meeting with the Empress.

It was all very cordial but Louis would even plot against Eugenie.

In the memoirs of Augustin Filon, the Prince Imperial's tutor, published in 1920 only after Eugenie's death,[1] Filon declared that there was no truth in the popular belief that the Empress had been the leader of a reactionary party at Court dedicated to furthering the cause of the extreme right. He wrote that the idea had been put about by Louis himself. Why? Because the Emperor wished to create the impression that there were two contending parties in the government: one Liberal, looking to the future and eager for reform – with which he liked to show himself siding – and the other Conservative and Catholic, opposed to all and every change, with which he was constantly having to battle. According to Filon, what made this invention all the more difficult to understand was that Eugenie 'owed all her political ideals to the Emperor in whose wisdom she believed implicitly . . . She was like his second conscience. She lent him her intuition, her instincts and he, who believed in the power of intuition and in the infallibility of instinct, consulted her blindly although,' added Filon slyly, 'his high opinion of her abilities was not always borne out by events.'

---

[1] *Souvenirs sur l'impératrice* was published within months of Eugenie's death, although Filon himself had died four years earlier.

A typical example of this was when a diplomat from Mexico named José Manuel Hidalgo, a childhood friend of Eugenie, suggested to Louis at Biarritz in September 1861 the unlikely proposition that Louis should be the founding father of a great Catholic Empire in Hidalgo's native country. He said that Louis should sponsor a European Catholic prince as Emperor. Eugenie promptly suggested the twenty-nine-year-old Archduke Maximilian of Austria, and Louis at once saw the proposal's gleaming, short-term appeal.

It was three-fold. First, it would prevent the predominantly Protestant United States from achieving ascendancy over the Catholic ex-Spanish colonies of Latin America which had recently, after 300 years, won independence from the enfeebled Spanish Empire. Second, this was the best time to act: a typical 'quick fix'. The War of Secession in the United States had broken out five months earlier and President Abraham Lincoln would be distracted by this bloodiest of civil wars for quite some time from enforcing the famous Monroe Doctrine of 1823. This warned that the United States would regard any attempt by European powers to extend their influence in the Americas as dangerous to its own peace and security, a threat not to be taken lightly. And third, the Archduke Maximilian was the younger brother of the Austrian Emperor, Franz Joseph, and Louis hoped that somehow he might be able to persuade Franz Joseph – on a *quid pro quo* basis – to hand over Venetia to the newly created Kingdom of Italy. The continued Austrian occupation of that province still rankled in Louis' mind as a major piece of unfinished business left over from the Plombières Agreement and his involvement in the Piedmont-Austria War.

In the series of interviews that Eugenie conceded to Maurice Paléologue forty years later on condition that they would not be published until after her death, she specifically confirmed this devious ploy by Louis: 'I won't hide from you the fact that, in my husband's mind, the promotion of an Austrian Archduke to the Mexican throne would, one day, become an argument in favour of obtaining from Franz-Joseph the transfer of Venice to Italy.'

Sadly, for Mexico, for France – and for Maximilian and his twenty-one-year-old wife Charlotte, the Mexican adventure that began to unfold at Biarritz in September 1861 was a tragedy, one that could all too easily have been avoided.

*   *   *

Back in 1821 Mexico, then, like most of Latin America, a Spanish colony, had declared itself independent under a charismatic but hotheaded Spanish army officer named Agustin Iturbide. The following year he had declared himself Emperor as Agustin I and, despite Mexico's crushing poverty, had himself and his wife crowned in a lavish ceremony modelled on Napoleon I's coronation in Notre Dame.

Agustin proved hopelessly inadequate and disorganised as a ruler and reigned for only three years before being driven from his throne and executed by a firing squad.

Thereafter, for nearly forty years, the country was ruled by a seemingly endless succession of military presidents, some remaining in power for only a few months, all of them united by their corruption and ruthlessness. The overwhelming majority of the nation's eight million inhabitants were Indian or of mixed race but power was securely in the hands of the generals, the white landowners and the Roman Catholic bishops. These were all, almost to a man, diehard Conservatives.

But finally, in October 1860, after three year of civil war, Benito Juarez, a humbly-born Radical lawyer of pure Indian blood, defeated the last of the military Conservative presidents, General Miguel Miramón, and, three months later, in January 1861, entered Mexico City in triumph. Several prominent Conservatives had already fled the country, most to France, but now many others followed suit.

Among these wealthy émigrés, along with José Manuel Hidalgo, were José María Gutiérrez de Estrada, a landowner banished some twenty years earlier for advocating a foreign prince who had spent most of his exile living in luxury in Rome, two priests, Father Francisco Xavier Miranda and Bishop Labastida, and a general named Juan Almonte. It will be noticed at once that this exclusive group was hardly representative of the country as a whole but neither Louis nor Eugenie seems to have regarded that as a problem.

The tales that these individuals told – of Church property confiscated, large estates seized, priests killed and nuns raped – were sufficient to achieve their object. Forty years later, Eugenie told Maurice Paléologue, 'with a strong voice and piercing eyes', that she saw nothing for which she needed to excuse herself. 'I have no shame for what happened in Mexico,' she said. 'I deplore it but I don't blush for it . . . and I am always ready to talk about it, for it is one of the themes that injustice and calumny have most exploited against us. The Mexican adventure, as it has been called, whose origins have now such a bad name, was, on the contrary, the result of a very highly thought out plan, the accomplishment of an extremely high political and civilising aim.'

Paléologue had the courage to say to the former Empress: 'What I don't understand is that, from a practical point of view, the impossibility of success did not strike the Emperor at once.'

'Alas!' she replied. 'We underestimated the resistance and complications that were ahead of us. Or rather, we were misled . . . in good faith probably. I'm not accusing anybody, but you cannot imagine the wonderful perspectives that people made us believe in. We were assured that the Mexican people were against the Republic and would welcome a monarchy with enthusiasm; that a Catholic prince with great allure such as Maximilian would be welcomed everywhere with open arms, triumphal arches and flowers; that the United States, torn apart by their civil war, would soon resign themselves to our intervention, etc, etc.'

What Eugenie did not say, and probably never even knew, was that her husband's half-brother, Auguste de Morny, soon to be created a duke, had a substantial financial interest in the matter. Benito Juarez, the new Mexican President, had taken control of a country that was virtually bankrupt and in July 1861 he had announced the suspension for two years of all payments on foreign debts – including a 15 million peso loan to a Swiss banker called Jecker, in whose affairs Morny had a 30 per cent interest. Naturally he encouraged Louis in any action that would help bring about repayment of the 15 million pesos.

On 31 October 1861, France, Great Britain and Spain signed in London an agreement called the Tripartite Convention, the aim of which was to force Mexico to pay all her foreign debts. The three countries, in the time-honoured style of high-handed nineteenth-century power politics, undertook to send a joint naval force to seize the Mexican port of Vera Cruz, take over the local customs administration and pay their creditors out of the dues that they collected. When they had raised enough money, they would return home.

On 17 December 1861, some 6,000 Spanish troops disembarked

at Vera Cruz. They were soon followed by a small British force and some 2,000 French troops.

The enterprise was impractical and doomed from the start. Five months later, in April 1862, the Spanish and British left. The French troops remained. More than that, totally under-estimating the opposition which they would encounter, they set out, with no reinforcements, on a march to Mexico City. They did so without a firm commitment by Maximilian that he would, in fact, accept the Mexican throne. It is difficult to understand Louis' thought processes at this time.

Maximilian, with his blond hair and magnificent blond side-whiskers, and his wife Charlotte made a fine-looking couple. A dreamer with woolly, liberal ideas, he was only a reluctant emperor and had merely told Louis that he would consider his proposal. But the ambitious Charlotte, daughter of one king, Leopold I of the Belgians, and granddaughter of another, no less than Louis-Philippe of France, was delighted at the prospect of becoming an empress. Throughout the next few years until they finally boarded an Austrian warship for Mexico, she consistently pushed and pummelled her husband into welcoming his Imperial role. Maximilian was a pawn between two powerful women: Eugenie of France and his own wife.

On 5 May 1862, while Maximilian was still trying to make up his mind, the French army was decisively routed by Juarez's troops at Puebla, a town guarding the road to Mexico City from the Atlantic coast. It should have made the normally cautious Louis pause but that would be failing to take account of Eugenie's firm and fiery dedication to the cause. In September 1862, another 3,400 French troops disembarked at Vera Cruz, followed by 20,000 more in October. A full-scale military intervention was now under way.

Juarez's troops resisted bravely but they were consistently outgunned and outnumbered. By May 1863 the rout at Puebla had been revenged and the road lay open to Mexico City. Juarez was forced to abandon his capital and the fighting moved to guerrilla resistance in the north of the country. In June, the French commander, General Achille Bazaine, entered a resentful Mexico City at the head of his troops. On 10 July, a self-styled Assembly of Notables in the capital voted to offer the Imperial crown to

Maximilian. In the following month, a delegation headed by José María Gutiérrez de Estrada set sail for Paris and the Adriatic port of Trieste, on the rocks above which perched Maximilian's Miramar Castle.

On 3 October, Gutiérrez de Estrada's ten-man delegation, including the young diplomat Hidalgo, offered the Imperial crown to Maximilian in the Great Hall at Miramar but the Archduke was still wavering. In the words of the American historian Henry Bamford Parkes, 'Gentle and irresolute, weak when he should have been strong and obstinate when he should have been open to persuasion, he had all the innocence of those who have been born in palaces and whose lives have been guided by a trained bureaucracy.'

Before giving a final reply to the Mexican delegation, Maximilian asked that the Mexican people themselves should vote on whether they wanted him as Emperor. That was easily achieved: Louis merely ordered General Bazaine to obtain the necessary Yes vote on a nationwide plebiscite. Within months, by a combination of vote-rigging and judicious bribery, Bazaine had accomplished his task.

Yet despite the favourable plebiscite, Maximilian still agonised over whether to accept this far distant throne. In March 1864, he and Charlotte visited Louis and Eugenie in Paris and, much to Charlotte's liking, they were received as if they were already Emperor and Empress. To reassure Maximilian, Louis promised to keep 25,000 French soldiers in Mexico until they were replaced by native forces and that the French Foreign Legion would maintain a force there of some 8,000 troops for at least six years. In return, Maximilian, a baby in arms in the world of high finance or *realpolitik*, pledged himself to repay, out of Mexican state coffers, not only all the monies which Louis had expended to date on the French intervention, a staggering total of 270 million francs, but also the old debts due to Britain, France and Spain in 1861, which were still owing – and, so as to keep Morny happy, included, of course, the infamous Jecker loan. After the soon-to-be-Imperial couple's return to Miramar, this solemn agreement was confirmed in writing. Clearly, this was arrant folly on Maximilian's part: he was saddling his already almost bankrupt country with huge new debts before he even got there.

But Maximilian was still not convinced. He had one last reservation: he did not want to throw away his rights of succession to the far more mighty Austrian throne. Franz Joseph, his older brother, had always been wary of his liberal ideas. Furthermore, he had never managed to rid his mind entirely of the lingering suspicion that Maximilian was really only his half-brother, being the illegitimate child of their mother, Archduchess Sophia, and the Duke of Reichstadt, Napoleon I's son exiled to the Austrian Court. If Maximilian were to go to Mexico, Franz Joseph wanted at least finally to be rid of him by insisting that he renounce his rights of succession to the Austrian throne, which Maximilian refused to do.

Both Louis and Eugenie wrote to him of their despair. Louis wrote a letter which, in the light of his subsequent actions, does not redound to his credit: 'Your Imperial Highness has entered into engagements which you are no longer free to break. What, indeed, would you think of me, if once Your Imperial Majesty had arrived in Mexico, I were to say that I can no longer fulfil the conditions to which I have set my signature?' Hypocrisy, thy name is Louis Napoleon.

That letter, plus further pressure exerted by the Austrian Government as the direct result of Eugenie's personal intervention with Metternich achieved its object. On 10 April 1864, Maximilian, having a few days earlier formally renounced his rights to the Austrian succession in an emotional meeting with his older brother, received again José Maria Gutiérrez de Estrada and his Mexican delegation. In a brief formal speech, he paid tribute to 'the loyalty and the spirit of goodwill of the Emperor of the French' and told them that 'solemnly and with the help of Almighty God' he accepted from the Mexican nation the throne that they had offered.

But he remained full of foreboding. On the next day he told a friend: 'For me, if someone came to tell me that the whole thing was cancelled, I would lock myself in my room to jump for joy! But Charlotte? . . .'

Four days later, Maximilian and Charlotte left for Mexico on the Austrian frigate *Novara*, escorted by the French frigate *Thémis*.[1] Charlotte may have been ambitious but she truly cared for her

---

[1] I have stood on the landing stage at Miramar from which they embarked and it seemed as if an air of melancholy still lingers upon the scene.

husband. 'Look at my poor Max!' she said to a lady-in-waiting. 'How he is crying!'

Yet he was still, after all, a true Habsburg brought up in arguably the most protocol-minded Court in Europe. His chief occupation on the six weeks' voyage was to compile a manual of some 600 pages on etiquette for his new Court. One wonders if anyone had ever told him that his new country's first Emperor had been put up against a wall by his 'subjects' and shot.

Back in Europe, the early years of the 1860s calmly unfolded. In September 1862, an event occurred whose long-term significance few at the time appreciated. King Wilhelm of Prussia, a tough old soldier aged sixty-four, had succeeded to the throne the year before on the death of his older brother. Now he appointed as his Minister-President, a tall, bull-necked Prussian aristocrat named Count Otto von Bismarck. The two were to work together in harmony for twenty-six years until the king's death in 1888 and together they were to achieve the destruction of Louis' Second Empire and the establishment in its ruins of a new German Empire. Wilhelm took Bismarck from Paris where he had been his Minister for only a few months. That brief time had been enough to teach Bismarck all that he considered necessary to know about France under Louis' rule: 'Viewed from a distance, it seems very impressive. Close at hand, you realise it is nothing.' He had already decided on what he wanted to make his life-work: the creation of his native Prussia as the centrepoint of an all-powerful new German Empire with Wilhelm, his king, as Emperor.

He realised that meant he would first have to humble or destroy the two leading nations that stood in his path: Austria, Europe's single largest German-speaking country to the south, and France, anxiously looking on from across the Rhine. He was supremely confident that both he and his people would prove worthy of the challenge, and his few months in Paris had satisfied him that the dissolute, pleasure-loving Second Empire would be no match for Prussian strength and determination. He already believed passionately in the political philosophy that he was to articulate many years later, in a speech to the Prussian House of Deputies on 28 January 1886: 'Germany is looking not to Prussia's liberalism but to her power . . . The great questions of the day will not be decided by speeches and majority resolutions but by blood and iron.'

That was a philosophy that was to lead to the Franco-Prussian War of 1870–71 and, carried on by two later German leaders, Kaiser Wilhelm II and Adolf Hitler, to two World Wars.

In 1863, there were two notable domestic events. In May, Louis, visiting the *Salon*, the official showplace of every year's new French art, before its formal opening, was disappointed by the particularly dull and uninspired paintings on display. He demanded to see the pictures that had been refused. Among them was Edouard Manet's early masterpiece *Déjeûner sur l'Herbe*, one of the first great Impressionist paintings. Louis ordered that a new *Salon* – a *Salon des Refusés* (Hall of the Rejected) – should be opened, and within two weeks *Déjeûner sur l'Herbe* was on public exhibition. In future years, the *Salon des Refusés* became a standard feature of the Parisian art scene and many of what are now the world's most famous paintings including Monet's *Impressions, Soleil Levant* that gave its name to the Impressionist movement, were first shown there: all thanks to Louis.

In November, elections were held for the first time in six years and Louis' old friend and associate, Persigny, then Minister of the Interior and as single-mindedly loyal to Louis as in their days of exile together, was in charge. With typical efficiency, he did his best to ensure a massive victory for the Government: constituency boundaries were redrawn so as to merge poor districts with richer ones, anti-Government meetings were forbidden, the press was muzzled and 'official' candidates boosted with public promises of local benefits and private bribery. Despite all this, in Paris only 22,000 votes were cast for the Government and 175,000 against. In the country, it was the other way round: thirty-two seats went to the Opposition against 250 to the Government. That might look like a victory but in 1857 only 665,000 people had voted for the Opposition. Now their number had swollen to two million. This was the first crack in public confidence in the régime.

Morny told Louis there was only one answer: he must make concessions, allow greater freedom of speech, encourage social reform – and dismiss his two most notoriously hardline Ministers: Persigny and Walewski. Louis only paid lip service to liberalising the régime but, with the ruthlessness of which he was occasionally capable, he sacked both his oldest friend and his cousin. His decision to sack Persigny delighted Eugenie, who had never forgiven him for opposing their marriage because she was not of royal blood, and Louis insisted on making him a Duke as some form of consolation. But it did not work. Persigny, seeing the hand of Eugenie in his dismissal, accused Louis to his face of being dominated by his wife. Completely forgetting that the man to whom he had been so close twenty years earlier was now his Emperor, he ranted: 'You make it appear as if you have abdicated! You are losing your prestige and you discourage your remaining friends who serve you loyally.' But the decision was irrevocable and Persigny remained bitter for the rest of his life, both at the weakness of the Emperor and the evil influence of the Empress.[1]

Four years later the simmering enmity between Eugenie and Persigny was to erupt into a confrontation which led to Persigny's disappearance from Court. Talking in the early years of the twentieth century to Maurice Paléologue she described the incident with her typical vigour which perfectly gives the taste of what she must have been like:

'Since the day of my wedding, Persigny honoured me with his hatred, a disparaging and venomous hatred. He would even sometimes call me "The Spanish Woman" or "The Foreigner"! Priding himself on the distinguished services he had given to the Napoleonic cause, he could not bear anybody between the Emperor and him: the Emperor and the Empire belonged to him; he had invented and created them; he therefore considered himself the only one capable to advise one and govern the other. My husband needed so much calm to tolerate the recriminations, the jealousies, the bad moods, the tempestuous bursts of Persigny, you would not believe it. Try and imagine a boiler that would not stop exploding!

'One day, however, the Emperor had to do something about it. As far as I remember, it was in November 1867. The Emperor, who had caught a cold whilst hunting and suffered from rheumatism, had taken to his bed. I was alone with him, in his bedroom,

[1] After Louis went into his final exile, Persigny wrote to his wife: 'The Emperor has arrived in England where more than ever he is in the power of his stupid wife [the literal translation of the original French is even more pejorative: 'under the slipper of his stupid wife']. I felt that I had to write to him but he has not replied. So all is finished between us.'

and reading to him the principal reviews from the papers, as the usher brought him a big sealed letter, bearing the inscription: "Only for the Emperor from the Duc de Persigny." The Emperor looks at the envelope, without opening it: "I am sure that this is yet another recrimination," he says. "How tiresome he can be! . . . Read me the letter. I haven't got the strength for it today." I open the envelope: it contained, at least, a dozen pages. To tell the truth, it was not a letter but a note or more like a diatribe against me, against my presence in the *Conseil des ministres* [Cabinet meetings], against the loathsome ideas that I represented in the government that would lead the Empire to its fall! . . . He covered his attacks with occasional references to my beauty and the nobility of my soul; but the charge was no less odious. I trembled at each word. My husband was listening to me, impassive. When I finished reading, I burst into indignation: "Never again will I set foot in the *Conseil des ministres*, no, never! . . . I do not want to be exposed to such abuse ever again. It is too humiliating, too unfair! . . ." I was beside myself. The Emperor kept on saying, with a soothing quietness: "Calm down! This new stupidity from Persigny has no importance. I feel that your place is at the *Conseil des ministres* and you won't stop sitting there. I am the master." I knew well that, when he took this affectionate but authoritarian tone, I had to obey, so I obeyed. But to assuage my heart, I wrote immediately to Persigny a quite firm letter that broke our relationship. From then on he did not appear at Court.'

The year 1863 is memorable in Louis' personal life because, at the age of fifty-five, he fell deeply in love for what was to be the last time. The affair was to last for two years and to result in his third illegitimate son. It was autumnal love: the girl, Marguerite Bellanger, was only twenty-three, a pert, pretty country girl born with the much more humble name of Julie Leboeuf in a village near Saumur on the Loire.

Like many young people, she had come to Paris to better herself and for a brief while played small comedy parts on the stage under her new 'theatrical' name. She soon discovered that she could earn more money and have much more fun as what Frenchmen of the time called a *cocodette*, an untranslatable word to describe the sort of 'respectable' prostitute that Hector Fleischmann, the accepted

French expert on the women in Louis' life, has called: 'The very type of the eight-day mistress for the man-about-town of the Second Empire.'

She was a friendly, bouncy, uncomplicated girl whose nickname was '*Margot la Rigoleuse*' (The Laughing Margot) and it was that quality which, apart from her youth, her blonde good looks and her trim figure, made her so attractive to the ageing and increasingly jaded Emperor. She made Louis laugh and genuinely seems to have been fond of him. After his death she came from France to weep before the open coffin when his body lay in state at Camden Place. For his part, he adored her and, as we shall see, even withstood the fury of his wife's wrath to remain with her.

Several different versions exist of how they met, some of the most maudlin sentimentality, but the most likely explanation is that she was spotted at Court (where her current *amour* was a young officer) by either Bacciochi or Mocquard, Louis' usual procurers, and they arranged the inevitable interview with His Majesty. Louis was immediately smitten and set her up in two homes: a villa at 27, rue des Vignes in Passy, then already a fashionable suburb of Paris, and in a smaller house in the grounds of St Cloud with a small door built into its garden wall similar to the door he had had built into the side wall of the Elysée Palace when Lizzie Howard lived opposite.

Their relationship speedily became an open secret. It was commonplace to see the Emperor in his carriage bowling along the Champs Elysées in the evening on his way to the rue des Vignes where Margot would entertain some of the most interesting and sophisticated people in Paris. 'The gravest and most frivolous persons flocked thither,' wrote a contemporary. 'Ministers, senators, equerries, chamberlains, diplomats, tenors, soldiers and buffoons.' Louis had not enjoyed such pleasant, relaxed evenings since his soirées fifteen years earlier with Lizzie Howard and their joint friends. Many at Court scoffed at the cosiness of it all and at Margot's carefree attitude which they were happy to see as vulgarity.

They failed to realise that it was part of her appeal to her world-weary lover. She could be marvellously indiscreet – and Louis loved it. Once when she was to all intents and purposes staying with him while he was taking the waters at Vichy, Eugenie – who knew exactly what was going on – paid a short visit, and Emperor and Empress went for a walk together. Suddenly Margot's little cocker spaniel appeared and greeted Louis ecstatically, licking his boots and jumping up at him. Eugenie was not pleased, but Louis thought it rather amusing.

A similar incident occurred when he was inspecting his troops at the military camp at Châlons (with Margot installed in a comfortable villa nearby) and, in front of hundreds of soldiers rigidly on parade, the friendly animal appeared and greeted the Emperor like a good friend – which, of course, he was.

The affair continued to trundle along very happily and early the following year, on 24 February 1864, Margot gave birth to a son called Charles Jules Auguste François Marie, but with no surname on the birth certificate. Even so, he is generally accepted to be Louis' son and undoubtedly Louis later bought him a splendid estate at Liancourt-Rantigny to the south-west of Paris.[1]

Then in August, Louis came back home early one morning from a session and collapsed. He was simply too old and worn out to withstand with full vigour the hours of debauchery to which Margot – to his great pleasure – had subjected him. By the time that daylight arrived, he had fully recovered and made light of the incident. But Eugenie was furious. She summoned Mocquard (now in his seventy-fourth year and soon to die) and insisted on his taking her to Margot's house. She stormed in: 'Mademoiselle, you are killing the Emperor! If you have any affection for him, you will leave tomorrow,' she cried at Margot. 'This must stop. I command you

[1] After the fall of the Second Empire two undated letters from Margot were found among the papers at the Tuileries in an envelope with *Lettres à garder* (Letters to keep) written in Louis' handwriting on the front. They were published in *Papiers et correspondance de la Famille Impériale* the following year. In the first, written to Adrien Devienne, a senior lawyer at Court, Margot acknowledges that she had 'betrayed the man to whom she owes everything' and had lied to him about the child, saying that he had been born prematurely at seven months when, in fact, he was a nine months' baby. In the second, written to Louis (*Cher Seigneur*, as she always called him), she begs forgiveness for having deceived him. Even so, most experts believe that Charles really was Louis' son and that Devienne extracted the two letters from Margot because of Eugenie's fears that at some later date the child could appear as Louis' bastard son and, in some way, jeopardise her own legitimate son's title to the throne.

to leave. I shall pay you but you must leave. Off you go! Leave this house!'

But Margot was not overawed by the furious Empress. 'Your husband comes here because you bore him and tire him,' she calmly replied. 'If you want him not to come, keep him at home with your charm, your amiability, your good humour and gentleness.'

When Eugenie reported the incident to Louis, demanding that he reprimand this young upstart, he merely shrugged his shoulders and murmured words to the effect that young people do not always have the manners that they should have. He made it clear to his wife that he did not want Margot to leave Paris and that he had absolutely no intention of breaking off their liaison.

'Right! So I shall be the one to go!' said Eugenie and, regardless of the scandal that it caused, again travelling in her guise of the Countess of Pierrefonds, for the second time she left Paris hurriedly and went to take the waters at Schwalbach, a spa near Hesse in Germany. When Lord Cowley reported her departure and the circumstances that had provoked it to Lord Russell, his Foreign Secretary, Russell was suitably disapproving of this passionate display of Latin temperament: 'Spanish blood and Spanish jealousy have often begotten imprudencies,' he replied, 'but I have never heard of such an imprudence as the visit of the Empress to Marguerite. It was certain to end in miserable failure, as the damsel would feel sure of better provision from the husband than the wife.'

Even when Eugenie, at Louis' pleading, eventually returned from Schwalbach in October 1864, domestic relations were not improved. 'What occupies serious attention now are the intestine discords in the Imperial family,' wrote Cowley on 6 December to Lord Russell. 'I am told that the Emperor and the Empress are hardly on speaking terms. It has come to this, that she taxes him with his present liaison to his face – calling the lady the scum of the earth – and he defends himself . . . She has made confidants of the Walewskis, saying: "Do not suppose that I have not always been aware of the infidelities of this man. I have tried everything, even to making him jealous. It achieved nothing but, now that he has condescended to this *crapule* [scum], I can stand it no longer!" Some people think that Her Majesty is capable of insisting on a separation [but] I doubt it.'

Cowley proved right. Within six months, the affair was over.

In early May 1865, Louis went on a state visit to Algeria leaving Eugenie to rule happily in his stead as Regent. No outsider knows why but, for once, absence did not make the heart grow fonder. Upon Louis' return, it was made clear to Margot that all was over. He made her a generous cash settlement and bought her a splendid home in the country; and that was it. 'The Empress is rejoicing at having brought back the wandering sheep to a more respectable fold,' Cowley reported superciliously to London. In later years, Margot married a Prussian named Kulbach and died at the sadly early age of forty-five.

Louis seems to have withstood the break-up of their relationship with typical stoicism, but even during the days of his most passionate, heartfelt love for Margot, she had not been the only woman in his life. On 26 January 1865, when '*La Rigoleuse*' was still regarded as his *maîtresse en titre*, Valentine Haussmann, daughter of Georges (now Baron) Haussmann, Louis' accomplice in the rebuilding of Paris, gave birth to a boy named Jules Adrien whom most experts regard as another of Louis' illegitimate sons. It was only a month before her marriage to the Vicomte Pernetty and was obviously not a welcome cuckoo in her nest. The child never lived with the new Vicomte and Vicomtesse and was eventually adopted by a M. Hadot who had married a former mistress of Louis' own half-brother, Auguste de Morny.

In such a way were these unfortunate accidents managed during the Second Empire.

Chapter Twenty-Two

The Turn of
the Tide (1865)

WHEN LOUIS' 'GOLDEN YEAR' of 1860 ended, the Second
Empire had seemed more secure than ever before and
Louis' own position as 'the arbiter of Europe' accepted
without question. At fifty-two, he appeared to be in vigorous good
health, still sat finely upon a horse, still had more than just an eye
for a pretty woman. Within a decade all that was to change. The
proud edifice of the Empire would collapse like a house of cards,
its place on the European map taken by the new power of Imperial
Germany under the new 'arbiter of Europe', Prince Otto von Bismarck, its ruthless and dedicated Chancellor. As for Louis, he would
be a prisoner-of-war (albeit in the soft comfort of the new German
Emperor's summer palace) soon to be released to his last sad exile
at Camden Place, with his health so badly deteriorated that he had
become a pale, indecisive and sad version of the witty, commanding
and assured man he had once been.

Many, if not most, historians and biographers have seen a cause-
and-effect relationship between the failure of Louis' health and the
failure of his Empire. The one brought about the other. The sick
man in the Tuileries could no longer steer his country safely upon
the turbulent seas of nineteenth-century history.

That is an over-simplification. Everyone who has written about
Louis is aware that he died at Camden Place in January 1873 during
a series of operations to remove a gall-stone – described by his
surgeon as the size of a walnut or large chestnut – from his bladder.
From that indisputable fact, most writers have worked backwards
to postulate that for many years previously he must have been in
almost continuous pain, his physical strength and mental concen-

tration sapped by the inexorable build-up of the illness that eventually led to his death.

But too much importance has been attached to Louis' medical condition, at least in its earlier stages. Indeed, some French writers have positively used it as an excuse for his final defeat in battle and their country's agonising humiliation. For instance, in 1937, in his treatise on *Napoléon III: sa maladie – son déclin*, Georges Lecomte of the Académie Française claimed: 'It would probably be exaggerated to establish an absolute link between the Imperial health and the unfortunate events . . . in France's history. If Bismarck already sets his eyes upon our country, it is not Napoleon III's fault, but if mistakes are committed in the harsh and shifty diplomatic struggle that is beginning, if the traps prepared by the foreigner are closing in on us, it is because, opposite a hostile Europe, stands only a man weakened by a grave illness and stricken by pain.' Many writers, both in France and Britain, have asserted that – and Jasper Ridley has echoed it in *Napoleon III and Eugenie* – Louis 'first showed symptoms in 1861 of stone in the bladder'. That is not so. R. Scott Stevenson makes clear in his study, *Famous Illnesses in History*, that Louis *did* have his bladder washed out in that year by Dr Felix Guyon, Professor of Genito-Urinary Surgery in the Faculty of Medicine in the University of Paris, but that was not to get rid of any stone, but to clear his urethra of obstructions caused by ulceration due to gonorrhoeal infection. Louis, like many a man indiscriminate in his choice of sexual partners, had fallen prey to a major sexually transmitted disease. That was, no doubt, extremely unpleasant but not sufficient to help cause the dissolution of an empire; and the illness does not appear again in Louis' medical literature.

In fact, the presence of a stone in Louis' bladder was not diagnosed until four years later, in August 1865, at the military camp at Châlons-sur-Marne where he was, as usual at that time of year, attending manoeuvres. He had not been feeling well for several weeks, suffering from headaches and frequent bouts of fever, but suddenly there was a turn for the worse with violent pains in the lower part of his body. He was obviously in great distress and Baron Felix Larrey, the army's chief medical officer, was called in. For the first time, a doctor conducted an intrusive physical examination of Louis' genital and urinary region and discovered the presence of a stone in his bladder where it was causing a local infection and blocking the entrance to the urethra.[1]

How had the stone got into the bladder? One possible explanation is that it had formed originally in his kidneys and then passed down into the bladder but Mr James Bellringer, a modern British urinological consultant, thinks that is improbable. He says: 'The majority of bladder stones arise in the bladder itself, and that seems the likeliest explanation here. The Emperor was known to have a gonococcal urethral stricture (i.e. narrowing of the urethra caused by his gonorrhoeal infection), and therefore may well have had a degree of urinary retention. This would predispose to the formation of a bladder stone. Stones small enough to pass down from the kidney are almost always small enough to pass out of the bladder, and are not likely to have caused the considerable pain that he was obviously suffering.' In other words, Louis was paying the price for his sexual excesses.

Baron Larrey relieved the pain by 'sounding' his patient. This entailed inserting a solid instrument, called a sound, into the bladder to dislodge the stone from the mouth of the urethra. Any urine still in the bladder would, so long as Louis drank plenty of water, flow freely into the urethra and be expelled painlessly in the usual way. That process, followed by rest to help the infection to clear, was sufficient to restore him to full health within days.

Larrey did not deem the situation serious enough to suggest to Louis a more painful and unpleasant treatment in which he would have inserted into Louis' bladder an instrument, called a lithotrite, with which he would have crushed the stone into small fragments. These would then have been flushed out of the bladder by means of a tube called a catheter with, again, the aid of plenty of water; that would have been the end of the stone.[2] Bearing in mind that the stone would, at that early stage, only have been comparatively

---

[1] No doctor, not even Dr Conneau, had earlier suspected that a stone might be the cause of Louis' occasional bouts of pain in his lower body. Otherwise they would not have recommended his annual visits to Vichy where, in fact, the alkali in the water helped the stone to grow.

[2] I am indebted for much of these medical details to Sir David Innes Williams in an interview at the Royal College of Medicine in October 1995, and to Mr James Bellringer in an exchange of correspondence in January 1999.

small, Dr Jean-François Lemaire has commented in Jean Tulard's *Dictionnaire du Second Empire*: '[The use of a lithotrite] could easily have saved the Emperor.'

Hindsight makes geniuses of us all.

We know, therefore, that, from at least the summer of 1865, Louis had a stone in his bladder. But even allowing for the chronic haemorrhoids from which he also suffered, the stone's impact on his general health and ability to function properly as the political head of his country should not be exaggerated.

In fact, over the next five years, it caused only four more severe attacks: in the summers of 1866, 1867, 1869 and 1870. Admittedly, the attacks got worse as the stone got inexorably bigger and, sadly for France and for Louis, they coincided, as we shall see, with crucially important moments in French history. 'But between those attacks he would have been quite normal. His general way of living or frame of mind would not have been substantially affected. His condition would not have affected his mental processes nor, I would have thought, his sexual appetite.' That is the view of the doyen of modern British urinological consultants, Sir David Innes Williams. After having read medical reports on the final stages of Louis' illness, he gave me this authoritative insight into his condition:

> The pain would not always have been there. If the stone got stuck in the urethra, it would hurt but it would then fall back into the bladder and be peaceful. In between his 'attacks', he would have been quite normal ... The only complication is that on occasion it would have been extremely uncomfortable to be jogged up and down on a horse or in a horse-drawn carriage because the stone keeps hitting the neck of the bladder and giving an urgent desire to pass water which you cannot do because it is stuck there.
>
> But, generally speaking, his condition was the sort of thing that, until and unless it gets too bad, people learn to live with and in between attacks they carry on fairly normally but then are laid low from time to time. The prostate is not mentioned in the reports but there is the possibility that there was a prostatic obstruction as well.
>
> The stones would have been complicated by episodes of urinary infection. But when he had overcome the infection and they were

happily sitting quietly somewhere, he would be reasonably comfortable. How would they overcome the infection? Not by sounding. That would just remove the obstruction. They would then have to wait: give him buckets of water to drink to flush it all through. There wasn't any satisfactory way of overcoming infection in those days apart from nature.

It is not difficult to find corroboration of the fact that Louis functioned perfectly well when not actually suffering from an attack. For instance, in July 1868, a year which offered Louis brief respite, Prince Metternich reported to Baron Beust, his Foreign Secretary: 'I have never found the Emperor better, both in health and spirits, or more forthcoming, than he was during the short visit I have just paid.' Again, in November 1869, two months after Louis had had a severe attack, Celeste Baroche, the wife of one of his ministers, relates in her memoirs how, at Compiègne, his 'good health' impressed everyone and he 'astonished and charmed his guests with his gaiety and high spirits'.

Eugenie was in Egypt at the ceremonial opening of the Suez Canal and Louis was presiding in Compiègne as sole host. On the last evening before returning to Paris, he insisted that all the ladies, both young and old, join him in a dance. The male guests also came on the floor and, for nearly two hours, everyone – including Louis – whirled ceaselessly around until the players in the Imperial orchestra could hardly hold their violins in their hands. The dancers ended ravenously hungry but there was no food left in the château's kitchens. So Louis led them in a raid on the kitchens of the barracks forming part of the château and the happy guests devoured with great gusto the soldiers' humble bread, washing it down with champagne.

Even more striking is the fact that, on 15 September 1870, within two weeks of Louis having been pushed almost beyond endurance by the pain from the kidney stone blocking his bladder during the disastrous Battle of Sedan, Bismarck, when asked by Sir Edward Malet, a British diplomat, about the fallen Emperor's state of health in captivity in Germany, replied 'that he never in his life had seen the Emperor in the enjoyment of better health and he attributed it to the bodily exercise and the diet which late events had forced upon him'.

* * *

One cannot dispute that Louis' worsening state of health played a major role, especially towards the end, in both the loosening of his grip and his fatalist response to events that characterised his last five years as Emperor. But that was not the whole story. Other factors were also at work. This account of a ceremony outside the Tuileries Palace when the Prince Imperial, aged twelve, was drilling other cadets of his own age, is worth considering.

'On a bench overlooking the scene sat a very tired old gentleman, rather hunched together, and looking decidedly ill. I do not think I should have recognised him for his spiky moustache. He was anything but terrifying in a tall hat and a rather loosely-fitting frock coat ... Behind him stood the Empress Eugenie, a splendid figure, straight as a dart, and to my young eyes the most beautiful thing that I had ever seen ... wearing a zebra-striped black and white silk dress, with very full skirts, and a black and white bonnet ... She was a commanding figure and dominated the whole group on the terrace while the Emperor, huddled in his seat, was a very minor show.'

Those words were written in 1933 by the British historian Sir Charles Oman, recalling a scene from his childhood in the summer of 1868. The significance is that 1868 was the only year between 1865 and 1870 when Louis did *not* have an attack from the kidney stone in his bladder, yet he was still looking so obviously ill and demoralised.

In fact, I believe that two other factors, apart from his ill-health, led to his sad deterioration.

The first factor was the sexual dissipation of his energies. At that stage of his life in late middle age already weakened by at least one bout of gonorrhoea, he had expended too much of his physical strength in sexual excess. It sapped his energy. By the late 1860s, his sexual energy had dissipated.

The truth about the Emperor's sex-life was never generally known. In 1912, Hector Fleischmann was able to publish an extensive book entitled *Napoléon III et les femmes*, and Edmond and Jules Goncourt left this revealing account of his style with one of his many conquests: 'When a woman is brought into the Tuileries, she is undressed in one room, then goes nude to another room where the Emperor, also nude, awaits her. The chamberlain who is in charge gives her the following instruction:

"You may kiss His Majesty on any part of his person except the face".'

As the Emperor grew older, so his need for urgent, animal-like couplings with few or no preliminaries became ever greater. The attractive wife of one court official, seeking to advance her husband's career (a common motive), sought and obtained a private audience with her sovereign and, as she later reported to the Countess Walewska, one of his longer-serving mistresses, 'I did not even have time to make a token protest before he laid hold of me in an intimate place. It all happened so quickly that even the staunchest principles are rendered powerless.'

The Marquise de Taisey-Chatenoy, another with whom he enjoyed a brief encounter, has left this graphic pen-portrait of how, after making an assignation at a ball at the Tuileries, he arrived in her bedroom in the early hours of the morning 'looking rather insignificant in mauve silk pyjamas. There follows a brief period of physical exertion, during which he breathes heavily and the wax on the ends of his moustaches melts, causing them to droop, followed by a hasty withdrawal which leaves one unimpressed and unsatisfied.'

But few women were so privileged as to be visited by Louis in their bedrooms. There was at the Tuileries, hidden behind a secret door in Louis' study on the ground floor, a small, dark staircase which led straight up to his private apartments immediately above. To that study a succession of attractive young women, strangers to Louis, would be brought by Bacciochi in the hope that he might find them of interest.

There would then ensue a few minutes of preliminary polite conversation; if the woman was not to his liking, he would eventually murmur: 'My papers are calling' and politely ask her to leave. If, however, the initial impression was favourable, he would ring for Mocquard to come and collect his post. Mocquard would then take some papers from his desk and tiptoe out, only to return when summoned later by another ring of the bell. In the meantime, Louis would have escorted the young woman upstairs. Courtiers had grown accustomed to the silky rustling of crinoline dresses as the women hurried through the outer door of Louis' study and climbed the secret staircase to his apartment. The staircase was called '*le pas des biches*' (the passage of the birds, alluding, in colloquial

French to young women or girls). Louis' approach to his liaisons continued to be predictable.

'The Emperor,' wrote Prosper Mérimée to a friend, 'likes to chase the girls and thinks they are all angels, fallen from the sky. He gets all excited and for a full two weeks can think of nothing or no one else. Then he immediately cools down and doesn't think about her again.'

The process would then start all over again. He even took a small house on the rue du Bac in the Latin Quarter to use as a discreet meeting place. In Philip Guadalla's memorable words, 'He was still one of Nature's bachelors, and a closed carriage sometimes clattered through the dark streets to a silent house.'

This has to be contrasted with his wife Eugenie's views on sex: when trying to persuade her favourite lady-in-waiting, Princess Anna Murat, then in her early twenties, to marry the wealthy but much older English statesman, Lord Granville, she counselled: 'After the first night it no longer has any importance whether a man is handsome or ugly and at the end of the first week it is always the same thing.' Unlike – perhaps in reaction to – her mother, the passionate Manuela de Montijo, Eugenie truly had no interest in the subject.

From 1860 onwards, Louis' sexual adventures did not decrease, nor were they confined, as until then, to those moving in Court circles. Ever the snob (as in her reaction to the country girl, Marguerite Bellanger), Eugenie reacted violently and a Court gossip was overheard to say: 'I can tell you confidentially that the Emperor is so terrified by household rows that he would be capable of setting the four corners of Europe on fire in order to avoid one of those conjugal scenes which his indiscretions are always provoking.'

And so, partly through contrition, partly through weariness and perhaps also through inherent weakness, Louis allowed his wife to play a greater role in Cabinet meetings and to assume increasing political power, in some measure, at least, as a compensation for his lack of marital fidelity. Forty years later, Eugenie was to tell Maurice Paléologue that, from the days of her childhood in Spain, when her mother's house was full of statesmen, diplomats, generals and journalists, she 'had the taste for politics'. It was a taste that she was to exploit to the full.

*   *   *

The second, non-medical reason for the deterioration of Louis' physique and spirit relates to a fundamental flaw in his character that the fulfilment of his destiny has revealed. Put quite simply, the great conspirator became a victim of his own greatest conspiracy. There can be no doubt that he kept his charm to the end. As one visitor related, 'At first glance I took him for an opium addict. Not a bit of it; he himself is the drug, and you quickly come under his influence.'

But in many respects, he had become soft and indolent, seduced by the glamour, the luxury and the sheer self-indulgence of the Empire that he had brought into being. He became the ultimate hedonist. Hedonism does not breed men of action: it dulls the senses and makes strong men weak. As the 1860s ran their course, he no longer had a strategy, only tactics. 'I never form distant plans,' he said. 'I am governed by the exigencies of the moment.' He became increasingly content to flow with the tide, more and more willing to hand over the tiller of the ship of state to Eugenie. An ageing libertine, wracked from time to time by immense pain, does not often make a strong head of state.

The key to the weakness that now increasingly held Louis in its grasp is, in part at least, to be found in the spirit of the age, in the very hedonism that had become the quintessence of the Second Empire. 'Paris!', the writer and diplomat, Wilfrid Scawen Blunt, was to recall. 'What magic lived for us in those two syllables! What a picture they evoked of vanity and profane delights, of triumph in the world and the romance of pleasure! How great, how terrible a name was hers, the fair imperial harlot of civilised humanity!'

Louis and the upper classes of France were willing clients of Blunt's 'fair imperial harlot'. Although Louis financed better housing for the workers and lifted the ban on their collective associations and acknowledged their right to strike, the conditions under which most of the poor lived remained appalling, and the standard working day was a gruelling twelve hours. Meanwhile, at the Imperial palaces, Eugene and her ladies displayed their handsome shoulders in crinoline gowns which famous painters vied with each other to portray. Masked balls, glittering receptions, plays, charades, party games and, for many, flirting and lovemaking were the order of the day at Court. The finest selection of whores, from street-walkers to courtesans, avidly sold their wares as if sex was just another commodity. The world's first modern couturier, the Englishman Charles Frederick Worth, designed magnificent dresses for the rich and Europe's first department stores, Au Bon Marché (opened in 1853) and La Samaritaine, offered an exciting range of goods for the nearly-rich. Painters, musicians and sculptors prospered, and Paris swayed to the swirling melodies of Offenbach, aptly dubbed 'the Mozart of the Champs Elysées'.

Where Guizot, Louis-Philippe's Prime Minister, had exhorted the middle classes of his time 'Enrichissez-vous!', a latter-day Guizot might well have said to the now even more prosperous middle classes: 'Dépensez! Dépensez! (Spend! Spend!). It was not an empire, it was a carnival, and the carnival-master was a cosmopolitan roué, his physical strength seeping from him, who smoked innumerable cigarettes and is said to have spoken 'German like a Swiss, English like a Frenchman and French like a German'.

After nearly two decades of this kind of living, the French ruling classes were no match for the lumpen singlemindedness of the Prussians, resolute to build a new German nation.

After Sedan, Crown Prince Friedrich of Prussia remarked in his diary how 'the glittering new uniforms' of the French 'formed a strange contrast with ours, worn threadbare in war service'. In the same vein, his wife Vicky, the eldest daughter of Queen Victoria, wrote to her mother, with an inherited zest for underlining: 'It is a great satisfaction to me to see how Prussian character, discipline, habits, etc., is now appreciated and seen in its true light, its superiority acknowledged with pleasure and pride ... Gay and charming Paris! *What* mischief that very court and still more that very attractive Paris has done to English society ... *what harm* to our 2 eldest brothers[1] and to the young and brilliant aristocracy of London! ... Our *poverty*, our dull towns, our plodding, hardworking, serious life has made us strong & determined – is *wholesome* for us. I should *grieve* were we to imitate Paris and be so taken with *pleasure* that no time was left for self-examination & serious thought.'[2]

Sadly, they also apply to Louis himself. This is aptly confirmed by a letter which I have found in the Royal Archives at Windsor

---

[1] Albert Edward, Prince of Wales (later King Edward VII), and Alfred, Duke of Edinburgh.
[2] The letter is kept in the Royal Archives at Windsor Castle, reference: RA Z25/13, V to QV, 9/6/70.

Castle written by Queen Victoria's Principal Private Secretary, Colonel Sir Henry Ponsonby, to his mother shortly after Sedan: 'The Prince of Wales dined, and I had a hot and noisy but not angry discussion with him about the Emperor who he rather pities. I see nothing to pity. He has dragged down his nation to ruin, plunged them into an awful war when it was his duty to have known they were unfit for it, taken command when he could do nothing and finally in the midst of a starving disorganised army surrendered himself prisoner before them and drove out in the smartest carriage with splendid footmen, equerries, etc. to live at ease in a beautiful castle while France is at its last gasp.'[1]

How these strands – failing health, sexual debilitation and the insidious effect of nearly twenty years' pampered existence – when pulled together combined to help destroy Louis and his Empire is next to be considered.

[1] Reference RA VIC/Add A 36.215. Ponsonby would certainly have read the report in *The Times* a few days earlier that the horses drawing Louis' brougham, 'all unconscious of the former estate of their master, were worthy of the Imperial stables. The two postilions were as smart as if they were in the Bois or *en route* for St Cloud on a wet day. They and the two who sat behind wore long waterproof cloaks, glazed hats and the Imperial cockade.' But then how would he have wanted the Emperor to be driven into exile? At least Louis had style.

Chapter Twenty-Three

Running on
Borrowed Time
(1865–70)

THE YEAR 1865 BEGAN on a sad note for Louis. On 10 March, Auguste de Morny died unexpectedly after a short illness. He was only fifty-five and, although the half-brothers had never been particularly close, his death inevitably brought back memories of their mother, Hortense. On hearing that Auguste was failing fast, Louis immediately cancelled a concert scheduled for the Court that night and hastened, with Eugenie, to his bedside. They arrived in time to kneel beside the dying man as a priest administered the last sacraments. Their farewell was moving in the extreme.

Louis lost more than a brother. Auguste was perhaps the most able and intelligent of all his inner circle of advisers. In the years to come, the gap left by the absence of his clear, realistic mind would be considerable. As Lord Cowley wrote to Lord Clarendon in London: 'You will have been shocked at poor Morny's premature death. He had it in him, if he had been honest, to have become a very great man ... People may say what they please but Morny is a great loss to the Emperor and the latter is much cut up. In critical moments he had great calmness and firmness, and even his enemies admit that his judgement in political matters, when not warped by his own interests, was sound.'[1]

---

[1] In fact, this grandson of Talleyrand was one of the most interesting men of the Second Empire. Although without ministerial office since resigning as Interior Minister shortly after the coup d'état, he had been a skilful President of the Legislative Body for the last eleven years of his life. He had also been soldier, ambassador, lover, gambler, dandy, founder of the Jockey Club and the Longchamps racecourse, and an astute, if dishonest, businessman.

Within a month of Auguste's death, on 9 April 1865, the Civil War ended in America and Louis was soon faced with a problem on which Auguste's worldly advice would have been invaluable. Andrew Johnson, the Vice-President who had succeeded to the Presidency on Abraham Lincoln's assassination on 14 April, sent an ominous message to Louis by way of James Bigelow, the American Ambassador in Paris: 'The sympathies of the American people for the Mexican republicans are very pronounced and the continuation of French interference in Mexico is viewed with considerable impatience.' Clearly, the United States, with the Civil War now over, would not long tolerate Louis' continuing breach of the Monroe Doctrine.

Both Louis and Eugenie at last began to realise that they had made a grievous mistake in trying to foist an Austrian princeling upon a totally alien country, thousands of miles away on the far side of the Atlantic Ocean. General Bazaine, commander of the French troops in Mexico and promoted Marshal in 1864, continued to dispatch to Paris encouragingly optimistic reports; but Louis and his wife were now seeing events clearly. They realised that large parts of the country were, indeed, more or less under the Emperor Maximilian's control but only because of the French army's presence. Furthermore, with the ending of the Civil War, the triumphant Union began to pour arms and volunteers over the border to give practical aid to Benito Juarez, still holding out in his provisional capital at Chihuahua in northern Mexico. There were frequent and increasingly bloody encounters between his men and Bazaine's troops, with mounting French casualties.

The problem was compounded by the fact that Maximilian, full of good intentions though he was, had not even created a firm powerbase for himself among the very people who would have been expected to support him. He had appointed a moderate, liberal ministry to the disgust of the clerics and the landowners. This woolly-minded 'do-gooder' with a taste for pink champagne and strict Court protocol pleased no one. His new Constitution established equality before the law, gave workers the right to leave their employment at will, cut down on child labour, abolished corporal punishment of adult workers and gave Indian villages the right to own communal property. Such reforms might now seem desirable, but it was not the purpose for which the landowners and the Catholic Church had brought this foreigner across from Europe.

Mexico was fast becoming for Louis what Spain during the Peninsular War had been for his uncle: a running sore draining his national resources and military manpower. No less than 34,000 troops were in Mexico shoring up Maximilian's throne. The situation could not be allowed to continue.

So, in January 1866, when opening the Legislative Body's new annual session, Louis announced that he was about to order a phased withdrawal of the French expeditionary force from Mexico, claiming that Maximilian's régime was by then secure. Of course, that was untrue and it took another three months before Louis, with typical reluctance for any form of irreversible commitment, actually ordered Bazaine to make the necessary military arrangements.

But by then he had a new and even more urgent problem on his own doorstep in Europe.

The problem can be expressed in the phrase: Bismarck and Prussia. As far back as 1862, just before his appointment as Minister-President, Bismarck had frankly told Disraeli: 'I shall seize the first good pretext to declare war against Austria, dissolve the German Diet [the ineffectual Parliament of the loose-knit German Confederation], subdue the minor [German] states and give national unity to Germany under Prussian leadership.' By the autumn of 1865 Bismarck had so far advanced his plans that he was already in the last stages of masterminding his assault upon Austria. Although an ageing power, Austria was still the largest German-speaking state in Europe with at least double the population of Prussia's eighteen million and he needed, first, to ensure that France would not come to her aid. In October 1865 he took the train down to the Villa Eugenie at Biarritz, ostensibly to enjoy Louis and Eugenie's hospitality but, in reality, to obtain Louis' neutrality in the forthcoming conflict.

It proved a merry time, with enjoyable party games; Bismarck, always a trencherman, consumed vast quantities of food and drink, but the copious hospitality did not affect his judgement. In long walks with Louis along the shore as the Atlantic rollers came pounding in, the tall, erect Prussian and the short, ageing Frenchman talked for hours. It was just the two of them, together with Nero, Louis' pet dog, and, apart from Bismarck's subsequent report to his King, no written account of their conversations has survived. It is clear that Bismarck put his cards more or less on the table and obtained Louis' tacit approval of his plans for war against Austria. He left Biarritz with French neutrality assured.

What was the price that Louis exacted for this vital concession? Almost unbelievably, there was none. Bismarck would almost certainly have worked upon Louis' hopes that a defeated Austria would at last be forced to hand over Venetia and thus complete the unification of Italy, a cause notoriously dear to his heart. That would undoubtedly have been a personal satisfaction for Louis, but it would not benefit French political or material interests at all.

Yet not a single practical concession in favour of France was agreed or seemingly even requested: not even a slight redrawing of French territory along the Rhine where slivers of land and a few townships had been taken by Prussia and Bavaria after Waterloo as spoils of war. Louis asked for nothing.

Modern apologists have blamed his failure at Biarritz on his kidney stone, diagnosed only three months earlier at Châlons by the army doctor, Baron Larrey. But by the time Louis and Bismarck strolled on the shore beside the Atlantic, Louis' bladder had been washed out by Larrey's catheter, he had rested for several weeks and he was no longer in pain. There is only one conclusion: Bismarck was cleverer, stronger and, by then, sharper than Louis.[1]

The following year, in June 1866, Bismarck finally achieved his aim and the Seven Weeks War broke out, with Prussian troops overrunning Saxony. This small southern German state had the misfortune to lie between Prussia in the north and the former kingdom of Eastern Bohemia, which then formed part of the Austrian Empire and is now part of the Czech Republic.[2] The newly united Kingdom of Italy opportunistically joined in as Prussia's ally in return for the promise that – at last – a defeated Austria would be forced to hand over Venetia. Although Italian troops soon suffered a humiliating defeat at Custozza, the Prussian army totally humbled

---

[1] This view of events not only has its own logic to support it but also coincides with many modern academics' view that Bismarck's great achievement in creating a unified Germany owed perhaps as much to his opponents' blunders as to his own iron will.

[2] Despite the War's title, the decisive fighting lasted only ten days.

its Austrian counterpart on 3 July at the Battle of Sadowa.[1] Austria was forced to sue for peace and to hand over Venetia to Italy.

This all happened with France making no serious move to help or protect Austria. Louis' neutrality was as great as Bimarck could have wished to achieve when he had visited Biarritz the previous October. As we have seen, Louis had not then asked for any form of payment for French non-involvement but now he was sending his Ambassador in Berlin, the small, pug-faced Vincent Benedetti, to see Bismarck and claim his reward. But this was long after the event, when he had lost any true bargaining power. The experienced plotter had lost his touch.

Benedetti proposed to Bismarck a secret treaty between their two countries. In it, France would accept Prussia's annexation of the smaller German northern states (gobbled up as part of her preparation for the Seven Weeks War) and her seizing all the remaining smaller southern states. In return, Prussia would not oppose French annexation of her own two small neighbours, Belgium and Luxembourg. It is impossible to defend Louis' honour in making such a proposal. France had bound itself by the 1839 Treaty of London to respect the recently created Kingdom of Belgium 'as an independent and perpetually neutral state' under the collective guarantee of Britain, France, Prussia, Austria and Russia.

Indeed, it was Germany's invasion of Belgium in 1914 in breach of this guarantee that was to lead to Britain declaring war on Germany and entering the First World War. Yet here was Louis stating that, in return for his acceptance of Prussian territorial aggrandisement, he would without scruple annex a country whose borders France herself had solemnly guaranteed.

Apart from the lack of morality in the whole business, it was a stupid proposal to make. Why should Bismarck pay for what he had already obtained for nothing? In a famous phrase, Bismarck commented to his associates that Louis' suggestion was like 'an innkeeper's bill' or a waiter asking for 'a tip' (*Trinkgeld*).

Shrewdly, Bismarck asked Benedetti to put his proposal in writing, a request that the Ambassador could not refuse. After a few days he rejected it, but filed away Benedetti's document for future

---

[1] Sadowa was also called Koniggratz in German but today it bears the Czech name of Hradec Králové.

use. Four years later, at the start of the Franco-Prussian War, he was – like any modern spin doctor – to leak it to *The Times* in London with a disastrous effect upon British public opinion, deeply offended by Louis' unprincipled deviousness. As William Gladstone, then Prime Minister, wrote to Queen Victoria: 'Your Majesty will, in common with the world, have been shocked and startled.'

Prussia's defeat of Austria in the summer of 1866 changed the balance of power in Europe. Until then Prussia had been an important but not paramount nation while Austria had sprawled grandly across much of central and eastern Europe, seemingly impregnable. Louis, like most other national leaders, was sure that Austria would easily win its unwanted war with Prussia. Even Bismarck himself had his doubts. 'If we are beaten, I shall die in the last charge,' he told Lord Augustus Loftus, the British Ambassador in Berlin.

As it turned out, he had no need to worry. His men were better trained than the Austrians, had in the person of sixty-five-year-old Count Helmuth von Moltke a much better general than the sixty-one-year-old Austrian Count Ludwig von Benedek, and his war machine was the first modern one in history. It combined sophisticated new weaponry, including a breech-loading needle-gun with greatly increased fire-power, with a revolutionary new use of railways quickly to mobilise and move men and equipment.

The Austrians were routed at Sadowa. They fought bravely but with hopelessly outdated weapons. After a battle that endured grimly all day with Bismarck, in major's uniform with spiked helmet and jackboots, looking down from a nearby hill, the Austrian troops finally broke and ran. They left behind 24,000 men killed or wounded; 13,000 men rounded up and taken as prisoners.[1] The road to Vienna lay wide open.

The next day Franz Joseph telegraphed Louis offering to surrender Venetia to Italy and asking him to act as mediator. Louis promptly agreed but it was not a triumph for his diplomacy: negotiations dragged on for seven weeks until finally the Peace of Prague was signed on 23 August. Venetia became, at last, part of the Kingdom of Italy, and Austria undertook never again to meddle in German affairs.

---

[1] Many graveyards still remain strewn over the battlefield.

For Louis it was almost as much a humiliation as it was for the Austrians. He took it so much to heart that it made him ill. In his lowered mental and moral state, it brought on his second kidney stone attack and he had to leave Paris to take the waters at Vichy to try and find some relief. As wily old Adolphe Thiers, Louis-Philippe's ex-Prime Minister and then a leading Opposition Deputy, commented: 'It is France who has been beaten at Sadowa.'

Eugenie's reaction to the Austrian defeat was even more bitter, as in January 1905: 'You are touching a most painful memory in my life that has remained like a neuralgic pain ... The Emperor's stay in Vichy, during the summer of 1866, after Sadowa, that is the critical date, the Empire's fatal date; it is during those months of July and August that our fate was sealed! Of all that period, there is not a single fact, not a single detail that has not remained in my mind.'

It need not necessarily have worked out like that. If Eugenie and some of Louis' ministers had had their way and France had strongly opposed Prussia after Sadowa and launched a meaningful military challenge on the Rhine, cutting across its extended lines of communication to the soldiers fighting many miles distant in Bohemia, there is just a chance that Bismarck might have pulled back and softened his stance towards the French Emperor.

We know that he thought Louis weak and worthy of contempt. 'A sphinx without a riddle,' had been his description of Louis after returning from Biarritz the previous year. He is also known to have described Eugenie as 'the only man in his Government'.

What happened at a meeting of the French Cabinet hastily summoned at St Cloud on the evening of 5 July would seem to justify such sneering epithets. At the meeting, Louis presided and Eugenie sat facing him. She now takes up the story in her own inimitable way:

'The debate began with Drouyn de Lhuys [then Foreign Secretary] at once offering to take, when it came to Germany, an energetic attitude. The Emperor was listening, without voicing either objection or consent ... As for me, deep inside I approved. But, before making my own views known, I asked Marshal Randon, the Minister for War: "Are we fit to make a military demonstration on the Rhine?" He answered, and I still hear the sound of his voice: "Yes, we can immediately concentrate 80,000 men on the Rhine and

250,000 in about twenty days." As the Emperor was still not saying a word, I took up, with all my enthusiasm, Drouyn de Lhuys' argument for energetic action. I tell you that, at that precise moment, I felt that the fate of France and the future of our destiny was in the balance. It is one of the most important moments of my life . . .

'But La Valette [the Interior Minister] suddenly intervened, and in a peremptory tone, to dispute Drouyn de Lhuys' strong suggestion. Among his arguments, one in particular seemed to strike the Emperor. It was that in order to stop Prussia's progress, we would have to form an alliance with Austria and that would cause a dispute with Italy – which would be a complete reversal of the entire political manoeuvring to which the Emperor had applied himself over the past year, since Bismarck's ill-fated visit to Biarritz.

'As for the territorial compensations that the newly extended Prussia would enable us to claim, La Valette was in no doubt that we would obtain them without any difficulty through friendly negotiations with Berlin.

'At that, I jumped in: "When the Prussian armies will no longer be committed in the depths of Bohemia and are able to turn against us, Bismarck will make a mockery of our claims!" I even said to the Emperor: "Prussia did not have any scruples about blocking you after your victory at Solferino. Why should you be bothered about blocking her after Sadowa? . . . In 1859, we had to give in because we would not have had 50,000 men to bar the road to Paris. Today, it is the road to Berlin that is open . . ."'

Drouyn de Lhuys and Randon, encouraged by Eugenie's stance, fought back and the Council took three momentous decisions. The first was to convene immediately the Legislative Body to obtain the necessary funding for a general mobilisation of the army; the second was the immediate gathering of 50,000 men along the Rhine; the third was the sending to Berlin of a threatening note, in which the French Government would formally tell the Prussian Government that it would not tolerate any territorial changes in Europe of which it had not first approved. Furthermore, the official announcement of these three measures would be published on the very next day in *Le Moniteur*.

'But nothing appeared in *Le Moniteur*,' Eugenie cryptically told

Paléologue so many years later. 'During the course of the night, other influences had their effect upon the Emperor. And events followed the course that we know.' Tantalisingly, she gave no clues as to what those 'other influences' might have been.

Perhaps they merely existed in Louis' own mind: he had lost much, if not all, of his earlier taste for decisive action.

According to Eugenie, it took Louis only five or six days to recognise his error. 'But it was too late to go back on it. The fatal hour had passed. I then saw him so beaten that I trembled for our future. All that the Opposition newspapers had said in criticism of the Emperor at that time, he then said about himself. One evening, in particular, we were taking a stroll together at St Cloud: he was completely distraught; I could not get a single word out of him. As I could not myself find anything more to say, I burst into tears and cried bitterly; my soul was in agony. My God, we paid a high price for our splendours!'

For the first time, Eugenie thought seriously that Louis should abdicate. She told Prince Richard Metternich, the Austrian Ambassador who had become in many respects her confidant, that she had suggested to her husband that he should abdicate in favour of their son and appoint her Regent until the nine-year-old Prince Imperial reached the age of eighteen. Louis had at once rejected the idea, but 'I assure you', she said in a remarkable breach of confidence, 'that we are marching to our downfall and the best thing would be if the Emperor could disappear suddenly, at least for the time being'.

In softer vein, she told Maurice Paléologue much later: 'Sadly we had not seen the end of our troubles. On 7 August, the Emperor left Vichy but was still so ill and depressed that, when he arrived at St Cloud, he had to take to his bed. On the day after, we received a telegram, sent from [the port of] St Nazaire. It was the Empress Charlotte who had unexpectedly arrived back from Mexico! We were entering another tragedy!'

In Mexico, the situation had deteriorated badly. In April, the same month Louis finally ordered Marshal Bazaine to make the necessary arrangements for a phased French withdrawal and Drouyn de Lhuys formally told William H. Seward, the American Secretary of State, that 10,000 men would leave for home that November, another

10,000 next March and the remaining 14,000 in the following November. Even the starry-eyed Maximilian was now forced to accept reality – up to a point. He requested Bazaine to organise an effective Mexican army for him. Of course, this quickly proved an impossible task: the régime was too unpopular and impoverished to attract sufficient number of acceptable recruits. Bazaine bluntly advised him to admit failure and leave the country with the last French contingent.

But Maximilian refused. In a last despairing hope of salvation, he sent Charlotte to France to plead personally with Louis for at least a delay in the withdrawal of the French soldiers. In his post-Sadowa mood of deep depression, this was perhaps the very last encounter that Louis wished to endure. In fact, Eugenie tried to spare him the ordeal. When Charlotte arrived at St Cloud and was met by the young Prince Imperial wearing the chain of the Mexican Order of the Eagle, she alone was waiting to greet her fellow Empress at the head of the Grand Staircase, lined by soldiers of the Imperial Guard.

She assured Charlotte that her husband was not well enough to receive her but the distraught woman who had come so far to see him would not be put off. She burst into tears and insisted that the Emperor see her. A few days later she returned and, on two separate occasions, both Eugenie and a clearly unwell Louis were waiting to receive her. Their last meeting was decisive. It was a grim and highly emotional encounter.

Charlotte pleaded that even a fraction of the French Expeditionary Force should be left in Mexico until matters improved and the full measure of the United States' support to Juarez could be assessed. 'I could have done that before Sadowa,' said Louis, 'but now it is impossible. You must realise that by leaving Mexico I am inflicting a humiliation on myself. I would give ten years of my life not to do so. But Mexico is an abyss into which France is sliding. I must stop it.'

'Then we are condemned to death,' replied Charlotte.

Louis tried to placate her. 'Your disillusionment after so many struggles is cruel,' he said, 'but at the Emperor Maximilian's age there is no need for despair. I beg him to leave Mexico with the French troops ... I count on you to persuade him to do so and confound the hotheads who wish to push him to his doom.'

All that Charlotte could reply through her tears was: 'You are condemning him to death, my beloved Max.'

'No, my dear sister, you do not want to listen to me,' said Louis. 'I have been planning a throne for him in the Balkans.'[1]

But Charlotte could merely repeat obstinately: 'Maximilian will die. He will not run away. A Habsburg does not run away.'

Louis still tried to make her accept the inevitable. 'Giving up an impossible task is not running away,' he said. 'Europe will applaud a wise decision which will spare both blood and tears.'

Charlotte was now beyond all endurance. 'Blood and tears!' she cried. 'Both will flow again, and because of you! Rivers of blood! And on your head!'

At this point, she collapsed. A doctor was hurriedly sent for and, as Eugenie tried to bring her round with a glass of water, Charlotte seized the glass and threw its contents at her. She screamed: 'Assassins! Leave me alone! I won't swallow your poisoned drink!'

She had literally gone mad in front of the horrified Eugenie and Louis.

The next morning, before leaving Paris for a brief return to her former home at Miramar Castle, she wrote an impassioned letter to Maximilian which showed the mental incoherence that now held her in its grasp. 'To me,' she wrote, 'the Emperor is the Devil in person and at our interview yesterday he had an expression to make one's hair stand on end. He was hideous and that was the expression of his soul.'

As for Louis himself, on 29 August, when he had got over the worst effects of his kidney stone attack, he wrote to Maximilian a letter as gallant as it was ruthless. '*Monsieur* my brother,' he wrote. 'We have received with pleasure the Empress Charlotte and it has been painful for me not to be be able to acquiesce to her demands. In effect, we are at a decisive moment for Mexico and it is necessary for Your Majesty to take a heroic role, the time for half-measures is past.

'I begin by declaring to Your Majesty that it is henceforth impossible for me to give Mexico another *écu* or another man. That being

[1] There is very little, if any, evidence of this 'plan' to put Maximilian on yet another throne.

established, it is imperative to know what will be the conduct of Your Majesty.'

He then set out the Emperor's two grim alternatives: try and defend himself with his inadequate Mexican army or abdicate and return to Europe with the last French soldiers.

Meanwhile, Charlotte went to Rome to intercede with the Pope. Pius IX received her courteously on 27 September but he too could only utter soft words of comfort. The black mood suddenly returned to her damaged mind and she screamed at him that her entourage were trying to poison her. Next morning, dressed in deep mourning, she returned and begged him to arrest them.

Gently she was led away and taken back to her native Belgium where she was to spend the next sixty years in the merciful oblivion of total insanity. She died in 1927 at the age of eighty-seven.

Maximilian's fate was, if anything, even more tragic. In November, he irrevocably decided not to abdicate and appointed, of all people, General Miramón, the last Conservative President of Mexico, to command his under-manned and under-armed army. The following month, Drouyn de Lhuys told Secretary of State Seward that France was bringing forward her plans for withdrawal and that her whole army would be evacuated by March 1867.

And that is what happened. On 13 March 1867, the last French troops left Vera Cruz for Europe, leaving some 7,000 dead behind them during the three years of their disastrous intervention.

On the following day, Maximilian and General Miramón were surrounded with their troops at Querétaro, 125 miles north of Mexico City. A siege, in which 9,000 defenders were encircled by 25,000 Republican soldiers, endured for two months before Maximilian, betrayed by one of his own colonels, was forced to surrender. He and Miramón, together with another general named Mejía, were promptly thrown into gaol.

A month later, on 19 June, Maximilian, standing between his two generals, was executed on the *Cerro de las Campanas* (Hill of the Bells) at Querétaro. At least, that is how Edouard Manet's famous painting shows the execution taking place. In fact, Maximilian, chivalrous to the end, ceded his place of honour to Miramón in tribute to his bravery as a soldier. 'May my blood be the last to be shed and may it bring peace and happiness to my unhappy adopted fatherland,' he said in a firm, clear voice seconds before the shots rang out.[1]

The news of Maximilian's death reached Paris on 1 July 1867. The timing could not have been worse or more ironic, for Louis was just about to leave St Cloud for a splendid prize-giving ceremony at the Universal Exhibition that had been enchanting the capital since 1 April. The event was the last magnificent display of government by dazzle. Twelve emperors and kings, six reigning princes, nine heirs apparent, a viceroy and countless 'highnesses' had descended on Paris.

Two contemporary accounts give a vivid picture of the pomp and style of the Second Empire at its last hurrah. First, a review of the Army on Longchamps Racecourse.

Countless thousands of spectators formed a living wall round uniforms while gleaming weapons and flags of all colours shone brightly in the sun. Then a shout was heard rising from all sides – 'The Empress is coming!' – and bright, gratified, smiling, bowing, she drove through the serried ranks on her way to the Imperial grandstand. The sovereigns, on horseback, then appeared followed by the German Crown Prince and the heir to the throne of Russia. The troops presented arms, greeting Their Majesties with a deafening blare of trumpets.

Then, the scene at the first night of Offenbach's latest operetta, *The Grand Duchess of Gerolstein*.

The Empress, dressed in rose-coloured silk, shoulders bare, her throat adorned by a superb necklace of pearls, seemed to shine

---

[1] In the spring of 1869, Manet was told that his newly completed painting, *The Execution of Maximilian*, would not be displayed officially in Paris and that a lithograph would not be allowed to be sold. The reason almost certainly was that Manet had painted the soldiers of the firing squad wearing uniforms almost identical to those of French soldiers, so that he was, in effect, showing 'France shooting Maximilian'. The Second Empire was haunted by the ghost of Maximilian, and the painting was not shown in France until twenty years later, having first been exhibited in the United States. This major painting is now prominently displayed in the National Gallery, London.

with the brilliance of her greatest days. All these kings crowding into Paris for the Exhibition intoxicated her with the praise and admiration they showered on her head. The decor of power surrounding her still gave the illusion of greatness. The previous evening she had offered a night fête to her crowned guests at Versailles, the like of which had never been seen, not even in the time of Louis XIV: water tournaments in the lights of the park to the sounds of hidden violins, the Grand Canal a mass of gondolas, a supper for 600 in the Hall of Mirrors, a fireworks display reaching its climax as 100,000 rockets lit up the night sky.

It was amid such scenes of Imperial splendour that Louis learned the fate of the thirty-five-year-old executed Emperor of Mexico.

In truth, the sad news of Maximilian's death was much more in keeping with the reality of French life and the circumstances of Louis' rule than all the fine uniforms and magnificent spectacle. In that same year of 1867, his cousin 'Plon-Plon', disloyal as ever, summed up the situation to a bespectacled, earnest politician named Emile Ollivier, who was to play a decisive role in the dying stages of the Second Empire: 'The Emperor is tired, he no longer has any friends, he is bored. He is truly ill with his bladder.'

Power was slowly ebbing away from Louis' hands. In the memorable words of Philip Guadalla writing in 1922: 'After 1866, the brilliance of the Empire [for it still had brilliance] was a glow of evening, a vivid light upon quiet hills that face a sinking sun. The sky was still bright; but there was a strange chill upon the Empire. The clear dawn of 1852 seemed half a century away, and quite suddenly the Emperor had become an old man. Something in Eugenie's sad-eyed beauty was beginning to fade, and the Court had aged.'

This is a poetic but nonetheless accurate way of stating an unpoetic reality. On 16 January 1868, Lord Lyons, the new British Ambassador who had recently taken over from Lord Cowley, reported to London: 'The real danger to Europe appears to be in the difficulties of the Emperor Napoleon at home. The discontent is great and the distress amongst the working classes severe ... There is no glitter at home or abroad to divert public attention, and the French have been a good many years without the excitement of a change.'

Seven months later, Lord Cowley himself reported, after visiting Louis at Fontainebleau, that he had found him 'aged, and much depressed. He spoke gloomily of his own position in France and said that he had found, touring the provinces, that the country districts were still for him, but that all the towns were against him.'

Cowley thought that he was even thinking of abdication. Lord Lyons agreed: 'I hear that the Emperor is very much out of spirits,' he reported to Lord Stanley, his Foreign Secretary, on 11 August 1868. 'It is even asserted that he is weary of the whole thing, disappointed at the contrast between the brilliancy at the beginning of his reign and the present gloom – and inclined, if possible, to retire into private life. This is no doubt a great exaggeration but, if he is really feeling unequal to governing with energy, the dynasty and the country are in great danger.'

Two years earlier Louis had abruptly rejected Eugenie's suggestion that he should abdicate in favour of their young son with herself as Regent but now this unlikely talk of abdication would seem to have some substance.

It is not difficult to see why. Eighteen months earlier, on 19 January 1867, Louis had sacked his longest serving Prime Minister, Eugene Rouher, and in a letter to Rouher printed in *Le Moniteur* had announced his intention of instituting major constitutional reforms diminishing the power of the Senate and for the first time sharing legislative power between the elected Deputies in the National Assembly and the Emperor himself. The 'Liberal Empire' on which these reforms were to be based did not materialise until three years later, in January 1870, when he asked the earnest, well-intentioned Emile Ollivier to form a Government.

But the letter itself exposed a definite crack in Louis' obsessive belief, until that moment, in his destiny to be the absolute ruler of France.

When questioned many years later by Maurice Paléologue, Eugenie claimed: 'The Emperor's intention was to leave to our son the task of re-establishing in France the functioning of public liberties. This great reform the Emperor did not think he could carry through himself, because he was the very embodiment of the authoritarian principle: it was his *raison d'être*.

'Nevertheless, so as not to postpone it too long, he had made the resolve, which he confided to no one but myself, to abdicate in about the year 1874, when the Prince Imperial would be eighteen and old enough to ascend the throne. He had even planned the places of our retirement: we would live at Pau in the winter, Biarritz in the summer.

'The publication of the letter of 19 January – about which I knew nothing beforehand – was due to the Emperor's growing concern about his health, and the feeling that he could not bear the burden of Empire another seven years.'

Louis lived out his last few years as Emperor in a mist of autumnal melancholy and failing physical well-being. Even the pleasures of sex at last began to pall. His last known mistress, the beautiful, Belgian-born Comtesse Louise de Mercy-Argenteau, shared his bed on a more or less regular basis from 1866, when they first met, right through to the end. She certainly had not played hard to get. Upon their first meeting at Court, Louis is said to have murmured as he bent to kiss her hand: '*Comtesse*, why has such a jewel so long been kept from us?' To which she replied: 'A jewel, Sire! If jewel there be, it is at the service of Your Majesty.'

But the old roué had become impotent. He was quite literally played out. 'It has been often said,' Louise wrote in her memoirs, 'that I was his last love. Without any misconceived pride, I may admit that this is true. But his mistress I have never been.' In a somewhat coy way she was saying that the old philanderer was no longer physically capable of completing the sexual act.

By the time that the pages on the calendar flicked over to 1870, his last year as Emperor, Louis was in every sense no longer the man that he had once been.

Chapter Twenty-Four

The Beginning of the End (1870)

O N 2 JANUARY 1870, Louis asked Emile Ollivier, loyal to the Empire but well-known as a reformer, to form a Government. At forty-five, he represented a break with all the ageing politicians whom Louis had previously called upon to help him rule. But he was a break with tradition in another, much more important sense as well. For his appointment finally brought into being the Liberal Empire that, as we have seen in the previous chapter, Louis had promised three years earlier in his famous 'letter of intent' of 19 January 1867.

Typically, Louis had been reluctant for change and had put off the promised liberalisation of his régime as long as he could. But the general elections that had been held in the previous May, the first for six years, had given him precious little choice. The Government had received 4,438,000 votes as against 3,350,000 for the Opposition parties. The result had not been a positive disaster but it also had not been the clear-cut victory that the extreme authoritarian Bonapartists had hoped for. From then on they were no longer the largest single party in the Legislative Body.

As if that was not disappointment enough, in August Louis had fallen seriously ill again with his stone. It was his first attack for two years and it laid him low. He had to cancel his annual visit to the military camp at Châlons and, even worse, his long-planned visit to Corsica to celebrate the hundredth anniversary of the birth of Napoleon I: instead Eugenie and the Prince Imperial had to go on their own. *Le Moniteur* spoke soothingly about the Emperor's 'rheumatism' but the real facts soon emerged and the rumour even spread that he was dying, causing shares to plummet on the Stock Exchange.

As usual, Louis soon recovered and went again riding in the Bois de Boulogne, but the image of a failing Emperor and a Government in stalemate persisted. What could be done about it? As Eugenie had written to him on 27 October 1869, sailing down the Nile en route to the opening ceremony for the Suez Canal: 'I do not believe that one can carry out two coups d'état in one reign.'

At last, Louis accepted the inevitable and at the New Year's Day reception on 1 January 1870 he told the assembled Deputies that, although he had been entrusted by the nation with the sole power of government, he would thenceforth share it with them. The next day he asked Emile Ollivier to form a Ministry[1] – and Ollivier promptly flexed his muscles by persuading Louis to dismiss Haussmann as Prefect of the Seine and stop Eugenie attending Cabinet meetings.

Yet, despite his seeming willingness to bow to the inevitable, Louis soon showed Ollivier that he had not lost his skill in manoeuvring. In April 1870, for the first time since 1852, he called upon the people to support him in a plebiscite, that old stand-by of Bonapartist rule. He asked the nation to vote Yes or No to the statement: 'The people approve the liberal reforms in the Constitution carried out since 1860 by the Emperor with the co-operation of the great bodies of the State and ratify the Senate's decree of 20 April 1870.' This decree emasculated the Senate, leaving real power shared between the Deputies in the Legislative Body and the Emperor himself. This was the very essence of the Liberal Empire.

The result of the plebiscite held on 8 May 1870 was an overwhelming victory for the Liberal Empire and for the Emperor himself. The Yes vote was 7,257,379, over four times as many as the 1,530,909 No votes. 'Sire,' declared the Speaker of the Senate, when announcing the final figures to Louis in a splendid ceremony at the Louvre, 'the country is with you. Advance confidently in the path of progress and establish liberty based on respect for the laws and the Constitution. France places the cause of liberty under the protection of your dynasty.'

Louis' private reaction was even more heartfelt. Taking his young son in his arms, he said: 'My child, your coronation is assured with

---

[1] Technically, Ollivier was not Prime Minister but Justice Minister, yet he was undoubtedly the paramount office-holder in the Administration.

this plebiscite. More than ever we can look to the future without fear.'

It was a time for righting wrongs in his personal life. Although he had never denied that the two boys, Eugene and Louis, born to Alexandrine Vergeot during his captivity at the Château de Ham in the 1840s, were his sons and had made financial provision for their welfare, he had never given them a title worthy of their status. Legally, they were both simply M. Bure. Now, on 11 June 1870, by Imperial decree, Eugene was made Comte d'Orx and Louis Comte de Labenne. Louis had had a somewhat humdrum life as a senior municipal official in Paris but Eugene had had a much more exciting time.

He had joined the army and gone, as part of his father's expeditionary force, to Mexico where he had settled, married a Mexican woman and set up in business. His life must have been somewhat bizarre since, two months after his marriage, his own mother-in-law tried to kill him. But still, he survived and only returned to France in the spring of 1870 when the collapse of his business made him almost destitute. So, on 29 April of that year, he wrote to Louis: 'Dear Father. I beg you to render unto me that which is my birthright. Take me into your paternal arms so that I may have at least the happiness of seeing you, of living beside you like an honourable man. If you love me as I love you, all coldness between us would be overcome. I want you to forget the past and I want people to say that I am the honour of my father and worthy of his name.'

He signed the letter, not Louis Bure, but Louis Napoleon.[1]

We do not know if Louis ever saw his son and 'took him in his paternal arms', but it cannot be pure coincidence that, having been Emperor for eighteen years, it was only six weeks later that he made both Louis and his brother counts. This was the same level of nobility that Napoleon I had bestowed upon his own acknowledged but illegitimate son, Alexandre Walewski. Almost to the very end, Louis was still following in the footsteps of his uncle.

---

[1] Orx and Labenne, the two small villages forming part of Louis' and Eugene's titles, are in the Landes in south-west France and I am most grateful to Mme Ursch and M. Jacques Pons of the Departmental Archives of the General Council of the Landes at Mont de Marsan for providing the material which has served as the basis of my text.

Meanwhile, the Second Empire seemed to have taken on a new lease of life and self-confidence. The malaise of the last few years had gone. Optimism was in the air, and it was infectious. On 30 June, Emile Ollivier told the Legislative Body: 'The Government has no uneasiness whatever. At no epoch has the peace of Europe been more assured. Irritating questions no longer exist.'

Sadly, they were all living in a fool's paradise. With its orchestras playing and its elegant passengers happily dancing, the liner was nearing the silent, frozen menace of the iceberg.

Within just over two months, it was all over. The Second Empire no longer existed and Louis was a prisoner-of-war in exile. Why? Because, at last, Bismarck got the war against France for which he had been longing and destroyed Louis' empire as the inevitable price of victory. The French Empire had to die so that Bismarck could proclaim over its prostrate body a new German Empire with his own King of Prussia as the first German Emperor. And Bismarck got his war because the French people, half-led by and half leading their Emperor, blundered into a senseless conflict for which they were totally unprepared.

But before we consider the final weeks of the Second Empire, the question of Louis' health has again to be addressed.

He had not suffered overtly from his stone since the crisis nearly a year before in August 1869 but he continued to feel unwell. He regularly saw blood and sometimes pus when he passed water; riding a horse was consistently painful. In his sixty-second year, he was determined to discover what was wrong with him. He was suspicious of his Court doctors many of whom, apart from the ever-loyal Dr Conneau, he considered, with their soothing words and bland assurances, as much courtiers as doctors. So he asked Dr Baron Lucien Corvisart, Conneau's assistant, to find an independently minded doctor to give him an honest, impartial opinion.[1] Corvisart recommended a university professor named Germain Sée who, to his immense surprise, found himself summoned to the

---

[1] Louis had utter confidence in Corvisart. He was the great-nephew of Napoleon I's doctor, Baron Nicolas Corvisart, who had looked after Louis' mother, Hortense, during her pregnancy.

Palace of St Cloud, on 20 June 1870, to conduct on his own a personal examination of the Emperor.

The consultation took place in the utmost secrecy. Sée was not allowed to come direct to St Cloud. He was met on the road leading out of Paris, made to change carriages and let in to the Palace by a secret door. If the Stock Exchange had come to hear about his visit, there would have been widespread panic and shares would again have plummeted. Sée has recorded that, with the exception of the Empress, Corvisart and (almost certainly) Conneau, no one even knew he was at the Palace.

After Louis had briefly described his symptoms, Sée at once realised the probable cause of his problems. 'After a few words,' he later wrote, 'the Emperor lent himself willingly to my examination which lasted an hour. It had been said that the Sovereign was afflicted with diabetes, that he was suffering from heart disease, and so on. But I saw immediately that this was not true. Moreover, I understood at once where to direct my diagnosis.' Sée, with great care (and, no doubt, considerable trepidation), inserted a finger into his patient's backside and probed around inside as thoroughly as he could. This highly intrusive physical examination confirmed his preliminary diagnosis: Louis had a large stone in his bladder.

'I did not, however, make my opinion known to the Emperor,' says Sée, 'but I told him that a consultation was necessary. "I believe you understand me thoroughly and I have full confidence in you", the Emperor replied. "So arrange for a consultation with the other doctors".'

Sée contacted Auguste Nélaton, Louis' surgeon, and his three principal doctors, Corvisart, Ricord and Fauvel. Dr Conneau was to attend the consultation but only as a witness. The five doctors agreed to meet on 1 July.

Sée again picks up the narrative:

'We met at Dr Conneau's residence at 8 am. I had thought that the consultation would not last more than half an hour but it occupied three hours. I began the proceedings in the following words:

'"Gentlemen, I am the youngest, and I therefore require you to listen to me first. I shall not say much. The Emperor is suffering from stone." They all exclaimed against this view. Corvisart said it was a cold, Fauvel an abscess. I maintained that I was right, and proceeded to prove it. I described all the Emperor's symptoms: the pains he suffered when riding and driving. In short, I explained all I had discovered when I had examined His Majesty on 20 June, and I wound up as I had begun: "The Emperor has stone, and nothing else."

'When I had finished, Dr Fauvel withdrew what he had said as to the abscess and Corvisart his declaration respecting the cold. All were unanimous in expressing the opinion that I was right. Only one thing remained to be done – to examine the Emperor again with a view to operating. But Nélaton would not hear of that. "It is absolutely necessary," I insisted, "and to operate immediately." Ricord upheld my opinion and said that the Emperor should have had a sound passed long ago to relieve the pain [as Larrey had done at Châlons five years before but Fauvel and Corvisart were of Nélaton's opinion. "You must understand," they said, "that we cannot treat the Emperor as though he were an ordinary patient."

'At this point, Nélaton drew me aside and said: "My dear colleague, you are still very young.[1] You do not understand what it is to have the care of a sovereign. He is not a patient like other patients; one has to know when to wait and sometimes to dissemble. Remember the great responsibility we are taking upon ourselves."[2] I replied: "That does not affect my judgement. The operation ought to have been performed six months ago. The patient is seriously threatened. There is only one thing to do, and that must be done at the earliest possible moment." By then Ricord had come completely round to my point of view. He said: "It must be done tomorrow. In any case, it must not be delayed beyond the day after tomorrow."

'Then the discussion recommenced. Unfortunately, it came to a question of voting. Only Ricord and I considered the operation an urgent matter. The other three asked for time to pronounce an opinion. "Let the summer pass;" said Nélaton, "in September, we

---

[1] In fact, Sée was fifty-two and the pompous, condescending Nélaton was only eleven years older.

[2] Sée added a footnote about the responsibility that would fall on Nélaton's shoulders as the surgeon who would actually have to carry out the operation. 'Only the year before, he had performed such an operation, with fatal results, on Marshal Adolphe Niel [then Minister of War]. Part of the lithotrite [a surgical instrument] had broken off, and an incision had to be made to remove it. The Marshal died of septicaemia.'

will see about it." [By September, Louis was a prisoner in Germany, and Eugenie and the Prince Imperial were in exile in England.] In vain, I supplicated. In vain, I insisted on the Emperor's courage in bearing pain; but nothing I said was of any use. We were two to three.

'The examination of the Emperor, and consequently the operation, were postponed. I was charged with the duty of drawing up the result of our consultation, and it was agreed that, on the next day but one at the latest, the document should be given to Dr Conneau, who was to get the signatures of all the doctors affixed to it, and then to communicate its contents to the Emperor and Empress.'

The document was never signed by anyone other than Sée himself and it was found in an envelope among Dr Conneau's papers when his house was searched in September 1870 after the fall of the Empire. *All* the existing biographies of Napoleon III maintain that Louis was never told of these findings, at the time, if at all, and that, throughout that fateful summer of 1870 when France lumbered into war with Prussia, he knew nothing of Sée's grim diagnosis. Indeed, Eugenie assured Paléologue many years later that the envelope was not opened until after Louis' death, so that he never knew the true state of his health.

Louis' apparent ignorance of his stone has always struck me as odd, if not frankly unbelievable. Henri Conneau had been his mother's doctor before him and was one of his oldest and most devoted associates. Yet everyone seems to agree without demur – or apparently much thought – that, at a time when Louis' health was of supreme importance for the future of the nation, Conneau took the responsibility upon himself of not telling his patient and friend of the report's contents but simply left it in its original envelope in a drawer in his house.

I now know this to be not true, and I say that for two reasons. First, Sir David Innes Williams, Past-President of the British Medical Association and of the Royal Medical Society and Britain's most eminent urologist, has told me: 'I find it difficult to believe that the Emperor having submitted to the most personal physical examination – yes, you are quite right: Professor Sée would have had to stick his finger up the Imperial backside! – would not have asked his doctor what on earth was the outcome, what was the diagnosis, and his doctor would then have been under an ethical duty to give him a reply.' Second, everyone seems to have overlooked the fact that, tucked away in a footnote to a long-forgotten book, *Souvenirs sur L'Impératrice Eugénie* by Augustin Filon, ex-tutor to the Prince Imperial, published in 1920 after Eugenie's death, is this vital nugget of information: 'On the death of the Emperor, this diagnosis could not be found among his papers. On Prince Napoleon [i.e. "Plon-Plon"] questioning Dr Conneau and asking what he had done with it, the doctor replied: "I have given it to the proper person." What did he mean? Prince Napoleon concluded that "the proper person" was the Empress . . . However, nothing could be more untrue. The Empress had no knowledge whatever of this opinion of Dr Sée's.'

That surely means only one thing: 'the proper person' to whom Dr Conneau gave the contents of this vital report was none other than his patient, the Emperor himself, who, at that crucial time for his own personal destiny and that of his country and his Empire, chose to ignore it. However great the pain or the personal risk, he would not be deterred from doing his duty.

In another version of 'Plon-Plon's' encounter with Dr Conneau printed in an even more forgotten book, Edward Legge's portentous biography of Eugenie published in 1910, 'Plon-Plon' presses Conneau as to what that 'proper person' said when shown the report and the answer was: '*Le vin tiré, il faut le boire*' (The bottle having been opened, one has to drink the wine). Bearing in mind that by then France was careering into war with Prussia and for her Emperor not to have been on the field of battle with her troops would have been unthinkable, that sounds like the authentic voice of Louis speaking.

But the case for Louis knowing exactly what was wrong with him in the summer of 1870 and choosing to ignore it goes even further. At least one set of contemporary doctors seems intuitively to have divined the truth about the close relationship between Dr Conneau and his patient. After Louis' death three years later, news of the Sée Report reached the French newspapers and the *British Medical Journal* for 18 January 1873 said in an editorial: 'It remained in the hands of M. Conneau, to whom in the first instance it was forwarded; and it is now disinterred by the singular vicissitudes of a strange fortune to bear testimony to the terrible exigencies which the government of a State imposes upon its ruler, and the firmness with which he put aside personal consideration when the functions of the State called him to a position incompatible with his duty to himself.

'Napoleon III started for the frontier intent on the Franco-German War and on placing himself at the head of his armies, the prey to intolerable suffering, which was increased by every jolting of the carriage and which almost forbade him to sit in the saddle. He started, moreover, with the knowledge that the surgeons whom he had consulted were altogether opposed to the risk which he was running and that, as an individual, if not as an emperor, he was bound to stay at home and get rid of his stone.'

Louis undoubtedly had many failings but he truly was a man of exemplary bravery.

On 3 July 1870, the same day that Professor Sée and the other four doctors met at Henri Conneau's house, an official dispatch from the French Ambassador in Madrid reached the Foreign Office in Paris with the startling news that the throne of Spain had been offered to, and accepted by, Prince Leopold of Hohenzollern-Sigmaringen from southern Germany. The disquieting aspect for the French was that Leopold was a kinsman of the King of Prussia, head of the House of Hohenzollern.

The news was like a sudden thunder-clap in the quiet Parisian summer sky. For how could France possibly have accepted that the throne of Spain, on one side of her borders, vacant for two years since Isabella II had been deposed, should be occupied by a German prince, coming from the other side of her frontiers? It is little wonder that Bismarck had been scheming hard for the past six months to promote Prince Leopold's candidature. He knew full well that no French emperor could have tolerated such a potentially dangerous encirclement of his country.

Indeed, Louis was to say later to a German-Jewish journalist named Mels Cohen who came to interview him as a prisoner-of-war in Germany: 'It would have been to my advantage for family reasons to see the throne of Spain occupied by this prince of the House of Hohenzollern, who is doubly related to me, as the great-grandson of Caroline Bonaparte [Napoleon I's sister] and the grandson of Stephanie Beauharnais [niece of Louis' grandmother, the Empress

Josephine] ... Add to this that his father, Prince Antony, was one of the best friends of my youth – and years have not dimmed our memory of happier times – and you will realise that I should be trampling on the interests of my own house by opposing vigorously his acceptance of the Crown of Spain.'

Asked if it would have been so grave a danger for France if a Hohenzollern had reigned in Spain, Louis replied: 'Yes, for at the end of two or three years he would inevitably have fallen from the throne and then Prussia would have inevitably intervened in Spain ... The proud blood of Spain would have accepted no foreign masters, and the difficulties of the situation confronting Prince Leopold in a few years would have induced Germany itself to assume the supreme power in order to support him.'[1]

On 6 July, Duc Antoine de Gramont, the new French Foreign Secretary, an arrogant career diplomat in his first Cabinet post, having only been appointed two months before, told the Legislative Body that, if Prince Leopold's candidature was not withdrawn, 'We shall know how to fulfil our duty without hesitation and without weakness.'

The message was not lost on the Deputies. They rose to their feet, waved their hats in the air, and shouted like excited children: '*Vive la France! Vive l'Empereur!*' and, even more ominous, '*À Berlin!*' Most of the French press took up the cry. National glory was at stake and the country was not going to be found wanting.

The next day Gramont kept up the pressure. He sent an urgent telegram to Vincent Benedetti, the highly experienced French Ambassador in Berlin whom Louis had made a Count only the year before in recognition of six years of service in the Prussian capital. Gramont told Benedetti that the only hope of peace lay in his securing a personal undertaking from King Wilhelm, whom he knew well, disowning and forbidding Prince Leopold's acceptance of the Spanish throne. He gave the Ambassador these firm instructions: 'I insist upon your not allowing any time to be wasted by evasive answers. We must know whether it is to be peace, or

[1] Perhaps because of his Spanish wife, Louis knew the Spanish temperament well. Eventually, a foreign prince – Amadeus of Savoy – ascended the Spanish throne; he lasted only three years before, after a short, ill-fated Republic, the deposed Isabella's son became king as Alphonso XII. Juan Carlos, the present sovereign, is his great-grandson.

whether a refusal is to mean war. If you get the King to recall the Prince's acceptance, it will be an immense success, and a great service. The King will, of his own accord, have assured the peace of Europe. If not, it is war.'

Three days later, on 10 July, he wrote again to Benedetti: 'You must absolutely insist upon having the King's answer – "Yes or No". We must have it tomorrow: the day after will be too late.' On that same day, Lord Lyons reported to London: 'If the Prince of Hohenzollern's renunciation is announced in 24 or 48 hours, there will be peace for the moment. If not, there will be an immediate declaration of war against Prussia.'

The British Ambassador had read the scene well for, on the very next day, Gramont wrote again to Benedetti in the same peremptory terms as before.

In all this dangerous talk of war, Louis was the only leading figure in Paris to strive positively for peace, and he did so by using, even at this very late stage, his consummate skill as a conspirator. As ever, he tried to find a way around the problem rather than confront it face-on. Ignoring his Cabinet as if the Liberal Empire did not exist, he instructed the French Ambassador in London to ask the British Government to use its influence in Berlin and Madrid against the Hohenzollern candidature – and he succeeded. Lord Granville, the British Foreign Secretary, duly made the appropriate representations to both Governments.

But Louis did not leave it only to official diplomatic channels. He sent a personal emissary to Prince Leopold's father, Prince Antony, and he wrote a personal letter to King Leopold II of the Belgians urgently requesting him to write also to Prince Leopold and tell him that the peace of the world depended upon his renouncing the Spanish throne. The king not only did so but also communicated with his cousin, Queen Victoria, who wrote in similar vein to Prince Leopold's sister-in-law.

All this personal lobbying worked. On the morning of 12 July, Prince Antony telegraphed to General Prim, the Spanish Prime Minister, in Madrid that he had persuaded his son to withdraw his acceptance of the Spanish crown and sent an identical telegram to Paris. When the news arrived at St Cloud, Louis grabbed the piece of paper and joyfully announced: 'It is peace!'

But he was not reckoning with the warlike blusterings of the politicians and, it has to be said, of French public opinion in general. When that evening Emile Ollivier announced the news of Prince Leopold's withdrawal to the Legislative Body, it was not greeted with cheers. On the contrary, most of the Deputies – like most of the French nation – were certain of the superiority of the French army over all others in Europe and they angrily bellowed their war-lust.[1]

They scoffed at Prince Antony's telegram as only a private undertaking which made no reference to France or Prussia. What guarantees, they demanded, were there that it carried the consent of the Prussian king or his Government? Could it not be reversed? In speech after speech, the demand was made that Prussia must publicly and officially dissociate herself from the Prince's candidature. There must be a guarantee that the question would not be raised again.

On that same evening, at five o'clock, Louis, Eugenie and Gramont met in secret at St Cloud. The most senior Cabinet Minister, Emile Ollivier, was not even invited. At that private meeting, the fate of France was decided between the three persons present – or rather, only two of them.

Sadly, by this point, Louis had run out of steam, and the reason is tragic: perhaps brought on by the stress of the past few anxious days, the stone in his bladder had once again laid him low in a devastating attack. Valerie Feuillet, wife of the famous contemporary novelist, Octave Feuillet, relates in her memoirs how she was present at that time at a reception at the home of Princess Mathilde where Louis 'sat sombre and silent. His wan expressionless eyes were fixed on the Oriental carpet at his feet. The Empress appeared equally sombre. On the way out, he was heard to say: "Quick. I am in horrible pain!"'

At that crucial stage in her history, France did not have an emperor and an empress; she had only an Empress, determined to do her duty as she saw it.

---

[1] Four days earlier, Louis had asked Marshal Edmond Le Boeuf, the War Minister, if the French army were ready for war. His reply has become famous as one of the most stupid comments in European history: 'If the war were to last for a year, we would not need to buy a gaiter-button!' This totally unfounded assurance soon became public knowledge and fanned the agitation for war into a blaze.

In later life, Eugenie strenuously denied the story put about by both 'Plon-Plon', the next male adult in line of succession to the throne, and by the veteran Opposition deputy, Adolphe Thiers, that she had called 'my war' the conflict that would almost certainly soon ignite. 'Never!' she declared angrily to Maurice Paléologue in April 1906, 'did that sacrilegious phrase or anything like it come from my lips!'

Perhaps not, but now it almost does not matter. She was now the real ruler of France, and she clearly saw war with Prussia as the only course compatible with national honour.

After the crucial, secret meeting at St Cloud on the evening of 12 July, Gramont sternly telegraphed the long-suffering Benedetti in Berlin: 'In order that this withdrawal by Prince Antony may have its full effect, it appears necessary that the King of Prussia should associate himself with it, and assure us that he will not authorise the candidacy afresh. Will you immediately seek an audience with the King and ask him for a declaration in those terms. He can hardly refuse it, if his intentions are truly sincere. Although the renunciation is now public, tempers are so high that it is not certain whether we shall succeed in controlling them.'

The wording could not have been more provocative.

Eugenie later confirmed that Gramont had been acting with her entire consent and support, and she saw no reason to apologise for that. She genuinely believed that French opinion would not be satisfied with anything less than the King of Prussia's guarantee. 'Unless we obtained it,' she told Maurice Paléologue, 'France would have been humiliated and insulted in the face of all Europe. There would have been an outbreak of anger in every French heart against the Emperor. It would have been the end of the Empire ... No! After Sadowa and Mexico, we could not subject the national pride to a fresh ordeal. We had to have our revenge.'

On 13 July, an interview took place at the German spa town of Ems that has passed into history. King Wilhelm of Prussia was there on holiday. The old man had been delighted to hear of Prince Leopold's withdrawal and hoped that the whole matter was now settled, but he answered Comte Benedetti's urgent request for an audience by making an appointment for late in the morning 'after my promenade in the park'. However, Benedetti, normally a smooth professional diplomat, was so pressured by the succession of peremptory telegrams from his Foreign Secretary that he did not wait for the formal audience which the king had readily granted him but lay in wait for Wilhelm in the park while he was still having his walk. With his normal courtesy, Wilhelm came over and took off his hat in greeting, expecting merely to exchange a few polite words in anticipation of their formal meeting later in the morning. But Benedetti had so lost his normal calmness that he at once launched into a passionate demand for a 'guarantee'.

Taken somewhat aback, Wilhelm mouthed diplomatic niceties about his own personal view being that he hoped the matter was now behind them. He clearly did not want to go any further than that. Yet Benedetti pressed on: 'Well, Sire, I can then write to my Government that Your Majesty has consented to declare that you will never permit Prince Leopold to renew the candidature in question?' As Wilhelm wrote later, 'At these words, I stepped back a few paces and said in a very earnest tone: "It seems to me, Mr Ambassador, that I have so clearly and plainly expressed myself to the effect that I could never make such a declaration that I have nothing more to add." Thereupon I lifted my hat and went on.'

He cancelled the formal appointment for later that day and ordered his personal secretary to send a telegram to Bismarck describing the incident.

In fact, Bismarck had been so worried that Wilhelm might weaken in the face of French persistence that he had started for Ems on the previous day to try and persuade him not to meet Benedetti. But, on hearing of Prince Leopold's withdrawal, he reluctantly assumed that the matter was closed and had returned to Berlin.

He was at dinner with Generals Roon and Moltke when the King's telegram arrived; he saw at once how a spin could be put upon the telegram, without fabricating a single word, so that, as he delightedly told the two generals, it would be, for the French, 'like a red rag to a bull'.

Here is the wording of 'the Ems Telegram', as it is known to historians, and how Bismarck shortened it so that readers can assess for themselves how effective his handiwork was. The words in brackets were deleted from the version that Bismarck released to the press:

Count Benedetti spoke to me on the promenade, in order to demand from me finally, in a very importunate manner, that I should authorise him to telegraph at once that I had bound myself for all future time never again to give my consent if the Hohenzollerns should renew their candidature. (I refused at last somewhat sternly, it is neither right nor possible to undertake engagements of this kind *à tout jamais*. Naturally I told him that I had as yet received no news, and as he was earlier informed about Paris and Madrid than myself, he could clearly see that my Government once more had no hand in the matter, His Majesty has since received a letter from the Prince.) His Majesty (having told Count Benedetti that he was awaiting news from the Prince,) has decided (with reference to the above demand) not to receive Count Benedetti again, but only to let him be informed through an aide-de-camp that his Majesty (had now received from the Prince confirmation of the news which Benedetti had already received from Paris and) had nothing further to say to the ambassador. (His Majesty leaves it to your Excellency whether Benedetti's fresh demand and its rejection should not be at once communicated both to our ambassadors and to the Press.)

Bismarck's brilliant scissor work made it appear that the King had felt insulted by Benedetti's request, and had refused to have anything more to do with him. That was, of course, a gross exaggeration.

The King's telegram, in Bismarck's truncated form, had exactly the effect he had hoped when published in Paris on the following day, 14 July. 'It is a blow in the face of France,' Gramont told Emile Ollivier.

On the next evening a young American woman, Lillie Moulton (a friend of Dr Evans), dined at the Palace of St Cloud. It was a sad, silent affair. 'The Emperor never uttered a word,' she wrote later. 'The Empress sat with her eyes fixed on the Emperor and did not speak to a single person. No one spoke.' They were not in the mood for small-talk for the Cabinet met no less than three times that day. At the final meeting, at 10.00 pm, Eugenie was present – for the first time in the Liberal Empire – and the decision was taken to go to war with Prussia. An official announcement would be made the next day.

At 1 o'clock on 15 July, Ollivier reported to the Legislative Body and Gramont to the Senate the Cabinet's decision and announced that the army reserves had been called up. 'With your consent,' they declared in identical speeches, 'we shall take immediate steps to safeguard the interests, the security, and the honour of France.' Both Deputies and Senators received the news with rapturous applause.

Later that afternoon France formally – and joyously – declared war on Prussia.

The enthusiasm for war was not confined to the capital. At Marseilles, over ten thousand people marched in a torchlight procession singing the *Marseillaise* and crying '*À bas la Prusse!*' and '*À Berlin!*' And there were similar scenes in many provincial cities.

France had plunged into the conflict unprepared, with a brave army but grievously disorganised with hopelessly outdated equipment and generals whose mind-frame was still set in the Crimean War. And they had no allies. As the editor of *The Times* sanctimoniously wrote: 'That noble, patient, deep, pious and solid Germany should at length be welded into a nation, and become Queen of the Continent, instead of vapouring, vainglorious, gesticulating, quarrelsome, restless and oversensitive France seems to me the hopefullest public fact that has occurred in my time.'

Following in his illustrious uncle's footsteps, Louis immediately assumed personal command of the army, but, unknown to all except his closest circle, he was in such pain from his stone it would have been impossible for him to be in effective control. The day after the declaration of war, his cousin Princess Mathilde, who despite their many differences of opinion, had remained extremely fond of him, insisted on visiting him at St Cloud. She found him almost unable to rise from his armchair to greet her, his cheeks sunken, his skin like wax, his eyes devoid of expression. In her direct way, she went in at once to the attack:

'Is it true that you are taking personal command of the army?' she asked.

'Yes.'

'But you are not in a fit state to do so. You cannot mount a horse. You cannot even stand the shaking of a carriage!'

'You exaggerate, you exaggerate!' said Louis.

'No, I do not. Look at yourself in a glass!' said Mathilde.

Louis made a forlorn gesture with his hand, and said with a wan smile 'Oh, I dare say I'm not very beautiful!'

And that was it. Mathilde had done her best but, as Jean Autin has written, 'she did not know that the Empress had demanded his presence at the head of his troops. A Napoleon does not remain in the rear. Honour demands that he goes to battle, that he take with him his son and that they both return victorious.'

Eight days later, on 28 July, Louis and the fourteen-year-old Prince Imperial in a specially tailored uniform embraced Eugenie and left for the front, but not on horseback or in a jolting, horse-drawn carriage. Like two travellers going on a business trip, they departed in a train from a small private railway station in the grounds of the Palace at St Cloud. It was the only way that Louis could join his troops.

Mathilde's entry in her diary for that day makes sad reading: 'Unlike others, I do not sing, I do not laugh. The reasons for this War do not excite my enthusiasm and renew all my fears, all my apprehensions. The butchery that will follow is not, to my mind, proportionate to the causes that have provoked it. *She* [Mathilde's own italics] displays herself as a heroine, is delighted to see depart her husband and her son. The spectacle makes me more melancholy than ever.'

Yet Louis' proclamation to the army had a ringing tone: 'Whatever road we may take beyond our frontiers, we shall find glorious traces of our fathers. We will prove ourselves worthy of them.'

In truth, Louis was starting on a road which would lead only to defeat and exile. He would never again see Paris, the glorious city whose rebuilding had been his accomplished dream, or ride in triumph, handsome on horseback, through its crowded streets. The Second Empire was entering the last few weeks of its existence.

Chapter Twenty-Five

The Empire Falls (1870)

ALTHOUGH IT WOULD BE six months before Paris fell, and nearly ten before peace was finally made, the Franco-Prussian War was over, as far as major battles were concerned, within six weeks.

From the very beginning, the whole French army was undermanned, short of equipment, and unprepared to advance. Reservists who should have swelled the numbers of the regular troops were hunting up and down France looking for uniforms and arms; the railways were blocked with supplies still lacking at the front; officers could not find the units they were supposed to command; generals at the front found they had plenty of maps of the German side of the frontier but none of the French; and they had no canteens, ambulances or baggage-carts. 'There is an utter lack of everything,' said one frustrated commander.

With the easy capture on 2 August of Saarbrücken, just two miles inside Germany, the French offensive, upon which so many hopes had been based, came to an end. There was to be no triumphal march on Berlin. Almost to their surprise, the speedily mobilised Germans soon found themselves on the attack, fighting in the enemy's country rather than their own. They crossed the Rhine and, on 6 August, at Fröschwiller on French soil, won their first major battle of the War. Brave French soldiers, on foot and on horse, died in their thousands beneath the onslaught of the German artillery. As Sir Michael Howard has written in his classic work, *The Franco-Prussian War*, 'The achievement of the German gunners on 6 August heralded the advent of a new age of applied technology in war. The disasters to the French cavalry emphasised that an epoch in warfare was now ended.' Napoleon I, that brilliant artillery general, would have smiled sadly at the Germans' use of their vast superiority in gunpower and shellpower. On the same day, further north, at Forbach, German guns thundered again and French troops were forced to flee.

That evening false rumours of victory reached Paris, and crowds paraded the streets singing the *Marseillaise*. But at midnight Eugenie, whom Louis had appointed Regent before he left for the front, was awakened at St Cloud to receive his telegram telling her of the twin defeats at Fröschwiller and Forbach. He urged her to proclaim a state of siege and prepare to defend Paris. Already he appears to have smelt defeat in the air.

But the news only fired Eugenie's resolve. She replied that the invaders would soon be driven back to the frontier and that she would answer for Paris. 'Take courage,' she said. 'With energy, we shall dominate the situation.' And she ordered posted in the streets placards acknowledging a temporary setback but calling for a united effort to save the national honour.

Two days later, she told Prosper Mérimée that Paris was being garrisoned for a siege, and that she would stay there while a second government at Tours would organise the defence of the south. 'We shall dispute every foot of ground. The Prussians do not know what they are in for. Rather than accept humiliating terms, we will keep up the fight for ten years.'

These were brave words but the shrewd Mérimée, only months from death, wrote to a friend the same day advising her not to come to Paris. 'There is nothing to be seen here but drunken or despondent crowds . . . Chaos everywhere! The army has been and still is admirable; but it seems that we have no generals. All may still be put right but it would need something like a miracle.'

Sadly, though nominally the commander-in-chief, Louis was not the man to accomplish that miracle. At times, doubled up with the agonising pain from his illness, with the sweat standing out on his face, unable to sit on a horse and almost unable to tolerate being driven in a carriage, he was physically and mentally incapable of leading his men. He was forced to accept the unpalatable truth that he could never again, as at Solferino in 1859, even attempt to emulate his great uncle on the field of battle. Even if he was occasionally decisive and gave a military order, all too often within a very short time he would countermand it. He simply was not up to the task.

On 9 August, he telegraphed Eugenie that he was handing over command to Marshal Achille Bazaine, who was with him and 180,000 men at Metz in central-eastern France, and would return at once to Paris. She was furious. In an urgent response she demanded that he consider 'all the consequences which would follow from your return under the shadow of two reverses'.

Once more he changed his mind and said he would not come. But he was now so ill, so racked with pain, so half-drugged with ineffective tablets that, on 14 August, he insisted on handing over command to Bazaine and left Metz with his son in a third-class railway carriage (the only one available) bound not for Paris but for the military camp at Châlons where another army was encamped under Marshal MacMahon.

Three days later, on 17 August, Louis called Marshal MacMahon, General Louis Trochu and Prince Napoleon ('Plon-Plon') to a Council of War. 'Plon-Plon', usually so wild and impatient of Louis' indecision, realised how morally and physically beaten his cousin was and urged him to send Trochu, a competent, fair-minded soldier, to Paris with emergency powers and to return there himself, leaving MacMahon in command of the army at Châlons. But Louis was so uncertain of himself that he insisted they must first consult 'the Regent' (Eugenie) before any decision was made. This brought forth a furious outburst from 'Plon-Plon'. 'Consult the Regent? Aren't you the Sovereign? This must be decided at once!'

But it was not. Louis sighed, as if almost to himself: 'It's true, I seem to have abdicated.'

Trochu left Châlons for Paris that same evening but Louis still would not return until he had received the 'Regent's' response.

On the following day, in a desperately hard-fought battle near the village of Gravelotte, north-east of Metz, where the final issue was in doubt until almost the last moment, the Germans won a decisive victory, at a cost to them of over 20,000 men. Coupled with an earlier success at nearby Vionville, they now totally cut off Bazaine's eastern group of French forces centred at Metz from the western group based at Châlons.

Gravelotte really ended the war. Bazaine's army was now surrounded at Metz, and it was useless for him to talk of forcing his way out.

Yet in Paris Eugenie seemed to remain in a dream world of her own, remote from grim reality. Three days after France's numbing defeat at Gravelotte came her reply to the message that Louis had sent after his Council of War on 17 August. 'Under no circumstances,' her telegram insisted, 'should the Emperor or the Prince Imperial return to Paris. No matter what their capacity, their place is with the Army.' As for Marshal MacMahon, Eugenie ordered him to 'march resolutely' to raise the siege on Bazaine at Metz and for the two marshals, with their combined armies, to strike a great blow for France. Neither she nor the ageing Comte Charles de Palikao, the retired general whom she had appointed Prime Minister in place of the more docile Emile Ollivier, gave any guidance as to how they were to accomplish this desirable task.

The telegram was the final blow to Louis' pride. He had relinquished his post as commander-in-chief and now, except in name, he was no longer even Emperor. He no longer gave orders, he only received them – and from his wife. He was no longer in command of his generals, he was merely an appendage jogging along with them as if a member of their staff.

The soldiers soon realised this humiliating truth about the man who had begun the war only a few weeks earlier as their commander-in-chief. However great the pain from his stone, however deep his misery and distress, Louis was still a man of the Second Empire, pampered and self-indulgent. The troops, surviving on only meagre army rations and forced to pillage the surrounding countryside in order to have any reasonable kind of sustenance, quickly became contemptuous of the many carriages bearing cases loaded with sumptuous food, silver tableware and bottles of champagne that accompanied Louis and his son wherever they went. The weather was foul. Driving rain churned the roads to mud and the sun seemed to have deserted the summer skies as they grimly marched on towards Metz. One day, a soldier seeing the normal convoy of Louis' luxurious cases approaching, stepped forward, waved his hat in the air and cried: 'Here is the Emperor Baggage! Long live Baggage 1st! Here is the Emperor Baggage and the little Prince of Baggages!' Thereafter, his own soldiers had only one name for Napoleon III: 'Emperor Baggage.'

Yet, in one respect, Louis still showed himself in control. No one, not even the Regent, was going to tell him what to do with his own son. Six days later, on 27 August, he told the Prince

Imperial, with tears in his eyes, that they must separate: he could no longer take the risk that the youngster might be killed or taken prisoner. 'That is an order!' he said to the weeping boy. The two embraced and they were not to see each other again until both were safely in exile in England.

MacMahon, under Eugenie's and her Prime Minister's strict but quite unrealistic orders from Paris, dourly pressed on in an increasingly impossible attempt to break the Germans' iron grip on Metz and liberate Bazaine and his men. Progress across country was painfully slow as his men trudged wearily across the rain-drenched landscape.

But the Germans had not stood still. Another powerful army was now intent on encircling MacMahon as well as Bazaine. As the last days of August passed, MacMahon found himself isolated, his communications cut, and with no line of escape except over the Belgian frontier. A series of local actions soon closed even this exit, and late on the evening of 31 August his bedraggled army, with Louis in tow, was penned like sheep into the little town of Sedan, still more than ninety miles from Metz and surrounded on all sides by a narrow circle of hills. Moltke, the Prussian general, poring over his maps, exclaimed with delight: 'We have them in a mouse-trap!'[1]

He gave the order: 'We attack at dawn.'

The Sedan of today is a typical small French country town of some 21,000 inhabitants. Its main tourist attraction is a seventeenth-century château fortress where, in the seven-page glossy leaflet which boasts of it as the largest fortified castle in Europe and recounts proudly its long military history, there is no mention whatsoever of the fact that it served as Marshal MacMahon's headquarters during the battle that raged on 1 September 1870. To the foreign visitor, Sedan seems to be a town which does not know if Napoleon III ever existed or, if it does, would prefer to forget it. The former sub-prefecture in the middle of town where Louis spent

---

[1] Auguste Ducrot, a French general poring over his own maps, came to much the same conclusion but he expressed himself even more forcefully: 'Nous sommes dans un pot de chambre, et nous y serons emmerdés.' (We are in a night-pot and we are going be shat upon.)

his last two nights as emperor now stands empty and derelict, perhaps awaiting demolition. But, again, no one knows and, even more cruel for the shade of Louis, no one cares.

This is where an emperor and a man's dream ended, and in the Sedan of today one cannot even hear a sigh in the air.

The battle that was to destroy the Second Empire and humiliate France for two generations began at 5 am on 1 September, when Prussian troops, supported by divisions from the Southern German state of Bavaria, attacked the comparatively open south-east side of the French position at the two villages of Bazeilles and La Moncelle. Here fighting went on all morning, and the German line was gradually extended northwards until, early in the afternoon, it met another extension from the west, and the whole French position in front of Sedan was encircled in a text-book German army pincer movement. Desperate cavalry charges could not break through the enemy line and the French infantry began to retreat into the town. MacMahon had been wounded early in the day and some of his corps commanders were minded to try and break through the German encirclement, which was not as strong in some places as in others, and beat an orderly retreat. But General Emmanuel Wimpffen, an old campaigner from the colonial wars in North Africa, designated by Paris as MacMahon's successor if the Marshal were incapacitated in battle, would not hear of it. 'Use all your energy and skill to secure a victory,' he said in a note to General Ducrot. 'We must have a victory!' 'You will be very lucky, *mon général*,' Ducrot replied, 'if this evening, you even have a retreat!'

Sadly, he was right but the only other person who seems to have come to the same grim conclusion was Louis. Despite the posturing of Wimpffen and most of the other generals, he realised that all was lost and, at about 9.00 am rode out onto the battlefield from the protection of the château fortress at Sedan.

For five hours, holding tightly on to the pollard of his saddle to help ease the excruciating pain from his groin, he rode through the hail of bullets and exploding shells hoping to find death with honour among his soldiers. Twice he had to come off his horse to pass water. Another time he had to dismount to throw his arms around the trunk of a tree to try and cope with the pain. Two of his officers were shot dead in front of his eyes. Later, in England, Sir William

Gull, his physician, was to exclaim: 'How could this man have sat on a horse at Sedan for five hours like that!'

Returning to the fortress, demoralised and sickened by the slaughter that he had seen at first hand, Louis gave the order at 2 o'clock in the afternoon for a white flag to be raised but Wimpffen countermanded the order, as was his right.

The German attack continued unabated. Sir Michael Howard has noted tellingly, 'Never before had gunfire been used in war with such precision.' After two more hours of hell, with casualties mounting by the minute, Louis, for the last time, asserted his prerogative as Emperor and demanded that the white flag be hoisted. This time, Wimpffen gave way and two German staff officers came in under a flag of truce. To their amazement, they found themselves in the presence of the Emperor. No one in the German camp, neither the King of Prussia nor Bismarck himself, had known he was there. They asked Louis to appoint an officer to negotiate but he referred them to Wimpffen, saying that he was in command.

However, he said that he would send a personal letter to King Wilhelm.

A little later, at about 6.00 pm in the fading sunlight, a French officer rode out with Louis' letter, written in French, to the Prussian King. It was as dignified as it was final: '*Monsieur mon Frère*, Having been unable to die in the midst of my troops, it only remains for me to place my sword in Your Majesty's hands. I am Your Majesty's good brother, *Napoléon*.'

Wilhelm and Bismarck studied the letter and Bismarck dictated the answer, also in French:

'*Monsieur mon Frère*,' Regretting the circumstances in which we find ourselves, I accept Your Majesty's sword, and I beg you to name one of your officers furnished with full powers from you to negotiate the capitulation of the army, which has fought so bravely under your orders. For my part, I have designated General Moltke for this purpose. I am Your Majesty's good brother, *Wilhelm*.'

At the time of his surrender and almost in the words of his letter to King Wilhelm, Louis sent this chilling telegram to Eugenie: 'The Army is defeated and captive; not having been able to have myself killed in the middle of my troops, I have had to constitute myself prisoner to save the Army. *Napoléon*.'

But Eugenie never received the telegram. Communications

between Paris and Sedan had been cut, and the Empress Regent and her capital had to wait two full days until, late on the afternoon of 3 September, the news of the disaster finally got through.

By then, Louis, weary, in pain and totally demoralised, had yet tried – unsuccessfully – still to serve his country and the defeated soldiers for whom he felt responsible.

Back in November 1863, Louis had proposed that a Congress of Sovereigns should be held in Paris to settle two current European disputes, one between Denmark and Prussia over the future of the two provinces of Schleswig and Holstein between their borders, and the other a situation that had arisen between Russia and Polish revolutionaries who had risen in insurrection against the Russian occupying forces. In effect, he was suggesting what nowadays would be called a 'summit conference' between national leaders. Today such an event is a commonplace but then it was a rarity. Nothing came of the proposal for the simple reason that neither the King of Prussia nor the Tsar of Russia was prepared to attend such a meeting.

But Louis had always maintained a visionary belief that major questions of dispute between nations should be settled by discussion rather than by war. He favoured an International Council of national representatives, meeting at regular intervals, that would secure the peace of Europe by endeavouring to talk through problems before they could ignite into armed conflict. One hundred and sixty years later, in June 1993, the *Académie du Second Empire* was to hold a 'celebration' in Paris in honour of his proposals that were 'well in advance of his times'.

Perhaps because of his belief in his own charm, Louis remained convinced to the end of his days in personal confrontation and discussion. In the aftermath of his surrender to the King of Prussia, he thought that he saw one last chance to put his views into effect and for leader to speak directly to leader.

In a tense meeting that took place between General Moltke and General Wimpffen on the evening of 1 September, the Prussian Chief-of-Staff had demanded that the entire French army at Sedan should surrender as prisoners-of-war and go into immediate captivity. To this, Wimpffen had argued for an 'honourable capitulation' with his troops marching out with arms and baggage and full military honours while making a solemn engagement not to take up arms against Prussia and her allies for the duration of the War. Moltke scoffed at the proposal and, when Wimpffen threatened to defend Sedan to the last man, he quietly pointed out that the French army, reduced to 30,000, with food for another forty-eight hours only and very little remaining ammunition, was in no state to continue to fight a besieging force now 250,000 strong, armed with 500 guns. Wimpffen asked for time to consult with his colleagues before giving a final response to the German demands.

'Very well,' said Moltke. He prolonged the truce until 9 o'clock the next morning – but with the added threat that, at 10.00 am, he would give the order for his guns to start shelling the town of Sedan itself.

When Wimpffen reported back to Louis and his fellow generals this fearsome news, Louis resolved that only he could bring honour out of defeat and persuade the Germans to accept something less than full surrender of an entire army. He announced that he would go and see the Prussian King and, ruler to ruler, negotiate better terms.

At first light the next morning and attended by a few of his staff on horseback, Louis left Sedan in an open carriage. He was wearing a general's uniform and decorations under a blue cloak with scarlet lining and was smoking his usual cigarettes. He was on his way to talk to King Wilhelm: man to man.

But within an hour Bismarck, who had ridden out to meet him, blocked his path near the small village of Donchéry. He dismounted, uncovered his head and bowed; courteous to the end, he nonetheless would not let Louis continue on to see his King. Using the excuse that Wilhelm was too far away (at his headquarters in the Château de Bellevue) to be fetched, he invited Louis to rest at a wayside cottage[1] beside the road and there, sitting in chairs outside the door in the early sunlight, they talked. But once he realised that Louis considered himself a prisoner, incapable of conducting any political negotiations, Bismarck lost interest. He stonewalled any possibility of seeing the King until the terms of surrender of the French army had been agreed. He 'respectfully' pointed out that discussion of those terms could only take place between the two generals nominated

---

[1] The cottage is now a restaurant and the Château de Bellevue has been converted into fine apartments.

by Wilhelm and Louis the previous day: Moltke and Wimpffen.

Moltke and Wimpffen talked together again that morning but the French general realised that the military situation was so close that he had very little room for successful negotiation. With the German guns still turned towards the defenceless town of Sedan, he had to accept the substance of the German terms. He managed to secure only one concession, in accordance with 'gentlemanly' ideas of warfare at that time: French officers who gave their word 'not to take up arms against Germany nor to act in any way prejudicial to her interests until the close of the present War' would be allowed to go free. Five hundred and fifty officers were thus able to preserve their liberty but, in addition to the 21,000 prisoners already taken during the battle itself, the staggering total of 83,000 more men was now added: together with over 1,000 wagons, 6,000 horses and 419 guns.

Only after all this had been clinched, with Wimpffen signing the formal Terms of Surrender at the Château de Bellevue at 11.30 am, was Louis at last allowed to meet King Wilhelm. They had met several times before in totally different circumstances and now they talked embarrassedly for about half an hour. There was little for Louis to say, except to compliment Wilhelm on his army – above all on his artillery. He realised that he would have to go into captivity in Germany – and Wilhelm generously offered his own summer palace at Wilhelmshöhe as his lodgings – but he had one favour to ask. He said that he did not wish 'to be exhibited to his own soldiers' and requested that he might go into Germany not along the same long road as his army but through neutral Belgium which was only seven miles away. Wilhelm readily agreed. When Louis left the meeting, onlookers saw him brush tears from his eyes.

Returned to the château fortress at Sedan, he sent this telegram to his wife, using the familiar 'tu' and not the more conventional 'vous': 'My dear Eugenie, it is impossible to tell you what I have suffered and what I am suffering. We have made a march contrary to all the rules and to common sense: it was bound to lead to a catastrophe, and it is complete. I would rather have died than be witness to so disastrous a capitulation, and yet, in the circumstances as they are at present, it was the only way of avoiding a butchery of 60,000 men.

'Then again, if only all my torments were concentrated here! I think of you, of our son, of our unfortunate country. May God protect it! What is going to happen at Paris?

'I have just seen the King. There were tears in his eyes when he spoke of the sorrow that I must be feeling. He has put at my disposal one of his châteaux. But what does it matter where I go? . . . I am in despair. Adieu, I embrace you tenderly. *Napoléon*.'

When the breakdown in communications between Sedan and Paris had finally been repaired and that telegram arrived in the French capital on the afternoon of the following day, 3 September, it was the first that Eugenie or the French Government knew of the appalling disaster that had taken place.

Eugenie's immediate reaction was perhaps predictable. As she later told Maurice Paléologue, 'For three or four days, I had not received any telegram from the Emperor nor any letter. And that long, inexplicable silence, kept me in a deep anxiety. I did not eat anymore, I did not sleep anymore; I was constantly sobbing.'

So when Louis' telegram eventually arrived, it was even more of a shock. She literally screamed for her two secretaries, Eugene Conti and Auguste Filon who, with his pupil the Prince Imperial away at the war, was helping out with the extra burdens caused by her being Regent. 'I called them with a scream, as one would call for help; I showed them the telegram. And then . . . and then, all I had in my heart came out . . . I won't tell you anymore,' she said.

But Paléologue, safe in the knowledge that his book would not appear until after Eugenie's death, has filled in the story himself. He has told his readers what Eugenie herself did not want them to know: 'The Empress let go of all the anger, rage and humiliation that had built up for weeks in her stormy mind. Full of convulsion and her eyes vague, she shouted: "No, the Emperor has not surrendered! A Napoleon does not surrender. He is dead! . . . Do you hear me: I tell you that he is dead and that the news is hidden from me! . . ." Then, contradicting herself, she exclaimed: "Why did he not have himself killed? Why did he not bury himself under the walls of Sedan? . . . Did he not feel that he was losing his honour? What kind of name will he leave for his son?"

'After this explosion, she broke into tears, kneeling and begging her husband to forgive her the aberrations and excesses that pain had brought to her. Then the scene ended with her fainting.'

*   *   *

By the time that Louis' telegram had arrived, he had already been driven off into exile.

The battle itself had been fought in unexpectedly glorious sunlight but heavy rains had come back again and, at 9 o'clock on the morning of 3 September 1870, Louis' carriage passed through the main street of Donchéry below the window of W. H. (later Sir William) Russell, *The Times'* Special Correspondent at Sedan. During the Crimean War some fifteen years earlier, he had been the first British journalist to serve as a war correspondent. Now he reported in his newspaper: 'The Emperor wore a kepi and the undress uniform of a Lieutenant-General, with the star of the Legion of Honour on his breast. His face looked exceedingly worn – dark lines under his eyes, which were observant of what was passing around, for he saluted an Englishman who ran out to see him, and who raised his hat. By his side sat a French officer, I think Achille Murat;[1] but who could look at anyone but the one man? and it was only a glance any person with good feeling would care to give at such a moment.' Yet the skilled journalist did not avert his eyes. He was, after all, reporting history: 'His Majesty had his hand to his moustache, which had the well-known pointed and waxed ends . . . Then he brushed the tears from his eyes with the gloves he had in one hand, and was overcome for several seconds.'

With that unique picture of Louis trundling into exile through the rain, we shall leave him for the moment.

Our attention must now turn to Paris: what was to become of Eugenie? What were to be the final hours of the Second Empire?

Not only in the capital but all over the country, those who had cried '*À bas la Prusse!*' were now crying '*À bas l'Empire!*' and '*La Déchéance!*' (Dethronement!). Crowds thronged the streets of central Paris and there was, once more in France's chequered history, the smell of revolution in the air.

At midday on 4 September, the new Republic was proclaimed to rapturous cheers at the Hôtel de Ville and a crowd some 200,000 strong gathered around the Tuileries Palace where the flag flying from the masthead indicated that Eugenie was still in residence.

---

[1] This was a pardonable mistake, in the heat of the moment, for General Joachim Murat, Louis' cousin. Achille was another cousin, also descended from Napoleon I's sister, Caroline.

She had refused all morning to leave but now Joseph Piétri, the Prefect of Police, warned her that her very life was in peril. 'I had no fear of death,' she said later, 'but I dreaded falling into the hands of viragos who would defile my last scene with something shameful or grotesque, who would try to dishonour me as they murdered me. I fancied them lifting my skirts, I heard ferocious laughter.' So at last, as the cries of the mob outside could be heard through the locked windows of the Palace, she yielded to the entreaties of two good friends, Prince Richard Metternich and Count Constantino Negri, the Italian Ambassador, who had hastened to the Tuileries, and agreed that she must go.

But it was impossible to leave the building directly: it was entirely surrounded by the angry crowd. Eugenie, accompanied by Mme Lebreton, her reader, the two ambassadors and a few loyal servants, made their way through an underground passage linking the Palace to the Louvre Museum. Then, in a bizarre, almost surrealist scene, with Eugenie having ordered the servants to turn back, the two fleeing women and their two brave comrades hurried through the Museum's galleries with some of the most beautiful paintings in the world gazing down upon them. Finally, they managed to slip out unnoticed into the street. Metternich hailed a passing cab which, after a couple of false stops at the empty homes of absent friends, eventually dropped them off at the house of Louis' dentist and long-standing confidant, Dr Thomas W. Evans. Alone in Paris, he gave them shelter and a night's lodging.

Eugenie had escaped from the Tuileries with only the clothes that she was wearing; there had not even been time to pack a suitcase. The irony was not lost upon them. 'Only a few days ago,' she told Evans, 'I declared that I never would leave the Tuileries in a cab, as Louis-Philippe did. And that is exactly what I have done!'

She obviously had to be taken safely out of the capital as quickly as possible. Early next morning she and Mme Lebreton left the Evans home on the rue Malakoff in the dentist's own carriage, with passports supplied by Piétri describing her as an English invalid being taken to London by her doctor (Dr Edward Crane, Evans' nephew). She was accompanied by her 'brother' (Evans himself) and her 'nurse' (Mme Lebreton). They travelled hard all day, with frequent changes of carriage and horses, heading for Deauville on the Channel coast where Mrs Evans was on holiday.

At 3 o'clock the next morning, they finally rang the front door bell at the Hôtel du Casino where Mrs Evans warmly greeted them. At midnight the next day, they boarded Sir John Burgoyne's yacht riding at anchor in the harbour. Although a perfect stranger, Dr Evans had appealed to him as an English gentleman for his help. After a rough passage they landed at Ryde on the Isle of Wight a little before 7 am on 8 September. Eugenie left the same day for Hastings where, at the Marine Hotel, the Prince Imperial was waiting for her.

In Paris, meanwhile, the crowds had torn down all street nameplates and removed all signs at shops, buildings and intersections that bore the name or Imperial title of Napoleon or Eugenie. The Second Empire had ceased to exist.

PART FIVE

THE END

Chapter Twenty-Six

Going into Exile
(1870–71)

O N THE EVENING OF 5 September, as the rain continued to
pour down, Louis arrived at his new 'prison', King Wilhelm of Prussia's summer palace at Wilhelmshöhe outside
Kassel, near the Rhine. With its large lake, its trees and elegant
lawns laid out as a Baroque park, it was, of course, far more
comfortable than his previous gaol, the Château de Ham, thirty
years earlier. Furthermore, his uncle, Jerome Bonaparte, had lived
there from 1807 to 1813 when he was Napoleon I's puppet King
of Wesphalia, and it contained several family mementos. One of
the first things that Louis saw when he entered the vast, ornate
building was a full-length portrait of Queen Hortense, his mother,
as a young woman: he could hardly bear to look at it, for his mood
was sombre. On his way into Germany, as his train stood in a
Belgian station, he had heard a newsboy shouting along the platform: '*Chute de l'Empire! Fuite de l'Impératrice*' (Fall of the
Empire! Flight of the Empress!).

His cousin, Prince Joachim Murat, a general in the campaign so
brutally ended, was with him, together with a personal suite including his two doctors, Corvisart and Conneau, and his ever loyal
valet Charles Thélin, another link with the château at Ham. Slowly
Louis began to unwind and soon was in much better health. Count
Karl von Monts, the Military Governor at Wilhelmshöhe and, in
effect, Louis' captor, even reported that after a while Louis would
from time to time mount a horse and spend several hours riding
for pleasure. That would have been typical of the topsy-turvy state
of his medical condition.

For the first fortnight of his captivity, Napoleon did not hear
from Eugenie and was saddened by her silence. Then, on 17 Sep-

tember, three letters arrived together. She seems to have relented of her former ferocious anger at his having surrendered and now wrote in terms of fond affection that had seldom been her wont in recent years. 'My tenderness and love for you only grow,' she wrote. 'To be together at last, that is all I wish for. The more the world falls away from us, the more closely shall we be attached and, hand in hand, we shall await the judgement of God . . . Poor, dear friend, if only my devotion can bring you an instant's forgetfulness of the trials through which your great soul has passed. Your adorable long-suffering makes me think of Our Lord. You, too, believe me, will have justice one day.'

Three weeks after wishing him dead, she was comparing him to Jesus Christ. It is little wonder that all Louis could find to reply was: 'The affectionate expressions in your letters have raised my spirits . . . Your letters are a wonderful consolation and I thank you for them. To what can I attach myself, if not to your affection and that of our son?' In a subsequent letter, he wrote: 'When I am free, it is in England that I wish to live with you and Louis, in a little cottage with bow windows and creepers.'[1]

On 30 October, without prior warning or invitation, Eugenie presented herself unannounced at Wilhelmshöhe. For the first time in three months, husband and wife met and talked earnestly together. Count von Monts did not listen to their private conversations but what he saw of their behaviour together made him later write: 'All her manner convinced me that she had always known how to impose her views on her husband's policy. She displayed great assurance in her observations. I derived the absolute impression that she was accustomed not only to make herself listened to, but to have the last word. She affected a certain superiority over the Emperor, a sort of tutorship; and if it is true that she had been at the head of the War Party in Paris I fully understand that her opinion was the decisive one.'

Indeed, it was not personal considerations but the war – or rather the prospect of peace – that had prompted her visit. Once the Emperor had been defeated at Sedan, Bismarck was anxious to

---

[1] Too much attention should not be paid to that word 'cottage'. Eugenie was later in the habit of calling the large, many bedroomed house in Hampshire which she bought after Louis' death and is today Farnborough Hill School: 'My little country cottage'.

end hostilities as quickly as possible. But Paris, although entirely surrounded, was still holding out – as was Marshal Bazaine with his 180,000-strong Army of the Rhine besieged at Metz – and the new Republican Government of National Defence refused even to talk about peace so long as Bismarck insisted on France handing over the provinces of Alsace and Lorraine.

In an effort to outflank the new Government, Bismarck had opened delicate negotiations with Eugenie, in exile in England, hinting that Bazaine's army might be allowed to act as a shield behind which a restored Empire, to which the Marshal still formally owed allegiance, could be restored. Refusing to be party to the dismemberment of France, Eugenie had appealed direct to King Wilhelm to 'offer terms which your defeated enemy can accept'. On 25 October, he had replied, courteously but firmly, as 'her good brother Wilhelm', stating that Germany was demanding Alsace and Lorraine not for territorial aggrandisement but for its own security: 'to be better prepared to repel the new aggression against us on which we can count as soon as France will have repaired her forces or gained allies.'

Two days later, unexpectedly and, to many Frenchmen, traitorously, Bazaine had surrendered with his entire garrison. On hearing the news, Eugenie had at once left for Wilhelmshöhe, but nothing came of her heartfelt discussions with Louis. After only three days, she left. 'If the King of Prussia had restored the French army to us,' she told von Monts, 'we should have been able to make an honourable peace and restore order in France.'

That would seem to be one more example of her poor grasp of reality.

Four months after Eugenie's visit, Louis received another female visitor. Approriately for him, it was not his wife, returned to see him again, but the Comtesse Louise de Mercy-Argenteau. They had been corresponding almost since his arrival at Wilhelmshöhe and he seems to have opened up to her in a way that he never did to Eugenie. On 4 February 1871, in a letter lamenting the chaos and indiscipline of the new Republic that had replaced him, he wrote that, if he were in King Wilhelm's place, with so many brave soldiers at his command, he would 'enter Paris at the head of my Army. I would scatter the demagogues who have usurped power. I would decline to treat with any but the legitimate Government, and I would propose to that Government a less onerous peace than that offered to the National Assembly and an alliance based upon an equitable appreciation of the interests of both countries.'

At a more personal level, he wrote in the same letter: 'The attachment to me of which you give evidence touches me deeply.'

Later in February she came to see him at Wilhelmshöhe, and he received her in a room where Queen Hortense's portrait hung over the marble fireplace. Gesturing towards it, he said, with his usual wan smile: 'You can see that my mother was here, waiting for me.' In a corner of the room, by French windows looking out onto the grounds, was a grand piano on which stood a vase of hortensias.

Louise opened the piano, sat down, and began to sing to her own accompaniment: '*Plaisir d'amour ne dure q'un moment . . .*' For a few moments, Louis, stretched out on a sofa and with his eyes closed, found a brief, sad happiness. The next morning, as she was leaving, Charles Thélin handed her a farewell gift on behalf of his master: a string of pearls that had once belonged to Queen Hortense.

The two lovers were never to see each other again.

On 18 January 1871, France suffered the indignity of King Wilhelm being proclaimed German Emperor at the Palace of Versailles to the acclaim of assembled German princes and generals. Paris herself still fought bravely on, but only for a short while longer. Ten days later, the capital surrendered at the end of a four months' siege and three weeks' bombardment.[1] The Government immediately asked for an armistice, and a three weeks' truce was agreed to allow for an Assembly to be elected to negotiate a permanent peace.

Those elections were held on 8 February 1871 and Thiers, the veteran deputy, was appointed 'Head of the Executive Power' of the Republic.[2] Even so, despite all the wily old lawyer's efforts, he had to accept that France was to hand over the two provinces of Alsace and Lorraine to Germany and pay a war indemnity of

---

[1] Four hundred people had been killed or wounded. This was one of the first times in history that a city with a large civilian population had been systematically shelled.

[2] Within a few months he was President of the Republic, which office he held until May 1873.

5,000,000,000 francs over the next three years. During that time German troops of occupation were to remain on French soil.[1] The nation's humiliation could not have been greater.

On 1 March, these terms were ratified by the Assembly which, on the same day, passed a resolution not only deposing Louis as Emperor but, for the sake of the Deputies' injured pride, also declaring him 'to be responsible for the ruin, the invasion and the dismemberment of France'. The official version of events then – and, still to some extent, today – is, that it was all the fallen Emperor's fault. He had somehow managed single-handedly to bring his country to disaster. That was then, and still is now, a gross overstatement.

At least, the armistice meant that Louis, like all other French prisoners-of-war, could return home, and on 19 March 1871 he left Wilhelmshöhe. But, in his case, where was 'home'? Where could the defeated Emperor now go?

Within days of arriving in England after her flight from Paris on 4 September, Eugenie had found a comfortable Georgian country house, not too far from London and internally refurnished in the style of a French château. The house – Camden Place at Chislehurst in Kent – belonged to Nathaniel William John Strode, Lizzie Howard's trustee, to whom the Imperial Household records show Louis had in the early 1860s, in the heyday of the Second Empire, given à titre inconnu a total of 900,000 francs. This amount would generously cover Strode's purchase of the empty mansion in 1860 and its subsequent internal remodelling as a suitably prestigious French home.

The man who pointed Eugenie in the direction of Camden Place was the worthy Dr Thomas W. Evans, as an American and a complete outsider, Louis' trusted confidant. Evans shared none of the vested interests of the rest of Louis' close associates, forever concerned to preserve their own positions in the hierarchy of Imperial power.

The fact that Eugenie chose Camden Place as their home in exile cannot be put down to mere coincidence, a chance of nature. I am convinced that, even in the early 1860s at a time when Louis'

---

[1] In fact, thanks to Thiers' astuteness in obtaining advantageous foreign loans, the indemnity was paid off and German troops departed after only two years.

stability and fame seemed assured, he was still plotting to give his family and himself a possible bolt-hole in case of crisis. As a child, after Napoleon I's first abdication in 1814 and again in 1815 after Waterloo, he had had to flee from luxury and pomp. 'When I am happy, I feel frightened,' he later told Eugenie. For all the Second Empire's glitter and panache, Louis was never sure, in his heart, how long it was going to last. Hence, the purchase *à titre inconnu* of a possible safe haven in case of emergency, a secret that he shared only with an outsider, Dr Evans.

Consider how Evans himself claims in his memoirs to have come across this unbelievably appropriate residence for an exiled French Emperor and his wife. It is worth quoting at length.

'Camden Place, Chislehurst, which afterwards became so well known as the home of the Imperial family, I discovered by a fortunate accident, after searching many days in vain for a residence for the Empress in the neighbourhood of London . . .

'In a conversation which I once had with the Emperor, he told me that some of the most agreeable days during his long sojourn in England had been passed at Tunbridge Wells. He praised the beautiful scenery, and spoke of the magnificent trees which he had seen there, and manifested a strong predilection for the place. [This is surely an irrelevance. Louis had been happy there – for about two weeks in July 1831 when he was twenty-three and much more interested in a local girl named Sarah Godfrey.[1]] The remembrance of this conversation induced me to see if it was possible to find a residence for the Imperial family at Tunbridge Wells for we all hoped that the Emperor would soon be permitted by the Prussian Government to leave Wilhelmshöhe and rejoin his wife and son in England.

'I consequently went to Tunbridge Wells, and succeeded in finding a place which I thought would probably meet all the immediate requirements of the Imperial household; but just before speaking to the owner upon the subject, a gentleman [who? why no name?] mentioned to me Camden Place, at Chislehurst. He described it as a large and beautiful country seat, close to London, and yet secluded, saying it was just what I wanted, but that, unfortunately, it was not to let. Believing from the description he gave me that the place

[1] See page 99 of Chapter Six.

was really a very desirable one, Mrs Evans and I took tickets for this place.

'On arriving at Chislehurst station I hailed the first conveyance I saw, and a few minutes later we halted at the gate in front of Camden Place. Mrs Taylor, the lodge-keeper, received us, and I asked her a few questions . . . She replied that Camden Place could not be rented, and expressed doubt as to whether it could be visited. Hearing me, however, speak a few words in French to Mrs Evans, she seemed to reconsider the matter, and exclaimed: "Oh, if you speak French you may perhaps be admitted into the house. There is a gentleman living here – Mr Foder – who also speaks French – and if you would like to see him I will go and call him."' [Could it be that Strode had left word for anyone arriving and speaking French to be allowed entry? French-speaking strangers were far less likely in those days than now.]

Mrs Taylor duly went to fetch Foder who 'very kindly offered' to show Dr and Mrs Evans over the place. ·

'The house was a large, well-constructed building, built of brick and stone, with projecting wings in front, surmounted by balustraded parapets. The facade was well exposed and very handsome. The house was approached by a fine sweep of roadway, and contained several large living-rooms, twenty or more bedrooms, and the offices for a full establishment. The stable accommodation also was ample. I saw at once that the grounds were quite extensive, and handsomely laid out. The main avenue from the gate to the house was lined with elms and beeches, and the broad stretches of well-kept lawn were broken by foliage plants and beds of flowers, and decorated by statuary; [Including an ornate well-head that Strode had had built as the exact replica of one in the grounds of the Palace at St Cloud] while, not far from the house, a massive group of cedars branched out conspicuously and threw into relief the body of the building.

'The impression produced upon us, as we passed through the park, was extremely pleasing; the colour was so soft and yet so varied, the calm, the restfulness, so complete, that the place seemed to be indeed an ideal retreat for one seeking a surcease from the turmoil and trouble of the world.

'Upon entering the house, we were surprised to find in it so many articles of French manufacture. The long hall lighted by a skylight, the large drawing room, the fine staircase leading to the floor above, and the arrangement of the very handsome rooms, with the furniture and other fittings, gave me at once the impression of being in a veritable French château. I was consequently not surprised when told that some of the furniture came from the Château of Bercy; but it was certainly remarkable, as was discovered some time afterward, that several of the pieces of carved mahogany in the dining-room were exactly similar to a number that, on the demolition of this château, had been purchased by the Empress at the same auction sale of the woodwork and other fixtures, and had been placed in the residence she had built in Paris for her sister, the Duchess of Alba.

'Observing the excellent French taste with which Camden House was furnished, I made to Mr Foder the plain statement that our object in coming here was to inquire if Camden Place could possibly be obtained for Her Majesty the Empress of the French. When Mr Foder heard this, he told me that, although Camden Place was not to be leased, he believed that Mr Strode, whose French sympathies were very strong, and had often spoken with admiration of the Imperial family, would gladly place his property at the disposal of the Empress and her son, without asking any remuneration for it.'

In fact, Evans claims that Strode agreed on the following day to let the house to Eugenie, although he does not state the amount of the rent. In other books, the rent varies from £200 to £500 a year.

Existing biographies give no really satisfactory explanation as to how the exiled Louis ended up in so unlikely a place as a country house that has now become, prosaically, the clubhouse of the Chislehurst Golf Club.

The Comtesse Marie des Garets, an intimate friend of Eugenie who served as her maid-of-honour throughout her long years of exile and would surely have known the situation at first hand, does not even mention a lease or rent in her memoirs. Published in translation under the title *The Tragic Empress* in 1929, they merely state: 'Among the numerous offers which she [Eugenie] received, she accepted that of Mr Strode, a rich Englishman, who had placed his country house at her disposal.' In 1932, Octave Aubry, an accomplished French historian, claimed in his *L'Impératrice Eugénie* that the Empress 'rented the house for 6,000 francs, a singularly low price, since it was furnished with luxury, even with taste.' Professor William Smith, the author of *Napoleon III*, the last major biography to appear in Britain, avoids the issue completely. He merely writes that the Emperor died 'in a house in Kent which, far from being a Bonapartist shrine, is today a golf club'. Jasper Ridley, author of *Napoleon and Eugenie*, the most recent non-academic, full-length British biography, comments noncommittally: 'Eugenie accepted an offer from Mr Strode of a lease of his house, Camden Place, at Chislehurst. Strode had known Louis Napoleon in England thirty years before; he was a friend of Miss Howard, who appointed him as her executor.'

In 1978, David Duff states in *Eugenie and Napoleon III*: 'After fleeing to England, Eugenie, with her complete trust in Dr Evans (an American dentist friend who had accompanied her from Paris), she asked him to rent for her a country house within easy reach of London. Evans, *by strange coincidence indeed* [my italics], selected Camden Place, Chislehurst, where long ago Prince Louis Napoleon had courted Emily Rowles and which, stranger still, now belonged to an executor of the late Elizabeth Howard.'

And Augustin Filon, the young Prince Imperial's tutor, has told in his *Souvenirs sur l'Impératrice Eugénie* how, when settling in to his new home, he found in an empty wardrobe a portrait of Jean Mocquard, Louis' Principal Private Secretary, who had not died until December 1864 and would have handled all Louis' private financial transactions in the early 1860s when Strode was officially 'buying' and refurbishing Camden Place. Filon mentions the possibility that Strode had been Louis' nominee in the purchase of Camden Place as an eventual refuge but, ever the loyal courtier, adds noncommittally: 'These points remain obscure.'

All this is remarkably suspicious. The case in favour of Louis having secured himself in advance a comfortable refuge, if the need arose, seems proved beyond reasonable doubt.

As for Louis himself, he only made typically enigmatic comments on his ending up at Camden Place, a house that he had known so well thirty years earlier. When, for instance, his old friend Sir William Fraser came to visit him there, Fraser commented that he would probably not remember but Fraser had presented him with a personal letter of introduction when Prince-President from Mrs Rowles, Emily's mother. Louis at once said that he remembered it. 'She was a great friend of mine. I used to be here frequently in former years.'

Undoubtedly Eugenie herself knew nothing of the background to their living at Camden Place. In a letter to her mother, Maria Manuela, still alive and well at seventy-six, she had written on 11 September 1870 from the Marine Hotel in Hastings: 'I cannot tell you yet about my plans. I want, if I am allowed to, to join the Emperor, but I will only know for sure later. I do not have the courage to talk to you about us, we are very unhappy; providence is crushing us, but may its will be done. I would very much like to embrace him but I cannot move for now, when I still do not know myself where to go.'

But the truth seems to be self-evident. Until Louis joined Eugenie at Camden Place and during the remaining two years of his life thereafter when the two of them lived there together, neither of them ever paid a penny in rent to Strode or anyone else. Unknown to Eugenie, to whom the arch-conspirator told few, if any, of his secrets, Louis did not need to pay rent. The house was morally, if not legally, his own property.

This would seem to be further confirmed by the fact that, when in March 1873, two months after Louis' death, Eugenie did take a seven-year lease from Strode, it made no reference to an earlier lapsed or surrendered lease to the deceased Emperor himself, which it would have done if such a document had existed. I have held in my hands the negatives of a photograph of that lease kindly supplied by Mr William M. Mitchell, a Chislehurst resident who has written a history of the Chislehurst Golf Club and Camden Place.

What about Strode himself? Did he ever comment on the 900,000 francs that he received from Louis, or on the strange 'coincidence' that the fallen Emperor came to rest at Camden Place? If he did, nothing has survived and it is perhaps worthy of note that, when he died in 1889, leaving an estate valued at £30,000 – over £1 million at today's prices – his will made no reference whatsoever to his substantial land holdings. His great-granddaughter, Julia Cowper Smith, has told me: 'Apart from the fact that he was a financier, we know very little about him – particularly about what happened to his land.' Strode remains a man of mystery.

When, on the afternoon of 20 March 1871, Louis arrived at Camden Place from Wilhelmshöhe and found a bedroom prepared for him next to Eugenie's with a portrait of his cousin, the Duc de

Reichstadt, hanging on the wall the virtual certainty is that he had, in a very real sense, arrived home. He may have been in exile but he was under his own roof.

Chapter Twenty-Seven

The Last Exile
(1871–3)

ON 20 MARCH 1871, the spring sun shone down at Dover on the large crowds gathering to await Louis' arrival from Ostend. With typical British love of the underdog, they cheered warmly when Eugenie opened her arms in greeting and, as Louis walked along the pier with his fifteen-year-old son on one side and his wife on the other, he kept lifting his hat and bowing. Within a few hours his carriage was swinging through the wrought-iron gates at Camden Place, bought by Strode at the Universal Exhibition at Paris in 1867,[1] and he alighted beneath the Latin motto inscribed in stone over the front door: *Malo mori quam feodari* (I prefer to die rather than be dishonoured or, as the young Prince Imperial translated it: Death before dishonour). When Eugenie had first seen it six months earlier, she had said: 'It is a motto made for me.'

She had done her best to prepare the house for Louis. His bed was canopied with a white satin coverlet embroidered with golden bees. His study next door was so small that there was only room for two armchairs, his desk, and a large cupboard for his papers. But it could be kept nicely warm in the coldest weather, and Louis was to spend many hours there in the hot, stuffy atmosphere he liked, with miniature portraits of Eugenie and Loulou and a small travelling-clock facing him on his desk, his collection of firearms arranged on the wall.

---

[1] The lamps on these fine gates were topped, appropriately, with golden Imperial crowns. When Queen Victoria first visited Eugenie at Camden Place in November 1870, she wrote in her journal: 'Everything was like a French house and many pretty things about.' Eugenie had not brought with her any of those 'pretty things': she had fled Paris empty-handed.

To add to the small Court in exile that had already built up around Eugenie, Louis had brought with him a small suite from Wilhelmshöhe including Comte Davillier, his equerry, Franceschini Pietri, his secretary and brother of the former Paris Police Prefect, and Baron Corvisart, one of his two doctors. His other doctor, Henri Conneau, had gone straight back to France from Wilhelmshöhe to rejoin his family and would soon bring his son with him to live at Camden Place as a young companion for the Prince Imperial.

The house was only of modest size, and there was not a great deal of unoccupied space. The Imperial family and their suites numbered about twenty and there were also some twenty-five servants to accommodate. It was a fairly tight squeeze. When there were guests, Piétri had to use his bedroom as a combined dressing-room and office. The building was comfortable and its grounds were splendid but it was most certainly not the Tuileries or the Palace of St Cloud.

Within a few days, the Prince of Wales came with a warm invitation from his mother for Louis to visit her at Windsor Castle where Eugenie had already been a guest on a number of occasions. On 27 March, only a week after his arrival in England, Louis paid a formal visit to the Queen.

'I went to the door with Louise [one of her daughters],' Victoria wrote in her journal, 'and embraced the Emperor *comme de rigueur*. It was a moving moment, when I thought of the last time he came here in '55, in perfect triumph, dearest Albert bringing him from Dover, the whole country mad to receive him, and now! He seemed much depressed and had tears in his eyes, but he controlled himself and said: *'Il y a bien longtemps que je n'ai vu Votre Majesté* [It is a long time since I have seen Your Majesty].

'He led me upstairs, and we went into the Audience Room. He is grown very stout and grey, and his moustaches are no longer curled or waxed as formerly, but otherwise there was the same pleasing, gentle and gracious manner. My children came in with us. The Emperor at once spoke of the dreadful and disgraceful state of France, and how all that had passed during the past few months had greatly lowered the French character ... There seemed to be *point d'énergie*. He was dreadfully shocked at *tout ce qui se passe à Paris.*[1] He said he had been most kindly treated at Wilhelmshöhe, and that he had kept well all through the winter. He expressed renewed admiration of England and spoke of it being sixteen years since he came to Windsor . . . I took him to the Corridor where all my people were assembled . . . The Emperor said a kind word to all.'

The visit was returned a few days later, on 3 April. It was a foggy, mild day, and Victoria drove from Chislehurst station to Camden Place in an open carriage. 'Immense cheering crowds and quantities of carriages out,' she noted. 'At the door stood the poor little Prince Imperial, looking very much better, and inside the Emperor and Empress, with their suite. The Emperor led me into the Drawing-room, where we sat down. Prince Joachim Murat came in with us. He is very good-looking and gentlemanlike. The dreadful state of Paris was talked of; and the Empress was greatly excited at it, the Emperor quieter. He only said: *Je ne vois pas comment ils peuvent payer.* . . I gave the Empress a nosegay of violets and primroses, which seemed to please her much. Left again at quarter to five . . . Felt very tired and sad.'

At first, Louis was steeped in melancholy. His old friend, Lord Malmesbury, then once more a member of the British government, came down to see him on the day after his arrival at Camden Place. 'After a few minutes he came into the room alone,' he later wrote in his memoirs, 'and with that remarkable smile which could light up his dark countenance he shook me heartily by the hand. I confess that I never was more moved. His quiet and calm dignity and absence of all nervousness and irritability were the grandest

---

[1] This was a reference to the riots that had broken out in Paris in which Socialists and Communists in Montmartre had refused to surrender their arms to the troops of the Republic and had seized and hanged the two generals commanding them. This led directly to the Commune in which for nearly two months Paris was in the hands of left-wing extremists with murders and atrocities committed on both sides. During this time, the Tuileries Palace was burned down just as, some months earlier, the Palace at St Cloud had been destroyed during the Prussian bombardment of the city. In the 1880s, both ruins were razed to the ground so that today nothing whatsoever remains of Louis' two principal palaces, not even the small railway station in the grounds of St Cloud from which he departed for the Franco-Prussian War. It is as if he had never existed. But Haussmann's Paris remains!

examples of human moral courage that the severest Stoic could have imagined.'

Another early visitor, the Earl of Cork, noticed the difficulty that Louis had in controlling his feelings before remarking simply: '*Enfin, je suis bien heureux de me trouver en Angleterre!*' [Well, I'm happy to find myself in England!]. He seemed, if only as a form of unconscious self-defence, to have mentally distanced himself from the horrific events of the past year. When Henry Brackenbury, a famous military writer of the time, visited him, he turned away from his game of patience to talk of Sedan and Marshal MacMahon's strategy in so detached a way that he might have been discussing peace-time manoeuvres rather than the campaign that had brought about his own downfall. When finally Brackenbury bowed himself out, he saw Louis pick up his cards again without a moment's pause as if they had been talking about something that had left him unconcerned and unmoved.

Gradually the melancholy mood passed and Louis began to lead, at least superficially, the life of a typical English country gentleman whose home happened to be conveniently close to the capital. The local railway company offered to place a special train at his disposal but he preferred to travel to London in an ordinary, first-class carriage and could be seen sitting on a seat at Chislehurst station or waiting patiently on the platform at Charing Cross. He came up to London to be a witness at Nathaniel Strode's wedding and he would sometimes dine in town at his old club, the Junior United Service, which had invited him to resume his honorary membership. At the Prince of Wales' request, he was elected a member of the highly select Marlborough Club. Ever courteous, he wrote to express his gratitude and to say how much he was looking forward to visiting the Club 'when I go to London'.

He settled into a domestic routine: reading his papers, entertaining his friends, playing patience, listening to the piano, walking in the grounds of Camden Place, sometimes attending a local bazaar or a cricket match on the neighbouring West Kent ground. Everyone was struck by how friendly, polite and unassuming he always was.

In this calmness, his health much improved and he even travelled around the country to some extent, as he had often done in the years of his earlier exile: visiting friends, inspecting factories and schools, occasionally visiting the Queen at Windsor or Buckingham

Palace. In the autumn of 1871, while Eugenie was visiting relations in Spain, he took the Prince Imperial with him to Torquay and Bath. In the summer of 1872 they all stayed at Brighton and then at Cowes, where they rented two villas on the parade. Time seemed to pass pleasantly enough.

For eighteen months, from March 1871 until September 1872, his bad health seemed to be a thing of the past. During all that time, his kidney stone did not stop him from leading an almost normal life. The absence of stress seems to have brought with it the absence of pain.

The conventional view, taken by many of Louis' biographers, is that, once established at Camden Place, he accepted his fate and, in a spirit of resignation and worsening health, finally lost the will to follow in his illustrious uncle's path. Beaten and ill, he gave up the ambitions of a lifetime: that is the popular theory.

The truth is quite the opposite. After the inevitable period of initial grieving, he determined once again to prove that the blood of the great Napoleon still flowed in his veins and that he was a worthy bearer of his uncle's name. By the time that 1872 came around, he had made up his mind that, just as Napoleon I had escaped from exile on Elba and returned in triumph to Paris at the head of his soldiers, so would he.

It was not only lofty ambition that motivated him. The constraints of exile in a rather cramped house, and the inclement weather of north Kent were beginning to affect a man whose roots were in Corsica and the Caribbean. It rained frequently and for days the house would be blanketed by dense yellow fog. 'I do not think that any of us expected to remain in England for long. An atmosphere of transience reigned with all its illusions,' later recalled the Comtesse Marie des Garets. 'The days were sad indeed under the misty sky in that great kingdom of fog and rain. By degrees, we began to rasp on each other's nerves.' As for Eugenie, she wrote to her mother: 'Here we are on the raft of the Medusa. There are moments when we feel like eating each other.'[1]

---

[1] A reference to Géricault's painting *The Raft of the Medusa*, now in the Louvre, in front of which Eugenie had paused for a moment during her escape from the Tuileries. It made a lasting impression on her.

Louis can hardly be blamed for wanting to escape from this genteel imprisonment. Napoleon I's return to power had lasted the infamous 'One Hundred Days' before the final, crushing defeat of Waterloo. But, for once, Louis had an advantage over his predecessor: in 1815, Napoleon I's son was only a sickly four-year-old, the future Duke of Reichstadt. Louis' own beloved son, the Prince Imperial, was a popular, handsome, serious-minded sixteen-year-old who already looked well in uniform and had ridden with his father on many glamorous military parades, and even into battle. We have already seen that, when still in power in 1868, Louis had seriously discussed with Eugenie abdicating in favour of Loulou in 1874, when the young man would have reached eighteen, the royal age of majority.

I am convinced that, in 1872, he was secretly plotting to return victoriously to France, not so much for himself but for his son.

In fact, one has to go back to first sources to help form a valid judgement on this. Sir William Fraser had the great advantage of knowing him well for more than forty years and last saw him only a few months before his death. In 1896, he wrote in *Napoleon III, My Recollections*: 'There can be no doubt that the Emperor intended to return to Paris. The popular idea was that his ambition was only for his son: no doubt this would be his ultimate object; but he was too sagacious not to know that the best method of ensuring his throne for his heir would be to regain it in the first instance for himself.'

Further direct confirmation of Louis' plans for a return to France comes from extracts from two other books languishing in the basement store of the Reform Club's Library. They are *Chislehurst-Tuileries, souvenirs intimes sur l'empereur* by Evariste Bavoux, a Counsellor of State of the Second Empire who also knew Napoleon well. It was published in 1873 within months of Napoleon's death. Describing a visit to Louis in the summer of 1872, he writes: 'His health! It has never seemed to me better and, as to his intellectual faculties, I would like his detractors to hear, as I did, fall from his lips judgements so full of depth and perception on the current state of affairs in Europe in general and in France in particular.'

The second book in the basement of the Reform Club is *Conversations with Napoleon III* by Sir Victor Wellesley, son of Lord

Cowley, the former British Ambassador's son, and Robert Sencourt. It describes a visit by Mels Cohen, the journalist who had interviewed Louis at Wilhelmshöhe and who visited the exiled Emperor at Chislehurst 'on a foggy morning in December 1872', less than a month before Louis' death. Cohen commented to Louis that the hope of an Imperial restoration in France had enormously increased of late, and Louis replied: 'Neither more nor less! It follows a path traced by the inexorable hand of Providence. It is a progressive march which nothing can stop, for the re-establishment of the Empire is an historical necessity.' When it came to bid the journalist farewell, he said ominously: 'Come and see me often here – or perhaps in France!'

For there still was time for the old conspirator to make one last, desperate throw. Bonapartism had not died in France along with the soldiers slaughtered at Sedan. There were still many voices ready to cry 'Vive l'Empereur!' The Republic that had taken Louis' place was dull, unpopular and incompetent. With Adolphe Thiers, it did not even have a permanent Head of State but only a temporary, acting President. For a while, so great had been the unpopularity of the Second Empire in the overwhelming sense of betrayal in the aftermath of Sedan and the fall of Paris that it seemed as if the old Bourbon monarchy might be restored under the sixty-year-old Comte de Chambord, whose grandfather, Charles X, had fled into exile as far back as 1830. But Chambord was a pompous nonentity who destroyed his chances by insisting on the return of the Bourbon flag of the fleur-de-lys and refusing to accept the much-loved tricolour that had taken its place. The country was passionate for strong government.

By early 1872 Louis had convinced himself that a new call to arms on the lines of his earlier attempts at Strasbourg and Boulogne would be more compelling than anything the grey men in power in Paris could muster. Eugene Rouher, his longest-serving Prime Minister, was amazed, during a visit to Camden Place, at the calm way in which, during a discussion about a social matter that interested them both, Louis said matter-of-factly: 'When I shall come back to Paris, I will arrange all that!' On another occasion when discussing events in France, Louis said to his son: 'The Empire has lost fifty per cent of its prestige but it still has the other half. As the monarchists and the republicans cannot organise themselves properly, that has to be enough to bring us back. We are the necessary solution.'

The wily Adolphe Thiers was so concerned to know what might be happening at Camden Place that he hired an English private detective named Edwin Levy to install agents in the windmill on the other side of the nearby West Kent cricket field and report the names of all visitors to the house. But Louis hired his own spies to spy upon Levy's men, and every morning a copy of their report was placed on his breakfast table.

In the summer and autumn of 1872 plans were made. The basis of a successful plot was hatched; and, just as Louis' half-brother, Auguste de Morny, had been his mainstay in the plans for his coup d'état in 1851, now another family member was his principal aide in this new attempt. It was none other than his cousin, Prince Napoleon, the normally unstable 'Plon-Plon' who now saw, in joint resolute action, the answer to his own inner feelings of inadequacy at a largely wasted life. He became a frequent visitor at Camden Place and for hours the two men were closeted together in secret, anxious discussions in Louis' small study. Neither Eugenie nor the young Prince Imperial were told anything of what was going on. Just as Louis had played his cards close to his chest and told his wife nothing of his plans to acquire a potential safe haven at Camden Place, now he also told her nothing of his plans to return and once again seize power. He carried non-communication of his innermost thoughts almost to the level of an art form.

What were those plans? They were strangely reminiscent of his two earlier endeavours at Strasbourg and Boulogne over thirty years earlier. For Louis was to leave England secretly and join 'Plon-Plon' at his home in Switzerland where, in general's uniform, he would set out for Lyons where Charles Bourbaki, a general whom Louis trusted implicitly, was in command. From there he would lead Bourbaki's soldiers in a triumphal march on Paris with garrisons en route joining in and declaring their support for his cause. A list of Cabinet Ministers had already been prepared and it was decided that he would live at the Louvre, since the Tuileries had been sacked by the Paris mob, and that his Court would be more austere than had flourished in bygone days. With money assured by secret funds raised through his London financier, James McHenry, the new coup was imminent.

But one further thing was essential: that Louis himself should be fit enough to ride on horseback at the head of his triumphant soldiers. The man who knew that he 'looked good on horseback' had to meet his last appointment with his destiny astride a horse.

On 9 December Louis and 'Plon-Plon' had a last meeting at Camden Place to finalise the details of their plan. As they were about to part, Louis said, as if almost half to himself: 'The worst that can happen to me is to be shot like the poor Emperor Maximilian. But that would be better than to die in bed and in exile.'

Suddenly alerted, 'Plon-Plon' asked: 'Are you certain that you can sit in a saddle and remain there for some time? A sick old man in a carriage like Louis XVIII cannot galvanise France.[1] We must, the two of us, march at the head of the troops. You must cut a fine figure, amid your general staff, cavalcading in front of the Dragoons down the Champs Elysées, just like in the good old times, with one hand on the reins and, with the other, saluting the crowd.'

'I feel that I can do it,' replied Louis with more confidence than he truly felt because, in fact, he hardly ever rode a horse these days and was – perhaps because of the renewed stress – beginning again to feel echoes of the old pains he knew so well when travelling in a carriage. Five months earlier, in July, when first experiencing the returned twinges of discomfort, he had called in Sir William Gull, Queen Victoria's private physician, who had allayed his fears with smooth, professional words. 'Do not worry,' he now told 'Plon-Plon'. 'I shall go and see Loulou at Woolwich[2] the day after tomorrow. I will try and make the journey all on horseback, and that will be conclusive.'

Two days later, as promised, he mounted his horse to ride to Woolwich but after only a kilometre he had to turn back: the pain was too intense. He gave orders for a carriage to be prepared but the journey had so tired him that he was forced to take to his bed and suffered three days of fever.

---

[1] A reference to the brother of the executed Louis XVI, who had returned to Paris in a carriage upon the Bourbon Restoration in 1814. Without the Allied armies' support, he would never have succeeded.

[2] To his parents' great joy, and with Queen Victoria's smiling approval for she treated him as almost an adopted grandson, Loulou had passed with flying colours his entrance examination for the celebrated Royal Military Academy at Woolwich a month before.

And that is why in the darkening days of mid-December 1872 he again asked Sir William Gull to come and see him. This time, Gull came with Sir James Paget, the Queen's surgeon-extraordinary. However, on examining the patient, Paget advised that Sir Henry Thompson, the country's most famous surgeon specialising in diseases of the bladder and kidneys, should be brought in and a further appointment was made for Christmas Eve.

Louis had not sought this medical help simply because he was worried about his health. He did it primarily because he needed to be able to ride a horse again. He confided to Sir William Fraser: 'I cannot walk on foot at the head of troops. It would have a still worse effect to enter Paris in a carriage. It is necessary that I should ride.'

So he called in some of the most fashionable medical men in the land to help him, and, with a combination of arrogance and incompetence, they killed him.

Chapter Twenty-Eight

An Unnecessary Death (1873)

S IR WILLIAM GULL AND Sir James Paget had been over-optimistic about the prospects of success when discussing the future with Louis. After they had departed, he sat down and wrote to his son: 'My dear child, Sir William Gull and Sir James Paget have come in consultation. They think that I will be cured in a month ... I embrace you tenderly. Your dear father, Napoleon.'

On Christmas Eve 1872, Sir Henry Thompson accompanied Gull to Camden Place where Dr Conneau was waiting for them and took them up to see their patient. Both Gull and Conneau were only general practitioners. Neither was a surgeon and neither had Thompson's expertise. Once surgery was involved, Thompson was, in the hierarchy of the medical profession, very much the man in command. As Sir David Innes Williams puts it: 'Gull would have taken no part in the operation. He was a physician, not a surgeon. He would only have been there as a token of Queen Victoria's concern for the Emperor but he would have played no part in the surgery – expect perhaps to get in the way.'

Thompson was a vain but talented surgeon; he was also a skilled painter, the author of two novels and later a pioneer of motoring and the leading advocate in Britain of cremation. He had built up a hugely remunerative practice and was a well-known social lion, celebrated in the best circles in London for his 'octaves': dinner parties for eight people, with eight courses and eight wines, served at eight o'clock in the evening. Queen Victoria had knighted him ten years earlier for successfully destroying the kidney stone of her uncle, King Leopold I of the Belgians. The operation, lithotrity, might, as we now know, have helped to cure Louis in the late

1860s, had Baron Larrey considered the condition serious enough at the time.

This now was the surgical procedure which Gull had brought in Thompson to consider performing upon Louis.

Sir David Innes Williams gives a unique account of performing a lithotrity: 'I did several of them in my younger days. You pass a metal instrument with two small blades at the end, called a litho-trite, into the bladder with the blades closed. Then you press it down at the back and open up the blades. Hopefully the stone falls between them and you work it up and down and you feel: "Yup, I've got it!" Then you fix the screw and turn it so that the blades close and break the thing. *In situ*. It's a great feeling!'

On Christmas Eve 1872, after the preliminary courtesies, Thompson probed Louis' bladder with a flexible catheter. Upon finding little or no urine left after Louis, at his request, had passed as much water as he possibly could, he announced that he suspected a large kidney stone was obstructing the flow and advised that without further delay he should return and examine him more fully under chloroform. He told Louis that, if such examination confirmed his provisional diagnosis, he would want there and then to remove it by crushing – as he (rightly) claimed he had done with great success many times before with other patients.

Louis readily gave his consent and endured a somewhat anxious Christmas and New Year until 2 January, the first available day when this crucial examination could take place. But he seemed full of hope, with no inkling of the fact that his life might be in danger.

Nearly forty years later, in February 1910, a French doctor in the South of France named Debout d'Estrées claimed that Sir William Gull had told him that he had warned Louis not to have an operation, 'the condition of his kidneys being such as to make me fear that any operation would be fatal'. By then Gull had been dead for twenty years and Thompson for six.[1] Did Gull say such a thing to d'Estrées in an attempt to extricate himself from any blame as to Louis' subsequent death or did d'Estrées invent it, as part of the long-standing and public animosity that prevailed between the British and French medical professions after the death of the fallen

[1] Edward Legge, a respected journalist and author, repeated the claim in his biography of Eugenie published in Britain that same year.

French Emperor? We are likely never to know but one thing is clear: whatever Gull may or may not have claimed after the event, he did not warn Louis beforehand against having the operation.

This is borne out by the fact that, in that somewhat fraught period over Christmas and New Year, Louis wrote delightedly to the Comte de la Chapelle, who was an active participant in his plot to return to France: 'In a month's time, I shall be in the saddle again.'

On 2 January 1873, Gull, Thompson and Conneau met again at Camden Place. This time they were joined by Baron Corvisart, Louis' other general practitioner, and J. T. Clover, a well-known anaesthetist.

A simple iron bedstead had been brought into Louis' bedroom to serve as an operating table. Louis took the chloroform quickly, and Thompson explored his bladder with a lithotrite. At once he detected a stone 'as large as a walnut or large chestnut'. So he carried on with a lithotrity to try and crush it.[1] He was only partially successful. He managed to crack the stone and remove a lot of fragments but a large chunk of the stone and some fragments were still left inside Louis, causing him a great deal of pain and discomfort.

On the following day, Thompson wrote to the Prince of Wales from Camden Place to tell him of his patient's progress. 'Altogether he is in *quite* as good a condition as I could have expected. Several more operations must follow before the stone can be entirely removed. I am installed here altogether, having given up all my London work for any period which may be necessary to complete my task, and allow nothing to happen, within my power to avert, which can possibly interfere with the successful result which I earnestly hope – not without misgiving – to obtain.'

The next day he was less optimistic: 'The Emperor goes on fairly well. Not quite so flourishing perhaps now as yesterday; on the whole about the same. I regard the case as a very grave one. In the *strictest confidence* I tell you this: the stone is so large; the Emperor is VERY SENSITIVE and is difficult to manage. I shall want all my

---

[1] According to the *British Medical Journal*, 11 January 1873, the mortality rate for lithotrity was as low as 4 per cent. Nowadays it is an even safer operation, called lithotripsy, where sound waves or a laser beam replace the metal lithotrite and pass through soft tissues without harming them but act as a shock that breaks up the stone into fragments.

force, all my resources to get him through, and I may fail. I am very anxious.'[1]

Like many an eminent specialist then and now, he seems not to have communicated his anxieties to his patient for, on that very same day, at 8.30 pm, Corvisart wrote to the Comte de la Chapelle, in French: 'My dear Count, I send you, with great pleasure, news of His Majesty. As you know, the operation of crushing goes on successfully. Today the Emperor dined. He has no fever. All is going on as well as we could wish, and you would read that upon our faces could you see them. I hope that each session will pass off as well, and that it will not be necessary to have many more. The Emperor wishes you to hear this good news, and directed me to write to you.'

So far, so good. Or so it seemed to the patient.

Two days later, on 6 January, Thompson performed a second lithotrity. The stone was once again crushed and more fragments washed out but the subsequent autopsy proved that half the stone was still left intact and two or three extremely small fragments 'none larger than a hempseed'. There would undoubtedly have to be, at least, a third operation when the patient – then aged nearly sixty-five – had sufficiently recovered his strength. Thompson's work was only partly done and Louis continued in pain.

'Where is Loulou?' he whispered to Eugenie.

'He is at Woolwich,' she told him. 'Would you like me to send for him?'

'No, do not disturb him. He is at work.'

On the evening of 8 January, as on previous evenings, Louis was given chloral, a popular Victorian sleeping potion. Throughout the night each of his doctors in turn visited him at regular intervals and, as Thompson reported to the Queen by telegram the next day, they all 'found him to be sleeping soundly and naturally, better than on the previous night'.[2]

At 9.45 am, Thompson and Clover, the anaesthetist, examined

---

[1] These two letters were forwarded by the Prince of Wales to Queen Victoria, who wrote in her journal: 'This alarmed me.'

[2] Later, attempts were made, especially by French doctors, to blame an overdose of the chloral for Louis' subsequent collapse. But the highly experienced Dr Corvisart had measured out the dosage and, as Sir David Innes Williams says, 'If it had killed the patient, I would have expected an immediate collapse upon it having been administered, not the next day.'

Louis and, finding his pulse to be regular and firm, decided to carry out at midday a third operation to wash out the remaining chunk of stone and fragments in his bladder. Shortly afterwards, Louis turned to Dr Conneau, who was then sitting by his bed, and whispered faintly: '*N'est-ce pas, Conneau, que nous n'avons pas été des lâches à Sedan?*' (We weren't cowards at Sedan, Conneau, were we?)

They were the last coherent words he uttered. At 10.25 am, Thompson looked into his room and at once noticed a change in his condition. As he later tersely expressed it in his telegram to Queen Victoria, 'signs of sinking appeared – the heart's action suddenly failed and he died at 10.45'. The date was Thursday 9 January 1873.

Meanwhile, Eugenie, who had been about to leave for Woolwich to see her son, was warned that there was 'a small crisis' and that it would be better if she waited. An aide went to Woolwich to fetch the Prince and Eugenie went upstairs to remove her hat. Then, as she approached Louis' room, the door suddenly flew open and Corvisart appeared, calling: 'Father Goddard, Father Goddard!'[1] With pounding heart, Eugenie hurried over to the bed. '*Voilà l'Impératrice, Sire*,' someone said as she bent down and kissed Louis' hand. He was breathing very heavily and seemed unable to see her but, as she later wrote to Victoria, his lips moved as though in a kiss.

'Loulou is coming,' she whispered, and his expression brightened. Then Father Goddard arrived and gently drew her away. While he was administering the Last Sacrament, the doctors told her that Louis was dying. She could not believe it. Running back to the bed, she fell on her knees and began to pray. A few minutes later, Louis died. Eugenie gave a shriek and fainted. When she revived, she wept unrestrainedly by the bedside.

Shortly afterwards, the carriage bringing the Prince Imperial was heard outside. Conneau and Corvisart hurried to the front door, and the young man saw at once that he had arrived too late. He ran upstairs so fast that he stumbled and fell several times before he found his mother waiting for him at the door of his father's

---

[1] The local Roman Catholic priest who had become a friend of the family and was at that time in constant attendance at the house.

room. She took him in her arms. 'I have nothing left but you,' she murmured through her tears. Then he went into the room, knelt by the bed and in a loud clear voice recited the *Pater Noster*.

Franceschini Piétri, Louis' secretary, immediately telegraphed the news to Queen Victoria's lady-in-waiting at Osborne: '*Veuillez annoncer à Sa Majesté la triste nouvelle. L'Empereur a cessé de souffrir. L'Impératrice est dans les larmes.*' (Will you announce to Her Majesty the sad news. The Emperor has ceased to suffer. The Empress is in tears.) The Queen showed her affection for Eugenie, only seven years her junior, by writing to her at once, as *Ma pauvre chère Soeur*, to express her heartfelt condolences. That single phrase – with that vital little extra word *pauvre*, bursting through the constraints of royal protocol – illumines Victoria's regard for the stricken Empress and the depth of their friendship.

For two days Louis' body lay on the little iron bedstead on which he had died, watched day and night by members of his household and two nuns. Then it was embalmed – sadly the process was defective and his face turned bright yellow – and dressed in the uniform of a French General of Division (a senior rank unique to the French army) with the ribbons of both the French Legion of Honour and the British Order of the Garter worn across his chest.

When his body had been placed in a lead coffin, with his sword lying beside it and Napoleon I's ring on one of his fingers, Eugenie came and placed a red rose on the blue tunic.

The Prince of Wales had wanted to attend the funeral but the Foreign Secretary, Lord Granville, had advised Victoria that the Prince Imperial might be proclaimed emperor and, fearing a Bonapartist demonstration, he advised her that her son should not attend. It would be more appropriate if he chose to visit Camden Place on the morning before the funeral to pay his respects to the Emperor as he lay in state.

So, on 14 January, the Prince of Wales came with his younger brother, the Duke of Edinburgh, and both stood in silence before the yellow-faced body, lying in its open coffin in the centre of the entrance hall, which had been transformed into a temporary chapel.

When they had departed, the gates were thrown open to the thousands of Frenchmen who had made the pilgrimage to Chislehurst to see their Emperor for the last time and who had been waiting outside since early morning. Some threw little bouquets into the deep folds of black velvet that draped the coffin. Many were sobbing quietly. An old soldier was heard to cry: '*Adieu, mon Empereur*', and an elderly woman begged to be allowed to see the body for one moment longer. Night fell, and still the procession made its way through the house and past the bier. At last, at nine o'clock, the gates were shut, and the family and the household came to kiss Louis' hand. Then the coffin was closed, and Eugenie came downstairs to pray beside it throughout the night.

At 11 o'clock on the morning of Wednesday 15 January, funeral bells rang out from the nearby Catholic parish church of St Mary's and the local Protestant church of St Nicholas, as the cortège passed through the wrought-iron gates of Camden Place on its way to St Mary's. The hearse was drawn by eight horses decked out in black velvet. Behind it the Prince Imperial walked alone, dressed in black relieved only by the broad red ribbon and the star of the Legion of Honour. He was followed by 'Plon-Plon' and other members of the Imperial Family, together with personal representatives of Queen Victoria and the Prince of Wales and many other distinguished mourners but the total number of the crowd, comprising men and women from all classes, was estimated at not less than 17,000. The Empress Eugenie could not bring herself to attend.

The church of St Mary's was far too small for the crush of people that wished to enter. Admission had to be limited to the 200 invited guests bearing cards, printed with a deep black border, and sealed in black wax with the seal of *La Maison de l'Empereur*. Jean Mocquard, Louis' secretary, Comte Felix Bacciochi, his court chamberlain and occasional procurer, Prosper Mérimée, his friend, and Persigny, at one time his closest associate, were all dead.[1] But, for the rest, the list of mourners read like a roll call of survivors of the Second Empire, with some surprising omissions. Among those in the church were: Comtesse Marianne de Walewska, Louis' ex-mistress and the widow of his cousin and Napoleon I's illegimate son, Comte Alexandre Walewski; General Comte Fleury; Lord

---

[1] When hearing a year earlier that Persigny was dying, Louis had written him a gentle letter of reconciliation but Persigny had died before it arrived.

Cowley, the former British Ambassador to Paris, and his wife whom Queen Victoria had asked to write a personal account of the ceremony; Marshals Canrobert and Le Boeuf; General Bourbaki; Eugene Rouher, Louis' longest-serving Prime Minister, and the Comte de Palikao, his last Prime Minister; Comte Benedetti and the Duc de Gramont, who had played so important a part in helping to bring about the Franco-Prussian War; and Baron Haussmann, who had helped to rebuild Paris.

Perhaps understandably, neither of his two illegitimate sons, the Counts Labenne and D'Orx, was present, nor their mother Alexandrine Vergeot (then Mme Bure) or, among his highly-placed former mistresses, the two Countesses, Virginia Castiglione and Louise de Mercy-Argenteau. Nor was there any sign of Princess Mathilde (who, ever the pragmatist, had not followed Louis into exile), Marshal MacMahon or Emile Ollivier.

'The funeral was the most touching scene I ever witnessed,' Lady Cowley wrote in her account for Queen Victoria. 'There was not a dry eye in the Church and the gentlemen who walked with, and stood by, the coffin, were all sobbing. All the pomps and obsequies at Notre Dame could never equal the scene in little St Mary's.'

When the Prince Imperial left the church, the crowd outside called 'Vive l'Empereur!' and there were cries of 'Vive Napoléon IV!' But he called back, in French: 'No, my friends. Do not cry: Vive l'Empereur!' The Emperor is dead. Cry: Vive la France!' But there were still some persistent cries of 'Vive Napoléon IV!'

Why had Louis died so suddenly? Why had the operation, with an average mortality rate of 4 per cent, proved so unexpectedly fatal?

The medical cover-up that followed Louis' sudden collapse and death has never been documented before. I have checked with the office of the present Coroner for Chislehurst and no records survive, if any ever existed, of any official intervention by the then holder of his office. There was merely a private autopsy carried out the next day by a famous pathologist named Dr Burdon Sanderson, Professor of Physiology at University College, London – with Thompson, the highly fashionable surgeon who had performed the suspect operations and all the other doctors in the case, standing beside him. It is perhaps no great surprise that Dr Sanderson's autopsy report, hurried out so that it could be delivered to the press at 6.30 that same evening, exonerated of any blame whatsoever Thompson and every other medical person involved.

The thrust of the report, signed by Sanderson, as well as by Thompson and his assistant, John Foster, Conneau, Corvisart and the anaesthetist, J. T. Clover, was that Louis had died not because of any negligence or wrongdoing by any of those participating doctors but solely because of Louis' own underlying kidney condition.[1] 'The most important result of the examination,' stated the report, 'was, that the kidneys were found to be involved in the inflammatory effects produced by the irritation of the vesical calculus [i.e. the stone] which must have been in the bladder several years to a degree which was not suspected; and if it had been suspected, could not have been ascertained . . .

'In the interior of the bladder was found a part of a calculus, the form of which indicated that half had been removed. Besides this, there were two or three extremely small fragments, none of them larger than a hempseed. This half calculus weighed about three-quarters of an ounce, and measured $1^{1}/_{4}$ inch by $1^{5}/_{16}$ inch. There was no disease of the heart, nor of any other organ excepting of the kidneys.

'Death took place by failure of the circulation, and was attributable to the general constitutional state of the patient.

'The disease of the kidneys, of which this state was the expression, was of such a nature and so advanced that it would in any case have shortly determined a fatal result.'

In other words, no one should worry too much about what had actually occurred during the two attempts at lithotrity that had taken place because the unfortunate Emperor would have died 'shortly' anyway. It is difficult to conceive of a more high-handed and arrogant attitude. And how much longer would he have had to live if they had not advised him to have the operation so that he would be able to ride a horse again in a month? How much time did that word 'shortly' allow him? Sir David Innes Williams' response is philosophical: 'Who can say?'

---

[1] Sir William Gull had not signed the report because he had left Camden Place immediately after the autopsy, but he recorded a separate opinion in a letter to *The Times* in which he wrote that he thought the stone was of longer duration than the others believed – but he 'entirely endorsed' the report's other observations.

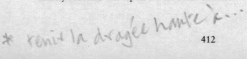

Indeed, no one can estimate for exactly how long Louis would have lived without the operations, or what would have happened to his plans to return to France, if he had not been able to ride into Paris at the head of his troops. The tragedy is that his doctors, and in particular Sir Henry Thompson, denied him the opportunity to find out.

It is implicit in the autopsy report that, if Thompson had known that the condition of Louis' kidneys was so bad, he would not have attempted the first operation. So what actually killed Louis? Sir David's conclusion is crystal clear: 'Obviously there was pre-existing, chronic damage to his kidneys. The consequences of stirring things up probably caused a fresh infection which tipped the balance against him. It was the infecting complication of his two operations which killed him, which finally finished the kidneys. If you have got renal failure and a severe infection on top of that, it's enough to kill you – even though he seemed to be recovering.'

The autopsy report may have pleased the eminent doctors most intimately connected with Louis' death but it did not satisfy everybody. On the following day, *The Times* thundered: 'It is melancholy to think that, notwithstanding all our discoveries and all our progress, several celebrated physicians and surgeons are still compelled to put their hands to a confession that the disease of the kidneys which must so soon have killed the Emperor existed "to a degree which was not suspected . . . and could not have been ascertained". A man may still, it appears, die under the hands of the first doctors of the world of a great organic disease without their knowledge of anything about it; and the only reflection which is not painful in this agonising dissection of human infirmities is that he who endured them now endures them no longer.'

Even some doctors agreed. In a letter printed in the *Lancet*, on 18 January, a Dr J. A. Wilson stated his clear conclusion: 'The case in question, under all the circumstances, was not suitable for the serial operations of anaesthetic lithotrity.' Stung into making a public reply, Thompson himself wrote to the *Lancet* a letter published in its next issue, on 25 January: 'The private physicians of the late Emperor have [expressed] their desire of drawing up a history of the case, which will afford full information on all matters possessing a scientific and practical interest for the medical profession.' *No such 'history' ever appeared.*

In the same issue of the magazine, a leader writer stated bluntly: 'It cannot be denied that the professional mind has been much exercised during the last three weeks on the subject of the treatment of stone in the bladder. Whilst universal regret is felt at the unfortunate result of the Emperor Napoleon's case, and much sympathy expressed for the eminent surgeon concerned, opinions have differed as to the propriety of the course pursued and the treatment adopted.'

In all the years that have passed since then, no biography has quoted a modern urinological surgeon's view of Louis' medical treatment. Mr James Bellringer has offered this assessment: 'The Emperor almost certainly died as a result of septicaemia (spread of infection by carriage of bacteria in the blood), itself caused by repeated instrumentation of an infected lower urinary tract ... Microbiology was in its infancy, and it was to be a further three years before Robert Koch demonstrated that Anthrax was caused by a bacterium (the first time that a disease had been shown unequivocally to be the result of bacterial infection). Many pathologists and surgeons of the day were still not believers in "germ theory". They would have observed that instrumentation was often followed by high fever and rigors, and that this often had a fatal outcome; but they would not have known why.'

Does this exonerate Louis' doctors from blame? Can they fairly be criticised in the light of medical knowledge, as it then existed? Bellringer is reluctant to criticise fellow members of his own profession who are now long dead and cannot defend themselves, but his conclusions are even more damning than those to which I had already come before consulting him: 'The mistake would appear to me to have been the decision to persist, in a sick patient, with a treatment which had already failed twice, despite the fact that they would have known the risks of sepsis (bacterial infection), if not the mechanism whereby it occurred. The refusal to accept defeat gracefully in such circumstances smacks of appalling arrogance, and I would respectfully suggest that if this were to be brought out by yourself as Counsel for the Prosecution, the jury (your readers) would be much more likely to reach a guilty verdict.'

He continues: 'The reason I put this forward is that I am aware how easy it is, as a surgeon, to refuse to accept that any operation performed by oneself will ever fail or go wrong. Sadly, this is not borne out by the evidence! The combination of an eminent surgeon of the day, a famous patient, and a new(ish) surgical technique remain even today a potent recipe for exactly this sort of disaster.'

As for my own opinion, it is quite clear why the promised 'history' of Louis' case never appeared in the pages of the *Lancet* or, indeed, anywhere else. Sir Henry Thompson and his colleages could not deliver it because it would have exposed their own diagnostic error and their own negligence, fuelled by arrogance.

And so the matter rests. On any basis, Louis need not have died when he did. In France today, many Frenchmen are still, wrongly, ashamed of their former Emperor. In Britain, we should be more ashamed of those doctors who tended him in the final days of his life.

EPILOGUE

THERE WAS A LONG, sad postscript to Louis' life. Six years later, his dear Loulou, grown to be a handsome twenty-three-year-old in Queen Victoria's army, was killed on 1 June 1879 fighting for Britain in the Zulu War in South Africa. Faced with death, he had shown a courage of which his father would have been proud. Left alone by his fleeing comrades when his saddle strap broke and he could not remount his horse, he saw seven warriors advancing upon him with assegais raised. One threw his weapon which struck him in the thigh. He pulled it out and threw it back, then ran towards the Zulus firing his revolver. His shots missed. A second assegai felled him and the Zulus clustered around him, stabbing him even after he was dead. The next morning, when British soldiers came to gather up his body, they found his clothes rent by seventeen vicious wounds – all in the front. At the Musée du Second Empire at the Château de Compiègne today, visitors can still see his tunic with those seventeen gashes in the fabric.

Both Queen Victoria, virtually his surrogate grandmother, and Eugenie were distraught with grief. When Eugenie was told the news, she collapsed into a chair staring into space and did not leave Camden Place for thirty-two days. Later she insisted on visiting South Africa and standing at the spot where her only child had met his death.

She resolved to leave Camden Place. It had become 'a house of gloom' for her. Loulou was laid to rest in nearby St Mary's, close to his father, but Eugenie was unhappy that both tombs should be in such a confined space. She set out to buy a much larger house for herself, with no sad memories and also with sufficient grounds in which she could have built a mausoleum to serve as a suitable final resting place for her husband and her son and, eventually, for herself.

In 1880, she found such a place at Farnborough Hill in Hampshire, a sprawling mansion built twenty years earlier by Thomas Longman, a well-known publisher who had recently died. It had its own extensive grounds and a wide stretch of adjoining, empty land was also up for sale. Eugenie bought both the house and the land, and ordered the house to be enlarged, remodelled and refurbished so as to turn it into a truly French and Imperial residence, with 'N' on all the outside drains, two glass-fronted doors for the dining-room saved from the pillage of the Tuileries Palace and a fine bas-relief of Napoleon III, his head crowned with a laurel wreath, on one side of the entrance hall.

On the adjoining land, she asked the French architect, Gabriel Destailleur, to build, in the flamboyant late French Gothic style, an abbey and a monastery dedicated to St Michael. The two buildings took five years to construct and when, in 1885, all was finished, Louis' and Loulou's tombs were removed from St Mary's and transferred to the crypt of the abbey. To this day, visitors (admitted on Saturdays) can see Louis' large granite sarcophagus, Queen Victoria's gift. A small wooden plaque reads: 'With affectionate sympathy. V. R.'

From Eugenie's sitting-room, *le grand salon de Sa Majesté*, she could see the dome of the Abbey over the rhododendrons that she ordered to be planted and she never allowed trees to be grown beyond those bushes to block her view. The house is now a thriving public school for girls and trees now block the view from the school library which Eugenie's *grand salon* has now become. But mementos of the Empress survive and a lovely story is still told at the school about a room on the ground floor, now little changed, in which she used to receive Queen Victoria, and the two old ladies would say to each other, on entering: 'After you my sister', 'No, after you my sister', often ending up by walking in together, hand in hand.

To the end of her days, Eugenie remained Spanish and she did her best to lighten the mid-Victorian heaviness of Thomas Longman's house by adding on to the sitting-room a glass-walled conservatory (her *jardin d'hiver*), by replacing wooden doors with sliding glass doors, and by providing space for many house plants by the windows, the areas tiled with bright Spanish colours, many of which still remain.

She lived on for forty-seven years after Louis' death, an indomitable old lady, travelling a great deal, maintaining her mental faculties right up to the end and, even in extreme old age, with eyes that were, according to Jean Cocteau, of 'a heavenly blue'. Whenever she visited Paris, she took rooms overlooking the Tuileries Gardens where the Palace had stood. When once a lady-in-waiting summoned up the courage to ask how she could bear to do so, she replied: 'I am not the same woman as used to live there. She died a long time ago.'

Eugenie did not in fact die until eight o'clock in the morning on 11 July 1920 when, at the age of ninety-four, her physical strength finally ran out and, on a visit to Madrid, in her beloved sister Paca's room, and on the bed which had once belonged to Paca, she quietly closed her eyes for ever. They brought her body back to England to be buried at St Michael's, in the presence of King George V and Queen Mary, the present Queen's grandparents, King Alphonso XIII and Queen Victoria Eugenia of Spain, Prince Victor Bonaparte, 'Plon-Plon's' son, and many other mourners who filled the abbey to capacity. She was buried in a nun's habit, and she rests today in a tomb placed in a recess in the wall over the altar in the abbey's crypt, with Louis and Loulou's tombs on either side.

Seven months before she died, she had told Maurice Paléologue at their last meeting that she was glad to have lived to see Alsace and Lorraine returned to France by a defeated Germany at the end of World War One. 'I have had the supreme consolation of seeing France re-established in her national integrity,' she said. 'I have had the solace of being able to tell myself that those heroes who died in 1870 are at last repaid for their sacrifice.'[1]

And what about Louis? How can one end this account of his life and that of those dearest to him? There can be no doubt that he was clever, brave and charming. But, in the ultimate, he proved to be lacking in staying power. His tragedy was that, having arrived at the exalted level which he regarded as his birthright, he did not know where to go or even how to maintain himself where he was.

Bismarck dismissed him as a sphinx without a riddle, but that is much too harsh. It is easy to understand what the ruthless Iron Chancellor, with a firm idea of what he wanted to achieve and how to attain it, could be so dismissive of someone like Louis, forever scheming and manoeuvring behind his inscrutable façade.

Let him lie in peace, dressed still in the uniform of a French

---

[1] As for the remaining lesser figures in Louis' life, 'Plon-Plon' died in 1891 and his sister, Princess Mathilde, in 1904.

general, with the sword that he surrendered to the Prussian king lying beside him and Napoleon I's ring on his finger. The two are perfect symbols of his high destiny and his ultimate defeat.

BIBLIOGRAPHY AND OTHER SOURCES

Académie du Second Empire. Bulletin No. 11. Paris, 1993.

Anonymous. *Papiers et correspondance de la Famille Impériale* (2 vols). Paris, Garnier Frères, 1871.

Aronson, Theo. *Napoleon and Josephine: A Love Story.* London, John Murray, 1990.

Aubry, Octave. *L'Impératrice Eugénie.* Paris, Fayard, 1932.

Autin, Jean. *L'Impératrice Eugénie.* Paris, Fayard, 1990.

Bac, Ferdinand. *La Cour des Tuileries sous le Second Empire.* Paris, Hachette, 1930.

—*Napoléon III inconnu.* Paris, Librairie Félix Alcan, 1932. (Of unique authority because of his father's long friendship with Louis.)

Barnett, Correlli. *Bonaparte.* London, George Allen & Unwin, 1978.

Baroche, Mme Jules (Céleste). *Second Empire. Notes et souvenirs.* Paris, Les Editions G. Crès et Cie, 1921.

Barrot, Odilon. *Mémoires posthumes,* Vol. III. Paris, 1875–6.

Barthorp, Michael. *The Zulu War.* Poole, Dorset, Blandford Press, 1980.

Baudelaire, Charles. *Œuvres complètes.* Paris, Robert Laffont, 1980.

Bavoux, Evariste. *Chislehurst-Tuileries, souvenirs intimes sur l'empereur.* Paris, E. Dentu, 1873.

Bertault, Jules. *Napoléon III secret.* Paris, Bernard Grasset, 1939.

Berthet-Leleux, François. *Le Vrai Prince Napoléon.* Paris, Editions Grasset, 1929.

Bluche, Frédéric. *Le Bonapartisme.* Paris, Presses Universitaires de France, 1981.

Boumier, Alain. *Le dernier séjour de Napoléon III en Angleterre.* Paris, Bulletin de l'Académie du Second Empire, 1996.

Bourgeois, Émile. *Modern France,* Vol. I. Cambridge, Cambridge University Press, 1922.

Bourrienne, Louis-Antoine. *Mémoires.* Paris, Garnier, 1828–30. *British Medical Journal,* London. 11 January 1873.

Briais, Bernard. *Grandes courtisanes du Second Empire.* Paris, Jules Tallandier, 1981.

Brogan, D. W. *The French Nation.* London, Hamish Hamilton, 1957.

Bruce, Evangeline. *Napoleon and Josephine: An Improbable Marriage*. London, Weidenfeld & Nicolson, 1995.

Bushell, T. A. *Imperial Chislehurst*. Chesham, Bucks, Barracuda Books, 1973.

Carpentier, Jean and Le Goff, Jacques. *Histoire de France*. Paris, Le Seuil, 1996.

Castelot, André. *Napoléon et l'amour*. Paris, Presses Pocket, 1968.

—*Napoléon Trois: Des prisons au pouvoir*. Paris, Librairie Académique Perrin, 1973. (All three volumes of Castelot's trilogy on Napoleon III form a valuable and fascinating collection of anecdotal material.)

—*La Féerie impériale*. Paris, Perrin, 1973.

—*Napoléon Trois ou l'aube des temps modernes*. Paris, Perrin, 1974.

Castillon du Perron, Marguerite. *La Princess Mathilde*. Paris, Amiot Dumont, 1953.

Chapman, Maristan. *Imperial Brother (Duc de Morny)*. London, Allan, 1932.

Christiansen, Rupert. *Tales of the New Babylon*. London, Sinclair-Stevenson, 1994.

Cobban, Alfred. *A History of Modern France*, Vol. 2. London, Penguin Books, 1965.

Cochelet, Louise. *Mémoires sur la reine Hortense et la Famille Impériale*. Brussels, 1836–7.

Colin, Gerty. *Rois et reines de Belgique*. Paris, Presses de la Cité, 1993.

Corty, Count Egon Caesar. *Maximilian and Charlotte of Mexico* (trans. Catherine Alison Phillips) (2 vols). New York, Alfred A. Knopf, 1928.

Cowley, 1st Earl. *The Paris Embassy during the Second Empire* (ed. Col. The Hon. F.A. Wellesley). London, Thornton Butterworth, 1928.

Crankshaw, Edward. *The Fall of the House of Habsburg*. London, Longmans, 1963.

Cronin, Vincent. *Napoleon*. London, Penguin Books, 1973. (In my view, the leading modern English biography of the Emperor.)

Dansette, Adrien. *Les Amours de Napoléon III*. Paris, Fayard, 1938.

—*Louis-Napoléon à la conquête du pouvoir*. Paris, Hachette, 1961. (Still the best French biography of the early years but not in the same class as his *du 2 Décembre au 4 Septembre* for the later years).

—*du 2 Décembre au 4 Septembre*. Paris, Hachette, 1972.

Decaux, Alain. *La Castiglione*. Paris, Perrin, 1964.

Desternes, S. and Chandet, H. *Napoléon III: homme du XX siècle*. Paris, Hachette, 1961.

Diaz-Plaja, Fernando. *Eugenia de Montijo, Emperatriz de los Franceses*. Madrid, Editorial Planeta, 1992.

Duff, David. *Eugenie and Napoleon III*. London, Collins, 1978.

Eugenie, Empress. *Lettres familières de l'impératrice Eugénie* (ed. 17th Duke of Alba and G. Hanotaux). Paris, Le Divan, 1935.

Evans, Dr Thomas W. *Memoirs* (2 vols). London, Unwin, 1905.

Feuillet, Madame Octave. *Quelques années de ma vie*. Paris, Calmann-Lévy, 1896.

Fierro, Alfred. *Histoire et dictionnaire de Paris*. Paris, Robert Laffont (coll. 'Bouquins'), 1996.

Fierro, Alfred, Palleul-Guillard, André and Tulard, Jean. *Histoire et dictionnaire du consulat et de l'empire*. Paris, Robert Laffont (Coll. 'Bouquins'), 1996. (A masterly assembly, in easily accessible form, of useful but sometimes obscure facts.)

Filon, Augustin. *Souvenirs sur l'impératrice Eugénie*. Paris, Calmann-Lévy, 1920.

Flaubert, Gustave. *L'Éducation sentimentale, in Œuvres Complètes* (ed. Bernard Masson). Paris, Le Seuil, 1964.

Fleischmann, Hector. *Napoléon III et les femmes*. Paris, Bibliothèque des Curieux, 1913.

Fleury, General Comte de. *Souvenirs*. Vol. I. Paris, Librairie Plon, 1897–8.

Forbes, Archibald. *The Life of Napoleon the Third*. London, Chatto & Windus, 1898.

Fraser, Sir William. *Napoleon III (My Recollections)*. London, Sampson, Low, 1888.

Frèrejean, Alain. *Napoléon IV*. Paris, Albin Michel, 1997.

Garets, Marie, Comtesse des. *The Tragic Empress* (ed. Marie-Louyse des Garets, trans. Hélène Graeme). London, Skeffington & Son, 1930.

Gayot, André. *François Guizot et Mme Laure de Gasparin*. Paris, Bernard Grasset, 1934.

Girard, Louis. *Napoléon III*. Paris, Fayard, 1986.

Giraudeau, Fernand. *Napoléon III, intime*. Paris, Paul Ollendorf, 1895.

Gombrich, E. H. *The Story of Art* (16th edn). London, Phaidon, 1995.

Goncourt, Edmond et Jules de. *Journal*. Paris, Robert Laffont (Coll. 'Bouquins'), 1989.

Gooch, G. P. *The Second Empire*. London, Longmans, 1960.

Gorys, Erhard. *Czechoslovakia* (trans. by Sebastian Wormell). London, a Pallas Guide sponsored by Shell International, 1995.

Guedalla, Philip. *The Second Empire*. London, Hodder & Stoughton, 1922 (1946 edn). (Stylistically marvellous but sadly not always entirely correct historically.)

Guest, Ivor. *Napoleon III in England*. London, British Technical & General Press, 1952. (A painstakingly detailed work of original research.)

Henri-Pajot, Jeanne. *Napoléon III: l'empereur calomnié*. Paris, Beauchesne, 1972.

Herold, J. Christopher. *The Age of Napoleon*. Harmsworth, Middlesex, Penguin Books, 1969.

Hibbert, Christopher. *The French Revolution*. London, Penguin Books, 1982.

—*Wellington*. London, HarperCollins, 1997.

Hirrigoyen, Francis. Articles in *Bulletin de la Société de Borda*, 1981 and 1988.

Hodgson, Godfrey. *A New Grand Tour*. London, Penguin Books, 1995.

Horne, Alistair. *The Fall of Paris*. London, Macmillan (PaperMac), 1990.

—*How Far from Austerlitz?* London, Macmillan, 1996.

Queen Hortense. *Mémoires de la reine Hortense*. Paris, Plon, 1927. (A too-often overlooked treasure-house of information.)

Howard, Michael. *The Franco-Prussian War*. London, Rupert Hart-Davis, 1961.

Hugentobler, Jacob and Meyer Bruno. *Château d'Arenenberg*. Musée Napoléon, Arenenberg, 1984.

Imbert de St Aman, Baron Arthur Léon. *Napoleon III and His Court* (trans. Elizabeth Gilbert Martin). London, Hutchinson & Co., 1900.

James, Constantin. *Des Causes de la mort de l'empereur*. Paris, 1873.

Jerrold, Blanchard. *The Life of Napoleon III*. London, Longmans, Green, 1874. (All four volumes are almost unreadable because of their pompous, late-Victorian literary style and Jerrold's obvious prejudice in favour of Louis whom he knew in exile in the last few years of his life, but the original documents quoted and the author's insight into Louis through personal knowledge are of immense value. Yet he is more often cited by French writers than British!)

Johnson, Douglas. *The French Intervention in Mexico*. London, National Gallery Publications, 1992. (A valuable and most helpful essay, forming part of *Manet: The Execution of Maximilian*, a publication issued in conjunction with the National Gallery's exhibition of that name.) *Journal des Landes*, 24 February 1910.

Keen, Benjamin. *A History of Latin America* (4th edn). Boston, Houghton Mifflin Company, 1992.

Ketelbey, D. M. *A History of Modern Times*. London, George G. Harrap & Co. Ltd (revised edn), 1940.

Kurtz, Harold. *The Empress Eugenie*. London, Hamish Hamilton, 1964.

Lacretelle, Pierre de. *Secrets et malheurs de la reine Hortense*. Paris, Hachette, 1936.

Lancet, London. 11, 18 and 25 January 1873.

Lebey, André. *Les trois coups d'état de Louis-Napoléon Bonaparte*. Paris, Perrin et Cie, 1909. (An early work containing much useful information to which not enough acknowledgement is made by many modern writers.)

Lecomte, Georges. *Napoléon III: sa maladie – son déclin*. Lyons, Laboratoires CIBA, 1937.

Legge, Edward. *The Empress Eugenie*. London and New York, Harper & Brothers, 1910.

—*The Empress Eugenie and Her Son*. London, Grant Richards, 1916.

—*The Comedy and Tragedy of the Second Empire*. London and New York, Harper & Brothers, 1916.

Lentz, Thierry. *Napoléon III*. Paris, Presses Universitaires de France, 1995.

Leprévost, Laurent. *Le Bonapartisme après Sedan*. Paris, paper in a symposium, *Pourquoi Réhabiliter le Second Empire?*, organised by Souvenir Napoléonien, 1995.

Loliée, Frédéric. *Le Duc de Morny* (trans. Bryan O'Donnell). London, Longman, 1910.

—*La Vie d'une impératrice*, Paris, Tallandier, 1928.

McMillan, James F. *Napoleon III (Profiles in Power)*. London and New York, Longman, 1991.

Malmesbury, 3rd Earl of. *Memoirs of an Ex-Minister*, Vol. I. London, Longmans, Green, 1884.

Martineau, Gilbert. *Le Roi de Rome*. Paris, Editions France-Empire, 1982.

Masuyer, Valérie. *Journal*. Paris, Revue des Deux Mondes, August 1914–November 1915.

Maurois, André. *Olympio ou la vie de Victor Hugo*. Paris, Hachette, 1954.

Maurois, Simone André. *Miss Howard: La femme qui fit un empereur*. Paris, Gallimard, 1956.

Melchior-Bonnet, Bernardine. *Restaurations et révolutions*. Paris, Librairie Larousse, 1984.

—*Napoléon, consul et empereur*. Paris, Librairie Larousse, 1984.

Mémoire des Landes, biographical dictionary published under the direction of B. Suau.

Mercy-Argenteau, Comtesse Louise de. *The Last Love of an Emperor*. London, Iris, 1916.

Minc, Alain. *Louis Napoléon revisité*. Paris, Editions Gallimard, 1997.

Mitchell, William M. *Chislehurst Golf Club*. Worcestershire, Grant Books, 1994.

Monts, Count Karl von. *La Captivité de Napoléon III en Allemagne* (trans. from German by Paul Brucks-Gilbert and Paul Lévy). Paris, Pierre Lafitte, 1910.

Moorehead, Caroline. *Dunant's Dream*. London, HarperCollins, 1998.

Mostyn, Dorothy A. *The Story of a House: Farnborough Hill*. St Michael's Abbey Press, 1989.

Napoléon III. *Œuvres de Napoléon III* (5 vols). Paris, Henri Plon, 1869.

—Letter to HRH Prince of Wales (4 March 1872). RA VIC/T 5/103 in Royal Archives, Windsor Castle.

Newton, Lord. *Lord Lyons*. London, Edward Arnold, 1913.

Normington, Susan. *Napoleon's Children*. Stroud, Alan Sutton Publishing, 1993.

Oman, Sir Charles. *Things I Have Seen*. London, Methuen & Co., 1933.

Pakula, Hannah. *An Uncommon Woman. (The Empress Frederick)*. London, Weidenfeld & Nicolson, 1996.

Paléologue, Maurice. *Les Entretiens de l'impératrice Eugénie*. Paris, Henri Plon, 1928.

Parkes, Henry Bamford. *A History of Mexico*. Boston, Houghton Mifflin Company, 1960.

Parturier, Maurice. *Morny et son temps*. Paris, Cercle du Nouveau Livre d'Histoire, 1969.

Peregrine, Anthony. 'Following Napoleon's Route from Elba'. London, *Daily Telegraph*, 10 May 1997.

Piétri, Franceschini. Telegram to Queen Victoria's lady-in-waiting, 9 January 1873. RA VIC/J 84/11 in Royal Archives, Windsor Castle.

Planche, J. R. *Recollections and Reflections*. London, 1872.

Plessis, Alain. *The Rise and Fall of the Second Empire* (Trans. Jonathan Mandelbaum). Cambridge, Cambridge University Press, 1985.

Pol, Stéfane. *La Jeunesse de Napoléon III*. Paris, Librairie Félix Juven, 1902.

Ponsonby, Col. Sir Henry. Letter to his mother (9 September 1870). RA VIC/Add A 36.215 in Royal Archives, Windsor Castle.

Pradalié, Georges. *Le Second Empire*. Paris, Presses Universitaires de France, 1957.

Rait, A. W. *Prosper Mérimée*. London, Eyre & Spottiswoode, 1970.

Richardson, Joanna. *The Courtesans*. London, Weidenfeld & Nicolson, 1967.

—*Princess Mathilde*. London, Weidenfeld & Nicolson, 1969.

Ridley, Jasper. *Napoleon III and Eugenie*. London, Constable, 1979. (A valuable, well-researched collection of facts, almost too many, with a tendency not to see the wood for the trees.)

Robb, Graham. *Victor Hugo*. London, Picador, 1997.

Rodzinski, Witold. *A History of China* (vol. 2). Oxford, Pergamon Press, 1979.

Roux, Georges. *Napoléon III*. Paris, Flammarion, 1969.

Sadleir, Michael. *Blessington-D'Orsay, A Masquerade*. London, Constable, 1933.

Savant, Jean. *L'Énigme de la naissance de Napoleon III*. Paris, Cahiers de l'Académie de l'Histoire, 1971.

Schutz, Jutta. *Corsica*. London, Insight Guides, 1993.

Séguin, Philippe. *Louis Napoléon le Grand*. Paris, Bernard Grasset, 1990.

Sencourt, Robert. *Napoleon III: The Modern Emperor*. London, Ernest Benn, 1933.

Sheehan, James A. *German History 1770–1886*. Oxford, Clarendon Press, 1989.

Simpson, F. A. *The Rise of Louis Napoleon*. London, John Murray, 1909. (An early academic work written in a style little accessible to modern readers but with much useful thought and information.)

—*Louis Napoleon and the Recovery of France* (3rd edn). London, Longmans, Green, 1951.

Smith, William. *Napoleon III*. London, Wayland Publishers, 1972.

—*Eugenie, impératrice et femme*. Paris, Olivier Orban, 1989.

Stracton, David. *The Bonapartes*. London, Hodder & Stoughton, 1967.

Starkie, Enid. *Baudelaire*. London, Penguin Books, 1971.

Stevenson, R. Scott. *Famous Illnesses in History*. London, Eyre & Spottiswoode, 1962.

Taylor, A. J. P. *Bismarck: The Man and Statesman*. London, Hamish Hamilton, 1955

Thompson, Sir Henry. Telegram to Queen Victoria, 9 January 1873. RA VIC/J 84/11 in Royal Archives, Winchester Castle.

Thompson, J. M. *Louis Napoleon and the Second Empire*. Oxford, Basil Blackwell, 1965. (Despite subsequent new research, this remains an outstanding biography by a British academic.)

The Times, London, 1 July, 1870.

The Times, London, 25 July, 1870.

The Times, London, 6 September 1870.

The Times, London, 11 and 16 January 1873.

Trevelyan, O. M. *History of England* (reissued 3rd edn). London, Longmans, Green, 1952.

Tulard, Jean. *Napoléon*. Paris, Fayard, 1977.

—(ed.). *Dictionnaire du Second Empire*. Paris, Fayard, 1995. (A monumental work of modern scholarship.)

Turnbull, Patrick. *Eugenie of the French*. London, Michael Joseph, 1974.

Vannucci, Marcello. *Storia diFirenze*. Rome, Newton Compton editori, 1986.

Queen Victoria. *Letters, 1870–78, Second Series, Vol. II*. London, John Murray, 1926.

—Letter to Empress Eugenie, 9 January 1873. RA VIC/ J 84/12. in Royal Archives, Windsor Castle.

Viel-Castel, Comte Horace de. *Commérages en marge du Second Empire*. Paris, Œuvres Représentatives, 1930.

Vigoureux, Claude. *Comment fait-on un coup d'état?* Paris, paper in a symposium, *Pourquoi Réhabiliter le Second Empire?*, organised by Souvenir Napoléonien, 1995.

Wagener, Françoise. *La Reine Hortense*. Paris, J-C Lattès, 1992.

Weintraub, Stanley. *Victoria*. London, John Murray, 1987.

Wellesley, Sir Victor and Sencourt, Robert. *Conversations with Napoleon III*. London, Ernest Benn, 1934.

Wingate, Peter with Richard. *Medical Encyclopedia* (4th edn). London, Penguin Books, 1996.

Zins, Ronald. *Les Maréchaux de Napoléon III*. Lyons, Editions Horvath, 1996.

Interviews

Bellringer, James F., FRCS (Urol.). Correspondence, January 1999.

Cowper-Smith, Julia. Telephone interview in London on 31 July 1996.

Father Cuthbert, Prior of St Michael's. Interview at St Michael's Abbey on 10 May 1997.

Gémain d'Orx, Marie-Hélène. Interview in Paris on 22 June 1996.

Salandre, Eric. Interview at the Château de Ham, 24 April 1996.

Williams, Sir David Innes, MD, MChir. Cambridge, FRCS. Interview at the Royal Society of Medicine, London, 9 October 1995.

Yarnold, Miss Ann. Interview at Farnborough Hill School on 10 May 1997.

Various Publications

French National Tourist Office, London, Sundry brochures, maps and leaflets on modern Martinique.

Sundry documentation supplied by M. Pierre Laperrade, owner of the Hôtel des Voyageurs in Gavarnie.

Anonymous. *Boulogne sur Mer: Guide Touristique*. Office de Tourisme, 1996–7.

Anonymous. *St Michael's Abbey, Farnborough*. St Michael's Abbey Press.

Anonymous. *Cauterets sera toujours Cauterets*. Cauterets Tourist Office, 1996.

INDEX

N III in subentries = Napoleon III (Louis Napoleon)